Cities of Ideas

Historical Urban Studies

Series editors: *Jean-Luc Pinol* and *Richard Rodger*

Titles in the series include:

*Printed Matters: Printing, Publishing and Urban Culture
in Europe in the Modern Period*
Malcolm Gee and Tom Kirk (eds)

*Identities in Space: Contested Terrains in
the Western City since 1850*
Simon Gunn and Robert J. Morris (eds)

Body and City: Histories of Urban Public Health
Sally Sheard and Helen Powers (eds)

*Urban Fortunes: Property and Inheritance in
the Town, 1700–1900*
Jon Stobart and Alastair Owens (eds)

Advertising and the European City: Historical Perspectives
Clemens Wischermann and Elliott Shore (eds)

Urban Governance: Britain and Beyond since 1750
Robert J. Morris and Richard H. Trainor (eds)

The Artisan and the European Town, 1500–1900
Geoffrey Crossick (ed.)

*Cathedrals of Urban Modernity:
The First Museums of Contemporary Art, 1800–1930*
J. Pedro Lorente

Capital Cities and their Hinterlands in Early Modern Europe
Peter Clark and Bernard Lepetit (eds)

*The Representation of Place: Urban Planning and Protest
in France and Great Britain, 1950–1980*
Michael James Miller

David Reeder

Cities of Ideas

Civil Society and Urban Governance
in Britain, 1800–2000

Essays in honour of David Reeder

Edited by
Robert Colls
and
Richard Rodger
University of Leicester, UK

ASHGATE

© Robert Colls and Richard Rodger, 2004

All rights reserved. No part of this publication may be reproduced, stored in a retrieval system, or transmitted in any form or by any means, electronic, mechanical, photocopying, recording, or otherwise without the prior permission of the publisher.

Robert Colls and Richard Rodger have asserted their moral right under the Copyright, Designs and Patents Act, 1988, to be identified as the editors of this work.

Published by
Ashgate Publishing Limited
Gower House
Croft Road
Aldershot
Hants GU11 3HR
England

Ashgate Publishing Company
Suite 420
101 Cherry Street
Burlington, VT 05401-4405
USA

Ashgate website: http://www.ashgate.com

British Library Cataloguing in Publication Data

Cities of ideas : civil society and urban governance in
   Britain 1800–2000 : essays in honour of David Reeder. –
   (Historical urban studies studies)
   1. Cities and towns – Great Britain – History – 19th century
   2. Cities and towns – Great Britain – History – 20th century
   3. Civil society – Great Britain – History – 19th century
   4. Civil society – Great Britain – History – 20th century
   I. Rodger, Richard, 1947– II. Colls, Robert, 1949– III. Reeder, David
   A. (David Alec), 1931–
   307.7'6'0941

ISBN 0754606503

Library of Congress Cataloging-in-Publication Data

Cities of ideas: civil society and urban governance in Britain 1800–2000: essays in
   honour of David Reeder / edited by Robert Colls and Richard Rodger
      p. cm. – (Historical urban studies series)
      Includes bibliographical references and index.
      ISBN 0-7546-0650-3 (alk. paper)
      1. Cities and towns – Great Britain. 2. Civil society – Great Britain. I. Reeder, David A.
   II. Rodger, Richard. III. Colls, Robert. IV. Historical urban studies.

HT133.C4925 2003
307.76'0941 – dc21

2003042171

ISBN 0 7546 0650 3

Typeset by SetSystems Ltd, Saffron Walden, Essex
Printed and bound in Great Britain by MPG Books Ltd, Bodmin, Cornwall

Contents

	List of Figures	ix
	List of Tables	xi
	Notes on Contributors	xiii
	Foreword	xvii
1	Civil society and British cities *Richard Rodger and Robert Colls*	1
2	Taxation and representation in the Victorian city *Martin Daunton*	21
3	The metropolitan and the municipal: the politics of health and environment in London, 1860–1920 *Bill Luckin*	46
4	Resolving the sewage question: Metropolis Sewage & Essex Reclamation Company, 1865–81 *P.L. Cottrell*	67
5	The Sheffield Democrats' critique of criminal justice in the 1850s *Chris A. Williams*	96
6	A year in the public life of the British bourgeoisie *R.J. Morris*	121
7	The 'common good' and civic promotion: Edinburgh 1860–1914 *Richard Rodger*	144
8	David Reeder's 'alternative system': the school boards in the 1890s *Brian Simon*	178

9 Futures from the past: the rise and fall of university liberal
  adult education 207
  Bill Williamson

10 Women and citizenship: gender and the built environment
   in British cities 1870–1939 231
   Hellen Meller

11 Citizenship, civil society and quality of life: Sutton Model
   Dwellings Estates 1919–39 258
   Patricia L. Garside

12 When we lived in communities: working-class culture
   and its critics 283
   Robert Colls

   David Reeder: career and publications 308

   Index 317

Figures

Frontispiece   David Reeder

6.1	Steam engines erected in Leeds up to 1829	123
6.2	The subscribers of Leeds 1832	124
6.3	Meetings in Leeds 1829	125
7.1	Ceremony of laying the foundation stone, General Post Office, Edinburgh 1861. W.H. Macfarlane, Edinburgh City Arts, catalogue reference HH 697/1913	155
7.2	The royal panorama, Edinburgh 19 July 1911	159
7.3	Public expenditure and civil priorities, Edinburgh 1860–1914. Edinburgh City Archives SL 35/1–46, Abstract of Accounts, between 1860 and 1914	161
7.4	Charitable relief and donations in Edinburgh 1860–1914	168
7.5	The basis of the Common Good fund: lands and properties held by the City of Edinburgh 1905	170
7.6	Annual revenue available to the Common Good fund, Edinburgh 1644–1914 (logarithmic scale)	171
11.1	Models for building civil society	277
12.1	Laygate Lane, South Shields 1930. Reproduced by permission of South Tyneside Public Libraries	285
12.2	Back lane girls, Lyton Street, South Shields 1938. Reproduced by permission of Mrs S. Tweddell	287
12.3	Back field boys, Eglesfield Road, South Shields 1957	287

Tables

5.1	The relative successes of the Democrat slates in Sheffield in 1851	116
6.1	Public meetings in Leeds 1829: meeting places	127
7.1	Promoting the city: civic receptions in Edinburgh 1879–1913	148
7.2	Presentations of the Freedom of the City: Edinburgh 1863–1912	151
7.3	Royal ceremonies and public entertainments, Edinburgh 1911	157
7.4	Town council donations to clubs and societies, Edinburgh 1911	165
7.5	Charitable and relief payments by Edinburgh Town Council 1860–1914	168
9.1	Extra-mural library acquisitions, Durham University 1950 and 1998	210
9.2	Tutorial classes and enrolments 1910–1950, Great Britain	216

Notes on Contributors

David Cannadine was Director of the Institute of Historical Research, University of London (1998–2003), and is currently Queen Elizabeth The Queen Mother Professor of British History at that university. He is also a Fellow of the British Academy and the Royal Society of Literature. His books include *The Decline and Fall of the British Aristocracy*; *Class in Britain*, and *In Churchill's Shadow*.

Robert Colls is Professor of English History in the School of Historical Studies at the University of Leicester. He worked with David Reeder at Vaughan College on Department of Adult Education Certificate programmes in social history and social studies, and on the BA Humanities / World Humanities.

P.L. Cottrell is Professor of Financial History at the University of Leicester, where he has been a staff member since 1972. Previously, he taught at the University of Liverpool, and has been a Bye Fellow of Robinson College, Cambridge, a Visiting Professor at Nihon University, Tokyo, and a Professeur invité, Département d'Histoire économique et sociale, Université de Genève. He was a co-founding editor of *Financial History Review*, after having previously edited *Business Archives*, *Business History* and *Journal of Transport History*. With David Reeder he had the pleasure of helping to develop the Victorian Studies Centre at Leicester and, over some summer weeks, teaching (and other things more convivial) with him at Maddingley Hall.

Martin Daunton is Professor of Economic History at the University of Cambridge and Fellow of Churchill College. His work on urban history includes books on Cardiff and on working class housing. He edited the third volume of the *Cambridge Urban History of Britain*, and recently published two volumes on the politics of British taxation since 1799. He is currently completing a general survey of British economic history from 1851 to 1951.

Patricia Garside is Research Professor in the European Studies Research Unit at the University of Salford. Her research interests lie chiefly in twentieth-century social and political history, with particular reference to London. She is concerned with the development of public policy, especially housing, health and town planning and is currently contributing to a comparative study of open space provision in London and Baltic capitals including St Petersburg, funded by the Finnish Institute. Recent publications include *A Model Guide to Lancashire Mental Hospital Records*, 2001 (with Bruce Jackson) and *The Conduct of Philanthropy: The William Sutton Trust*, 1999.

Bill Luckin is Professor of Urban History at Bolton Institute. He is the author of *Pollution and Control: A Social History of the Thames in the Nineteenth Century* (1986) and *Questions of Power: Electricity and the Environment in Interwar Britain* (1990). Bill Luckin is also coeditor, with Roger Cooter, of *Accidents in History* (1997) and with Dieter Schott and Geneviève Massard-Guilbaud of *The Environment and the City: Modern European Cities and the Management of their Resources* (Ashgate, 2005).

Helen Meller is Professor of Urban History at the University of Nottingham and Director of the Centre of Urban Culture. She has published widely on themes relating to leisure in cities, women and cities, philanthropy and planning. Her previous books include: *Patrick Geddes: social evolutionist and city planner* (1990), *Towns, Plans and Society in Modern Britain* (1997) and *European Cities 1890–1940: history, culture and the built environment* (2001). Current research interests are on green open spaces in European cities in the twentieth century.

R.J. Morris is Professor of Economic and Social History at Edinburgh University where he has taught since 1968. He has written widely on urban and class history. His publications include *Class, Sect and Party* (1990) and the forthcoming *Men, Women and Property*, both studies of the urban middle classes in 19th-century Britain. He was founding editor of *History and Computing*, President of the European Urban History Association, 2000–2002, and was active in the revival of the Urban History Group in the 1980s. He has benefited over many years from the advice, support and wisdom of David Reeder.

Richard Rodger is Professor of Urban History and Director of the Centre for Urban History at the University of Leicester. In 1987 he succeeded David Reeder as Editor of *Urban History*. He has published widely on the social, business and legal history of urban Britain; his most recent book, *The Transformation of Edinburgh: Land, Propert and Trust in the*

Nineteenth Century, was awarded the Frank Watson Prize for the best book on Scottish history in 2001 and 2002. He has collaborated with David Reeder in both teaching and research, publishing jointly 'Industrialisation and the City Economy' (2000).

Brian Simon, who died 17 January 2002, was Emeritus Professor of Education at the University of Leicester. His four volume history of English education, 1780–1990, remains the classic work. He was a lifelong campaigner for a more egalitarian and effective system of education in Britain. Along with H.J. Dyos, he was a key influence on David Reeder.

Chris A. Williams is a Lecturer in the History Department of the Open University, and a member of the OU's European Centre for the Study of Policing. He has published several articles on the history of policing in Britain between the early nineteenth century and the 1970s, specifically on urban policing.

Bill Williamson is Emeritus Professor of Continuing Education at the University of Durham. He grew up on Tyneside where his grandparents had worked in the coal mines. The two books he is most proud to have written are *Class, Culture and Community; A Biographical Study of Social Change in Mining* (Routledge 1982) and *Lifeworlds and Learning; Essays in the theory, philosophy and practice of Lifelong Learning* (NIACE 1998).

Foreword

David Cannadine

This book is an important contribution to two of British history's most flourishing sub-specialisms: urban history and the history of education. But it also celebrates the Golden Jubilee of David Reeder's association with the University of Leicester, which began in 1952 when he became a student in the School of Education, and it salutes his many-sided contribution to our understanding of both of these exciting fields. For as a teacher, writer, editor, lecturer, facilitator, entrepreneur and networker, David Reeder has always lived a double life, and he has done so more easily and openly than some scholars on whom that epithet has recently been bestowed. In one guise, he has been successively an RAF Education Officer, Leicester school teacher and Head of the Faculty of Education at Garnett College, Rochampton. But in another, he has been a Lecturer in Education and Urban Studies at the University of Leicester, where he has been closely identified not only with the School of Education but also with the Victorian Studies Centre, the Centre for Urban History and the Department of Adult Education. Appropriately enough, it was Leicester which gave him the chance to indulge both of his historical interests, and it brought him into contact with two of the most important figures in these fields: Jim Dyos, the founder and first Professor of Urban History in the country, and Brian Simon, the most controversial and influential Professor of Education of his day.

From his earliest historical writings, David Reeder established himself in the nineteenth century, producing general surveys which were much influenced by his experiences in schoolteaching. But by the time he returned to Leicester to undertake graduate work in the early 1960s, history was both fermenting and fragmenting, and urban history and the history of education were both poised to take off and come of age in the knowledge boom of that decade. The growth in Victorian studies, and the large-scale demolition of nineteenth-century cities in the name of progress and improvement, brought the urban past to the top of the historical agenda, while the raging debate over comprehensive schools, and the unprecedented expansion of universities and colleges of further education, urgently needed some serious historical perspective. Jim Dyos and Brian Simon were ideally placed to discern these developments and to respond to these challenges, and David Reeder worked closely with both of them, initially as a student and from 1973 as a colleague, helping them put Leicester at the forefront of these new and expanding fields. The heady excitement of these pioneering days is well caught in the perceptively affectionate appreciations he would eventually write of both these mentors; and he also co-edited (with myself) a posthumous collection of Jim Dyos's essays and (with Ali Rattansi) a Festschrift for Brian Simon.

In the meantime, David Reeder had begun to publish extensively on his own account. As an urban historian, his early researches were in the appropriately Dyosian subject of London suburbia, and from his dissertation he crafted classic essays on Paddington, Hammersmith and Fulham – neighbouring communities in some ways similar, in other ways not. This was followed by 'Slums and Suburbs', the chapter he co-authored with Jim Dyos, in *The Victorian City: Images and Realities*, which remains unsurpassed in its evocation and analysis of the complex forces making for the creation – and degradation – of the whole metropolitan environment. But the provinces also beckoned, and in the last decade David turned his attention to the local economy and municipal provision in twentieth-century Leicester, and to Maidstone from the Victorian era to the First World War and beyond. These researches have also informed a succession of review essays, where he has surveyed the subject, discerned trends and suggested new directions. All these writings have been powerfully informed by the belief that urban historians must combine a recognition of the broader processes making for city growth with a capacity to evoke the particularities and peculiarities of specific places. For towns and cities, he insists, are not just the outcome of economic and social and political forces: they are themselves a significant historical variable – as he has recently argued (with Richard Rodger) in an essay in the *Cambridge Urban History of Britain*.

This belief that the city is in itself an independent influence on the past and the present has also informed, and provided a link with, David Reeder's parallel work on the history of education. In 1977, he published a symposium on *Urban Education in the Nineteenth Century*, a pathbreaking collection which abandoned the narrowly traditional and institutional approach which had so often characterized the subject, and sought to open it up to new methodologies, taking in urban politics, social class, literacy and Anglo-American comparisons. To that volume, Reeder contributed an essay on late-Victorian and Edwardian perspectives on education in an urbanized society, which he later developed into the extended introduction he contributed to *Educating Our Masters*, published under the auspices of the Victorian Studies Centre at Leicester

University, where he surveyed some of the most seminal writings by liberal Victorian commentators on the problems and possibilities of urban schooling. The history of education, Reeder rightly insists, is thus in part the history of ideas, and no one has done more than he to insist that that is so. But it is also the history of much else besides, as he has shown in his pioneering account of secondary education in England from the 1860s to the 1920s, and his most recent assessment of the uneven impact of comprehensive schooling in England and Wales since the 1960s.

This is a substantial and significant scholarly *oeuvre* which any historian might contemplate with pride and satisfaction. But David Reeder has never been a selfish or self-absorbed scholar, getting on with his own research and writing to the exclusion of all else. Quite the contrary: he has been the most generous and collegial of historians. He has taught a remarkable range of courses at Leicester University, including the pioneering Humanities and World Humanities BA at Vaughan College. David was a great teacher with a flair for adult education; his students appreciated the treasures he put in their way. At one time and another he has directed both the Victorian Studies Centre and the Centre for Urban History at Leicester. He was an active supporter of the History of Education Society and a founder member of the Urban History Group. For much of the 1960s, he was editor of *The Vocational Aspect of Education*, and for most of the next decade he was editor of the *Urban History Yearbook*. He wrote the conclusion to David Owen's *The Growth of Victorian London*, prepared most of the massive bibliography and helped to steer the book through the press. He has organized seminars and conferences galore, served as general editor of two major series and participated in international gatherings and projects in France, Germany, Italy and the Netherlands. In addition to the fine example and high standards he has set in his own work, he has always been a great *enabler*, making spaces and creating opportunities for many other scholars; and this splendid volume is an eloquent and distinguished testimony to their gratitude, appreciation and affection.

The Institute of Historical Research
16 February 2003

CHAPTER ONE

Civil society and British cities

Richard Rodger and Robert Colls

In March 1967 an elegant and powerful argument was set out in a conference paper in Bloomington, Indiana. This paper was saturated with ideas about the city and urban relationships. The argument, underpinned by sources both historical and literary, genuinely deserves the accolade of 'seminal'. Entitled 'Slums and Suburbs', the paper developed a significance far beyond the simplicity of the title, concerned as it was not just with housing but with the inner dynamics of Victorian capitalism.[1] The argument owed much to David Reeder; the stylistic elegance owed much to Jim Dyos. Their *credo* was that towns and cities themselves added an extra dimension to social and economic relationships, a view subsequently expressed by Fernand Braudel:

> Towns are like electrical transformers. They increase tension, accelerate the rhythm of exchange and ceaselessly stir up men's lives.[2]

In its published form, explicitly and subliminally, the paper informs much of the current scholarship about towns and cities. Its analysis not only affected a generation of urban historians, some of whom have contributed to this volume, but also informed the agenda for social history in Britain, then still in its infancy.[3]

As a 'land of fragments' Victorian London was portrayed as a mosaic of streets unfolding from one neighbourhood into another. Coherence was not immediately apparent. Despite the 'stumbling logic' that was the London leviathan, a rhythm was revealed in which the city by day and the city by night was shown to have a pair of logics since both diurnal and nocturnal patterns introduced common purposes and forged common identities for sub-sets of Londoners. The coherence of the city was also revealed through the organizing principles of commerce and employ-

---

[1] H.J. Dyos and D. Reeder, 'Slums and Suburbs' in H.J. Dyos and M. Wolff, (eds), *The Victorian City: Images and Realities*, (London, 1973) vol. II, pp. 359–86. For a list of David Reeder's publications see pp. 308–15.

[2] F. Braudel, *Capitalism and Material Life* (London, 1973), p. 382.

[3] This contribution was reprinted in A. Sutcliffe and P. Thane, *Essays in Economic and Social History* (Oxford, 1986), pp. 216–46.

ment, since for most city dwellers it was the forces of demand and supply, of scarcity and choice, that determined their daily rhythms.[4] The rules of the market inserted their own logic on the space, time and mentalities of Londoners.[5] Tacit acceptance of these rules implied compliance, deference, order and control.

In London, as elsewhere in Britain, late eighteenth-century urbanization was achieved without much investment in the infrastructure. Urban administrative structures and jurisdictions were unsuited to changing circumstances, and their officers were often paralysed by fear should they transgress their legitimate authority. The adverse impact of this under-investment was accentuated by the pace of in-migration in the early decades of the nineteenth century when urban population increase between 1801 and 1831 was greater than the total population of Britain in 1801. It would be the equivalent in 2001 of adding 50 million people to the towns and cities of Britain by 2031, *without* the benefit of planning codes, building regulations, sewerage and water supply systems, and assurances over the quality of building materials and the competency of architects and builders.

Slums and suburbs were a response to market forces and to the impediments to circulation that were posed by rapid urbanization.[6] Solutions to urban breakdown were numerous. In their paper 'Slums and Suburbs', however, David Reeder and Jim Dyos broke new ground when they explained:

> Centrifugal forces drew the rich into the airy suburbs; centripetal ones held the poor in the airless slums. But the compelling pressures of expansion caused ripples of obsolescence, which overtook places once dancing with buttercups and left them stale as cabbage stalks. Suburbs begat or became slums, rarely if ever the reverse, and the town never coalesced. Whole districts lost ordinary contact with their neighbours, and London became, in the most indulgent terms, an island of villages; in the most heartless, a geographical expression of increasing vagueness. Yet this disintegration was not a disconnected process. The fact of the suburb influenced the environment of the slum; the threat of the slum entered the consciousness of the suburb.[7]

---

[4] M.J. Daunton (ed.), 'Introduction', *Cambridge Urban History of Britain*, vol. III: *1840–1950* (Cambridge, 2000), pp. 3–9.

[5] L.D. Schwarz, *London in the Age of Industrialisation: Entrepreneurs, Labour Force and Living Conditions 1700–1850* (Cambridge, 1992); G. Kearns and C.W.J. Withers, 'Introduction', in G. Kearns and C.W.J. Withers, (eds), *Urbanising Britain: Essays on Class and Community in the Nineteenth Century* (Cambridge, 1991).

[6] M.J. Daunton, 'Introduction'.

[7] Dyos and Reeder, 'Slums and Suburbs', p. 360.

Here, then, was a new, explanation of urban development. In a relatively short time, at most three generations, the elites of the new Georgian quarters of so many eighteenth and early nineteenth-century towns increasingly abandoned their city centres for the suburb. 'Ripples of obsolescence' consigned desirable homes to the vagaries of the market as sub-division and multiple occupancy overwhelmed the former exclusivity of city-centre addresses. Market mechanisms – principally pricing and profits – functioned to redistribute resources, a position powerfully presented by Dyos and Reeder as:

> the manipulators of capital, the middle classes helped to make possible the expansion of house-building in the suburbs, the parts of the city in which they were shaping their own environment, but in diverting resources for these purposes they also helped to determine the environment of those left behind in the city centre.[8]

If, through purchasing power and market forces the middle classes siphoned resources to the suburbs to the detriment of the slums, then this process of social segregation was reinforced by the simultaneous diversion of municipal infrastructural investment to the suburbs. Indeed, it was recognized by Adam Smith as inherent in the system of property relations. Smith noted that:

> Civil government, so far as it is instituted for the security of property, is in reality instituted for the defence of the rich against the poor, or for those who have some property against those who have none at all.[9]

As Bob Morris has explained elsewhere, and as Martin Daunton explains in this volume, manufacturers and business interests gained doubly from municipal investment in pure water and public utilities: first, through the indirect subsidy to their business interests and, second, through business and personal benefit to their new residential districts.[10] Thus, urban power structures were used to enable those with power to advance their interests beyond the scope delivered purely by market forces. How market penetration and political domination intersected depended upon time and place, though the withdrawal of the middle class from the governance of London was more marked than in the industrial and manufacturing districts of the north. London became 'an island of villages' with a disunited system of local government

---

[8] Ibid., p. 361.

[9] Adam Smith, *The Wealth of Nations* (1776; Harmondsworth, 1974), book 5, part 1, p. 321.

[10] R.J. Morris, 'Externalities, the Market, Power Structures and the Urban Agenda', *Urban History Yearbook*, 17 (1990), pp. 99–109.

administered by over 30 separate boroughs, the by-product of the middle classes' disengagement and a preference for their own suburban 'island'. 'Two nations' co-existed, uneasily, as confirmed in Benjamin Disraeli's novel *Sybil* (1846) and pamphlets with titles such as *The Dens of London Exposed*, *The Million Peopled City, One Half of London Made Known to the Other*, and perhaps most famously, *Town Swamps and Social Bridges* (1859).[11]

Social polarization as represented by 'slums' and 'suburbs' was part of an argument for economic efficiency based on low wages.[12] Efficiency, productivity gains and international competitiveness were paraded as a consequence of this approach in the nineteenth century, in much the same way that a revival in the British economy in the 1920s and a 'return to normalcy' was predicated on cost-cutting. In another incisive view of Victorian cities, the authors commented that slum dwellers were 'merely the residuary legatees of a kind of house-processing operation which was started by another social class with little or no idea or concern as to how it would end'.[13] Adam Smith, however, was in no doubt half a century earlier: 'No society can surely be flourishing and happy, of which the far greater part of the members are poor and miserable.'[14]

In the face of these issues, David Reeder's historical interests fanned out to include democratic participation, social exclusion, education and class, community and neighbourhood, metropolitanism and provincialism, poverty and social classification.[15] These are the intellectual threads in a remarkably rich and diverse scholarly life. Most of these threads Reeder wove into the tensions of property relations. For example, he noted that as immigration proceeded, so the physical and moral fabric of communities came under pressure. Even though these things were not new, and the early modern town or city was not a tranquil place, by the

---

[11] Reprinted as G. Godwin, *Town Swamps and Social Bridges* (Leicester, 1972).

[12] See especially, G.S. Jones, *Outcast London: A Study in the Relationship between Classes in Victorian Society* (Oxford, 1971); part I.

[13] For a long run view of these processes see R. Rodger, 'Slums and Suburbs: The Persistence of Residential Apartheid', in P.J. Waller (ed.), *The English Urban Landscape* (Oxford, 2000) pp. 233–68; D.R. Green and A. Parton, 'Slums and Slum Life in Victorian England', in S.M. Gaskell (ed.), *Slums* (Leicester, 1990), pp. 17–91.

[14] Smith, *The Wealth of Nations*.

[15] See, for example, D. Reeder, 'Conclusions: Perspectives on Metropolitan Administrative History', in D. Owen, *The Government of Victorian London 1855–1889: The Metropolitan Board of Works, the Vestries and the City Corporation* (Cambridge, Mass, 1982), pp. 347–69, which synthesizes brilliantly many of these strands.

early nineteenth century decennial population growth rates of 30–40 per cent in the inner districts gave impetus to changes on a scale never previously experienced. The construction of new suburban communities on the periphery of cities produced a realignment of social relations. Existing systems of family and kinship support, of mutuality and trust, were revised. New agencies were formed and, as the actions of one firm or agency impinged on others, so the problems were gradually addressed.

As life expectancy at birth dropped from 35 to 29 years in the 1820s and 1830s (a level not previously experienced since the Black Death), a deepening ecological breakdown was apparent.[16] Several complementary approaches to this urban crisis were developed. One response was suburbanization, a trickle of middle class migration in the 1830s that became a flood after 1850.[17] In London, suburbanization, together with relatively modest population growth rates, was itself a decongestant. Another response was infrastructural investment in the city. Private and public finance initiatives were involved. Phillip Cottrell's chapter in this book shows how a privately financed scheme in the mid-1860s attempted to deal with London's sewage problems. In the public sphere, predictions of biological collapse proved unfounded, Bill Luckin argues, as London invested heavily in its sewage system. As a result, by the last quarter of the nineteenth century, it enjoyed a period of renewed environmental and epidemiological progress as one of the healthiest capitals in the world. This achievement had much to do with the efforts of the Metropolitan Board of Works (MBW), wrongly reviled as corrupt and inefficient. Indeed Luckin offers an important reminder that the MBW and the Metropolitan Asylums Board, which from 1870 played a significant role in reducing the extent of epidemic diseases such as typhoid, typhus, smallpox and scarlet fever, are typical of a dense network of Victorian institutions that have attracted unfair criticism. This adverse assessment owes more to a 1960s reaction against managerial and bureaucratic structures than to a systematic assessment of mid-Victorian institutions, and it has taken a revised interest in institutional economics to demonstrate that important, if indirect, productivity gains result from administrative reorganization and economies of scale. According to Edwin

---

[16] S. Szreter and A. Hardy, 'Urban Fertility and Mortality Patterns' in Daunton, *Cambridge Urban History of Britain*, vol. III, pp. 629–72; S. Szreter and G. Mooney, 'Urbanisation, Mortality and the Standard of Living Debate: New Estimates of the Expectation of Life at Birth in Nineteenth Century Cities', *Economic History Review*, 51 (1998), pp. 84–112.

[17] For a review of the literature, see R. Rodger, *Housing in Urban Britain 1780–1914* (Cambridge, 1995), pp. 70–95.

Chadwick, the public health movement allied administrative efficiency with political stability.

Indeed it was Chadwick himself who remarked that air pollution in large towns 'operates as a tax increasing the wear and tear of linen and expense of working to all who live within range of the mismanaged chimneys'.[18] At one level this was an early version of cost–benefit analysis with gains and losses on opposite sides of the social welfare balance sheet. The utility function of industrialization factored in environmental damage and human exploitation and measured this against employment creation and rising standards of living. In the Victorian city, as Martin Daunton explains, there was a paradigm shift as monopoly power was replaced by free-trade power. However, by mid-century unrestrained free trade had produced acute urban environmental damage and the lowest life expectancy since the Black Death. Private and public interest coincided over health and, as Luckin and Cottrell both show, intervention was legitimated to contain the contamination of the cities. Where public funds were exclusively used to address environmental concerns, however, the newly reformed municipal councils resurrected the spectre of public monopolies – gas, water and sewage companies initially – and in effect handed tax-raising powers to them without due accountability and transparency. Echoes of the clarion call 'No taxation without representation' were not to be taken lightly. What Daunton explores remains a conundrum: how is it possible to secure the consent of taxpayers to spend without also giving them the power to block desirable public investments in the social infrastructure?

Philosophical issues to do with liberty and constraint were not confined to political tracts. In the business of drains, dirt and disease, they involved political choices and practical limitations on liberty.[19] Urbanization threw up problems of land use, sanitation, services and the organization of markets. The city needed systems by which to define nuisances, to proscribe unacceptable behaviour, to number houses, to protect rights to trade and to regulate traffic.[20] These problems were immediate. If left unresolved for long, they impeded daily life and commercial activity. Most responses to them involved a measure of imposed authority. But whose authority should that be? At the core of

---

[18] E. Chadwick, *Report on the Sanitary Condition of the Labouring Population of Great Britain 1842*, ed. M.W. Flinn (Edinburgh, 1965), p. 356.

[19] C. Pooley, 'Choice and Constraint in the Nineteenth Century City: A Basis for Residential Differentiation' in J.H. Johnson and C. Pooley (eds), *The Structure of Nineteenth Century Cities* (London, 1982), pp. 199–233.

[20] S. and B. Webb, *The Development of English Local Government 1689–1835* (Oxford, 1963), p. 5, described English local government as 'a confused network of local customs'.

this question, and one that preoccupied early and mid-Victorians, was the balance that had to be struck between central administration and local government.

In the 1830s local self-determination was a powerful legacy. 'Local provision, for local wants, locally identified' was how Hennock described the diversity that existed, despite the superficial uniformity associated with county, borough and parish administration.[21] The latitude of early nineteenth century local officials was considerable, and what local powers they lacked could be obtained either by petitioning Parliament themselves or by prompting local turnpike trusts or street commissioners to do so.[22] Either way, local needs were paramount. By the 1830s, however, the statistical revolution was underway.[23] Reinforced by the collection of data for births, deaths and marriages by the Registrar-General from 1837 onwards, inspectors and government agents collected information which in effect produced targets and league tables – accident rates in factories, literacy rates in schools, policing levels per head of population, and other similar 'performance indicators'. National norms and deviations from them were set to plague reformed local councils ever after. The centralization of knowledge was underway. As J.S. Mill noted in his highly influential work on government, 'power may be localised but knowledge, to be useful, must be centralised'.[24]

A rift between knowledge and power had emerged in the first decade of Victoria's reign. Centralizers were ranged against what Chris Williams describes as 'ultra-localists' – defenders of the faith as far as local self determination was concerned. The 'faith' was the sovereignty of local administrative units of government, as expounded by Joshua Toulmin Smith.[25] The main unit of local administration was not the town council

---

[21] E.P. Hennock, 'Central/Local Government Relations in England: An Outline 1800–1950', *Urban History Yearbook* (1982), p. 39. See also R.A.W. Rhodes, *Control and Power in Central–Local Government Relations* (Aldershot, 1983) and subsequent work on inter-governmental relations.

[22] R. Sweet, *The English Town 1680–1840: Government, Society and Culture* (Harlow 1999); J.M. Ellis, *The Georgian Town 1680–1849* (Basingstoke, 2001). See also S.M. Gaskell, *Building Control: National Legislation and the Introduction of Local Bye-laws in Victorian England* (London, 1983), pp. 3–20.

[23] M.J. Cullen, *The Statistical Movement in Early Victorian Britain: The Foundations of Empirical Social Research* (Brighton, 1975).

[24] J.S. Mill, *Considerations on Representative Government* (1861; New York, 1958), ch. xv, section 2, p. 1.

[25] J.T. Smith, *Local Self Government and Centralization: The Characteristics of Each, and its Practical Tendencies* (London, 1851). W.H. Greenleaf, 'Toulmin Smith and the British Political Tradition', *Public Administration*, 53 (1975), pp. 25–44; W.C. Lubenow, *The Politics of Government Growth: Early Victorian*

itself, but the folk or ward-mote, monthly meetings of burghers whom Toulmin Smith claimed had a right to determine public policy and whose engagement in community issues was directly descended from Adam Ferguson's conception of 'civil society'.[26] The idea of the ward-mote was an attempt to develop a highly localized form of political consciousness based on household and neighbourhood, examined in this volume in relation to Sheffield in 1851. Compared to conventional politics, the ward-mote offered a less gendered view of participation since neighbourhood and household were the basis of common political participation.

It is worth remembering that the 'mismanaged chimneys', cellars and middens that so offended Edwin Chadwick and his brigade of informants were the responsibility of the police, who were obliged to identify and report to the Improvement Commission. Alongside their responsibilities in the criminal justice system, therefore, the police had wide-ranging powers in relation to urban civil codes, local improvement acts and general statutes.[27] The Sheffield Democrats, as they were termed, were opposed to centralization and the extensive new powers assigned to 'undemocratic' institutions spawned by government boards and commissioners. Such views found considerable popular support. Crucially, however, the Democrats were opposed also to the 'immense power' accorded to police and magistrates. Ward-motes, the Democrats claimed, should have jurisdiction over criminal justice and it was over this issue that the movement eventually self-destructed. It was one thing for Sheffield burghers to advocate repairs to drains and pavements, but quite another to intervene in the criminal justice system by deciding who, and who not, to prosecute.

Ward level representation and the jurisdiction of the police were key issues that arose out of the centralizing tendencies that developed in mid-century cities. The fact that the Sheffield Democrats failed to replace municipal authority with local political activists may seem hardly surprising, but we should not forget the intensity of the opposition they encountered. As de Toqueville explained:

> Among democratic nations it is only by association that the resistance of the people to the government can ever display itself; hence

---

Attitudes Towards State Intervention 1833–1848 (Newton Abbot, 1971), pp. 86–94.

[26] A. Ferguson, *An Essay on the History of Civil Society*, ed. F. Oz-Salzburerger (Cambridge, 1995). Chris Williams also refers to the Saxon origin attributed to the local or folk unit of organization.

[27] Adam Smith, *Lectures on Justice, Police, Revenue and Arms* (1896; New York, 1956), p. 154.

the latter always looks with ill favour on those associations which are not in its own power.[28]

Central–local tensions were not new in 1851, and as Williams notes, parish level accountability was a proposal that had been advanced when the Metropolitan Police force was first formed in 1829.[29] However, if the popular Democrats were thwarted in Sheffield, another form of activism, 'subscriber democracy', was busy in Leeds.

If 1829 was an extraordinary year in London, it was not so in Leeds, according to Bob Morris. In that year there were no riots, political demonstrations, franchise campaigns, no strikes and no slumps. The Leeds middle class were constructing the local state as a place of order established through a programme of public, committee and annual general meetings, convened through a series of printed notices and published announcements, and gazetted by rules, regulations and annual reports. As the voice of local authority, the bourgeoisie developed complementary systems. On the one hand, through commercial and industrial organizations, market structures and property management, their economic power was established. On the other hand, concentrated in the halls and meeting rooms often funded by commercial firms, the social and cultural activities of the middle classes provided a stage for civil society. Viewed in this way, middle class associational life and volunteer activists, described by A.J.P. Taylor as 'a great army of busybodies', take on a different complexion, coloured more by political rationality and a sense of civic responsibility.[30]

The bourgeois 'public' that had established an urban presence during the late eighteenth century in literary and philosophical discussions took on an increasingly political role. Clubs and coffee houses, salons, soirees and a developing free press created opportunities for a critical forum in the eighteenth and early nineteenth centuries.[31] This was prompted in the 1830s by the inequality of the existing system of franchise, and by an urgent need to influence economic policy at state level. With the expansion of trade and industry, there was a shift in the relationship between state and society. State policy assumed an importance that had been absent in workshop production. Accordingly, knowledge, and thus information, particularly commercial information, gained

---

[28] A. de Tocqueville, *Democracy in America* (London, 1840), book 4, ch. 5.
[29] Quoted in L. Reith, *British Police and the Democratic Ideal* (London, 1943), p. 51.
[30] A.J.P. Taylor, *English History 1914–1945* (Oxford, 1965), p. 175.
[31] P.A. Clark, *British Clubs and Societies 1580–1800: The Origins of an Associational World* (Oxford, 2000), pp. 94–140.

a vital new importance.[32] Against the conventional view that the growth of the city was instrumental in the expansion of industry and commerce, it has been recently observed that 'the talk of the bourgeoisie, not the smoke of the factory was the defining characteristic of the modern city economy'.[33]

'The talk of the bourgeoisie' spilled over into the political domain. Slums and suburbs, sewers and sanitation were part of that dialogue, and the political inclusion of the middle class after 1832 on which it was founded produced structural transformations in the public sphere.[34] Public opinion, public interest and public policy coincided in a series of urban interventions by municipal authorities. Binding these actions together were the meetings of the middle class which Morris describes as 'part of a process of ordering of order' in the growing industrial town.[35] Voluntary associations, through their agendas and accounts, provided a discipline and a transparency that contributed to the development of standards of public probity. In addition, as the reformed corporations embarked on their administrative journeys to raise revenues and address environmental concerns, procedures for the conduct of public meetings were established. The choreographed ritual of 'the meeting' enabled participants to act out their roles just as it subordinated areas of potential disagreement. Urban association was an important element in class formation, cultural hegemony and ethnic inclusion and exclusion. Yet this apparent divisiveness obscures the positive contribution that association made to the development of civil society and citizenship. Plurality was tolerated. Social tensions were mediated. Identity was established.

In 'Slums and Suburbs' then, Reeder and Dyos presented an approach to a deepening environmental malaise in the city in terms both spatial and social. Recent scholarship, presented here, shows two mutually reinforcing strategies were also at work. One emphasized administrative reorganization and public investment as a means to address the threat to life that cities posed. The other, Tocquevillian in

---

[32] D.A. Reeder and R. Rodger, 'Industrialisation and the City Economy', in Daunton, *Cambridge Urban History of Britain*, vol. III, pp. 554–5.

[33] C.J. Simon and C. Nardinelli, 'The Talk of the Town: Human Capital, Information and the Growth of English Cities 1861–1961', *Explorations in Economic History*, 33 (1996), pp. 384–413.

[34] J. Habermas, *The Structural Transformation of the Public Sphere* (Cambridge, 1989). See also J. Garrard, *Democratisation in Britain: Elites, Civil Society and Reform since 1800* (Basingstoke, 2002), pp. 42–83.

[35] On this point see also R.J. Morris, 'Governance: Two Centuries of Urban Growth' in R.J. Morris and R. Trainor (eds), *Urban Governance: Britain and Beyond since 1750* (Aldershot, 2000), pp. 1–14.

character, stressed the emergence of a political consensus, structured around middle-class culture, developing hesitantly into a participatory democracy. The common denominator in both these strategies was the idea of civil society. Even before the Registrar General began to collect data on deaths it was evident that industrialization and urbanization together posed a serious threat to the health of the nation. To redress the balance of social disadvantage and environmental damage that resulted from the unfettered operation of the market or the clumsy tyranny of the state required a 'third way'. This was seen as achievable through the medium of 'civil society', where 'in the area between family and the state, or the individual and the state; in non-state institutions which organise citizens for political participation' it was possible to construct a new consensus.[36] The city is especially instrumental in this process because it offers so many interstices between individuals and institutions where a community of interest, or civic virtue, can flourish. De Tocqueville termed this 'local public spirit' and claimed that 'there is no surer guaranty of order and tranquillity, and yet nothing more difficult to create'.[37]

The idea of a 'local public spirit', termed 'the common good' in Scottish burghs, is explored by Richard Rodger and owes more than a little to the concept of 'civil society' developed first by the Scottish moralists Adam Ferguson and David Hume.[38] An ancient term, dating from 1493, the common good assumed renewed significance in the years after 1860 to municipalities who used the revenues derived from property and customs dues mainly to assist a diverse group of private clubs and associations. In Edinburgh, for 50 years before the First World War, Rodger shows how the town council cemented loyalties and encouraged participation by offering small donations, prizes and subsidies to private organizations. In so doing, he demonstrates the enduring nature of public–private partnerships and their capacity for forging alliances between the agencies within the local state. In another strand of activity, the Edinburgh town council mounted vigorous publicity campaigns to attract conferences and exhibitions, offered the freedom of the city to prominent (and well-disposed) individuals, and conducted intensive

---

[36] K. Kumar, 'Civil Society: An Inquiry into the Usefulness of an Historical Term', *British Journal of Sociology*, 44 (1993), p. 383; C.G.A. Bryant, 'Social Self-organisation, Civility and Sociology: A Comment on Kumar's 'Civil society'', *British Journal of Sociology*, 44 (1993), p. 399. See also J.A. Hall, 'In Search of Civil Society', in J.A. Hall (ed.), *Civil Society: Theory, History, Comparison* (Cambridge, 1995) and E. Gellner, *Conditions of Liberty: Civil Society and its Rivals* (London, 1994).

[37] de Tocqueville, *Democracy in America* (1840; London, 1994), p. 68.

[38] Ferguson, *Essay on the History of Civil Society'*.

efforts to lobby parliament in defence of its own civic interests.[39] In addition, the expenditure to preserve the town's records and to commission paintings of historic scenes and significant local events were efforts to influence public opinion. All this can be seen as the construction of that public sphere which de Tocqueville deemed so difficult to create.[40] Together with the pomp and ceremony associated with royal visits, civil society was constructed after 1860 in Edinburgh by municipal actions which were both responsive to, and stimulated by, public opinion. These actions were legitimated in the name of the 'common good' and funded by revenues precisely assigned for the purpose.

Much of the discussion surrounding the role of associational culture and its contribution to participatory democracy is presented in relation to the formative years of 1780 to 1840. This is as it should be. But the evidence from Edinburgh and elsewhere is that this relationship continued throughout the nineteenth century and well into the twentieth century.[41] Even as collectivism gained a foothold, voluntarism remained a durable influence on the local state.[42] The increasing density of mid- and late-Victorian neighbourhood-based organizations – the self-help and thrift-based burial, cooperative and collecting societies, church and works outings, building clubs, trade unions and mutual aid societies – reinvented the socially integrative role of local organizations and contributed to the distinctiveness of communities. This is the world that Robert Colls says has been lost. His chapter in this volume reminds historians that communities do not last forever. Sometimes they become extinct. Sometimes, also, and in spite of appearances, they are difficult to 'see'. Colls's chapter stands as a warning to all urban historians who use words like 'community' and 'culture' lightly. It is also a record of a remarkable urban achievement. Somewhere between the middle of the nineteenth and the end of the twentieth century, hugely against

---

[39] On this point, see S. Gunn, *The Public Culture of the Victorian Middle Class: Ritual and Authority in the English Industrial City 1840–1914* (Manchester, 2000).

[40] Habermas, *The Structural Transformation of the Public Sphere*, pp. 140, 148, 236. Thus Habermas stresses the communicative aspects of public opinion in relation to civil society rather than placing the emphasis on associations.

[41] See for example, P.H.J.H. Gosden, *Voluntary Associations in Nineteenth Century Britain* (London, 1973); R. Price, 'The Working Men's Club Movement and Victorian Social Reform Ideology', *Victorian Studies*, 15 (1976), pp. 301–28; R.J. Morris, 'Clubs, Socieities and Associations', in F.M.L. Thomson (ed.), *Cambridge Social History of Britain 1750–1950*, vol.3: *Social Agencies and Institutions* (Cambridge, 1990).

[42] J. Harris, *Private Lives, Public Spirit: Britain 1870–1914* (London, 1994), p. 16.

the odds and in ways that went largely unnoticed until it was too late, British working-class people built a civil society in their own likeness.

Acting between the citizens and the government, civil society promotes a moral environment in which individual rights and civic virtues can be empowered. This theme runs through the work of David Reeder, especially in relation to the empowerment facilitated by educational opportunity.[43] Institutions tend to flourish within pluralist political cultures based on free association and individual rights.[44] And they tend to be less narrowly sectional, or partisan, than families and single-issue pressure groups, which often deny the validity of alternative viewpoints (one of T.H. Green's prerequisites for a civil society).[45] This idea of social inclusion is at the heart of Brian Simon's account of school boards in the 1890s, and Bill Williamson's account of university adult education from around the same period.[46]

Simon shows how the achievements of the school boards were so powerful, and threatening, that a new education act was forced through in 1902 to quash the challenge. Democratically elected school boards started to introduce a popular, non-selective and efficient system of education running from elementary to higher. Their most important innovation was the introduction of the 'higher grade' schools, which filled a gap in 'secondary' education, as it became known, that was unevenly and expensively provided by conservative-minded grammar schools (endowed and county). The new higher grade schools introduced science and technology, modernized the curriculum and encouraged

---

[43] D. Reeder, 'Predicaments of City Children' and 'The History of Urban Education', in D. Reeder (ed.), *Urban Education in the Nineteenth Century* (London, 1977); D. Reeder (ed.), 'Liberal Intellectuals, Education and the Franchise', in D. Reeder (ed.), *Educating our Masters* (Leicester, 1980); D. Reeder, 'Representations of Metropolis: Descriptions of the Social Environment in Charles Booth's *Life and Labour*', in D. Englander and R. O'Day (eds), *Retrieved Riches: Social Investigation in Britain 1840–1914* (Aldershot, 1995), pp. 323–38; D. Reeder, 'Schooling in the City: Educational History and the Urban Variable', *Urban History*, 19 (1992), pp. 23–38; and 'The Reconstruction of Secondary Education in England 1869–1920', in B. Simon (ed.), *The Rise of the Modern Educational System 1870–1920* (Cambridge, 1992), pp. 13–43.

[44] R. Dahrendorf, *After 1989: Morals, Revolution and Civil Society* (London, 1997), p. 79, described charities as 'untidy and imperfect', a reference to the fact that there are now so many charities that they are far from self-interested.

[45] T.H. Green, *The Principles of Political Obligation* (London, 1895), p. 121.

[46] Brian Simon died while this work was in press. His contribution to the history and philosophy of education is warmly acknowledged in a powerful tribute by David Reeder, *History of Education*, 31 (2002), pp. 307–10, in which he is described as the most significant figure in the field.

pupils to stay beyond the school leaving age.[47] Two further school board innovations transformed the educational climate. One was the introduction of pupil-teacher centres, which revised the system of entry into the teaching profession, and the other was the significant extension of education at all levels for all age groups in the 'education continuation schools' and the subjects they offered.

The rising popularity and power of the school boards represented another variant of the central–local government tensions evident in public health debates half a century earlier. Ministry officials, encouraged by Tory and Anglican criticisms of secularization in the curriculum and the challenge to the social order from an educated working class, opposed the work of the school boards. Cities with educational ideas were perceived as challenges to central authority. Sucessful as well as radical, school boards had to be suppressed. The 1902 Education Act abolished the boards, charged voluntary schools to the rates, and established a narrow system of selective fee-paying secondary education. With pupil teachers now obliged to attend the new secondary (grammar) schools, 400 pupil-teacher centres were undermined. But crucially it was the dismantling of the school boards that did the damage – a 'sombre story' in Simon's words and an 'act of vandalism' for which the country is still paying a high price.

Much the same could be said of the very recent dismantling of university adult education departments, founded from the late nineteenth century to make university teaching available to those who wanted it. Williamson's chapter is poised between the success of these departments in the making of a new civil society in Britain, and their failure to seriously challenge the snobbery and conservatism of their host universities. In the end, their reluctance to fight left them vulnerable to takeover. By the early 1990s it was a question of take over or be taken over, and, even if they had had the stomach for the fight, argues Williamson, they were not strong enough in the communities they served to be able to feel confident of victory. He is certain, however, that the pioneering work of university adult education departments with those whom the school system had failed granted the universities a moral high ground which they used to insinuate themselves into the affections of modern society.

School boards continued until 1928 in Scotland and still go on in America where the level of participation in their elections can be as

---

[47] For a more extended account of these developments see D. Reeder, 'The Reconstruction of Secondary Education in England 1869–1920', in D.K. Muller, F. Ringer and B. Simon (eds), *The Rise of the Modern Educational System 1870–1920* (Cambridge, 1987), pp. 135–50.

strongly contested as for state and federal posts. In Edinburgh, when 184 day schools were transferred to the jurisdiction of the Edinburgh School Board (ESB) in 1872, many acquired the motif of the ESB – a caring female teacher standing over a diligent child who has an open book. For middle class women, teaching offered steady and reasonably high status employment, and for the few, an opportunity to serve on school board committees. The moral environment that Helen Meller explores was based initially on neighbourhood and city. Constrained by limited educational and job opportunities, family ties and low pay, the scope for women's action was local. It was also practical, operating in the social spaces that existed between local government, churches and the charities.

Drains and building byelaws were part of a 'man's world'. The skills and ideas of women were developed primarily in informal arenas, principally household, cultural and leisure. Their practical, grass-roots knowledge in managing the household economy and knowing what was happening on the streets contrasted sharply with the emerging male-dominated professional and academic discipline of town planning, where an appreciation of the quality of the physical environment was different from the social needs of the people who lived there. Whereas civic improvers (male) sought to demolish and rebuild, women improvers focused on daily lives. In a complete inversion of the professional planners' perspective, the volunteers' efforts included internal redecoration, rooms for social purposes, gifts of flowers, garden plots, choral singing and the encouragement of open spaces. It was an environmental manifesto that owed its inspiration to Miranda Hill and the organization she founded in 1876, the Kyrle Society. A holistic approach to welfare was inherent in the Kyrle Society's philosophy and the variants of it scattered around British cities. Based on the total environment and not simply on housing construction, the Kyrle Society's approach appealed to the 'social biologist' Patrick Geddes, and his sponsorship found expression, though limited support, in planning circles where a vision for modern cities replaced that of piecemeal and pragmatic inner city improvement. It was the apotheosis of the idea that 'a good environment would produce a good society'. Crucially, however, garden city experiments distracted planners from the enduring environmental problems of the older cities. Women's demands for equal citizenship rights were closely identified with the moral responsibility that was enshrined in voluntary associations. However, as collective action and state provision gained sway, the voluntary activities underpinning the moral responsibilities of women were undermined. Voluntary work was left on the sidelines, according to Meller, and with it the civic role of women.

Any simple polarity between collective and voluntary action in social policy after the First World War would be inaccurate, however.[48] Sidney Webb's gloomy prognosis was that as democratic rights were extended and public authorities acquired increasingly extensive powers, then the private, pluralistic and voluntary associations that had constituted the social fabric in earlier times would be displaced, leaving only a two-way relationship between the state and the individual.[49] Pat Garside takes up this theme in her account of the Sutton Trust and its contribution to the housing stock between the wars. As she observes: 'The concern was that greater involvement in the market place on the one hand and the growth of state intervention on the other would erode people's sense of responsibility to one another.'

The Sutton Trust, initially a model dwellings trust, built almost 8000 homes throughout urban England between 1900 and 1939. Like Meller, Garside, shows how associational life and social responsibility were encouraged 'from outside' but that successes were overshadowed by local authority housing provision which was increasingly recognized as the principal agency for replacing housing stock.[50] The Sutton Trust's 'sociable and familial civil society' went unrecognized, therefore, even though lack of this dimension was exactly the criticism that was levelled at 'failing' council estates.[51] The Trust's vision of Athenian democracy was extolled and its practical encouragement for social responsibility was given through community centres. These were promoted by powerful agencies, particularly the National Council for Social Service and the New Estates Community Council, and were supported financially by influential business and civic leaders. The centres provided activities intended to educate and integrate the newly relocated tenants on the Sutton estates. They sought to foster an involvement in local affairs. This done, it was hoped that an interest in civic duty would be translated into political involvement. Chris Williams's ward-motes in mid-nineteenth century Sheffield were not so far removed.

---

[48] The patchwork of private, public and voluntary hospital and fire service provision has been noted by M. Gorsky, 'Voluntary hospitals . . .', paper presented to the Centre for Urban History seminar, December 2000, and Shane Ewen, 'Power and Communication in Two Midland Cities: Birmingham and Leicester, 1870–1940' (work in progress).

[49] S. Webb, 'Social movements' in *Cambridge Modern History*, vol. 12: *The Latest Age* (Cambridge, 1910), pp. 730–65.

[50] P.L. Garside, *The Conduct of Philanthropy: The William Sutton Trust 1900–2000* (London, 2000). For a similar viewpoint on the largest Scottish housing association (with 100 000 homes in 1989), see H. Al-Quaddo and R. Rodger, 'The Implementation of Housing Policy: The Scottish Special Housing Association', *Public Administration*, 65 (1987), pp. 313–29.

[51] A. Olechnowicz, *Working Class Housing in England between the Wars: The Becontree Estate* (Oxford, 1997).

Did the inter-war housing estates fail to build a civil society? Council tenants did participate in mutually supportive activities but did so principally on a family and friendship basis, not in the manner of participatory politics. Citizenship was passive, 'culturally and politically impoverished', and limited to pubs, cinema and football. By comparison, Sutton tenants, who were significantly poorer than council tenants, were provided with libraries, infant nurseries, baths and wash-houses, and gymnasiums, until 1927 when financial 'prudence' persuaded the trustees that, given the small size of the Sutton estates, residents could make use of local community. The emphasis now was to embed Sutton tenants in the local area. Access to local shops became an important consideration in developing new Sutton estates after 1927.[52] Garside's judgement on the elements essential for the construction of a durable civil society should be circulated to all housing associations and all local authority housing departments. She observes:

> Directly and indirectly, the Sutton Trust's policy on shopping built confidence – between tenants, between tenants and traders, between tenants and neighbours beyond the estate boundaries, and between tenants and their landlord. Sutton tenants were less likely to suffer the strangeness, alienation and loneliness that afflicted tenants of large council estates while the trustees avoided being perceived as an inadequate, hostile and remote landlord.

The Sutton Trust's provision of the Leeds bowling green, the Bradford institute and the Sheffield meeting hall deepened associational life and empowered residents through their management of the facilities.

By these means, some forms of common life were developed in some parts of inter-war Britain. Were these not the embodiment of de Tocqueville's 'local public spirit' which offered 'no surer guaranty of order and tranquillity' but of which there was 'nothing more difficult to create'.[53] The fragility of the common life that was developed is evident in the contrasts between accounts of council housing estates and Sutton Trust estates, but it is de Toqueville's latter remark that most concerns us today.

The 'public spirit' on which community is based depends on a delicate balance between public and private interests. In the early nineteenth century the indirect consequences of private actions caused unreasonable damage and social costs on other citizens, individually and collectively. Is it possible in post-industrial, post-modern Britain to create a society

---

[52] I am grateful to Ruth Brown, a current Sutton tenant in Leicester, for information on this point.
[53] de Tocqueville, *Democracy in Amercia*, p. 68.

coherent enough to restrain 'anti-social behaviour'? In a sense, the very meaning of 'post-modern' and 'post-industrial' would seem to deny the possibility, but in our everyday lives the practical question remains: in the area between the individual and the state, is it possible to develop a society strong enough in its valuation of the common life to defend what's left of the public good, and perhaps even promote it?[54] But in a world where civil society has been damaged and denied, and where the common life has been deconstructed, what constitutes the 'public good'? In the final chapter in this volume, by explaining the making and then the breaking of a community that had lived the common life day to day and celebrated the public good in its associations and politics, Robert Colls raises these vital questions.

The *Guardian* recently devoted an entire supplement, twice, to an account of the public service activities of over 150 individuals in which their commitment to the public interest was reported as strong and, if anything, strengthening.[55] Another account reported on the proliferation of public interest groups in twentieth-century Britain and commented that this was unprecedented in British history, though media disquiet has been expressed concerning the numbers, status and assets of charitable trusts and philanthropic organizations and their roles have been questioned.[56] These 'nurseries of democracy',[57] as charitable organizations have been described, are clearly flourishing even if the sceptic might think this is more to do with their tax-exempt status than their being the cradle of civil society.[58] Alternatively, the disestablishment of boards of inspectors and commissioners accountable to local or central government and their replacement by quasi-autonomous non-governmental associations (quangos) and private businesses has produced what has been termed an 'elective dictatorship' in local and national affairs. These unelected bodies, formed in considerable numbers in the 1980s and 1990s, effected a 'hollowing out' of the state by means of systematic cutting away at existing social institutions.[59] It was a reversal of the nineteenth-century approach by which a matrix of agencies built social

---

[54] Kumar, 'Civil society', p. 383.

[55] 'Public Voices', *Guardian*, 21 March 2002; 'The Common Good', *Guardian*, 21 March 2001.

[56] S.H. Beer, *Britain Against Itself: The Political Contradictions of Collectivism* (London, 1982).

[57] Committee on Charitable Trusts, 1952–3, para. 53.

[58] Charitable trusts received from government in the 1990s three times more resources than they did in the 1980s. See Parliamentary Debates, 5th Series, House of Lords, vol. 163, pp. 89, 95–6, 105.

[59] R.A.W. Rhodes, 'Hollowing out the State: The Changing Nature of Public Service in Britain', *Political Quarterly*, 65 (1994), pp. 138–51.

institutions intended to construct the civic life – 'guardians', literally, to oversee, to institute and to promote social cohesion, albeit in their own way.[60]

This dense network brokered change and continuity in the modern city. These are the communities that have been deconstructed, claims Robert Colls. This is the 'world we have lost'. Or is it the world that is mutating? Fixed in time and space, around workplace and, as Morris has shown, around the triad of 'class, party and sect', communities were bound by their identities.[61] These identities, though often spatially defined, were also systems of shared values.[62] They are, or were, communities of ideas. And what distinguished earlier 'communities' was their overlapping memberships and the extent of their engagement with urban agendas beyond their own sectional interests. This diverse urban culture produced plural visions of urban society that were negotiated through written statements and oral testimony delivered in the public arena of local newspaper columns and open meetings.

This rich associational culture still exists in Britain. The monthly Leicester publication *What's On?* identifies nineteen different dance groups in the city and seven different walking groups, including Red Rope, a socialist walking and climbing club, each holding regular meetings.[63] Sports, educational courses, exhibitions, concerts, historical and religious interests each have their own listings. 'Right to Roam', ramblers, friends of the philharmonia, alumni associations, wine tasting, science fiction readers' meetings and Macintosh users' groups each are self-contained communities, some of which meet only virtually. These activities have their democratic DNA in eighteenth, nineteenth and early twentieth-century British associational life. Whether twenty-first century urban associations will be able to think beyond their own agendas to link up and engage that 'political habitus' sufficiently to turn it into a civil society again is too early to say. Whether single-issue political organizations – poll-tax protestors, anti-vivisectionists, asylum seekers – can gel in the future around broader-based issues to produce a coherent

---

[60] T.A. Markus (ed.), *Order in Space and Society: Architectural Form and its Context in the Scottish Enlightenment* (Edinburgh, 1982), pp. 25–113.

[61] R.J. Morris, *Class, Party and Sect: The Making of the British Middle Class, Leeds 1820–50* (Manchester, 1990). See also D. Hayden, *The Power of Place: Urban Landscape as Public History* (Cambridge, Mass., 1995); R. Sennett, *Flesh and Stone: The Body and the City in Western Civilisation* (London, 1994).

[62] S. Gunn and R.J. Morris (eds), *Identities in Space: Contested Terrains in the Western City since 1850* (Aldershot, 2001).

[63] In addition to salsa, country, tango, line dancing, lindy hop and swing, there is also 'not quite belly dancing'. For further details, see <www.leicester.gov.uk/link>.

civic community remains uncertain.[64] Nineteenth-century associations, for all their imperfections, were constitutionally significant because they shielded 'an unusually stable and diverse civil society from the arrogance of politicians in temporary command of the state'.[65] Contemporary associations and single-issue organizations are the raw materials of social inclusion. But, as the essays in this volume show, if they do not develop beyond the narrow confines of their sectional interests, then civil society is impaired. The arrogance of politicians will then be difficult to arrest.

---

[64] The Countryside Alliance provides a rural model.
[65] D. Marquand, 'Commentary: After Tory Jacobinism', *Political Quarterly*, 65 (1994), p. 125.

CHAPTER TWO

Taxation and representation in the Victorian city

Martin Daunton

Cities involve a huge transfer of costs and benefits, of external economies and diseconomies. They generate rents and monopoly profits for some, and pollution, exploitation and disease for others. The relationship between these gains and losses troubled those responsible for the government of cities in the pre-industrial past, and still trouble politicians in the post-industrial present. However, they created particular intellectual and conceptual problems in early Victorian Britain. At this point, Britain had emerged as the most urbanized nation in human history; it was also experiencing an unprecedented shift from organic to mineral fuels and raw materials.[1] The result was to free the economy from the limits of a Malthusian world in which population pressed against the limit of resources, at the cost of a greater capacity to pollute. At the same time, economic policy was debated and contested with the shift from protectionism to free trade. By the middle of the nineteenth century, the Rent-seeking power of the old monopolies of the East India Company or the protected producers of Caribbean sugar had been swept aside. The result might simply be to create a new group of monopolists with power to exploit the consumer – railway, gas or water companies. Could the benefits of free trade and liberty from the exploitative power of monopolists be subverted?[2]

These concerns link with two other debates in the second quarter of the nineteenth century: the franchise and taxation. The parliamentary, poor law and municipal franchises were reformed in 1832, 1834 and 1835

---

[1] The argument of E.A. Wrigley, *Continuity, Chance and Change: The Character of the Industrial Revolution in England* (Cambridge, 1988).

[2] On the culture of free trade, see F. Trentmann, 'Civil Society, Commerce and the "Citizen Consumer": Popular Meanings of Free Trade in Modern Britain', in F. Trentmann (ed.), *Paradoxes of Civil Society: New Perspectives on Modern German and British History* (New York and London, 2000), pp. 306–331; and on debates over the nature of companies and their power over consumers, T.L. Alborn, *Conceiving Companies: Joint Stock Politics in Victorian England* (London, 1998).

to create a responsible property-owning electorate, which would be prudent and shrewd in its control of spending, not least because it would pay taxes. However, prudence can be myopic and self-interested, concerned for the immediate savings from lower taxes on the individual, with scant regard for the social implications and long-term costs of deteriorating public health and the burdens imposed on others by the activities of free riders. The franchise might create irresponsible prudence and prevent responsible spending, or it might allow political myopia to be corrected and long-sighted policies adopted. The debate over the structure of voting was less concerned with notions of a rise of democracy, than with the most appropriate qualifications and voting systems to link taxpaying and desirable levels of spending. The debate was not confined simply to public bodies, for the issues of taxpaying and representation also informed the private sector. Might it be that monopolistic companies supplying services were both unaccountable to the public, and able to impose charges that were tantamount to taxes? The result might be taxation without representation, a theme informing the discussion of natural monopolies in the Victorian city. Similarly, industrialists pouring wastes into the river systems or smoke and fumes into the air were in effect taxing the local inhabitants.

A sense of these connections, and the way that the debates over franchise reform and free trade permeate the politics of Victorian cities, is provided by two quotations. In 1842, Edwin Chadwick remarked that the pollution of air in large towns 'operates as a tax increasing the wear and tear of linen and expense of working to all who live within range of the mismanaged chimneys'. A few years later, John Stuart Mill complained that gas or water companies had taxing powers, and that their ability to charge a high rate for gas had the same impact on the owner of a cotton mill using gas for lighting as did granting power to an individual or association to impose a duty on all raw cotton imported into the country, for their own private benefit.[3] These comments suggest that debates over nuisances, monopolies and public governance were framed by a common discourse of the power to tax, and of how best to shape the franchise to control taxing powers. The franchise should be considered in a much wider way than the right to vote in parliamentary or local elections, for the same issues applied to the right to vote within companies. In both public bodies and commer-

---

[3] E. Chadwick, *Report on the Sanitary Condition of the Labouring Population of Great Britain, 1842*, ed. M.W. Flinn (Edinburgh, 1965), pp. 355–6; J.S. Mill, *Principles of Political Economy, with Some of Their Applications to Social Philosophy* (London, 1848; new edition ed. W.J. Ashley, London, 1909), pp. 962–3.

cial concerns, there was a similar discussion of the form of the franchise to create responsibility and financial probity, which may be considered in three locales.

The first locale is 'nuisances' created by economic growth and urbanization. Smoke and noxious vapours polluted the air; effluent and wastes poisoned watercourses; noise annoyed and smell offended. These nuisances created major legal and philosophical problems: how was one person's freedom to pollute to be restrained? In modern parlance, we might ask how free riders on the urban system were to be controlled. The issue was addressed, using a different vocabulary, by John Stuart Mill in *On Liberty*.[4] As he realized, the liberty of one person ends where harm is done to others – but what counts as harm? This was not only a major issue in political philosophy, for it was dealt with in an immediately practical way by courts grappling with the question of what constituted a 'nuisance', and how far pollution was an acceptable price to pay for economic prosperity and employment.

The second locale is the franchise. Taxpayers or ratepayers had an interest in voting for cheap government, the view satirized by Dickens in 1853 when he imagined an election address in the fictitious town of Cess-cum-Poolton: 'Ratepayers: Cess-cum-Poolton! Rally around your vested interests. Health is enormously expensive . . . Be filthy and be fat. Cesspools and Constitutional Government! Gases and Glory! No insipid water!!!'[5] The construction of the franchise and its relation with taxpaying was crucial in order to escape the hold of these parsimonious ratepayers over urban government, to break the constraints of short-sighted economy or 'myopia' arising from a preference for the immediate reduction of taxes over the long-term benefits of a healthy, efficient urban economy. How could the franchise be shaped to allow investment in the social infrastructure and an increase in public goods? There were conflicting needs: on the one hand, how to ensure that collective action was possible and free riders paid; on the other, how to ensure that the outcome was not excessive expenditure. There was a fine line between irresponsible or myopic economy and irresponsible expenditure; the local government franchise was critical to creating a *via media* of responsible spending. By what means was it possible to secure the consent of

---

[4] J.S. Mill, *On Liberty with The Subjection of Women and Chapters on Socialism*, ed, S. Collini (Cambridge, 1989), pp. 13, 94; the modern discussion of social costs starts with R.H. Coase, 'The Problem of Social Cost', *Journal of Law and Economics*, 3 (1960), pp. 1–44, reprinted in his *The Firm, the Market and the Law* (Chicago and London, 1988), pp. 95–156.

[5] C. Dickens, 'Our Last Parochial War', *Household Words* (1853), p. 265, quoted in S.E. Finer, *The Life and Times of Edwin Chadwick* (London, 1952), p. 435.

taxpayers to spending without giving them the power to block desirable investment in the social infrastructure, and without giving power to the beneficiaries of expenditure at the expense of those who provided the funds?

The third locale is natural monopolies or utilities. Investment was not only an issue in the public sector, for there was a new scale of private investment in the hands of large companies for railways, gas, water, tramways and electricity. The emergence of these large companies created a similar problem to the old chartered monopolies and imperial producers sheltered by protective duties and the navigation laws: monopoly power over the consumer. The rhetoric used in debates over the navigation laws and protection was transferred to discussion of the monopoly powers of gas or water companies, of how to ensure that free trade did not recreate monopolies in a new guise. Further, taxation and representation emerged as a significant political issue, for the nature of the franchise was crucial in companies as well as in public bodies: how should the electorate and voting powers in the company be constructed to ensure that its taxing powers were not used against the interests of the consuming public, yet without harming the right of the shareholders to a decent profit?

These issues are variations on a single theme: how should costs and benefits be allocated within the Victorian city? The focus of this chapter is on the period from about 1830 to 1870, when systemic problems arising from Victorian urban and industrial growth were debated in the same vocabulary as the discussion over free trade and parliamentary reform. The concern for social costs and externalities – for free riders who took without paying, and rent-seeking monopolists who extracted profits without responsibility – was placed within the same language as debates over the East India Company, the reintroduction of the income tax or the abolition of the corn laws.

Nuisances: who should be responsible?

In 1842, Edwin Chadwick suggested that one person's freedom to pollute was another person's cost, equivalent to a tax imposed by the state. Should this freedom be restrained, on what terms and by what means? In medieval and early modern towns, individuals could seek redress under the common law of nuisance, making a claim for damages against the person causing the nuisance. The basic legal maxim was that a man should use his own property so as not to injure that of others: *sic utere tuo ut alienum non laedas*. The application of the maxim was not straightforward, for it implied a decision on the *balance* of interests and not *absolute* rights and wrongs.⁶ Where was the line to be drawn between freedom to do with one's property as one wished and the duty not to injure a neighbour? In the early nineteenth century, common law precedents gave some guidance.

A nuisance might be justified on the grounds that the activity had a general utility to society. The principle rested on a case of around 1560, in which a barrister complained that the calm of his chambers was disturbed by the 'jabbering of the boys' in a neighbouring school. His complaint failed, for schools were useful and it was lawful to set them up anywhere; the lawyer could always move his chambers to the other side of the house.⁷ However, in the case of *Aldred* v. *Benton* of 1610, Aldred's complaint against Benton for erecting a pig sty was upheld. Aldred complained that the 'fetid and unwholesome stink' of the pigs made his house uninhabitable. In his defence, Benton argued for the utility of pigs as food (as of schools for educating boys) and claimed that 'one ought not to have so delicate a nose that he cannot bear the smell of hogs'. The crucial consideration deciding the case in favour of Aldred was the claim that the smell led to a risk of infection, to actual damage rather than discomfort.⁸ Utility alone was not a sufficient defence, and there was a further test: did the nuisance cause actual damage? This principle was applied in the case of *Jones* v. *Powell* of 1628. The complaint was against a brew-house, using coal whose fumes affected the health and papers of the bishop's registrar whose office was six feet away. Everyone needs beer, and the defendant argued that he had to use coal given that wood was in short supply. The nuisance could therefore be justified on the grounds of utility, but the court held that much depended on location. Whether or not the complainant could reasonably be expected to tolerate the nuisance depended on the established trade of any district. In this case, the court found that a nuisance was committed.⁹

Such rulings allowed neighbours to adjust disputes, but were they applicable to more general, systemic nuisances which were of increasing importance in the late eighteenth and early nineteenth centuries? The stench of a pig sty affected close neighbours; what about the copper works of Swansea or St Helens that spread poisonous fumes over a wide

---

⁶ J.H. Baker, *An Introduction to English Legal History* (3rd edn, London, 1990), p. 483.

⁷ See J.H. Baker and S.F.C. Milsom, *Sources of English Legal History: Private Law to 1750* (London, 1983), p. 592; Baker, *English Legal History*, p. 487.

⁸ Baker, *English Legal History*, p. 487; J.F. Brenner, 'Nuisance Law and the Industrial Revolution', *Journal of Legal Studies*, 3 (1974), p. 405.

⁹ Baker, *English Legal History*, p. 488; Brenner, 'Nuisance Law', p. 405; A.W.B. Simpson, *Leading Cases in the Common Law* (Oxford, 1995), p. 171; Baker and Milsom, *Sources of English Legal History*, p. 601.

area? In the case of a private nuisance, a landowner complained of an injury to his property rights, and it was entirely possible for an individual to complain of the damage caused by a large copper smelter. It was also possible for a public body to complain of a public nuisance caused to the community as a whole. The two approaches were not exclusive, for a private action could be taken against a common problem causing a public nuisance where it was also injuring private property rights. The issue became a political one. A large landowner might be able to pay the costs of a legal action in defence of his private property rights, whereas many small occupiers suffering a loss of health and the inconvenience of smuts and fumes would not be able to protect their interests unless a public body were willing to act. In principle, public bodies had considerable scope to take action; in practice, any decision to take action was highly contested. Could a council afford to act against major employers and ratepayers in the town, who might indeed be represented on the corporation? In Swansea, one of the most severely polluted towns in the country with its massive use of coal to smelt copper ore which produced poisonous fumes, the corporation only once took action. In 1820, a petition led to a meeting of inhabitants to consider the problem of smoke pollution, and the corporation contributed £200 towards a total of £1000 offered as a reward for developing a technique to reduce emissions. It did not use the law of public nuisance, and action continued to rely on private actions brought by landowners.[10]

Even if action were taken, how would the courts decide whether an activity should be considered a nuisance? As we have seen, utility was not a complete defence, and the answer might turn on what was reasonable, for as one judge remarked, 'what would be a nuisance in Belgrave Square would not necessarily be one in Bermondsey'.[11] Might an action against a polluter simply throw workers out of their jobs? These issues caused considerable concern in early Victorian cities, where it was increasingly obvious that nuisances were systemic and not simply matters of good neighbourliness. In the opinion of some legal historians, the courts could not operate to control free riders and prevent one person's freedom harming other members of society. On this view, the courts interpreted *Aldred* v. *Benton* in an increasingly restrictive way in the 1850s and 1860s, so giving greater opportunities to large-scale

---

[10] Baker, *English Legal History*, p. 492; Fleming, *The Law of Torts* (9th edn, Sydney, 1998), p. 461. I would like to thank Roderick Bagshaw of Mansfield College, Oxford, for clarifying this point. On Swansea, see E. Newell, 'Atmospheric Pollution and the British Copper Industry, 1690–1920', *Technology and Culture*, 38 (1997), pp. 655–89.

[11] Brenner, 'Nuisance Law', p. 414, quoting a judge in 1879.

industrial concerns to pollute. Hence the courts failed (so it is argued) to extend the law from good neighbourliness to the entire urban environment.[12]

The issue was the balance to be struck between individual suffering and public amenity. Critics of the courts and judges suggest that they were inclined to favour the industrialists as creators of prosperity against those who bore the costs of pollution. Their case rests on opinions such as Vice-Chancellor Bruce's denial in 1851 that anyone had an absolute entitlement to completely unpolluted air; all that could be expected was air 'not rendered incompatible with the physical comfort of human existence'. How should this quality of air be defined? He took a robust attitude about English character:

> ought this inconvenience to be considered in fact as more than fanciful, more than one of mere delicacy or fastidiousness, as an inconvenience materially interfering with the ordinary comfort physically of human existence, not merely according to elegant or dainty modes and habits of living, but according to plain and sober and simple notions among the English people?[13]

Similarly, in *Hole* v. *Barlow* (1858) the Court of Common Pleas accepted that no nuisance existed from the reasonable use of a lawful trade in a convenient and proper place, even where it caused annoyance. Any other view, argued the judge, would mean that

> the neighbourhood of Birmingham and Wolverhampton and the other great manufacturing towns of England would be full of persons bringing actions for nuisances arising from the carrying on of noxious or offensive trades in their vicinity, to the great injury of the manufacturing and social interests of the community.[14]

The issue was well put by Lord Wensleydale in 1863, in the case of St Helen's Smelting Co. against William Tipping, a former cotton master who bought a landed estate and mansion in the grim industrial town of St Helens. Not surprisingly, Tipping soon complained of damage to his property. In the opinion of Lord Wensleydale,

> where great works have been created and carried on, and are the means of developing the national wealth, you must not stand on extreme rights and allow a person to say, 'I will bring an action

---

[12] Ibid., pp. 408, 431; J.P.S. McLaren, 'Nuisance Law and the Industrial Revolution: Some Lessons from Social History', *Oxford Journal of Legal Studies*, 3 (1983), p. 220, argues that the failure was not doctrinal, but arose from the fact that the law was no match for the social problems of industrialization.

[13] Brenner, 'Nuisance Law', p. 410.

[14] Ibid.

against you for this and that, and so on.' Business could not go on if it were so.[15]

In other words, complaints could not be made about billowing smoke and fumes from factory chimneys which caused *general* damage, but only about the actual physical damage caused by a specific piece of smut from a particular chimney to a particular person or property. The interpretation put on these cases by some legal historians is that judges were favourably disposed to polluters and to industrial capitalism.

However, it should not be assumed that the courts simply interpreted the law in favour of industrial firms at the expense of the community. Indeed, the celebrated dispute between Tipping and the St Helen's Smelting Co. was not a straightforward victory for the industrial polluter. The case went to appeal and then to the House of Lords, which rejected the view that the private rights of individuals were subordinate to the public interest of economic development. In other words, a business in a suitable location was *not* immune; it was left to the jury to consider the facts of the case. Hence the legal principle could be tempered by common sense or discretion. The outcome was not so much a charter for industrial polluters, as some legal historians have argued, as confusion in the common law.[16]

Not all judges were tenderly disposed to industrial polluters, and they took account of a number of considerations. Much depended on who came first, or the doctrine of *prior appropriation*. This doctrine held that there was no case for a nuisance if industry were in the area prior to residential development; where industry was the newcomer, a nuisance could be upheld.[17] Some judges went further and argued that a polluter could not simply argue that the complainant had come to an existing nuisance. At least in the case of water rights, prior appropriation could be modified by the doctrine of *natural flow* which held that users downstream had a right to water undiminished in quality from its source. The issue facing judges was how the doctrine of natural flow fitted with prior appropriation. Did the owner of land downstream from a large town have a right to pure water, or was pollution by industry and sewage

---

[15] Ibid., p. 415.

[16] The best account of the case is A.W.B. Simpson, 'Victorian Judges and the Problem of Social Cost: Tipping v St Helen's Smelting Co. (1865)', in his *Leading Cases*, pp. 163–94; *Revised Reports*, CXLV 1863–66 (London, 1914), pp. 348–56.

[17] McLaren, 'Nuisance Law', p. 172; see the judgement in *Rex* v. *Cross*, 1826, *Revised Reports*, XXXI, 1826–30 (London, 1897), pp. 684–5. The noxious trade of slaughtering horses in Islington was held to be a nuisance because the houses already existed; it would not be a nuisance if the houses came to the nuisance.

justified by the long existence of the town? Although the doctrine of prior appropriation might be used as a defence against a charge of committing a nuisance, the doctrine of natural flow would uphold the complaint.[18]

The courts were not entirely sure of the relative weight of these doctrines. In the case of *Wood* v. *Waud* in 1849, the judge ruled that a landlord had an absolute right to pure water according to the doctrine of nature flow. Although residential pollution from human effluent and domestic smoke was acceptable and natural, he ruled that the pollution of the air and water by manufacturers was not acceptable.[19] However, not all judges took the same approach, and there was a wide divergence of legal opinion between doctrines of prior appropriation and natural flow. The courts were debating the nature of market relationships, in much the same way as Margot Finn argues in the case of small debts. As she shows, judges did not in any simple way impose political economy or the laws of the free market. They were concerned to protect women debtors from exploitation by devious traders, while urging strictness against men in the labour market.[20] The same ambivalence is found in the case of nuisances.

The doctrine of natural flow affected the development of sanitation in large cities. In 1858, a landowner with property on the river Tame downstream of Birmingham complained of the nuisance caused to his property by Birmingham Corporation, which had built a new system of sewers and was dumping raw sewage into the river. The landowner claimed a right to enjoy the river in an unpolluted state, 'or at all events so far unpolluted that fish could live in the stream and cattle would drink of it', and he sought an injunction to stop the practice. The court found against the corporation. Similarly, landowners complained of the pollution caused to the river Aire in Leeds by the discharge of unpurified sewage from sewers constructed under Improvement Acts of 1847 and 1848. In 1870, the appeal court found in favour of the landowners, despite the facts that the river was already polluted, that no complaint was made until the sewers had operated for 16 years, and that the health of Leeds would suffer. The judgement rested on the explicit statement in the improvement acts that the sewers 'shall in no case become a nuisance'. Leeds Corporation was required to ensure that its sewage was

---

[18] McLaren, 'Nuisance Law', p. 173.
[19] Ibid., pp. 173, 176–7; *Revised Reports*, LXXVII, 1848–9 (London, 1905), pp. 809–31.
[20] M.C. Finn, 'Working-class Women and the Contest for Consumer Control in Victorian County Courts', *Past and Present*, 161 (1998), pp. 116–54.

purified and deodorized so as not to cause a nuisance.[21] Similarly, when Doncaster council planned to discharge sewage into the river Don, both the Aire and Calder Navigation Co. and the Manchester, Sheffield and Lincolnshire Railway Co. secured an injunction and obliged the council to construct a sewerage works in the early 1870s.[22] Judges argued in other similar cases that it was feasible or reasonable, at little cost, to purify the sewage before it entered the stream.[23] Courts could therefore force through sanitary change, depending on the definition of what is 'natural' (which raises issues of philosophical meaning and scientific authority) and what solutions were economically 'reasonable' (which raises complex questions of costs). Rather than imposing some simple notion of political economy, the courts were seeking to define relations in a free market in a highly contested process of assessing costs and benefits, and defining where the liberty of one person to do harm to another should be constrained. These issues were to reappear in the case of 'natural monopolies'.

The outcome was more complex than a simple shift in favour of polluters, for many judges stressed the need of industrialists and corporations to behave in a responsible manner. The problem was not so much that courts were favouring industry, as a division of opinion that made the use of courts risky to *all* parties and limited their usefulness in balancing the interests of polluters and complainants. The problem was not simply the confusion caused by continued debate over legal principle. There were also issues of proof and of political will. It was one thing to take action against a neighbour's pig sty where cause and effect may be easily proved. How was it possible in a town such as St Helen's or Swansea to prove that a particular smelting works caused damage to a particular property? There was even a suspicion that copper smelters built taller stacks in order to make proof more difficult, by spreading smoke and fumes over a wider district. Where there were several polluters in a district, the complainant needed to show the exact proportion of pollution caused by each, and each pollutant had to be traced back to its precise source. Further, the cost of private actions was high, and even when a successful common law action awarded damages, it was still necessary to take a further action in an equity court to obtain an

---

[21] *Attorney-General* v. *Leeds Corporation*, 1870: *The Law Reports: Chancery Appeal Cases, V, 1869–70*, pp. 583–96.

[22] K.S.M. Goschl, 'A Comparative Study of Public Health in Wakefield, Halifax and Doncaster, 1865–1914', Ph.D. thesis, Cambridge University, 1999, p. 87.

[23] McLaren, 'Nuisance Law', pp. 177–8; Brenner, 'Nuisance Law', pp. 423–4.

injunction to stop the pollution in future. Hence most cases were brought by large landowners, or by one industrial concern against another to protect their water supply or to stop free riders who reduced their costs by using cheaper, dirty methods. Whether town councils or other public bodies would take action was doubtful, given their reliance on the tax revenue from large industry, and the fear of creating unemployment.[24]

Common law was therefore supplemented by statute law and institutional innovation. In the case of sewage and water pollution, new bodies were created to adjudicate between the different claims on water. In 1888, the new county councils could apply to the Local Government Board to establish a joint committee for a river with powers under the Rivers Pollution Prevention Act 1876. This committee allowed the competing interests of different authorities to be moderated in a highly political, contested process.[25]

In the case of air pollution, common law was supplemented by statute law, without entirely resolving the contestation of costs and benefits, for the terms used in the acts were open to dispute. The Nuisances Removal Act 1846 defined a nuisance as anything 'injurious to health' – a criterion requiring proof that smoke or fumes actually caused respiratory disease. The phrase was usually interpreted in a restrictive, narrow way. The Smoke Abatement Act 1853 required steam engines to use the 'best practicable means' to consume their own smoke. A similar phrase was used in the Alkali Act of 1863, which limited the emission of muriatic acid gas, and of 1874, which extended the law to noxious vapours. Manufacturers were required to use 'the best practicable means for preventing their discharge into the atmosphere'. How would the courts define what was 'practicable'? The word could be defined as 'technically feasible', so that a workable method of limiting emissions would be enforced regardless of cost. In fact, the term was defined as *economically justified*. The Royal Commission on Noxious Vapours concluded in 1878 that 'those means of improvement cannot properly be called practicable which involved a ruinous expenditure' and would prevent the continuance of trade and employment. Hence the issues of utility and reasonableness found in the common law were debated in the formulation and interpretation of statute law. As with natural monopolies, where the measurement of profit and capital were so important, so with nuisances there were complex issues of assessing the cost of new equipment and the impact on profits and prices. What was reasonable or practicable might also vary according to the stage of the trade cycle, or of international

---

[24] The difficulties are outlined in McLaren, 'Nuisance Law', pp. 194–9, 205–15.

[25] Goschl, 'Comparative Study', pp. 98–100.

competition: what might be reasonable in a period of boom might not be bearable in time of depression or serious competition from abroad.[26] These considerations gave considerable importance to the definition of capital and profit: were profits sufficiently generous to afford new methods of limiting emissions, or would the cost erode profits and threaten the survival of the industry? Further, standardized measurements of emissions and their chemical composition were needed, and some sense of the cost implications of any reduction in emissions. The development of financial accounting and of chemical measures were central to the regulation of industry – a point which reappears in the case of utilities.

These issues of pollution were expressed in the same language and continued the same discourse as debates over protection and free trade. What were the conditions for employment and prosperity; how should the balance between growth and amenity be struck; and what was the social desirability of forms of economic activity? The supporters of protection argued that industry subverted the economic order, creating over-dependence on exports at the expense of a balanced and harmonious domestic economy. Furthermore, urban-industrial interests were corrupting the political system with their selfish pursuit of profit and the misuse of power.[27] Supporters of free trade argued, on the contrary, that protection of agriculture and trading monopolies corrupted politics, and distorted the efficient and natural distribution of resources. Such concerns reappear in debates over pollution. Were industrialists to be given freedom to pollute in the pursuit of prosperity and employment – or did their activities create an imbalance in the political order and economic system, imposing costs on other members of society in the same way as protection for landowners? Courts had to consider these issues, and local authorities had to strike a balance between competing interests within the community. Did they show more concern for industrialists and employment, or health and amenity – for whom did they speak?

This vexed question leads to another crucial issue in the early Victorian city: the structure of the franchise and the conditions for collective action. Indeed, another solution to the problem of pollution was investment in public works such as great water works at Loch Katrine for Glasgow or the new sewers and Embankment in London, which could provide pure water or prevent polluted water from causing harm. These projects were amongst the major investments of the nineteenth century, demanding large-scale 'lumpy' capital at considerable cost to the taxpay-

---

[26] Brenner, 'Nuisance Law', pp. 426–7.

[27] A. Gambles, *Protection and Politics: Conservative Economic Discourse, 1815–52* (Woodbridge, 1999).

ers before any benefit would be apparent. How was collective action to be encouraged and the costs of this large investment justified, in the face of myopic self-interest for cheap government?

Public works: who should pay?

In 1858, Disraeli fled the House of Commons, overcome by the stench of the Thames that could not be masked even by the expedient of soaking the curtains of the chamber in chloride of lime. The Thames had become an open, fetid drain, as sewers designed only for storm water poured the contents of water closets into the river water that was supplied to the customers of the water companies. The result was not only stench; it was death from cholera and typhoid. Obviously, the problem was well beyond the scope of the law of nuisances designed to deal with a neighbour's privy seeping into the adjacent property. The nuisance could not be rectified without large-scale public investment: who should pay, on what terms?

The problem of pollution of the Thames arose from a disjuncture between the desire of the water companies to increase their profits by installing more water closets, and the financial resources of the commissioners of sewers. The sewers were intended to cope with storm water, and until the early nineteenth century it was an offence to make a connection with domestic sanitation. This rule was changed in 1815, which increased the demand for water closets – but nothing was done to increase the fiscal resources of the commissioners of sewers. They resigned in protest in 1852, and in 1853 their successors failed to raise a loan on the security of the rates. The task of improving sanitation was taken over by the Metropolitan Board of Works (MBW) in 1855, and £4.1m was eventually invested in new sewers, which then raised the major question of who should pay. Initially, ratepayers were only obliged to pay if they derived a direct benefit from the new sewers, and they could apply to Quarter Sessions to be excused from payment. In other words, they were treated as individual consumers of a service, like gas, rather than as contributors through their taxes to collective investment in the health of the metropolis. This approach was abandoned in 1858, when the MBW was given power to raise a loan of £3m on the security of a main drainage rate paid by all parts of London, without a right of appeal.[28]

---

[28] S. Halliday, *The Great Stink of London* (Stroud, 1999), pp. 33, 35–47; S. Halliday, 'Sir Joseph Bazalgette and the Main Drainage of London', Ph.D.

The relationship between taxation and representation was critical for the nature of collective action. Despite a common desire for retrenchment and economy, both by penny-pinching ratepayers and advocates of cheap government, expenditure on major capital projects was also needed. The ambitions of the new poor law could only be fulfilled if expensive workhouses were constructed to impose deterrent, indoor relief; and the crisis of pubic health could only be resolved by large-scale investment in the urban infrastructure. High levels of spending might be irresponsible and wasteful – but so could parsimony. Great care was therefore needed in shaping the local franchise in order to prevent 'policy myopia', the preference of taxpayers for low taxes that might lead to long-term problems of poor public health and urban diseconomies. How could a more far-sighted approach to public spending be created, without falling into the danger of removing constraints on spending and alienating taxpayers?

At the start of the nineteenth century, most municipal corporations were closed, self-electing oligarchies. The municipal corporations often had some sense of civic identity and pride, and their members were often drawn from the Tory-Anglican patricians of the town. They might well have some interest in sponsoring urban improvements and defending the economic prosperity of the town, but they were also open to criticism. They might wish to defend the interests of the freemen of the town through the use of apprenticeship and trade regulations, an approach increasingly open to attack as irrelevant to a competitive, commercial society. The closed oligarchies were criticized for using the resources of the town for partisan ends, and the finances of the corporation lacked transparency and accountability. As a result, ratepayers were reluctant to pay their taxes, and the finance of urban improvements came to rest on borrowing and a mounting burden of debt – a situation difficult to sustain in the longer term in the absence of a buoyant tax base to service the loans. By the early nineteenth century, the relation between taxation and representation in the existing corporations needed to be reformed in order to remove constraints on collective spending. Further, many of the expanding towns of the eighteenth and early nineteenth centuries fell outside the existing corporations, and they needed to be brought within the structures of corporate governance.[29]

---

thesis, London Guildhall University, 1998, pp. 22, 36–7, 41–2, 50, 56–7, 82–3, 106–10, 201 and appendix 3.

[29] J. Innes, 'Governing Diverse Societies', in P. Langford (ed.), *The Short Oxford History of Eighteenth-Century Britain* (Oxford, 2002), pp. 103–39; E.J. Dawson, 'Finance and the Unreformed Borough: A Critical Appraisal of Corporate Finance, with Special Reference to the Boroughs of Nottingham, York

In addition to the municipal corporations found in some older towns, all parishes in town and country had responsibility for poor relief, the maintenance of roads, the provision of watches and general order. These services were controlled by the vestry meeting, which appointed officers from the inhabitants of the parish and imposed a rate or labour charge. Unlike the closed and self-electing municipal corporations, parishes were usually 'open', allowing all householders in the parish to attend – a practice more applicable to rural villages than to populous urban districts. The danger of open meetings, in the eyes of critics, was not merely chaos and inefficiency; it was that control might fall into the hands of the potential beneficiaries of welfare spending, with high levels of taxation on the better-off members of the parish. On this view, taxation could be used irresponsibly by giving power to residents who paid little or no rates but did have political voice. The issue was how to give more power to 'responsible' taxpayers in order to impose discipline on spending and to force the poor to become self-reliant participants in a free labour market.[30]

The limited coverage of the municipal corporations, and the failings of parish vestries in responding to the demands of the urban environment, led to the emergence of a third, ad hoc, set of institutions: improvement or police commissioners who regulated the use of the streets through watches, lighting and cleansing. These commissions were established by local acts of parliament that laid down the franchise. In many cases, the commissions were dominated by large owners of property, as in Great Bolton where the act of 1792 gave control to 40 trustees with property of £1000, who were appointed for life with the power to fill vacancies by co-option. This closed, oligarchic system of governance was challenged in the early nineteenth century by smaller ratepayers who wished to overturn the dominance of Tory-Anglican cliques and to impose economy. In 1831, the franchise in Bolton was changed so that

---

and Boston', Ph.D. thesis, University of Hull, 1978; S. Szreter, 'Economic Growth, Disruption, Deprivation, Disease and Death: Or the Importance of the Politics of Public Health for Development', *Population and Development Review*, 23 (1997), pp. 693–728.

[30] On the operation of the old poor law, see R.M. Smith, 'Charity, Self-interest and Welfare: Reflections from Demographic and Family History', in M.J. Daunton (ed.), *Charity, Self-Interest and Welfare in the English Past* (London, 1996), pp. 23–49. The precise outcome depends on the social structure and cultural assumptions of any parish: in some cases, the vestry was dominated by small proprietors who were not inclined to favour high taxation of themselves and general poor relief to those who were considered to be irresponsible and feckless. See S. King, 'Reconstructing Lives: The Poor, the Poor Law and Welfare in Calverley, 1650–1820', *Social History*, 22 (1997), pp. 318–38.

vacancies were filled from a list of candidates nominated by the vestry meeting. A similar change occurred in Manchester, where the commission was created in 1765 as a self-appointed body with the power to co-opt new members; in 1792, the commission consisted of any owner or occupier of property with a rental of £30; and in 1828, 240 commissioners with a property qualification of £28 were appointed by electors with a qualification of £16. In some towns, the property qualification was higher, and was biased towards owners rather than occupiers. For example, in Burnley the qualification was set in 1819 at the ownership of property with a yearly value of £50 or occupation of property of £100. In other towns, the qualification benefited occupiers, as at Oldham where owners needed property with an annual value of £50 compared with occupiers who only needed £30. These conflicts over the franchise involved a radical attack on a propertied oligarchy which was accused of imposing rates on others in order to undertake public works of benefit to themselves. However, a change in the relation between taxation and representation also created the prospect of lower middle-class parsimony or myopia. Small shopkeepers or traders attempted to reduce public spending and the burden of the rates in order to protect their profits, at the expense of the health of the community.[31]

In each case, the relationship between taxation and representation needed to be redefined. The process was highly contested, with two competing principles emerging in the early nineteenth century. One approach was associated with the Sturges Bourne Act 1818, a permissive measure available to parishes wishing to move from open to select vestries. It was implemented at a national level in the new poor law of 1834, which gave more votes to large owners and ratepayers. Owners of property up to £50 had one vote, with an additional vote for each £25 to a maximum of six; ratepayers had one vote for assessments up to £200, rising to a maximum of three votes for property rated at £400 and above.

---

[31] M. Winstanley, 'Owners and Occupiers: Property, Politics and Middle-class Formation in Early Industrial Lancashire', in A. Kidd and D. Nicholls (eds), *The Making of the British Middle Class? Studies of Regional and Cultural Diversity in Early Industrial Lancashire* (Stroud, 1998), pp. 97–100; for detailed studies of some of these conflicts, see J. Garrard, *Leadership and Power in Victorian Industrial Towns, 1830–80* (Manchester, 1983); P. Taylor, *Popular Politics in Early Industrial Britain: Bolton, 1825–50* (Keele, 1995); M.J. Turner, *Reform and Respectability: The Making of a Middle-Class Liberalism in Early Nineteenth-Century Manchester*, Chetham Society, 40 (1995); D. Fraser, *Urban Politics in Victorian England: The Structure of Politics in Victorian Cities* (Leicester, 1976); V.A.C. Gatrell, 'Incorporation and the Pursuit of Liberal Hegemony in Manchester, 1790–1839', in D. Fraser (ed.), *Municipal Reform and the Industrial City* (Leicester, 1982).

The aim was to prevent irresponsible spending, by removing the ability of potential beneficiaries of the poor law to impose charges on other members of the community who paid the bulk of the taxes. The result (so it was hoped) was to constrain irresponsible spending on outdoor relief and relief in aid of wages; it might be to create responsible spending by directing capital investment into deterrent workhouses or (as in the case of the Public Health Act) improved sanitation. The system of plural voting would remove the ability of non-taxpayers to dominate spending, without falling into the other trap of handing power to myopic small traders.[32]

The second approach was associated with Charles Hobhouse's permissive act of 1831, which allowed parish vestries to become select with a franchise of one vote for each ratepayer. The duke of Wellington was concerned that this franchise would leave property 'at the disposition of the rabble of the parish', by giving voters with little property and minimal contribution to taxes a controlling voice. The principle was not accepted in the new poor law of 1834; it was accepted in the reform of municipal corporations of 1835. The outcome was rather different from Wellington's fear, for the franchise was dominated by small ratepayers with a concern for parsimony and cheap government. They pursued a policy of *irresponsible economy* or myopia, which led to a failure of public spending and collective action with alarming consequences for urban mortality.[33]

In the case of the improvement commissioners, separate local acts to set up each body gave way to general legislation establishing the framework of powers. Initially, the Lighting and Watching Act of 1830 followed the lines of Sturges Bourne, with a graduated franchise of one vote for property assessed at £50 and an additional vote for each additional £25 up to a maximum of six votes. In 1833, the act was amended on the principle of one ratepayer, one vote. The franchise of 1830 was more likely to lead to responsible economy and spending – with the complaint that a small number of large ratepayers and property owners could impose costs on other taxpayers. The franchise of 1833 meant that a larger number of small ratepayers could capture the commission, and impose strict economy or myopia. The franchise of

---

[32] For the background to debates over the reform of the poor law, see P. Mandler, 'The Making of the New Poor Law *redivivus*', *Past and Present*, 117 (1987), pp. 131–57.

[33] The best discussion of the changing nature of the franchise is J. Prest, *Liberty and Locality: Parliament, Permissive Legislation and Ratepayers Democracies in the Nineteenth Century* (Oxford, 1990), pp. 8–9, 12–13, 15–16. On the 1835 Act and its implications, see Szreter, 'Economic Growth', pp. 705–6 and E.P. Hennock, 'Finance and Politics in Urban Local Government in England, 1835–1900', *Historical Journal*, 6 (1963), pp. 212–25.

existing commissions was not standardized, so there was a wide variation in the relationship between taxation and representation.[34]

In the second quarter of the nineteenth century, collective spending was at a low level and the urban death rate started to rise.[35] The problem facing sanitary reformers was how to shape the franchise to reduce myopia and to permit responsible public spending by controlling cautious or myopic small ratepayers. However, there was also a danger in transferring too much power to a reforming minority of sanitary reformers: there could be resistance from the disaffected majority and a loss of consent to taxation. Such a danger was apparent in the Public Health Act 1848, which allowed a small minority of ratepayers – 10 per cent – to petition for the creation of a local board of health and to borrow on the security of the rates; the franchise also gave more votes to large property owners and ratepayers. In 1858, the approach was changed so that a majority of two-thirds of ratepayers was needed to set up a local board, so imposing a barrier to spending and at the same time creating consent for taxation. Further, support for spending on new purposes was secured through the use of ratepayers' plebiscites or referenda to obtain powers to levy a rate for a specific proposal. The Museums Act 1845, the Bath-houses and Wash-houses Act 1846 and the Libraries Act 1850 and 1855 allowed a local authority to spend tax revenue on these purposes, if a majority of the ratepayers agreed. Similarly, the Borough Funds Act 1872 required a municipality to secure approval of a public meeting before promoting a private bill to take on new powers. Although these plebiscites permitted 'economists' to block spending and to impose a myopic approach to collective action, they also established consent to specific forms of spending as socially desirable. Consent was constructed by hypothecation of taxes, with each case being fought on its merits and so ratcheting up and legitimizing higher public spending.[36]

Meanwhile, the hold of ratepayers' myopia was weakened by changes in the franchise for borough councils in 1867 and 1869. The local electorate rose fourfold to about 60 per cent of working-class men, most of whom paid their rates as part of their weekly rent to their landlord rather than directly to the council. As a result, the franchise was no longer dominated by lower middle-class ratepayers concerned for the impact of local taxes on their profits, and inclined to take a myopic view

---

[34] Prest, *Liberty and Locality*, pp. 8–9, 11.

[35] S. Szreter and G. Mooney, 'Urbanization, Mortality, and the Standard of Living Debate: New Estimates for the Expectation of Life at Birth in Nineteenth-century British Cities', *Economic History Review*, 51 (1998), pp. 84–112.

[36] Prest, *Liberty and Locality*, pp. 30, 35, 42–5.

of spending. A new cross-class alliance could emerge, bringing together working-class electors with larger industrialists and professionals, in a positive municipal culture of improvement and investment.[37]

Monopolies: who should provide?

Resolving the problems of public health in early Victorian cities required both public collective action and large-scale *private* investment in utilities such as gas, water and transport. Investment in these utilities was 'lumpy', requiring large amounts of fixed capital before a profit could be secured, and could only be undertaken by the creation of a corporate organization. Here, it seemed to many supporters of free trade and a liberal economy, was a serious threat: the old chartered companies and protection of special interests had been eroded or swept away, and now a new form of monopoly threatened to exploit consumers.

The rhetoric of free trade did not assume that the economy was to be left to the invisible hand of the market and laissez-faire, to unfettered competition and blind obedience to the laws of the market. Rather, it assumed a world of active participation in a commercial economy, and was linked with attempts to create an active associational life of 'Athenian democracy'. The economy of Victorian cities was dominated by small-scale units, owned by families or partnerships, whose success depended on the creation of trustworthiness and a reputation for probity in order to secure credit. The survival of this economic system depended on active participation in clubs, charities, churches and chapels, in the creation of networks of sociability and family connections as trustees of marriage settlements or executors of wills. The management of industrial or trading firms depended less on internal managerial hierarchies than on external institutions. Chambers of Commerce provided methods of commercial arbitration and legal forms for contracts; boards of conciliation set wage levels; exchanges provided information on markets and prices.[38] Urban externalities were therefore vital to the success of a world

---

[37] E.P. Hennock, *Fit and Proper Persons*: Ideal and Reality in Nineteenth Century Urban Government (London, 1973), p. 12; Szreter, 'Economic Growth', p. 717.

[38] F. Trentmann, 'Political Culture and Political Economy: Interest, Ideology and Free Trade', *Review of International Political Economy*, 5 (1998), pp. 218–19, 232; E.F. Biagini, 'Liberalism and Direct Democracy: John Stuart Mill and the Model of Ancient Athens', in E.F. Biagini (ed.), *Citizenship and Community: Liberals, Radicals and Collective Identities in the British Isles, 1865–1931* (Cambridge, 1996), pp. 21–44; D. Reeder and R. Rodger, 'Industri-

of small firms; there were also considerable urban diseconomies of disease, pollution and congestion that could threaten profitability and efficiency. The attempt to remove these diseconomies through the provision of urban services by private monopolies might lead to new threats, from the rent-seeking behaviour of large companies imposing high charges for poor quality service, which posed a threat to the active associational life of Victorian towns and cities. The rhetoric of free trade and criticism of monopolies continued into the mid-Victorian period, as attention moved from the destruction of old privileges and restrictions on trade, to the preservation of small firms and active associations from the abuses of new monopolies.

Attacks on corporate privileges were transferred – very explicitly – to the new 'natural' monopolies of Victorian cities. What was the point of permitting merchants to import raw materials without paying protective duties only to become the captives of railway companies able to charge high freights? Herbert Spencer, the leading advocate of laissez-faire economics feared that the corporate conscience of a railway company was inferior to the conscience of an individual, and realized that a group of men might undertake collectively an act which each would find repellent.[39] The issue was how to make sure that collective concerns behaved morally and did not abuse power. One answer was proposed by William Farr, who argued in 1873 that railway companies should follow the example of the East India Co., of 'absorption into the sovereign power'.[40] But there were alternatives to public ownership and control, and in particular the development of mechanisms to regulate privately owned monopolies in the public interest.

The leading historian of the law of contract, P.S. Atiyah, argues that between 1770 and 1870 courts and lawyers moved towards freedom of contract, developing general rules which applied to all people and circumstances rather than considering the circumstances of individual transactions or issues of fairness. On this view, the courts were part of the imposition of a hegemonic ideology of political economy. Atiyah argues that one important element of freedom of control was the notion of *caveat emptor*, which rejected the assumption that payment of a fair price for a commodity implied a warranty; rather, the price paid by the consumer took account of any risk that the good might be

---

alisation and the City Economy', in M.J. Daunton (ed.), *Cambridge Urban History of Britain*, vol. III: *1840–1950* (Cambridge, 2000), pp. 554–7, 560–61.

[39] H. Spencer, 'Railway Morals and Railway Politics', from his *Essays*, vol. III (London and Edinburgh, 1891), p. 60 quoted in P.S. Atiyah, *The Rise and Fall of Freedom of Contract* (Oxford, 1979), p. 281.

[40] Alborn, *Conceiving Companies, pp. 51–2.*

defective.⁴¹ However, this simple account of the rise of freedom of contract and the dominance of political economy neglects some important areas of debate, and not least the power of monopolistic utilities. Could the buyer beware in the purchase of water or gas or electricity, in the absence of alternative suppliers and in ignorance of the quality of the commodity?

The concern over the power of utilities connects with debates over the franchise, for the crucial question was what power did shareholders have to 'tax' consumers, and to whom were they accountable? The creation of companies to provide gas depended on parliamentary sanction through a private bill. In order to simplify procedures, parliament appointed 'surveyors', men trained as lawyers and engineers who went to any town affected by a private bill in order to assess local opinion, and to report back on the proposals of the company. In 1847, in their report on private bills for the supply of gas to five industrial towns in the Midlands and Yorkshire, the surveyors attempted to define market relations. Above all, they were concerned with the 'franchise' of the companies – who had a 'vote' in its decisions and what were its taxing powers? Should the number of shares held by an individual be limited, and should ownership be confined to residents of the town? Should new shares be offered to existing shareholders at par, in a form of a closed corporation, or should they be sold at public auction to anyone who cared to pay? The issue was discussed in the same vocabulary as debates over voting for public bodies, with similar concerns about the precise relationship between the owners and consumers of gas as between those who paid taxes and benefited from public spending. Thus the gas company in Ashton argued that public concerns owned by improvement or police commissioners (as in Manchester) were less representative, for the franchise was skewed to large mill-owners and ratepayers who could secure lower prices for gas at the expense of the general public or use high profits to reduce their payment of rates. Thus 'public' ownership could result in a small group able to exploit consumers, and the company argued that it was more accountable and representative. Indeed, its new bill proposed to limit the number of votes of large shareholders to 13 so that a few large owners could not dominate; and new shares would be sold at public auction to allow anyone who wished to become enfranchised. Critics of the companies doubted the proposals, arguing that a few large shareholders from beyond the town could still impose high charges on the residents. The authors of the report were not convinced by either the company or the commission. Instead, they recommended that shares in the gas companies

---

⁴¹ Aytiah, *Freedom of Contract*, Part I, especially pp. 398–405; and on *caveat emptor*, pp. 178–80, 471–9.

should only be available to consumers within the town, with a limit to the number of shares, so that 'the members of the Gas Company should, as far as possible, be identical with gas consumers'. The efficiency of the plant, and control over dividends, should then be enforced by government officials, with a maximum dividend of 5 per cent.[42]

The outcome was the creation of model clauses for future bills. The maximum dividend was fixed at 10 per cent, and any two consumers (termed, significantly, 'gas ratepayers') could apply to the Quarter Sessions for the appointment of an accountant to check the books and enforce a reduction in price when the maximum dividend was reached.[43] In the opinion of many consumers, these model clauses did not go far enough, for no maximum *price* was fixed. Further, the maximum *dividend* could be evaded by offering more shares to existing owners at par, so increasing the capital base on which the dividend was paid rather than borrowing money at low interest rates in order to construct plant at less cost and permit the reduction of prices. Indeed, there was less incentive to use capital efficiently, in order to raise productivity, than to manipulate the capital of the firm to maximize the amount of dividend received by shareholders. Of course, the provision of additional shares to existing shareholders also limited the franchise of the company. One way of limiting the ability of shareholders to exploit consumers was to insist that new shares should be sold at public auction, so that the franchise would be widened to any consumer who wished to secure a vote. Moreover, the attempt to limit dividends and prices posed major technical issues of how to define capital and profits, and how to ensure that a fall in the price did not entail deterioration in the quality of gas.[44]

Such concerns were major political issues in London from the late 1850s, when the Metropolitan Board of Works, the City Corporation and the gas consumers mutual protection association pressed for maximum prices and standards of 'illuminating power' as well as maximum dividends. The outcome of the campaign was to introduce a maximum price, which could only be exceeded if costs rose. If local authorities felt

---

[42] PP 1847 XXII, *Minutes of Evidence ... on a Preliminary Enquiry respecting the Ashton Gas Amendment Bill*, Qq 903–89, 996, 999–1020; on the ownership of shares, see Qq 480–520 and list of owners on pp. 211–12; PP 1847 XXII, *Local Acts: Preliminary Enquiries*, 'Observations or General Report on the Existing System of Lighting Towns with Gas by Messrs Johnes and Clegg', pp. 95–100.

[43] 10 Vict. c. 15, 'An Act for consolidating in one act certain provisions contained in acts authorizing the making of gasworks for supplying towns with gas'.

[44] These issues were discussed in PP 1859 III, *Select Committee on Gas (Metropolis)*.

that the increase was not justified, they could object to the Home Secretary who would appoint an arbitrator. This procedure might prevent an increase in price, but it did not resolve the complaint that the maximum price was too high, and that it was difficult to reduce. The issue remained of how to give more voice to consumers against the rent-seeking behaviour of the companies. One possibility was to hand power to arbitrators appointed by the Board of Trade, who would audit accounts and inspect works to make sure that capital was being used efficiently and that profits were not being hidden away. Such an approach would use experts to assess whether the companies were showing 'due care and management', and were in reality making a profit 'attaining as near as may be' 10 per cent. But the approach was still open to the criticism that it gave priority to profits and offered no incentive to cut prices and increase efficiency. The interpretation of the phrase 'due care' was open to dispute, for it could still permit the issue of new share capital to benefit owners rather than consumers. These issues were debated in parliament in 1867–8, and connected with discussion of the second reform act and the concern for the correct relationship between voting and taxpaying.[45]

The issue came to a head when coal prices rose in the early 1870s and the companies sought higher prices to maintain their maximum dividend of 10 per cent. The MBW argued that the price should not be increased, for the companies failed to show due care and management, and their capital was excessive as a result of offering shares to existing shareholders in order to evade controls on dividends. The political difficulties were resolved in two ways. One technique was the adoption of sliding scales, which emerged from a select committee chaired by W.E. Foster and were applied for the first time in 1875. A company could only increase its dividend by reducing the price of gas, and could only increase the price of gas by cutting the dividend. The aim was to create symmetrical interests between owners and consumers, for the only way of paying high dividends was through the adoption of efficient, high productivity technology that also allowed a reduction in prices. The task of assessing whether a company showed 'due care and management' was no longer

---

[45] 23 and 24 Vict. c. 125, 'An Act for better regulating the supply of gas to the metropolis'; 31 and 32 Vict. c. 125, City of London Gas Act 1868; *Parliamentary Debates*, 3rd ser. 186, 4 April 1867, cols 1107–8; 11 April 1867, cols 1576–9; 2 May 1867, cols 1914–24; 3rd ser. 187, 9 May 1867, cols 362–3; PP 1866 XII, *Report from the Select Committee on the London (City) Corporation Gas etc Bills*, pp. 67–8; PP 1867 XII, *Special Report from the Select Committee on the Metropolis Gas Bill*, pp. 5–16; D.A. Chatterton, 'State Control of Public Utilities in the Nineteenth Century: the London Gas Industry', *Business History*, 14 (1972), pp. 170–73.

determined by the personal opinion of judges and arbitrators; it could be left to an automatic accounting mechanism. As Foster said, it would 'bring the consumer and the producer into the one common interest of maintaining a low price of gas'. The contest was over accounting practices – where to fix the upper and lower limits of movement and the precise extent of variation. Further, the method of creating share capital was changed in order to change the nature of representation. New shares could no longer be issued to existing shareholders at par, with the danger of a self-electing, closed corporation with opportunities for inefficiency and private gain. The 'auction clauses' required that they be sold openly to the highest bidders, so that the company received any premium and could then invest in new plant. Although shareholders and consumers were not entirely coterminous as proposed in the report of 1847, their interests were now symmetrical, with a mutual interest in efficiency and productivity gains in order to combine high profits and low prices. The alternative approach was public, municipal ownership, which did make consumers and owners coterminous through participation in local elections. The consumers were the electors and owners, so removing the opportunity for a small group of shareholders to act as rent seekers against the public. The result was not necessarily to reduce prices to the consumers, for most municipal gas undertakings charged commercial prices and used the profits to increase the revenue of the municipality.[46]

What was involved was far more complex than a simple rise of freedom of contract or political economy dependent on the invisible hand of the market. Rather, there was a contested, contingent and highly visible set of institutional and accounting arrangements in order to allocate productivity gains between different parties. As in the case of polluting industries, someone had to define what was reasonable and showed due care, how capital was to be defined and profit measured, and

---

[46] PP 1874 LVII, *Copies of Certificate of Commissioners Appointed by the Board of Trade in 1873 on an Application of the Gaslight and Coke Co. for a Revision of the Illuminating Power and Price of Gas*; PP 1875 XII, *Report from the Select Committee on the Metropolis Gas Companies Bill*; PP 1876 XI, *Report, Select Committee on Metropolis Gas (Surrey Side) Bill*, pp. 11–51; PP 1899 X, *Report from the Select Committee on Metropolitan Gas Companies*, pp. 21–9, 347–51; PP 1918 III, *Report from the Select Committee on Gas Undertakings (Statutory Prices), Report*, pp. 591, 604–8; Chatterton, 'State Control of Public Utilities', pp. 173–4; on municipalization, R. Millward and R. Ward, 'From Private to Public Ownership of Gas Undertakings in England and Wales, 1851–1947: Chronology, Incidence and Causes', *Business History*, 35 (1993), pp. 1–21 and R. Millward, 'The Market Behaviour of Local Utilities in pre-World War I Britain: The Case of Gas', *Economic History Review*, 44 (1991), pp. 102–27.

how the quality of gas or the pollution of smoke was to be assessed. Could lawyers be given the freedom to make such decisions, or should authority be removed to new bodies of experts – to accountants and chemists? Such issues were important not only in the case of gas, but in the railways and tramways, electricity and water, where the outcome was not necessarily the same, with differing consequences. The result could be a stand off, with measures designed to protect the consumer resulting in low profits and investment. Arguably, the solution in the case of gas did allow the interests of consumers and investors to be balanced to their mutual benefit, showing how it was possible to regulate private capitalism in the interests of the wider community. The precedent was not followed in other sectors, and the longer term solution was public ownership which in turn led to a new stand off and privatization.

Conclusions

The allocation of costs and benefits, of profits and taxes, extended into others areas besides the examples given in this chapter. One was considered by David Reeder in his first article – the land, which became so important a theme in urban politics. Did landowners extract socially created value from higher land prices created by urban growth? Did high land prices and the reversionary rights of the leasehold system create slums and block urban development? Should the unearned increment be taxed away, and should landowners contribute to betterment?[47] It would be possible to extend the analysis to other utilities, such as water and electricity or tramways, and to take the story forward in time to nationalization and privatization. For the moment, the point to stress is that the major philosophical issues of liberty and constraint can be traced – as John Stuart Mill himself realized – in the mundane realities of urban drains, gas and sanitation as well as in works of political philosophy. These issues were crucial to investment in social overhead capital, to the death rate of the growing cities of Victorian Britain and to the efficiency of a major sector of the economy. Debates over free trade and protection were continued in a new form, with contests over the social costs of industrial growth and the nature of 'balance' in the economy. They divided lawyers and the courts: it is not a simple story of the rise of freedom of contract, of liberty to pollute or the triumph of moral over political economy.

---

[47] These issues emerge in David Reeder's first research: 'The Politics of Urban Leaseholds in late Victorian Britain', *International Review of Social History*, 6 (1961), pp. 1–18.

CHAPTER THREE

The metropolitan and the municipal: the politics of health and environment in London, 1860–1920[1]

Bill Luckin

As David Reeder pointed out in a major historiographical survey in the early 1980s, many contemporaries were convinced that Victorian and Edwardian London remained 'out of step politically [and] not much affected by the radical movements of the century, or, for that matter by the main thrust of the Industrial Revolution'.[2] In terms of control of the environment and maintenance of public health, relatively recently created bodies in the capital frequently found themselves having to cooperate with 'pre-modern' institutions established in the seventeenth, eighteenth and early nineteenth centuries. This random mix of the old and new gave rise to a system – or, as many called it, an 'anti-system' – characterized by unparalleled governmental complexity. The Metropolitan Board of Works (MBW) and (after 1889) the London County Council (LCC), the City, the Metropolitan Asylums Board (MAB), Poor Law authorities, voluntary hospitals, the Thames and Lea Conservancy Boards, the Port of London Authority (PLA) – each was individually or jointly responsible for an astonishingly convoluted body of legislative and administrative practice. Until 1904 regulation of the eight private water concerns rested with the notoriously prejudiced company engineers, the Registrar-General's Office (RGO), the Local Government Board (LGB) and the semi-official metropolitan water analyst, the most

---

[1] I would like to thank the editors for very helpful comments on an earlier draft of this chapter. I am also greatly indebted to Graham Mooney for his insights into and patient elucidation of metropolitan demographic and epidemiological history.

[2] D. Reeder, 'Conclusions: Perspectives on Metropolitan Administrative History', in D. Owen, *The Government of Victorian London 1855–1889: The Metropolitan Board of Works, the Vestries and the City Corporation*, ed. R. MacLeod (Cambridge, Mass. and London, 1982), p. 349.

influential of whom was the distinguished chemist Sir Edward Frankland.³ Parks and open spaces were individually or jointly controlled by the Crown, the MBW, the LCC, miscellaneous trusts and charities and private individuals or groups of individuals. The task of applying sanitary legislation at local level might appear to fall to the vestries and, after 1900, the boroughs. But in many spheres – inspection of factories and workshops, prosecution of purveyors of adulterated food, anti-smoke measures and the 'protection of infant life' – responsibility was divided with the MBW in control until 1889, and afterwards the LCC. Little wonder that, confronted by so impenetrable an institutional jungle, reformers repeatedly resorted to the generalized rhetoric of democratic accountability. Castigating the practice of nomination rather than direct election, they insisted that nothing less than a restructuring of the London government system would bestow unity or coherence on day-to-day life in the capital. According to this ubiquitous discourse, the power of the vestries and their successor-bodies – the boroughs – must be radically reduced, thereby making it possible to secure standards as high as those assumed to be in place in urban provincial England.⁴ Among major metropolitan authorities in the late nineteenth century only the school board appeared to be moving in the right 'progressive' direction, and, as Brian Simon's contribution to this volume indicates, reformist Londoners had high hopes of an increasingly democraticized educational system.⁵ But the school board was also widely cited as an exception which proved the rule: taken as a whole, metropolitan administration conformed to heavily loaded images of amateurism combined with an antediluvian contempt for the spirit of representative control.

This critique was linked to the notion, invariably owing more to the

---

³ C. Hamlin, 'Edward Frankland's Early Career as London's Official Water Analyst, 1865–1876: The Context of 'Previous Sewage Contamination'', *Bulletin of the History of Medicine*, 56 (1982), pp. 56–76 and the same author's *A Science of Impurity: Water Analysis in Nineteenth Century Britain* (Bristol and Berkeley, 1990).

⁴ The full range of arguments is surveyed in J. Davis, *Reforming London: The London Government Problem, 1855–1900* (Oxford, 1988). See also K. Young and P.L. Garside, *Metropolitan London: Politics and Urban Change, 1837–1981* (London, 1982). Other excellent overviews include P.J. Waller, *Town, City and Nation: England 1850–1914* (Oxford, 1983), pp. 24–67; P.L. Garside, 'London and the Home Counties', in F.M.L. Thompson (ed.), *Cambridge Social History of Britain*, vol. I: *Regions and Communities* (Cambridge, 1990), pp. 471–539; R. Dennis, 'Modern London', in M. Daunton (ed.), *Cambridge Urban History of Britain*, vol. III: *1840–1950* (Cambridge, 2000), pp. 95–132; and A. Briggs's seminal *Victorian Cities* (London, 1963), pp. 311–60.

⁵ See B. Simon, chapter 8 this volume.

cadences and logic of progressive rhetoric than demographic or epidemiological reality, that poverty and disease were persistently and at times traumatically present in the late nineteenth and early twentieth-century capital. Recent research has confirmed that between the 1680s and the 1760s London constituted a desperately unhealthy environment. Repeated outbreaks of smallpox and fever struck down adults and rampant gastro-enteritic infections, convulsions, pneumonia and bronchitis triggered exceptionally high levels of infant and early childhood mortality.[6] However, from the late eighteenth century onwards, local environmental reform, increased access to rudimentary medical care and partial domestication of childhood infections led to a significant reduction in death rates in every age group.[7] Following two generations of improvement, the second quarter of the nineteenth century witnessed a pronounced deterioration, a development which was almost certainly closely linked to unprecedentedly high levels of in-migration, severe infrastructural shortcomings and increased levels of pollution. Epidemiological regression was experienced throughout urban Britain during this period, though London was significantly less severely affected than newly industrializing towns in the Midlands and north.[8] Nevertheless, and despite the capital's relative advantage, many mid-century metropolitan commentators were gloomily convinced that there might be a return to the desperate conditions that had prevailed between the 1680s and the 1760s. In the event cholera, typhus, typhoid, smallpox and influenza failed to gain a permanent foothold in the capital, and by the early 1870s public health activists were beginning cautiously to predict that London

---

[6] J. Landers, *Death and the Metropolis: Studies in the Demographic History of London 1670–1830* (Cambridge, 1993). See also L.D. Schwarz, *London in the Age of Industrialisation: Entrepreneurs, Labour Force and Living Conditions, 1700–1850* (Cambridge, 1992), part 2 and the same author's 'London 1700–1840' in P. Clark (ed.), *Cambridge Urban History of Britain*, vol. II: *1540–1840* (Cambridge, 2000), pp. 649–55.

[7] R. Floud, K. Wachter and A. Gregory, *Height, Health and History: Nutritional Status in the United Kingdom 1750–1980* (Cambridge, 1990), pp. 207, 275 and 326: Landers, *Death and the Metropolis*, p. 354; and R. Porter, 'Cleaning Up in the Great Wen: Public Health in Eighteenth Century London' in W.F. Bynum and R. Porter (eds), *Living and Dying in London: Medical History Supplement* no. 11 (London, 1991), pp. 61–75. See also D. Sunderland, 'A Monument to Defective Administration? The London Commissions of Sewers in the Early Nineteenth Century', *Urban History*, 26 (1999), pp. 349–72.

[8] Floud, Wachter and Gregory, *Height, Health and History*, pp. 205–7, 288–95 and S. Szreter and G. Mooney, 'Urbanization, Mortality, and the Standard of Living Debate: New Estimates of the Expectation of Life at Birth in Nineteenth Century British Cities', *Economic History Review*, lx (1998), pp. 108, 110.

would never again experience the slaughter associated with this earlier era of exceptionally high epidemic mortality.

Compared with other major European cities and many other towns in Britain in the later nineteenth and early twentieth century the capital was a relatively healthy city. However – and this also greatly strengthened the progressive case – well-to-do districts frequently contained large, in fact very large, pockets of abject poverty. Thus in late nineteenth century Kensington some of the very richest of Londoners lived no more than a stone's throw away from some of the most miserably deprived. In comfortable Wandsworth in the early 1870s, the unhealthy Clapham sub-district registered a population density of approximately 18 persons per acre compared to a figure of less than 10 for the rest of the area. During the same period in suburban Camberwell, St George's sub-district recorded a population density of more than 75 individuals per acre, while the figure for the suburb as a whole was no more than 25. Twenty years later, Hackney Wick – notorious throughout the late nineteenth and early twentieth centuries for squalor, substandard housing and lack of access to social infrastructure – registered a mean infant mortality rate of 263: the comparable figure for the more affluent and socially stable Hackney sub-district declined to 122.[9] During that same decade, the 1890s, Shirley Forster Murphy, the first medical officer to the London County Council, initiated a series of investigations into poor and socially deprived areas in north Kensington, Holborn, Fulham, Lambeth and Rotherhithe and concluded that in localities in which 'administration [was] lax', only radical intervention would 'prevent the conditions of life falling to a point where they may endanger the safety of the whole community'.[10] In these areas, medical officers frequently sided with the LCC and the LGB in an attempt to persuade their pay-masters to give a higher priority to effective public health and environmental intervention. Temporary alliances of this kind may be detected in Southwark in 1893 and Rotherhithe, Fulham and Lambeth in 1895.[11] In Kensington in 1898 the medical officer, Thomas Orme Dudfield, strenuously supported the LCC's attempt to compel his vestry to take 'special action' in relation to the desperately poor Notting Dale area.[12] Local opposition to reform

---

[9] *Annual and Decennial Reports of the Registrar-General. Annual Report of the Medical Officer of Health: Hackney*: 1895, pp. 49–54.

[10] London Metropolitan Archive. 15.0 (1899) 'London Government Bill, 1899. Report by the Medical Officer upon the Provisions of the London Government Bill', p. 3.

[11] *Annual Report of the Medical Officer of Health to the London County Council*: 1893, appendix 4, pp. 1–7; ibid., 1895, p. 73.

[12] *Annual Report of the Medical Officer of Health to the London County Council*: 1899, appendix 2, pp. 1–23.

could be intense. In 1896 Holborn found itself rebuked for employing a wholly inadequate sanitary staff, under-investing in domestic refuse services and failing to provide alternative accommodation for individuals whose homes had been subjected to compulsory disinfection. The vestry stonewalled and it was only following additional veiled threats on the part of the LCC and the LGB that a kind of victory – in the form of the appointment of a single additional sanitary inspector – was finally achieved.[13]

Yet these deprived areas only very rarely dragged district death rates down to the deplorable levels experienced in the most environmentally insalubrious of new industrial towns in the Midlands and north. Certainly, the worst affected sectors of the capital – densely overcrowded districts in the East End and immediately to the south of the river – were devastated by cholera in 1831–2, 1848–9 and 1853–4.[14] During the second of these outbreaks, Rotherhithe was nearly as savagely afflicted as Methyr Tydfil, widely believed to be the most polluted town in Britain. Five years later, Bermondsey experienced the highest death rate in Britain but London as a whole escaped with mortality approximately nine times lower than that recorded in its own most heavily hit inner southern districts.[15] During the final epidemic in 1866, it was again a metropolitan locality – Stepney – which recorded the highest death toll in urban Britain. The capital as a whole now escaped with much lower mortality than Swansea, Liverpool or Exeter.[16]

Cholera made no more than a minor contribution to long-term death rates. But, despite progressive protestations to the contrary, other indicators confirmed that London's health record was significantly superior to that of the great majority of newly industrialized towns. Thus during the 1850s adults in Blackburn, Hull, Liverpool and Sheffield were between 20 and 50 per cent more likely to die from typhus than their counterparts in the capital.[17] A generation later, only Bristol, Birming-

---

[13] *Annual Report of the Medical Officer for the London County Council*: 1896, appendix 7, pp. 1–6.

[14] M. Durey, *The Return of the Plague: British Society and the Cholera 1831–2* (Dublin, 1979), pp. 50–76: S.E. Finer, *The Life and Times of Sir Edwin Chadwick* (London, 1952), pp. 333–54; R.A. Lewis, *Edwin Chadwick and the Public Health Movement 1832–1854* (London, 1952), ch. 9; R.S. Lambert, *Sir John Simon 1816–1904 and English Social Administration* (London, 1963), pp. 123–31 and 202–8.

[15] British Parliamentary Papers (hereafer BPP) (4072) 1866 xxxvii, p. 120,'Report on the cholera epidemic of 1866 in England'.

[16] BPP (3949) 1867 xxxvii, p. 339, 'Ninth Report of the Medical Officer of the Privy Council'.

[17] B. Luckin, 'Evaluating the Sanitary Revolution: Typhus and Typhoid in

ham and Bradford recorded lower typhoid death rates than London.[18] During this same period, infants in Leicester, Hull, Birmingham and Norwich were between one and three times more likely to succumb to summer diarrhoea than those born in the capital and mortality from all causes within this most vulnerable age group was significantly lower in London than in the great majority of newly industrialized centres.[19] Thus in no year between 1840 and 1910 did infant mortality in any single metropolitan district rise above that registered in the worst provincial city.[20] The most revealing index of all – life expectation at birth – certainly indicates that many towns made significant progress between 1870 and 1900. However, Londoners born in 1891–1900 could still expect to live for eight years longer than Mancunians, six years longer than Liverpudlians and two years longer than inhabitants of Birmingham. (Among a representative sample of cities with populations of more than 100 000 only Bristolians – with a life expectancy of 47, three years higher than the figure for the capital, and a year above the national average – enjoyed a superior level of health.[21])

Nevertheless, and despite the detailed findings of broadly optimistic social statistical and epidemiological investigations, a widely canvassed contemporary perception of 'London life' continued to be one of unremitting poverty and disease. The unprecedented scale and uniquely complex social, economic and spatial configuration of the capital provides a partial explanation for this contradiction. In addition, a massive body of documentary and fictional literature devoted to the 'rediscovery of poverty' in the capital between 1870 and the outbreak of the First World War did indeed incontrovertibly reveal scandalously sub-standard conditions in the East End and the inner southern and central districts. As has already been noted, these accounts confirmed the ubiquitous proximity of outright deprivation to 'comfort' in 'respectable' parts of the city.[22] In addition, wretchedly adverse living conditions may have been more visibly prominent in the capital than elsewhere: provincial

---

London, 1851–1900', in R. Woods and J. Woodward (eds), *Urban Disease and Mortality in Nineteenth Century England* (London, 1984), p. 114, table 5.2.

[18] BPP 1893–4 (7172-ii) xl (ii), Appendix G.1, table 11, 'Report of the Royal Commission on the water supply of the metropolis'.

[19] W.E. Buck, 'On Infantile Diarrhoea', *Transactions of the Sanitary Institute of Great Britain*, vii (1885–6), p. 87.

[20] N. Williams and G. Mooney, 'Infant Mortality in an 'Age of Great Cities': London and the Provincial Cities, c.1840–1914', *Continuity and Change*, 9 (1994), pp. 191–2, tables 1 and 2.

[21] Szreter and Mooney, 'Urbanization and Mortality', p. 88, table 1.

[22] A. Lees, *Cities Perceived: Urban Society in European and American Thought, 1820–1940* (Manchester, 1985), pp. 106–17.

districts characterized by extreme poverty might contain 5000 people, but in the capital they often housed, or failed adequately to house, four times that number.[23] These bleak communal archipelagos of economic and social backwardness in a city which claimed to be the most materially advanced that the world had ever seen generated a massive body of work devoted to anti-urbanism and the utopian fantasy of dispatching the most impoverished inhabitants of the capital to an under-populated countryside. The allure of social Darwinistic theories predicting biological collapse among 'residual' sectors of London's working class became part of the *lingua franca* of the metropolitan intellectual elite, and as a result the capital, rather than urban provincial Britain, established itself as a primary focus for a fear of city life which both reflected and reinforced anxiety centred on the perceived economic and military decline of the nation as a whole.[24]

An environmental revolution

Recent research suggests that metropolitan historians should be less preoccupied with deeply ingrained depictions of the environmental and administrative 'backwardness' of the capital than with explanations of how London developed into so relatively healthy a capital city. Such an approach brings the demographic into closer proximity with the political while simultaneously drawing attention to the extent to which the municipal idea, *senso strictu*, may or may not have been relevant to the needs of the metropolis. It also allows us to interrogate the achievements of provincial administrations underwritten by self-consciously progressivist ideologies. In order to clear the ground for an examination of these issues, there is a need for an outline account of administrative and institutional change in London between the mid-nineteenth century and the 1920s.

Centralized and local expenditure on sewers, street cleaning and what David Owen has felicitously termed the 'miscellaneous duties' of London government depended heavily on increased supplies of water.[25] From mid-century onwards, reformers concentrated more intensively on the

---

[23] E. Hart, 'Mortality Statistics of Healthy and Unhealthy Districts of London', *Sanitary Record*, vi (1879), p. 57.

[24] G. Stedman Jones, *Outcast London: A Study in the Relationship between the Classes in Victorian Society* (Oxford, 1971): D. Pick, *Faces of Degenerationism: A European Disorder c.1848–1918* (Cambridge, 1989); J. Harris, *Private Lives, Public Spirit: Britain 1870–1914* (Oxford, 1993), pp. 241–5; and Lees, *Cities Perceived*, pp. 136–43.

[25] Owen, *Government of Victorian London*, ch. 6.

'water question' than on any other issue.[26] Depicted as corrupt, profit-maximizing bodies, the companies, operating under a body of private act legislation reaching back to the seventeenth century, became massively unpopular in the aftermath of the cholera epidemics of 1848–9 and 1853–4. Thereafter, technical improvements in terms of the selection, storage and filtration of water appeared to ensure Londoners of a less polluted supply. But in 1866 extreme and culpable incompetence on the part of the East London Company triggered a cholera epidemic which killed 5500 inhabitants in the East End and inner north-eastern suburbs.[27] By the mid-1870s, however, the capital was receiving a greatly improved service. Goaded on by a plethora of hard-hitting official and semi-official technical reports, the companies began to operate more reliable storage, filtration and delivery systems.[28] Sceptics continued to advocate the abandonment of the Thames, insisting that the capital must seek out non-river water in the Surrey hills. In the event, during the final 30 years of the century the single most sensitive indicator – the 'typhoid index' – confirmed that London was significantly less susceptible to the infection than most other cities in Britain and Europe. In addition, differentials in the rate of mortality from the 'autumn fever' in affluent and poor districts, which had been prominent in the 1850s and 1860s, narrowed between 1870 and 1900.[29] Controversy continued to rage around the issues of constant supply and large variations in city-wide consumption. Yet reformers who deeply distrusted the companies found themselves refuted by the mortality statistics. Epidemiologists and specialists in the fields of waterworks technology and the treatment and disposal of sewage had demonstrated that it was possible to subject river water to routine purification up to a point at which it would no longer

[26] The best account is still A.K. Mudhopadhyay, 'The Politics of London Water Supply, 1871–1971', Ph.D. thesis, University of London, 1972. But see also A. Hardy, 'Water and the Search for Public Health in London in the Eighteenth and Nineteenth Centuries', *Medical History*, 28 (1984), pp. 250–84 and the same author's 'Parish Pump to Private Pipes: London's Water Supply in the Nineteenth Century', in Bynum and Porter (eds), *Living and Dying*, pp. 76–94. The larger national context is well described by J.A. Hassan, *A History of Water in Modern England and Wales* (Manchester, 1998).

[27] B. Luckin, *Pollution and Control: A Social History of the Thames in the Nineteenth Century* (Bristol and Boston, 1986), pp. 81–95.

[28] See, for example, BPP 1867 [PP] (3949) xxxviii, 'Ninth report of the Medical Officer of the Privy Council'. Appendix 7. 'Mr J. Netten Radcliffe on cholera in London and especially in the eastern districts' and BPP 1870 (208) xxxviii, 'Twelfth report of the Medical Officer of the Privy Council'. Appendix 5. 'Report by Mr J. Netten Radcliffe on the turbidity of water supplied by certain London water companies'.

[29] Luckin, 'Evaluating the Sanitary Revolution', p. 108, table 5.1.

pose a severe threat to public health.[30] The companies continued to treat working-class consumers with arrogant indifference but public opinion, and surveillance on the part of a progressive scientific community, ensured that the capital was now moderately well protected against cholera, typhoid and dysentery. The MBW and the LCC repeatedly attempted to buy out the companies, but made little progress until the beginning of the twentieth century. When the private concerns were finally deprivatized and placed under the control of the Metropolitan Water Board in 1904, the recently created boroughs secured what supporters of the LCC considered to be blatant over-representation.[31] As we shall see, in relation to city-wide public utilities, deeply imbedded fears of rejuvenated Chadwickian centralization were repeatedly rekindled.

These developments were paralleled by the evolution of institutional means of reducing the incidence of disease. Nineteenth century Londoners were quite correct to be suspicious of the medical profession: doctors were able to provide relief for no more than a small number of non-infectious ailments. However, the city-wide isolation system, the Metropolitan Asylums Board, established in 1868, and accessible to non-pauper patients from the 1870s, played a significant role in reducing the outreach of epidemics of typhus, typhoid, smallpox and scarlet fever.[32] Voluntary hospitals may also have contributed to a reduction in mortality and morbidity. Formally, charters forbade the admission of individuals suffering from infectious disease. But regulations were frequently breached. Examination of hospital registers confirms that an increasing proportion of the metropolitan population now had access to a bed – or to out-patient treatment – for a wide range of infectious and non-infectious conditions. By the 1860s, London, with 16 per cent of its population ending his or her days away from a normal place of residence, was the most heavily medicalized city in the world. Forty years later, one third of all metropolitan inhabitants died in a voluntary or isolation hospital, Poor Law infirmary or charitable institution.[33]

At the same time, a rapid growth in applied scientific, medical, environmental and statistical knowledge injected a degree of order and rationality into the daily activities of bodies responsible for the mainten-

---

[30] Hamlin, *Science of Impurity*.

[31] Owen, *Government of Victorian London*, pp. 135–40; Davis, *Reforming London*, pp. 47–50; and Mudhopadhyay, 'Politics of London Water Supply'.

[32] G.M. Ayers, *England's First State Hospitals and the Metropolitan Asylums Board, 1867–1930* (London, 1971).

[33] G. Mooney, B. Luckin and A. Tanner, 'Patient Pathways: Solving the Problem of Institutional Mortality in London during the Later Nineteenth Century', *Social History of Medicine*, 12 (1999), p. 237, figure 1.

ance of public health and the protection of basic environmental standards. The establishment of the General Registry Office (GRO) in 1837 enhanced awareness of differentials in the incidence of disease according to locality and cause. Just as the construction of city-wide public works in the 1850s and 1860s encouraged vestries and district boards to concentrate more intensively on bolstering the quality of social infrastructure, so the growing sophistication of the GRO's annual and decennial reports exerted a highly positive influence over epidemiological surveillance within individual sanitary areas.[34] In the mid-1850s, medical officers frequently compiled annual reports which did little more than recycle the GRO's quarterly tables of births, marriages and deaths. This continued to be the case in poorer localities until the mid-1870s. A clear majority of late nineteenth and early twentieth-century districts recruited their medical officers at the lowest possible, part-time or 'piece-rate' salaries.[35] However, in a handful of genuinely progressive areas quite different priorities prevailed. There might be strong local political opposition to the assiduously argued specialist critiques of Thomas Orme Dudfield in Kensington, John Tripe in Hackney and Shirley Forster Murphy in St Pancras. But between the 1870s and 1890s the publication of the annual report of the medical officer developed into an important event in the vestry calendar. In Kensington and Hackney annual mortality statistics were broken down into even more detailed categories than those used at the GRO. By the 1880s progressive districts were setting the pace. Inter-communicating with the GRO, exchanging information at meetings of their professional association and at the Epidemiological Society, and publishing in the *British Medical Journal* and *The Lancet*, the new body of professionals became integral to the London government system. Participating in the proceedings of the Chemical, Meteorological and Statistical Societies, and the Royal Society of Arts, medical officers exchanged policy-oriented bodies of knowledge and expertise.[36] In the

---

[34] J.M. Eyler, *Victorian Social Medicine: The Ideas and Methods of William Farr* (Baltimore, 1979); M.J. Cullen, *The Statistical Movement in Early Victorian Britain* (Brighton, 1979); 'Special Issue. The General Registry Office of England and Wales and the Public Health Movement 1837–1914, A Comparative Perspective', *Social History of Medicine*, 4(3) (1991).

[35] A.S. Wohl, 'Unfit for Human Habitation', in H.J. Dyos and M. Woolf (eds), *The Victorian City: Images and Realities* (London, 1973), vol. I, p. 610. See also A. Hardy, 'Public Health and the Expert: The London Medical Officers of Health, 1856–1900', in R.M. MacLeod (ed.), *Government and Expertise: Specialists, Administrators, and Professionals, 1860–1919* (Cambridge, 1988), pp. 128–42.

[36] On this issue, see R.M. MacLeod, 'The X-Club: A Social Network of Science in Late Victorian England', *Royal Society: Notes and Records*, 24 (1970), pp. 305–22; J.V. Jensen, 'The X-Club: Fraternity of Victorian Scientists', *British Journal of the History of Science*, 5 (1970–71), pp. 63–72; and A. Desmond,

fields of waterworks technology, sewage treatment and disposal, as well as the identification of sources of infection associated with unsafe food and drink, local sanitary bureaucracies cooperated closely with public health specialists and epidemiologists who had served an apprenticeship with John Simon at the Medical Office of the Privy Council between 1858 and 1871, and who were now undertaking inspectorial work on behalf of the Local Government Board.[37] As with infrastructural investment, so also in terms of specialist knowledge, London enjoyed a head start of about 20 years over a clear majority of urban provincial centres.

Lest this seem too sanguine an interpretation, it is worth recalling that, in his history of metropolitan public health administration published in 1907, Henry Jephson concluded that the legislation of 1855 had

> put a term to the chaos of local government in 'greater London' and swept away the three hundred trumpery and petty existing local bodies. It created a legally recognisable metropolis defining its component parts and boundaries. It established a definite system of local representative government in that metropolis for the administration of its local affairs. It conferred upon the new authorities not only the powers vaguely possessed and imperfectly, if at all, acted upon by their predecessors, but a considerable number of new ones. It laid the basis for the sanitary supervision of the inhabitants of greater London.[38]

Jephson also conceded that the ignominious collapse of the MBW amid well-attested accusations of rigged building contracts and backhanders marked an 'unfortunate ending to a great public body which had done really great service to London'.[39] Thirty years later as sceptical an observer of the London scene as W.A. Robson readily acknowledged the scale of infrastructural progress between the 1850s and 1880s.[40] The official historians of the LCC, Gwilym Gibbon and Reginald Bell, ritually condemned the MBW as a 'glorified works contractor' but then praised its environmental legacy as 'a distinguished array of improvements that had altered the face of London and brought light and

---

Huxley: From Devil's Disciple to Evolution's High Priest (London, 1997), pp. 327–30.

[37] Useful details are contained in C.F. Brockington, 'Public Health at the Privy Council 1858–71', *Medical Officer*, xci (1959), pp. 173–7 *passim*: see also relevant biographical footnotes in Lambert, *Sir John Simon and English Social Administration*.

[38] H. Jephson, *The Sanitary Evolution of London* (London, 1907), p. 82.

[39] Ibid., p. 382.

[40] W.A. Robson, *The Government and Misgovernment of London* (London, 1939), p. 83.

cleanness into many of the foulest haunts of disease'.[41] Numerous other progressives lauded the performance of London's first semi-centralizing administrative authority. But the vestries were invariably treated with contempt. 'The great masses of the working classes', Jephson claimed, '... were by the deliberate decision of the great majority of [these bodies] deprived of the protection which Parliament had devised and provided for their sanitary and physical well-being.' Moreover, 'the great bulk of the local authorities deliberately ignored the remedy devised by Parliament, and with most reprehensible callousness let the evils go on and increase: ... the name 'Vestry' had become almost synonymous with incapacity'.[42] To the arch-rationalizer Sir Ughtred Kay-Shuttleworth, the inefficiency and corruption of London's local governing bodies reflected and reinforced a quasi-medieval administrative and spatial confusion. In 1878 he asked a 'typical' MP to imagine that he was making his way

> from Old Palace Yard, first to the Horticultural gardens, and, then, say, to Kensal Green Cemetery. He would first pass first through the district of St John's, Westminster, St Margaret's, Westminster, St George's, Hanover Square, Chelsea and Kensington, when he would come back to St Margaret's, Westminster. In his walk ... he would pass through the vestry districts of St Margaret's, Westminster, and Paddington, enter Chelsea again, near Kilburn; and, on reaching Kensal Green, find himself in Kensington again.[43]

To Kay-Shuttleworth, all this implied nothing less than irremediable functional incompetence. It was therefore imperative that amateurish London vestries should subject themselves to re-education and learn from what 'provincial corporations do for their own municipalities ... employ first-rate officers instead of the mere surveyors now employed; and do everything on a uniform ... system'.[44] Tried without benefit of jury, the vestries were found guilty of sabotaging rather than creatively contributing to London's nineteenth-century environmental revolution. A long-drawn out appeal is still being heard: but revisionist scholarship has already established that the original trial must have been rigged.[45]

---

[41] I.G. Gibbon and R.W. Bell, *History of the London County Council, 1889–1939* (London, 1939), pp. 25, 27.

[42] Jephson, *Sanitary Evolution*, pp. 302, 398.

[43] Sir U. Kay-Shuttleworth, *Reform of London Government: Speech in the House of Commons, 5 April 1878* (London, Municipal Reform League Pamphlet), p. 5.

[44] Ibid., p. 18.

[45] This may be concluded from Owen, *Government of Victorian London* and more emphatically from A. Clinton and P. Murray, 'Reassessing the Vestries: London Local Government, 1855–1900', in A. O'Day, *Government and Institutions in the Post-1832 United Kingdom* (Lewiston, 1995), pp. 51–84. Davis, *The London Government Problem*, ch. 1 and Dennis, 'Modern London', pp. 101–2,

Metropolitan exceptionalism

Compared with the capital, many towns and cities in England were faced with problems which ensured that an erosion of the health divide would only be slowly and unevenly achieved. New manufacturing centres paid a disproportionate price for being recent rather than anciently established large-scale urban communities. Since the beginning of the eighteenth century, and much earlier, London had suffered and adapted to numerous near-catastrophes. Crises in the relatively recent past – the Great Fire, the epidemiological setbacks of the 'hard' eighteenth century, the cholera and fever panics of the 1840s and 1850s – had seemed to many to threaten the very existence of the capital. Nevertheless, intermittent and extreme disequilibrium repeatedly gave way to a degree of stability, suggesting that the emergence of a late eighteenth century spatial and demographic critical mass may have played an important enabling role in cyclically re-establishing social and ecological balance. London, in other words, derived hard-won gains simply from its long experience and recovery from numerous crises over a period of centuries rather than mere decades. Differential demographic growth rates in the early nineteenth century were also central to the maintenance of the metropolitan–provincial divide. Although the population of the capital expanded at just over 2.5 per cent per annum during the peak period of national urbanization between 1801 and 1841, this was a low figure when compared with increases recorded in Bradford, Liverpool, Glasgow, Manchester, Wolverhampton and Leeds, each of which experienced a growth rate of between 5 and 10 per cent. In a number of cases – Bradford, Liverpool and Glasgow – comparisons with conurbations in the contemporary developing world are far from irrelevant.[46] Excessively rapid demographic expansion – and massive levels of in-migration – ensured that incremental, adequate consolidation of infrastructure was inherently unlikely to be secured in a city like Manchester, which grew from around

---

are more circumspect, while Young and Garside, *Metropolitan London*, p. 21, restrict themselves to the generalization that 'the vestries . . . varied widely in their size, wealth and responsiveness'. In *London 1808–1870: The Infernal Wen* (London, 1971), pp. 287–90, Francis Sheppard bases his assessment of the vestries almost wholly on Jephson, *Sanitary Evolution*, a work in which these bodies are lampooned as opponents of every initiative for social and environmental reform. The same author's *London: A History* (Oxford, 1998), p. 284, presents a slightly more favourable view. For a balanced account of the post-revisionist consensus see S. Inwood, *A History of London* (London, 1998).

[46] J. Langton, 'Urban Growth and Economic Change: From the Late Seventeenth Century to 1841', in Clark, *Cambridge Urban History*, vol. II, p. 473, table 14.4 and P. Sharpe, 'Population and Society 1700–1840', ibid., p. 500.

two and a half thousand in the mid-seventeenth century to 95 000 in 1801, and to no fewer than a third of a million in 1851.

The capital also derived clear-cut advantages from an exceptionally early movement towards mass suburbanization.[47] In some historical circumstances over-rapid decentralization can lead to temporary infrastructural instability: as already noted, every late nineteenth-century metropolitan suburb contained within its borders overcrowded and poverty-prone sub-districts which continued to record death rates significantly above the mean for the larger areas in which they were located. Nevertheless, the decline in population densities associated with the astonishingly rapid post-1850 expansion of city-sized localities such as Lambeth, Wandsworth, Lewisham and Hammersmith greatly reduced mortality from viral and bacterial droplet infections and made a decisive contribution to improvements in life expectancy for every age group.

In addition, London's status as an imperial city played a decisive role in ensuring that it maintained a clear health advantage over urban provincial Britain. During one of the most serious environmental crises of the century – the so-called 'great stink' on the Thames in 1858 – Members of Parliament adopted a wide range of attitudes towards municipal self-government and metropolitan exceptionalism. In the event, the House voted in favour of immediate intervention. The Metropolitan Board of Works was empowered to borrow up to £3 million at 4 per cent: this would be guaranteed by the government and the principal repaid by means of a sewer rate of threepence in the pound. The decision constituted a silent revolution in relations between the national executive and the MBW, as well as a subtle sea-change in dominant provincial perceptions of the capital.[48] In voting for the principle of metropolitan

---

[47] H.J. Dyos and D.A. Reeder, 'Slums and Suburbs', in Dyos and Woolf, *The Victorian City*, vol. 1, pp. 359–86.

[48] Luckin, *Pollution and Control*, pp. 17–20. See also S. Halliday, *The Great Stink of London: Sir Joseph Bazalgette and the Cleansing of the Victorian Metropolis* (London, 1998). In addition to Owen, *Government of Victorian London*, explicitly or implicitly revisionist accounts of the MBW are to be found in G. Clifton, *Professionalism, Patronage and Public Service in Victorian London: The Staff of the Metropolitan Board of Works 1855–1889* (London, 1992) and D.H. Porter, *The Thames Embankment: Technology and Society in Victorian London* (Akron, Ohio, 1998). For orientation on a generalized nineteenth-century provincial ethos see Briggs, *Victorian Cities*; D. Read, *The English Provinces c.1760–1960: A Study in Influence* (London, 1964); H.J. Dyos, 'Greater and Greater London: Notes on Metropolis and Provinces in the Nineteenth and Twentieth Centuries', in D. Cannadine and D. Reeder (eds), *Exploring the Urban Past: Essays in Urban History by H.J. Dyos* (Cambridge, 1982), pp. 37–55; E.P. Hennock, *Fit and Proper Persons: Ideal and Reality in Nineteenth Century Urban Government* (London, 1973); L.H. Lees, 'Urban Networks', in Daunton, *Cam-*

exceptionalism, members had tacitly lent their support to what Norman Davies has identified as the ideological construction of an Anglocentric 'British Imperial Isles'.[49] Furthermore, provincial representatives who questioned the wisdom of allowing London to spend money on so lavish a scale tended to deprecate increased social investment wherever it might be located. In deploring metropolitan extravagance, they deplored levels of expenditure that might have made provincial cities safer places in which to live. Within this larger political context, the local government 'revolution' of 1835 can only have played a minor role in enabling communities to engage more effectively with large-scale environmental and public health problems. Pre-existing traditions, which benefited privileged interest groups determined to maintain the political status quo, proved remarkably resilient. Eighteenth-century improvement trusts and commissions were in any case widely believed to be doing an adequate job for a minimum of public money.[50] Councillors vehemently opposed what appeared to them to be excessively ambitious and costly projects. Fiery radical denunciation cut across and complicated what might otherwise have constituted politically neutral debates about which tasks required immediate attention in overcrowded and deprived cities and townships. Thus in the eyes of Owenites, Chartists and independents, the deodorization and disposal of sewage emerged as explicitly ideological issues. In an environment in which there continued to be widespread support for the Benthamite orthodoxy that private contractors should undertake public works for individual localities, the spectre of businessmen growing fat on profits derived from transporting human waste to

---

bridge Urban History, vol. III, pp. 81–6; and R.J. Morris and R.H. Trainor (eds), *Urban Governance: Britain and Beyond since 1750* (Aldershot, 2000). See in particular in this volume, R.H. Trainor, 'The 'Decline' of British Urban Governance since 1850: A Reassessment', pp. 28–46.

[49] N. Davies, *The Isles: A History* (London, 1999), ch. 9.

[50] For background here see P.J. Corfield, *The Impact of English Towns 1700–1800* (Oxford, 1982), pp. 79–81, 156–8; B. Keith-Lucas, *The Unreformed Local Government System* (London, 1980); D. Fraser, *Urban Politics in Victorian England* (Leicester, 1976), pp. 55–90, 154–77: and E.P. Hennock, 'Urban Sanitary Reform a Generation before Chadwick?', *Economic History Review*, x (1957), pp. 113–20. See, also, Sunderland, 'A Monument to Defective Administration?'. Links between predominantly eighteenth and early nineteenth century ways of perceiving and intervening in the urban environment are definitively described in C. Hamlin, *Public Health and Social Justice in the Age of Chadwick: Britain, 1800–1854* (Cambridge, 1998). Continuing conflicts between new and longer established forms of local government in provincial Britain in the period after 1835 are confronted in D. Fraser, *Power and Authority in the Victorian City* (Oxford, 1979).

neighbouring farms, alienated radicals and economizers alike.[51] As Simon Szreter has emphasized, even when councillors agreed that a specific urban problem should be given absolute priority, deep ideological divisions invariably worked against meaningful collective action. Only in the 1860s would the economy-obsessed middle and lower middle classes finally demonstrate a willingness to contemplate increased expenditure out of the rates on public works and services designed to benefit every member of the community.[52] The gradual emergence of 'united fronts' of this kind proved to be greatly more significant than the precise historical moment at which a city adopted, or failed to adopt, the 'democratic' Municipal Corporations Act.

Nevertheless, as we have already noted, provincial centres with populations of over a hundred thousand made impressive progress during the final 30 years of the nineteenth century: the four-year advantage enjoyed by the capital in terms of life expectancy at birth in 1850 had narrowed to two or three by the beginning of the twentieth century. The process whereby outer metropolitan suburbs gained an advantage over all others in London was replicated outside the capital. Analysis of this issue is complicated by the fact that the registration districts comprising the largest cities in England were invariably few in number, giving the impression that each locality was divided into a unitary core and a unitary suburbanizing hinterland. But this evidential problem does not invalidate the larger picture. Between 1871 and 1900 life expectation at birth in Sheffield improved from 35 to 39: the rise in salubrious Eccleshall was from 42 to 46. Manchester experienced an increase of four years, from 32 to 36: in leafy Chorlton-cum-Hardy the rise was from 38 to 42. Socially and economically deprived Liverpool increased from 28 to 30:

---

[51] Individual case studies are summarized in B. Luckin, 'Pollution in the City' in Daunton, *Cambridge Urban History*, vol. III, pp. 213–17. See also N. Goddard, '"A mine of wealth": The Victorians and the Agricultural Value of Sewage', *Journal of Historical Geography*, 22 (1996), pp. 274–90 and J. Sheail, 'Town Wastes, Agricultural Sustainability and Victorian Sewage', *Urban History*, 23 (1996), pp. 189–210.

[52] S. Szreter, 'Economic Growth, Disruption, Deprivation, Disease and Death: On the Importance of the Politics of Public Health for Development', *Population and Development Review*, 23 (1997), pp. 698–723. See also S. Szreter and A. Hardy, 'Urban Fertility and Mortality Patterns', in Daunton, *Cambridge Urban History*, vol. III, pp. 633–49 and J.G. Williamson, *Coping with City Growth during the British Industrial Revolution* (Cambridge, 1990). A.S. Wohl, *Endangered Lives: Public Health in Victorian Britain* (London, 1983), pp. 112–16, provides a succinct account of the increasing uptake of central governmental loans for public works from the 1870s onwards among increasingly politically stable municipalities.

'comfortable' West Derby (Liverpool) progressed from 39 to 41.[53] During the period in which urban provincial England was narrowing its long-standing health deficit in relation to the capital, manufacturing centres in the Midlands and north were themselves undergoing a similar process of internal demographic and epidemiological differentiation. However, nearly half a century might separate adoption of the Municipal Corporations Act and a partial closing of the metropolitan–provincial health divide: little if any synchronicity is detectable between the formal democratization of urban governmental structures and measures rendering provincial centres significantly less dangerous places in which to live. In terms of health status in the period between the mid-nineteenth-century cholera crisis and the outbreak of the First World War, 'backward', 'irrational' and 'amateurish' London gained and maintained a slowly narrowing lead. Differentially reformed and infrastructurally modernizing urban provincial Britain struggled to close the gap.

Revisiting the revisionist agenda

With a population of two and a half million in 1851 and over eight million in the 1920s, London had always been far too populous and diverse a city to be governed by a single centralizing authority. Pondering this point – and the extent to which the capital now comprised a constellation of city-sized communities – an anonymous observer recorded in 1909 that

> only five of the boroughs have less than one hundred thousand inhabitants: sixteen between one and two hundred thousand; five between two and three hundred thousand, and three over three hundred thousand. Thus enclosed within the metropolitan area are a number of administrative bodies equal to most of the largest provincial towns.[54]

Sixty years earlier, Edwin Chadwick had been convinced that it would be necessary to replace traditional forms of metropolitan administration with a crown-appointed commission possessing a right to overrule parish

---

[53] Szreter and Mooney, 'Urbanization and Mortality', p. 90, table 2. Other work that has made use of spatial analysis and differential cause-specific death rates to examine intra-urban differentials includes M.E. Pooley and C.G. Pooley, 'Health, Society and Environment in Nineteenth Century Manchester', in Woods and Woodward, *Urban Disease and Mortality*, pp. 148–75 and R.I. Woods, 'Mortality and Sanitary Conditions in the 'Best Governed City in the World'', *Journal of Historical Geography*, 4 (1978), pp. 35–56. See also Luckin, 'Evaluating the Sanitary Revolution'.

[54] 'London Health in 1908', *Sanitary Record*, xliv (1909), p. 623.

elites, deprivatize the water companies and construct a main drainage system predicated on the controversial though by no means wholly misguided principle of arterial circulation. When Chadwick was ousted from the Commission of Sewers and the General Board of Health and then symbolically drummed out of the capital, untrammelled localism failed to re-establish itself. Far from making the world safe for the vestries, the subsequent impassioned mid-century debate paved the way for compromise rather than regression or full and immediate municipalization. Building on the environmental insights underlying Chadwick's vision of an idealized sanitary city, the MBW coordinated the construction of a massively ambitious intercepting sewage system. In so doing, the Board made it impossible for vestries and district boards to evade at least a degree of cooperation with the new and quasi-centralizing authority. Denigrated both by contemporaries and successive generations of historians for its gerontocratic ineptitude and corruption, the MBW may now be more realistically assessed in the light of what it actually achieved between the late 1850s and the late 1880s. Here there was broad contemporary agreement that later nineteenth century London witnessed nothing less than an environmental revolution: even those who insisted that the MBW must be replaced as rapidly as possible by a directly elected and fully centralizing authority possessing comprehensive powers in the fields of public health and environmental control failed to marshal evidence to controvert such a view.

As yet too little research has been undertaken into the micropolitics of day-to-day administration at local level in the capital between the 1860s and 1920.[55] However, no vestry or borough conformed to the caricature of amateurish and corrupt non-interventionism rhetorically circulated by metropolitan and provincial progressives. It is now known that, following a temporary setback during the second quarter of the nineteenth century, the capital experienced an era of renewed environmental and epidemiological progress; advances were achieved in a political climate in which central control over vestries and boroughs remained semi-formal rather than legislatively compulsory. Indeed, only in the 1890s – a period of high ambition on the part of the newly established

---

[55] An exception is A. Hardy, *The Epidemic Streets: Infectious Disease and the Rise of Preventive Medicine 1856–1900* (Oxford, 1993). Emphatically non-political in the conventional sense of the term, this study nevertheless reveals a great deal about bureaucratic conflict and compromise at local level. In *The Government of Victorian London* Owen confirms that in London, as in urban provincial Britain, differences over public health policies could trigger open political warfare. See, in particular, the Southwark fever saga of the 1860s, involving the irrepressible one-time medical officer and vestryman George Rendle, pp. 306–12.

LCC – would a potentially city-wide body, armed with relevant powers, briefly succeed in monitoring and pressurizing 'backward' districts. As we have seen, these detailed Public Health Department reports identified serious shortcomings at sub-district level in nearly every region of the capital. They also confirmed that it was unlikely that progress would be maintained unless reforming medical officers tacitly collaborated with the LCC and the LGB to convert low-spending authorities to the idea that universally positive benefits could be derived from increased expenditure on environmental infrastructure and personnel. In time, however, the Conservative government, capitalizing on its national political and ideological supremacy, undermined the LCC's universalistic project to play an ever larger role in the day-to-day administration of the largest city in the world. For their part, the vestries demanded that they be transformed into autonomous boroughs: the LGB reneged on its earlier commitment to semi-enforced metropolitan reform and encouraged the newly constituted authorities to declare what amounted to unilateral independence from the standard-setting LCC. At the same time, economic considerations proved decisive. As the Progressive T.J. Macnamara noted, the creation of the boroughs had less to do

> [with increasing] the dignity of local authorities [than] to enable the rich to slate off their obligations to the poor. The rich with their few needs want to cut themselves adrift from the poor parishes with their low rateable value and many needs.[56]

By the beginning of the twentieth century the political situation in London was no less complex than it had been in 1850. Formally, the struggle for the representative principle had been only partially successful. In 1855 the local governmental electorate in the capital had been approximately 195 000, or about 30 per cent of the total male population aged 20 and over. Forty years later, a million Londoners possessed the right to vote for two LCC councillors from each of the 60 metropolitan parliamentary divisions. In 1918 the Representation of the People Act increased the size of the electorate, so that by 1920 just over a million and a half inhabitants were authorized to vote in LCC elections. Comparable figures for the metropolitan vestries and boroughs rose from approximately 700 000 during the mid-1890s to about 800 000 just before the outbreak of war, and over a million and a half by 1920. However, by this latter date, only about half of the total adult metropolitan population possessed a legislatively legitimated right to play a full role in the political life of the capital.[57] To

---

[56] Cited in Waller, *Town, City and Nation*, p. 63.
[57] *Report of the County Council to 31st. March, 1919* (London County Council, 1920), p. 11.

progressives this represented near-failure and a betrayal of the mission to transform a generalized progressive impulse into the hard currency of effectively centralizing political and administrative power. Now, in the mid-Edwardian era, the massively self-confident advocate of capital-wide reform of the 1890s had degenerated into a weakened and strategically confused authority which was frequently relegated to the very margins of legislative and executive influence. The Council's 14 members on the Metropolitan Water Board were decisively outnumbered by 27 spokesmen nominated by the boroughs. Representation on the Thames and Lee Conservancy Boards amounted to no more than a paltry three out of 28 and two out of 15 respectively. Ten City-influenced river interests held the whip-hand on the 18-member Port of London Authority, with the Council being entitled to no more than four co-opted votes. The LCC would continue to be excluded until 1929 from the Metropolitan Asylums Board, which was administered by 55 members selected by the Boards of Guardians and 18 nominated by the newly created Ministry of Health.[58] Notable progress in the fields of education, transport and housing notwithstanding, the Council was rebuffed whenever it attempted to gain statutory power to intervene in boroughs which failed to meet minimum requirements under public health legislation, or to reprimand under-achieving bodies responsible for the generalized protection of the metropolitan environment.

All this carries important lessons for the metropolitan historian. First, a continuing preoccupation with the minutiae of the 'London government problem' reveals so much but no more about the dynamics of daily political and social life in the capital during the late nineteenth and early twentieth century. Second, the achievements of the LCC – and more specifically the extent to which it fulfilled the ambitions of the founding-fathers of the late 1880s and early 1890s – have now been fully and convincingly documented.[59] These interwoven themes – the introduction of a 'rational' system of metropolitan administration and the creation of a genuine and genuinely radical city-wide authority – were themselves rooted in common political and cultural concerns: reforming the governmentally unreformable, rationalizing the irrational and creating a materially and ethically regenerated metropolis. Thus, in terms of text and sub-text, what Mill, Jephson, Kay-Shuttleworth, W.A. Robson and other highly articulate progressives said and wrote about London had less to do with a real capital in real time than an imagined capital in unreal

---

[58] Ibid., pp. 9, 11, 15.
[59] See A. Saint (ed.), *Politics and the People of London: The London County Council 1889–1965* (London, 1989) and S.D. Pennybacker, *A Vision for London: London, Everyday Life and the LCC Experiment* (London, 1995).

time. All this implies that metropolitan history should now be less concerned with formally political than explicitly cultural approaches to the evolution of economy, society, environment and collective *mentalite* in the late nineteenth and early twentieth centuries.

Third, by the outbreak of the First World War, a clear majority of metropolitan boroughs were in the process of further consolidating the achievements of vestries which had themselves long since attained a high degree of institutional and bureaucratic maturity: London had finally evolved into a semi-municipalized city. At the same time, other elements of the administrative system – the Metropolitan Water Board, the Port of London Authority, the Thames and Lea Conservancy Boards – remained proudly and obstinately 'pre-modern', although no less functionally competent, and in a clear majority of cases more functionally competent than their counterparts in urban provincial Britain. In terms of the dynamics of early twentieth century metropolitan government, the evidence points to a ubiquitous tension between the drive for increased professional and technical competence on the part of these non-representative bodies and continuing demands for public control championed by the LCC and some though by no means every borough. As in the later nineteenth century, so now in the early twentieth, informal networking between the capital's scientific, medical and epidemiological elites and those who worked for committees and individuals at local level and for the independent, quango-like bodies discussed in this chapter, repeatedly saved the London government system from self-inflicted paralysis. Here, certainly, the coordinating role of the LCC – an astonishingly large, indeed profligate employer of free-floating 'experts', able to take a distanced view of the effectiveness of a thousand and one interventions at every tier of an intensely complex set of administrative structures – may well have been decisive.

Finally, recent scholarship has confirmed that the indisputable achievements of the Metropolitan Board of Works, the vestries and the boroughs constitute a retrospective refutation of the caricatured image of ineptness and corruption so expertly and persuasively constructed and rhetorically naturalized by successive generations of progressive reformers and historians. Now, more than ever, the task is to complete the revisionist agenda by undertaking detailed research into relations and structural and ideological contradictions between the 'modern' and the 'pre-modern' in the capital during the twentieth century as a whole.[60] Such work will be likely to throw light both on London's recent history and the multifaceted and ever-shifting nature of the metropolitan–provincial divide.

---

[60] Richard Dennis begins to explore this terrain in 'Modern London'.

CHAPTER FOUR

Resolving the sewage question: Metropolis Sewage & Essex Reclamation Company, 1865–81[1]

P.L. Cottrell

The City of London further developed over the mid-nineteenth century to become the world's premier financial mart.[2] Its global ascendancy was assisted by the liberalization of company law, while most displayed in the facilitation of a mounting volume of capital exports. Although the market's expanding capacity and increasing effectiveness are beyond question, considerable doubts have gathered over whether it adequately met all domestic needs.[3] David Reeder put this issue in particular terms through querying the extent to which City houses raised resources for investment within London itself. He noted the establishment of Metropolis Sewage & Essex Reclamation Co. in 1865 as an example.[4] This chapter further explores his specific concern and example by considering the context of this company's origins, its formation and subsequent 'life' during early and mid-Victorian England.

Such an examination is more than a case study in the business and financial history of London since the attempt to establish Metropolis

---

[1] I am very grateful for the kind assistance of Professor W. Brock, Professor E. Collins and Dr W. Mathew in developing drafts of this paper, and to the services of the Essex County Record Office, Chelmsford, and the National Archives, Public Record Office, Kew. Further research was assisted by study leave from the University of Leicester, 2nd semester, 2000–1, while the writing of the final version was greatly assisted by the editors' comments.

[2] For the most recent discussions, see R. Michie, *The City of London: Continuity and Change 1850–1990* (London, 1992) and D. Kynaston, *The City of London*, I: *A World of its Own* (London, 1994).

[3] For the latest, albeit particular, review of a very sizeable literature, see M. Collins, *Banks and Industrial Finance in Britain, 1880–1939* (Cambridge, 1991).

[4] D. Reeder, 'Conclusion: Perspectives on Metropolitan Administrative History', in D. Owen *The Government of Victorian London 1855–89: The Metropolitan Board of Works, the Vestries and the City Corporation*, ed. R. MacLeod (Cambridge, Mass. and London, 1982), p. 362.

Sewage & Essex Reclamation is also one instance, possibly the most important, of various private initiatives over the mid-century to resolve profitably the 'sewage question'. This was continuously debated from the 1840s until the early 1870s, provoked by increasing volumes of town effluent. The proper disposal of sewage posed a major dilemma for Victorians and, while unresolved, increasingly insalubrious conditions promoted fatal illnesses. Diarrhoea, gastro-enteritis, typhoid and typhus were all direct causes of especially infantile mortality and, thereby, major contributors to continuing high urban mortality.[5] Cholera outbreaks may have propelled the 'Sanitary Movement', while the great fear that they generated did much to overcome, eventually, ideological and other resistance to necessary remedial intervention.[6] Nevertheless, the persistent urban killers lay closer to home, with continuing pollution comprising their breeding grounds.

Historians have paid increasing attention to the consequent, albeit belated, development of urban sanitary systems, particularly sewerage and, more recently, to the related question of river pollution and how that was also eventually addressed.[7] Most have ignored contemporaries' visions of how sewage might be profitably transformed into agricultural fertilizer. From the late 1840s, repeated official inquiries into sewage, later joined by those concerned with river pollution, emphasized its 'utilization'. Furthermore, Edwin Chadwick saw an answer to London's problems in the sale of night soil to farmers, which would offset the considerable costs of providing the capital's growing population with both pure water and an effective waste disposal system.[8] The promotion

---

[5] S. Szreter, 'The Importance of Social Intervention in Britain's Mortality Decline c.1850–1914: A Re-interpretation of the Role of Public Health', *Social History of Medicine*, 1 (1988), pp. 17, 19.

[6] See A. Briggs, 'Cholera and Society in the Nineteenth Century', *Past & Present*, 19 (1960–61); R.J. Morris, *Cholera 1832: The Social Response to an Epidemic* (London, 1976); M. Durey, *The Return of the Plague: British Society and the Cholera 1831–2* (Dublin, 1979); A.S. Wohl, *Endangered Lives: Public Health in Victorian Britain* (London, 1983); and G. Kearns, 'Urban Epidemics and Historical Geography: Cholera in London 1848–9', *Historical Geography Research Series*, 15 (1985).

[7] See T. Richards, 'River Pollution in Industrial Lancashire, 1848–1939,' doctoral thesis, University of Lancaster, 1982; and L.E. Breeze, *The British Experience with River Pollution, 1856–1876*, American University Studies, Series IX History, 139 (New York, 1993).

[8] On London's growing sanitary problem over the first half of the nineteenth century, see Owen, *Government of Victorian London*, pp. 47–8; and B. Luckin, *Pollution and Control: A Social History of the Thames in the Nineteenth Century* (Bristol and Boston, 1986), pp. 11–34. Chadwick's ideas had something of a forerunner in those of John Martin: see Luckin, *Pollution and Control*, pp. 14–15 and Breeze, *The British Experience with River Pollution*, p. 10.

of Metropolis Sewage & Essex Reclamation Co. represents a subsequent endeavour to put much of his conception of a 'unified system' into practice. The following discussion of this particular attempt commences by examining the wider background – the extent to which farmers employed fertilizers and manures.

Town manure and agriculture

Generally during the 1830s farmers used readily available manures – bones, chalk and lime, hoof and horn, marl, salt, saltpetre and soot – together with farmyard muck and the folding of animals within rotations.[9] The practice of marling stretched back to pre-history, and had undergone a considerable revival from the seventeenth century, particularly to improve East Anglia's light soils. Of equal importance was farmyard manure. Otherwise, until the railway system's full development, transport costs forced farmers to employ what was close to hand. For instance, those around Sheffield applied industrial waste – bone and horn parings from the fashioning of knife handles – while all within carting distance of large towns used urban refuse: street sweepings, stable litter and night soil. Surrey farmers prized 'London muck' for making their clay soils workable.[10]

'London muck' was also applied to the light, gravelly river terrace soils of the emerging market gardening area to the east of the City[11] – as in the Barking area following the 1737 Roding Navigation Act. It was used for crops of potatoes and cabbages and, increasingly, for new produce such as apples, asparagus, currants, onions, plums, turnips and walnuts. 'Town manure' gained a further importance for this horticulture from the 1840s, when crop-forcing methods were introduced. By the mid-century, 200 cargoes of London night soil, together with slaughterhouse waste and even animal carcases, were discharged annually at the Town Quay, Barking, to meet the demand from the locality's 300 acres of market gardens. However, this noxious traffic led to a petition to the General Board of Health and its members were sufficiently alarmed to

---

[9] See R. Shiel, 'Improving Soil Productivity in the Pre-fertiliser Era', in B.M.S. Campbell and M. Overton (eds), *Land, Labour and Livestock* (Manchester, 1991) and L. Brunt, *'Where's there's Muck, there's Brass': The Market for Manure in the Industrial Revolution*, University of Oxford discussion papers in economic and social history, No. 35 (Oxford, 2000).

[10] J.D. Chambers and G.E. Mingay, *The Agricultural Revolution* (London, 1966), pp. 62–4.

[11] For context, see E.H. Hunt and S.J. Pam, 'Essex Agriculture in "the Golden Age" 1850–73', *Agricultural History Review*, 43 (1995).

institute an inquiry. Their investigation revealed the dangers arising from utilizing urban effluent as a soil treatment and fertilizer. Nevertheless, Barking's market gardens were not the sole employer within Essex of 'London muck'; it was also applied by farmers around Witham, some 25 miles to the north east.[12]

Essex and Surrey farmers' increasing reliance upon 'London muck' gave some substance to Chadwick's vision of a 'unified system'. It had a further basis in the working systems of Ashburton, Edinburgh and Leeds, together with those of some towns abroad. As in his other endeavours, Chadwick energetically attempted to realize his concept of a profitably 'cleansed' London, but Towns Improvement Co., registered in 1845, failed to receive the financial backing promised. Nonetheless, he persisted, and the Board of Health published *Minutes on Sewage Manure*. Its author claimed that, at an outlay of 6s. per acre for the necessary piping, agricultural land's fertility would be increased by a multiple of three to four through the application of night soil.[13] There was also a wider group of enthusiasts for aspects of Chadwick's 'unified system', including John J. Mechi, who employed locally generated sewage on his Tiptree Hall Farm at Kelvedon, Essex, and praised its effects. In turn, Chadwick lauded him: 'the population of Towns will be highly indebted to Mr Mechi for the example he has set in the application of liquid manure'.[14] This vigorous campaigner for the agricultural benefits of effluent and for what was to be subsequently called 'High Farming' pointed himself to John Morton's experiments at Lodge Farm, Barking, which involved 0.3 million tons of London sewage.[15] Mechi continued to

---

[12] J.E. Oxley, 'Barking and Ilford', in W.R. Powell (ed.), *A History of Essex*, V, in R.B. Pugh (ed.), *Victoria History of the Counties of England* (Oxford, 1966), pp. 216, 239.

[13] R.A. Lewis, *Edwin Chadwick and the Public Health Movement 1832–1854* (London, 1952), pp. 92–3, 118–19, 122, 237, 309–10; S.E. Finer, *The Life and Times of Sir Edwin Chadwick* (London, 1952), pp. 223–4; and A. Brundage, *England's 'Prussian Minister': Edwin Chadwick and the Politics of Government Growth 1832–54* (London, 1988), pp. 101–8. See also British Parliamentary Papers (hereafter BPP), X (1846), Select Committee on Metropolis Sewage Manure, *Report*; and R. Sheail, 'Town Wastes, Agricultural Sustainability and Victorian Sewage', *Urban History*, 23 (1996).

[14] Essex County Record Office (hereafter ECRO), T/A 804/1, extract, 24–9 May 1852, from Tiptree Hall Farm visitor's book 1846–1878 (British Library, Add. Ms 30015). On Mechi at Tiptree Hall Farm, see ECRO, T/P 114/12, collection of notes etc. by A.J. Dunkin, 1761–1858; and R.R. [R. Rolton], *Tiptree Hall Farm, Essex, J.J. Mechi, Esq.* (London, ?1853).

[15] See J.J. Mechi, *A Second Paper on British Agriculture: With an Account of his own Operations at Tiptree Hall Farm* (London, 1851); *A Fourth Paper . . .* (London, 1854); *How to Farm Profitably; or, Sayings and Doings of Mr Alderman*

bang the drum for what he regarded a 'vast food producing treasure' until the 1870s.[16] Individual pioneers were joined during the 1840s by potentially larger undertakings, such as London Sewage Co., which aimed to collect effluent from as far west as Chelsea for processing in reservoirs at Barking Creek.[17]

Despite a growing emphasis on 'sewage utilization', the continued use of 'natural' manures was challenged by the inception of agricultural chemistry and the growing availability of artificial fertilizers, further enhanced by the spread of the railway network. However, farmers were innately conservative and, although nitrate of soda was introduced in 1835, it was still considered a novelty 15 years later. Nonetheless, agricultural chemistry enabled knowledge, half a century old, of the importance of phosphates for plant growth to become eventually a practical aid. Justus von Liebig developed the treatment of bones with sulphuric acid, and wrote a manual – *Organic Chemistry in its Applications to Agriculture and Physiology* (1840) – which was to be much reprinted. Three years later, John Barnet Lawes found a method for manufacturing superphosphate of lime, initially using coprolite (fossilized dung), and transformed it into a practical process at his Deptford factory.[18]

One of the main checks to applying the industrial products of the new science over the mid-century came from another natural fertilizer, guano (desiccated bird faeces), primarily obtained from Peru. Its import began in 1835 and, from 1842, the sole concessionaires were Antony Gibbs & Sons, Latin American merchants in the City who also had branch houses along South America's Pacific coast. Farmers' increasing use of guano, partly spurred by Gibbs's own propaganda, also generated a greater interest in both agricultural chemistry and experimentation with natural manures. Yet, the first half of the 1850s witnessed a guano boom, with sales and prices rising to a peak in 1856, when 211 647 tons were sold within Great Britain alone. However, its base cost, which had risen from £9 to £11 a ton in July 1854, was increased again to, first, £12 in July 1856 and, then, £13 six months later, on instructions from the Peruvian

---

Mechi (London, 1859); and *Profitable Farming: Being the Second Series of the Sayings and Doings of Mr Alderman Mechi* (London, 1872).

[16] Letter to *The Times*, 4 August 1870, p. 12c.

[17] ECRO, D/Dop/B25, Notices concerning applications for Acts to incorporate London Sewage Co. 1846; Q/Rum2/29, Deposited plan and book of reference of London Sewage Co.; T. Wicksteed, *Report upon the Various Plans Proposed for Rendering Available the Manure Contained in the Sewage of the Metropolis...* (London, 1845); and J. Booker, *Essex and the Industrial Revolution* (Chelmsford, 1974), p. 181.

[18] Chambers and Mingay, *Agricultural Revolution*, pp. 13–14.

government. Two price rises within half a year pricked the bubble. Guano sales within Britain and continental Europe declined sharply despite its base cost falling back to £12 in July 1858. Although there was some recovery from 1861, the trade remained for some years thereafter at a lower level than during 1849.

Guano's high price from 1856 stimulated the greater output of industrially produced fertilizers, particularly superphosphate of lime, with claims by 1863 that every town had a manure manufactory. More effective processes for manufacturing sulphuric acid facilitated its production, which drew in mounting imports of bones, bone ash, Norwegian Apatite and Spanish phosphate. There was also a growing trade in nitrate of soda. All in all, by the late 1850s manufactured fertilizers enjoyed a very buoyant market. In particular, superphosphate was cheaper than guano and better suited for turnips, one of the major crops of 'High Farming'.[19]

While farmers employed increasing amounts of guano and then turned to factory-produced fertilizers, the continuing experience of cholera and a gathering new concern over river pollution led during the 1850s to widening efforts, private and public, to resolve the basic problem of urban pollution. For many, 'sewage utilization' remained the nub of the issue. Alum was rediscovered for deodorizing and purifying sewage, the process also producing 'sewage guano', a product description that was to re-occur during the early 1870s. However, the costs were initially too high for commercial exploitation.[20] At an official level, the problem was passed in January 1857 to a Royal Commission, largely comprising experts, charged with considering the 'best mode of distributing the sewage of towns and applying it to beneficial and profitable use'.[21] Following its second report in August 1861, a sub-committee of Lawes, the agricultural chemist, and John Thomas Wray, a fellow scientist, began to evaluate sewage as a fertilizer.[22] Their trials at Rugby, together with the Commission's other work, were the context for a 'sewage mania' of which *The Times* was a major promoter.

Despite considerable renewed interest, the economics of sewage as a

---

[19] See W.M. Mathew, *The House of Gibbs and the Peruvian Guano Monopoly* (London, 1981), pp. 36–9, 93–7, 135–47, 165–73, 180–83. See also Mathew, 'The Imperialism of Free Trade; Peru, 1820–70', *Economic History Review*, 2nd ser., 21 (1968), pp. 569–74.

[20] *The Times*, 6 August 1868, p. 6f.

[21] See *Reports*: BPP, XXXII (1857–8), *Preliminary*; XXXIII (1861), *Second* and XXVII (1865), *Third*. See also BPP, L (1863), *Speciality of the Inquiry entrusted to Particular Members of the Royal Commission on the Utilisation of Sewage, appointed 1857* . . .

[22] See *The Times*, 19 April 1865, p. 10b.

fertilizer remained problematic. This became clear when a Commons Select Committee published its second report in 1862,[23] provoking a debate in the *Journal of the Royal Agricultural Society* where Lawes concluded

> in the meantime, we must deal with the sewage as we find it, and the price which the farmer could afford to pay for it would certainly offer no inducement to capitalists to invest their money in distributing it in small quantities over extensive areas. The only persons benefited by such a scheme would be the contractors, and others, engaged in carrying out the undertaking.[24]

It was a prescient judgement but members of the Commons Committee were undoubtedly affected by the sewage mania, propelled by the belief that extraordinary profits could be made from the sale of urban effluent as a fertilizer.[25] As the construction of the Metropolitan Board of Works' main sewers neared completion during the early 1860s, London became the geographical focus of this continuing debate and craze over 'utilization'. However, it was not just a question of the profitable disposal of 'London muck'. In December 1864, both rural and urban interests approached parliament. Landowners were interested in applying sewage on their estates, while urban bodies sought powers to resolve their respective sewage problems, met to some extent by the 1865 Sewage Utilization Act, which enabled local authorities to distribute effluent for agricultural purposes.[26] A further Utilization Act, passed two years later, resulted in expenditures totalling £154 859 by the early 1870s.

Lord Robert Montagu pointedly raised the related issue of river pollution through a private bill. As discussed below, he had chaired a Select Committee that had once again reviewed the merits of sewage as a fertilizer. His bill addressing river pollution was a calculated measure, aimed to force a reluctant government to react, and succeeding to the extent of a Royal Commission being established. Like the 1857 Sewage Commission, it was primarily a technical inquiry, and two of its three members – Wray, the agricultural chemist, and Robert Rawlinson, a civil engineer – had previously acted as Sewage Commissioners. Furthermore,

---

[23] BPP, XIV (1862), Select Committee on the best means of utilising sewage of cities and towns of England, with a view to reduction of local taxation and benefit of agriculture, *First Report* and XIV (1862), *Second Report*.

[24] J.B. Lawes, 'On the Utilisation of Town Sewage', *Journal of the Royal Agricultural Society of England*, 24 (1863), p. 88. See also P.H. Frere, 'The Money-value of Night-soil and of Other Manures', in the same volume, pp. 124f.

[25] Owen, *Government of Victorian London*, p. 62.

[26] See J.B. Hutchins, *The Sanitary Act, 1866 . . . and the Sewage Utilization Acts of 1865 and 1867* (3rd edn, London, 1867).

Wray had been consulted by Montagu's 1864 Committee on Metropolitan Sewage. The Sewage Commissioners finally completed their work in the mid-1860s. It was taken further for another decade by the River Commissioners, who were to set the legislative framework for urban effluent disposal until the close of a century.[27]

Selling London's sewage

Although the sewage question's scope widened over the first half of the 1860s, with London's trunk sewerage system close to commissioning, it also came again to have a strong metropolitan focus. The Metropolitan Board of Works solicited tenders for the effluent that its sewers would otherwise discharge into the Thames in 1860, and again in 1863. The latter competition was affected in 1864 by yet a further Select Committee inquiring into sewage utilization.[28] Montagu, its chairman, not only maintained that London's night soil was a valuable commodity but was also a critic of the Board of Works. Consequently, his Committee was as much an investigation into the Board's recent activities as a further review of the business economics of sewage sales. Nonetheless, like its predecessors, it backed the Chadwickian vision,[29] with members having heard, for instance, that south Essex farmers, such as Wagstaff of South Oxendon, would be prepared to buy sewage at 2d a ton.[30]

Harried by Montagu's Committee, the Metropolitan Board of Works took forward the second tender competition for the sale of sewage through its Main Drainage Committee undertaking site visits of utilization systems. This entailed viewing not only the Edinburgh works, which had been one of Chadwick's examples, but also those at Carlisle, Croydon and Rugby, the last the location of experiments by Lawes and Wray on behalf of the Sewage Commission. These wide investigations resulted in a report acknowledging the obnoxious smell that some systems generated, but which contained no outright conclusions over the balance sheet for the sale of London's sewage. However, the Corporation of the City of London, totally ignoring the opinion it had solicited from

---

[27] Luckin, *Pollution and Control*, pp. 163–4 and Breeze, *River Pollution*, pp. 19–23. For the reconstitution of the River Commissioners, see Breeze, *River Pollution*, pp. 78–81.

[28] BPP, XIV (1864), Select Committee on plans for dealing with sewage of Metropolis and other large towns, with view to its utilisation to agricultural purposes, *Report*.

[29] Owen, *Government of Victorian London*, pp. 62–3.

[30] Booker, *Essex*, p. 182.

Justus von Liebig, maintained that the capital's sewage could be sold for at least £2 million per annum.[31]

The Metropolitan Board of Works received two tenders: one from Thomas Ellis and one jointly submitted by the Hon. William Napier and William Hope, and the latter was accepted by a majority of the Board.[32] Napier had worked for Chadwick in the development of a putative water supply scheme for London.[33] Although possessing a persuasive personality, his 1851 report on the Farnham area as a possible 'gathering ground' for water proved worthless.[34] Other aspects of his character had caused him to be sheltering from his creditors when his report was published, but he was sufficiently qualified to act as Clerk of Public Works for Hong Kong during the 1850s.[35] Napier's partner Hope was a military man and an inventor. He had served as an artillery officer, receiving the Victoria Cross for bravery during the Crimean War. Hope was also interested in sanitary reform, which may possibly explain how he became acquainted with Napier.[36] Furthermore, there is some evidence that Hope had become involved in sewage utilization. By the early 1860s, he lived at Parsloes Manor, Becontree, Essex, and so had his home within what was to be the business area of their future company – Metropolis Sewage & Essex Reclamation.[37] Of the two concessionaires,

---

[31] Owen, *Government of Victorian London*, pp. 63–4. Part of Liebig's opinion, provided to the Lord Mayor, is given in the minutes of the Corporation's meeting. See *The Times*, 25 January 1865, p. 5f. It was referred to the Coal, Corn and Finance Committee.

[32] There had been a prior pamphlet campaign, see W. Hope and W. Napier, *The Sewage of the Metropolis; A Letter to J. Thwaites* ... (London, 1865); *A letter ... in Reply to the Report of the Coal, Corn and Finance Committee to the Corporation of the City of London* (London, 1865); and *The Sewage of the Metropolis ... in Reply to the Second Manifesto of the 'Coal, Corn, and Finance Committee'* (London, 1865). But see also, R. Wason, *The Sewage Question: A Letter to the Chairman of the Metropolitan Board of Works, proving that the Plan of Messrs. Hope & Napier would be very injurious to the Health of the Inhabitants*, (London, 1865).

[33] E. Walford, *County Families of the United Kingdom* (London, 1865), p. 729.

[34] BPP, XXIII (1851), W. Napier, *Report and Papers of Suggestions on the Proposed Gathering Grounds for the Supply of the Metropolis ... ; addressed to the General Board of Health*, c. 1371.

[35] Lewis, *Edwin Chadwick*, pp. 263, 265, 353.

[36] *Who's Who* (1905), p. 793, and [This England], *Register of the Victoria Cross* (Cheltenham, 1981), p. 130.

[37] J. Howson, *A Brief History of Barking and Dagenham* (n.p., n.d.), p. 9. There is a fragmentary record indicating that the Metropolis Sewage scheme was first put forward in 1861; see ECRO, Q/Rum2/29, Deposited plan and book of reference of Metropolis Sewage, 1861; and D/DSt/E15/10 Wasey Sterry estate, accounts and correspondence, 1856–1864. See also D.W. Gramolt, 'The Coastal

it was Hope who proved the doughtiest campaigner for realizing at least some of this company's aspirations.

Under their scheme, London's effluent would be transported through a nine-foot six–inch culvert over some 44 miles from the Northern Outfall Main Sewer at Barking Creek to East Wick Head, Foulness and Dengie. The envisaged system would not only distribute sewage to farms in southern Essex but also convey the residue to the mouth of the Thames for the twinned land reclamation project.[38] The planned opening up of 12 000 acres of the Dengie and Maplin Sands to agriculture required the conclusion of agreements with South Essex Estuary & Reclamation Co. This concern had been established in 1852 by a private act and had begun, but no more, to take in the coastal flats.[39] Napier and Hope valued their concession at £1 million. Furthermore, the continuing sewage mania fuelled by *The Times* resulted in them estimating profits of £0.65 million,[40] to give a probable return of 20 per cent, shared equally between them and the Metropolitan Board of Works. In return, Napier and Hope deposited £25 000 as caution money, which would be lost should their scheme's culvert not be completed.[41]

The project was initially taken forward by Sewage Utilization & Essex Reclamation Co., which was permitted by the Metropolitan Board of Works to apply sewage to land at the recently completed Northern Outfall Sewer.[42] This trial investigation had a propitious context, arising from the publication of the Sewage Commissioners' third report in which Lawes displayed some change of mind over sewage's effectiveness as a fertilizer. Nonetheless, he was not a total convert, emphasizing that the potential financial rewards depended on the precise context, in particular whether expensive pumping engines rather than gravity applied the effluent. Furthermore, the Rugby trials undertaken by Lawes with Wray

---

Marshland of East Essex Between the Seventeenth and Mid-nineteenth Centuries', MA thesis, University of London, 1960, p. 111.

[38] On the technical aspects of the reclamation scheme, see J.M. Heppel, 'On the Closing of the Reclamation Banks', *Minutes of the Proceedings of the Institute of Civil Engineers*, 23 (1864).

[39] See South Essex Estuary and Reclamation Act 1852 (15 & 16 Vict.), c. lxvi; ECRO, T/M 264/1, Index plan of South Essex Reclamation and Improvement of Crouch and Blackwater, 1852; Gramolt, 'Coastal Marshland of East Essex', pp. 110–11; and J.R. Smith, *Foulness: A History of an Essex Island Parish*, Essex Record Office publications, No. 55 (Chelmsford, 1970), p. 44. The company was wound up in 1868.

[40] Booker, *Essex*, p. 182.

[41] Ibid., p. 182; and Owen, *Government of Victorian London*, p. 63.

[42] Minutes of the weekly meeting of the Metropolitan Board of Works, 17 March 1865, reprinted in *The Times*, 18 March 1865, p. 12c.

implied that heavy soils were less suitable for sewage application.[43] Whether buoyed up by this qualified support or simply impatient to realize their project, Napier and Hope pushed their bigger scheme forward by seeking a private act to incorporate Metropolis Sewage & Essex Reclamation Co.[44]

Seeking to raise the funds

As the bill to establish their concessionary company proceeded through parliament, Napier and Hope turned to the City for the necessary capital to exploit their scheme. Here they were well placed since Hope was manager of the International Financial Society, the leading finance company amongst the many recently established.[45] Furthermore, Metropolis Sewage was not the first proposal that Napier had brought before the merchant bankers who sat on the Society's board. Their mutual dealings over the previous two years had concerned various types of land finance companies, which had primarily stemmed from Napier being, by the 1860s, managing director of Lands Improvement.[46] This company, with other comparable undertakings, had been formed following the repeal of the Corn Laws to compete with funds supplied under the Public Money Drainage Act – the 'sweetener' for repeal. Lands Improvement had rapidly established itself as the market leader.[47] Furthermore, in June 1863, Napier joined the board of the newly formed Leasehold Investment Co.[48] As a result, by 1865 Hope and Napier had a firm connection with the City. Moreover, Napier had also gained strong links with landed wealth which he had utilized to aid a series of company promotions, particularly that of Land Securities, undertaken with Inter-

---

[43] *The Times*, 19 April 1865, p. 10b.

[44] *The Times*, 29 April 1865, p. 7f.

[45] For the International Financial Society, see P.L. Cottrell, *Investment Banking in England 1856–1881: A Case Study of the International Financial Society* (New York and London, 1985).

[46] Hull University Library (hereafter HUL); International Financial Society, minutes of board meetings (hereafter IB), 19 November 1863, 3, 17 and 21 December 1863; National Archives, Public Record Office, Kew, London (hereafter PRO); BT31/840/773C, BT 31/851/797C and BT31/866/852C; *The Economist*, 16 January 1864, p. 78; and *The Bankers' Magazine* (1864), p. 772.

[47] D.C. Moore, 'The Corn Laws and High Farming', *Economic History Review*, 2nd. ser., 18 (1965), pp. 545–56 and D. Spring, *The English Landed Estate in the Nineteenth Century: Its Administration* (Baltimore, 1963), pp. 154–8. See also F.M.L. Thompson, *English Landed Society in the Nineteenth Century* (London and Toronto, 1963), 251, 257.

[48] PRO, BT31/789/480C.

national. Through these various dealings, Napier had established himself with International as a provider of solid and profitable proposals.

On the same day that the bill to incorporate Metropolis Sewage & Essex Reclamation Co. received its third reading in the Commons (28 April 1865), Napier and Hope put their latest venture to International. They were prepared to sell their concession from the Metropolitan Board of Works to the company that they were attempting to incorporate by a private act for £50 000 in its fully paid-up shares, together with a proportion of its future profits, while looking to be reimbursed for their scheme's preparatory costs.[49] It subsequently transpired that Napier was so anxious to realize the project that he had simultaneously initiated negotiations with a rival issuing house.[50] He may have had good reason to deal with others as, despite his recent financial successes, not all of International's directors were receptive to the Metropolis Sewage proposal. Regardless of the great probability that International's directorate were already aware of the scheme – either as a result of the publicity it was receiving or directly but informally from Hope himself, their general manager – their debate over Metropolis Sewage on 28 April 1865 ran on over the day until 4 pm before qualms had been quelled.

When International finally agreed to pursue the project, it was on the basis of it being undertaken jointly with Antony Gibbs & Sons, past concessionaires for Peruvian guano. Gibbs had lost the guano contract in 1861 due primarily to Peruvian statesmen wishing to end foreign control of the trade. But Gibbs's recent substantial interest in guano made them ideal joint promoters of Metropolis Sewage, the more so since the focus of their business had turned from trade to investments and Stock Exchange speculation.[51] Furthermore, some Gibbs partners were already involved with one of Metropolis Sewage's concessionaires – Hope – in a Majorcan land speculation.

International agreed to guarantee the placing of half of Metropolis Sewage's £2.1 million nominal capital for a 10 per cent commission, with Antony Gibbs & Sons underwriting the other half. International was to be the lead house. Although the promotional expenses were to be borne jointly, Gibbs paid £5 000 to the finance company 'for their extra trouble in the affair'. It was recognized from the outset that this was a highly speculative project and, consequently, might not receive the support of a capital market that was in any case displaying general signs of being

---

[49] HUL, IB, 28 April 1865.

[50] International Financial Society, *Report of the Directors on the Subjects to be discussed at the Extraordinary General Meeting of the Shareholders* (London, 1871), pp. 3–4.

[51] See Mathew, *The House of Gibbs*, pp. 186–214, 223.

replete after three years of absorbing new issues. Therefore conditions were stipulated. First, Napier and Hope were to meet £10 000 of the issuing costs should less than 80 per cent of their company's shares be allotted to 'bona fide applicants'. And there were others. The civil engineering contract was to be agreed 'to the satisfaction of' the Society's solicitor regarding 'the amount of capital including interest at the rate of 5 per cent during construction'. Lastly, should it not prove possible to obtain the necessary private act to incorporate the company, Napier and Hope were to meet 'all the parliamentary and engineering expenses'.[52]

The company's bill eventually received the backing of the parliamentary committee that investigated its objectives. This was despite contrary opinion having been given once more by an agricultural chemist, Augustus Voelcker. He thought that, generally, there was no profit to be made from sewage. And, with regard to Metropolis Sewage's particular scheme, he considered that diluted raw sewage could not be applied with success to estuarine sand.[53] His assessment had been given as a result of yet a further intervention from the Corporation of the City of London, its members determined that the maximum price was obtained for the capital's sewage. The Corporation's intrusion had, in turn, resulted in the Metropolis Sewage bill at its Commons stage being put to two referees, but they had found the company's scheme 'useful and practical'.[54] Ultimately, the project gained the most prestigious backing, with the Prince of Wales casting the first vote in its favour when Metropolis Sewage & Essex Reclamation Co.'s bill received its third reading in the Lords on 2 June.[55]

International's agreement to float Metropolis Sewage's capital was subsequently revised: on 29 June and, again, on 3 July.[56] The second modification was necessitated by the discovery that the project's construction costs had been underestimated. Furthermore, concerns over the new issue market's possible lack of receptiveness had increased, which led to the requirement that, should the public subscribe for less than 50 per cent of Metropolis Sewage's shares, Napier and Hope were to pay a further £10 000 commission to International.

Within two days of the second modification to the agreement with Napier and Hope, International's board decided to float Metropolis

---

[52] HUL, IB, 28 April 1865. For other aspects of the affair, see D. Kynaston, *Cazenove & Co.: a history* (London, 1991), pp. 58–60.

[53] Owen, *Government of Victorian London*, p. 64.

[54] *The Times*, 8 July 1865, p. 7a. See also BPP, VIII (1865), Select Committee on Metropolis Sewage and Essex Reclamation Bill, *Special Report*.

[55] *The Times*, 3 June 1865, p. 7e and 28 & 29 Vict. c. cxxi.

[56] HUL, IB, 29 June 1865 and International Financial Society, Minutes of Committee Meetings [hereafter IC], 3 July 1865.

Sewage.⁵⁷ Its prospectus was published on 9 July, a Saturday, a not unusual point in the week for distribution as it was considered that likely investors in new companies reflected upon their respective financial affairs on Sunday mornings. More unusual was the initial division of the company's nominal capital into £100 scrip (provisional certificates). These were only to be converted into £10 shares in October, after subscribers had made a further 10 per cent payment upon their holdings. The project's construction costs were finally estimated at £2.4 million, it being planned to raise the balance of capital required through a subsequent £0.3 million debenture issue. The sewage distribution system was to be built by William Webster, who had been substantially involved in constructing the Metropolitan Board of Works' sewers, including the Southern, Crossness Outfall. On the basis of von Liebig's calculations, drawn from the well-established Edinburgh works' balance sheet, it was expected that the arising profits would give shareholders an annual return of 15 per cent.⁵⁸

Although prices were continuing to rise on the London Stock Exchange, International's management soon found that further inducements, besides advertising costing £5 000, were required for attracting applications for the scrip of the somewhat unusual concern they were promoting. A circular was issued to emphasize that shareholders would enjoy limited liability.⁵⁹ However, unlike some other company promoters, International's directors initially refused Hope's request to 'manipulate the market so as to produce a large artificial premium [on the company's share price] before allotment with the object of attracting public subscriptions'.⁶⁰ Instead, stockbrokers were paid a commission of 5s. per scrip certificate for applications that they personally attracted.⁶¹ However, this tactic was liable to let a wide circle within the City know that the flotation of Metropolis Sewage was not going well, and they, in turn, could act accordingly. Indeed, Metropolis Sewage's flotation proved to be a flop. By 20 July, out of 21 000 offered for subscription, applications for merely 7500 scrip certificates had been received. It was decided to allot just 6000.

Henry Huck Gibbs, a partner in Antony Gibbs & Sons, informed his Uncle William two days later that 'The Metropolis Sewage does not flow as smoothly as we could wish. You will see in The Times that it continues

---

⁵⁷ HUL, IB, 5 July 1865.
⁵⁸ *The Times*, 8 July 1865, p. 7a, and 10 July 1865, p. 7a.
⁵⁹ *The Times*, 15 July 1865, p. 6a.
⁶⁰ International Financial Society, *Report of the Directors on the Subjects to be Discussed at the Extraordinary General Meeting of the Shareholders*, p. 5.
⁶¹ HUL, IC, 7 July 1865.

to be quoted at 6 premium; but that may give you a false impression unless it is explained.' Indeed, that was the case. The market price of £6 per scrip certificate over the issue price was solely the result of the outcome of speculation involving Stock Exchange dealings in its scrip before allotment and the International's reaction, rather than the public's demand for its securities. Henry Hucks Gibbs told his uncle that 'The assault of the bears had been furious, and to prevent the stock going to a discount the International had to buy nearly 1,000 shares at 2 prem[ium].' This makes it very evident that some market operators had taken the early view that the flotation would not succeed, resulting in the collapse of the price for the scrip of Metropolis Sewage. Therefore, before the scrip had been allotted – distributed to applicants – these particular speculators had sold scrip on the Exchange in the expectation that they would ultimately make a profit by closing out their sale transactions through obtaining scrip at an even lower price. International had attempted to counter such speculative market manoeuvres – bear sales – by buying scrip prior to allotment. International had entered the market but not as Hope had earlier urged to drive up the scrip's price in order to attract applicants. Rather, its management had bought scrip to protect the nascent company by attempting to prevent the price of its securities from falling below their issue price.

Henry Hucks Gibbs further pointed out that 'You will see then that the bears were not only immoral enough to sell what they had not got, and might never have, but idiots enough not to apply for what they had sold.' Those who had sold short on the market immediately following the publication of Metropolis Sewage's prospectus had been so confident of a collapse in the price of its scrip that they had not submitted applications to the International by which to obtain the securities that they required to ultimately meet their sale bargains on the Exchange.

There had been other aspects to the flotation of Metropolis Sewage, with Henry Hucks Gibbs also remarking 'some of the applicants had asked for more than they wanted, in expectation that there would be large applications, and that in getting their share would get as much as they needed – some were known "Stags".' This shows that other market operators had taken a contrary view of the flotation through anticipating a very substantial general public demand for Metropolis Sewage scrip. If this had occurred, it would have resulted in the Stock Exchange price for the scrip rising significantly as a result of demand exceeding its supply, fixed by the size of Metropolis Sewage's capital. With this anticipation of a rising 'bull' market, they had applied to the International for large blocks of scrip. However, they intended to sell, either immediately before or immediately after allotment – conducting 'stagging operations' – to profit immediately from the difference between the market premium on the scrip and its issue price. 'Bulls', 'bears' and 'stags', along with 'lame ducks', were not new stock exchange operators as they had existed from when the market had been established during the late seventeenth century. Their predecessors had flourished or perished, as during the railway mania of the 1840s, and the flotation of limited liability companies over the mid-1860s had given them new opportunities.

Being aware of both short sales – bear operations – and 'stagging' in Metropolis Sewage scrip, 'the International therefore exercised their discretion in the allotment, and distributed about 4,500 shares'. Its management had decided to initiate a 'bear squeeze' by only allotting a small amount of Metropolis Sewage scrip to applicants, so restricting its supply to the Stock Exchange for those who had undertaken dealings before allotment. As Henry Hucks Gibbs forcefully remarked 'Then began the Bears to Roar. They hoped the stock would have gone down; but as there were few or no sellers it went up; because they who had to deliver, could not get the stock.' Market transactions in Metropolis Sewage had not been completed at allotment since speculators who had sold short had not been allocated scrip by International and, therefore, could not provide it to those to whom they had sold it. They were deliberately being squeezed at and after allotment, with the only source of scrip being the issuing house. The 'Urban Bears came to the International and roared for mercy'. However, the Society's management decided to show what Henry Hucks Gibbs called 'mercy' as, although those who had sold short 'might have been mulcted what the Society pleased, but in consideration that they were regular Jobbers, whose trade consisted in speculative buying and selling, they were let off for a £[?] each on the 1,500 shares they represented'. So, shortly after the allotment of Metropolis Sewage scrip had closed, 1500 certificates had been sold by the International at a premium – at a cost over their issuing price – to jobbers (market makers) on the London Stock Exchange to allow them to settle their respective bear (short) positions. The International's management may have thought it more than diplomatic to assist these jobbers, whose support they might need in the future for other flotations. However, no comparable 'mercy' was shown to other speculators who had similarly sold short but who were not members of the London Stock Exchange. As Henry Hucks Gibbs put it 'the Bears from the suburban forests who had wilfully maliciously beared the shares of the company and oversold themselves, they still remain roaring'.[62] The 'suburban Bears' may have been 'outside' brokers, or possibly provincial brokers.

---

[62] Guildhall Library, London (hereafter GL), Antony Gibbs & Sons papers (hereafter Gibbs papers), Ms 11036/3, H.H. Gibbs letter book, to W. Gibbs, 22 July 1865.

Of the 6000 allotted scrip certificates of Metropolis Sewage, only 4500 had gone to the general public ('bona fide' applicants). International's management applied to the Stock Exchange for a special settlement for the scrip certificates, which was granted, allowing them to be regularly traded. Holders of scrip could therefore henceforth sell these securities on the market for its fortnightly account and, conversely, those who wished to buy scrip could do so through the Exchange. However, solely seeking a special settlement was liable to cause adverse comment, and Metropolis Sewage's secretary wrote to *The Times* explaining why no related application had been made for a quotation in the Stock Exchange's *List*. This would only take place in the coming October, when holders paid a further 10 per cent and their scrip was converted into shares. It was a technical explanation and an unsatisfactory one, as any seasoned investor would have recognized. A quotation in the *List*, giving a daily published price, was not being sought in July 1865 since so few shares – merely 4500 – were in public hands as a result of the speculation that had taken place before allotment and the International's reaction to it. With so few scrip certificates available, the market in them would consequently be thin, would lack liquidity and jobbers on the Exchange, well aware of this, would not be prepared, when approached, readily to state buying and selling prices. Indeed, they might refuse to trade at all or, at best, require special negotiation over price and delivery since they would be uncertain over how they could either obtain scrip for delivery or sell on scrip. This all became fully evident when the Stock Exchange refused to give quotation for Metropolis Sewage in October 1865.[63] Yet Hope remained sanguine: '[he] still tells a flattering tale, that so soon as the public shall see that the farmers begin to take the sewage, and that it produces good results on their lands, they will come in fast enough, and at a premium'.[64]

Metropolis Sewage was not the only company whose birth was subjected to these various market operations during the new issues boom of the mid-1860s. The problems caused by dealings before allotment, especially for the inexperienced investor, were to be reviewed during the financial slump of the late 1870s by the Royal Commission on the Stock Exchange. Yet, it was realized, as attempts at legislation had shown, that it was practically impossible to suppress dealings before allotment. Most frequently, they had been used, and continued to be used, to aid a

---

[63] *The Times*, 10 August 1865, p. 6f; and BPP, XIX (1878); Royal Commission on the London Stock Exchange, *Report and Minutes of Evidence*, Appendix V, p. 367.

[64] GL, Gibbs papers, Ms 11036/3, H.H. Gibbs private letter book, to W. Gibbs, 30 July 1865.

promotion by artificially raising a nascent company's share price to attract applications for its securities. But, equally, they could be directed to cause its early collapse. As the International's management recognized, jobbers on the Exchange were professional speculators. If the law prevented them from dealing in securities in the process of being created, others would take their place – on the pavement outside the Exchange or elsewhere, as was equally the case with Metropolis Sewage.

Nursing a financial failure

With the failure of the flotation, International and Antony Gibbs & Sons involuntarily obtained the major interest in Metropolis Sewage as a result of the share-placing agreement made with Napier and Hope. Metropolis Sewage's working capital had consequently to be largely provided by International and Gibbs,[65] leading their managements to make immediate moves to obtain representation on the company's board. By August, two seats on the company's board had been secured, one for a representative of International and one for Gibbs.[66] Henry Hucks Gibbs thought that his house and International would 'have a clear majority in the direction during construction, – in order to enforce economy'.[67] In practice, Metropolis Sewage was subject to dual control since the overwhelming interest in it held jointly by International and Gibbs meant that any decisions involving significant expenditure required their separate approval.

International's management concurred with 'push[ing] forward experiments', which at the beginning of September led to Metropolis Sewage opening negotiations for 700 acres at Hainault, Essex, where the forest had been progressively felled since 1850.[68] However, within a month strategic policy underwent a major change; instead of waiting upon the results of the Hainault trials of 'London muck' as a fertilizer, the decision was taken to start the works 'at once'.[69] Nonetheless, the main concern

---

[65] HUL, IB, 27 July 1865.
[66] HUL, IB, 3 August 1865.
[67] GL, Gibbs papers, Ms 11036/3, H.H. Gibbs private letter book, to George [B. Crawley], 3 August 1865.
[68] HUL, IB, 31 August and 7 September 1865, and Howson, *Brief History*, p. 10.
[69] HUL, IB, 28 September 1865. See also ECRO; Q/Rum2/178, Deposited plan section and book of reference of Metropolis Sewage, 1865; PRO, BT 356/112888, Barking Creek, Essex; Reclamation works and proposed sewage pipe of Metropolis Sewage system, 1866; and BT 356/9232, Barking Creek, Essex; Sewage

of both International and Gibbs remained to minimize expenditure and, initially, their representatives attempted to achieve this by persuasion, with Henry Hucks Gibbs writing to Hope on 16 October 1865:

> Matters are not going as well with our sewage affairs as I could desire, your influence [?is necessary] in the direction of Economy and Prudence – [?with] those Directors (chiefly your own friends) who I think are rather inclined to disregard those two virtues – [?these are] my views and those of the International.[70]

The relationship between the two groups involved – International and Gibbs as majority shareholders and those led by Hope – and their respective attitudes towards the company became more defined after its first General Meeting on 24 November 1865. This had been called by International once its management had registered 'such number of shares as the solicitor may think necessary', which led to its nominees holding 5000 shares prior to the meeting.[71] Henry Hucks Gibbs subsequently summarized what he considered to have been a successful outcome:

> Our programme carried – construct first 3½ miles of culvert and a branch to Hainault Forest, little time be lost and full experiment made, if a failure – the most we should jeopardise would be that amount of shares allotted to which we have thought proper to have registered in our names and perhaps amount unallotted.[72]

International's management's attitude was displayed through Lachlan M. Rate being formally appointed to Metropolis Sewage's board. Amongst International's directors, he had been the most strenuously opposed to the scheme when Napier and Hope had first formally presented it.

The 'Hope party' fought back during the early months of 1866 with an application for International to register itself 'as shareholders in respect of the Script Certificates' that it held through the 1865 placing agreement. International's board considered the obligation

> to do so was uncertain and it was at present undesirable ... to register ... in view of the possibility of the Metropolitan Board of Works having a claim against the Metropolis Sewage for damages in the event of the scheme not being carried out.[73]

---

works, dredging and driving coffer of Metropolitan Sewage & Essex Reclamation Co., 1866.

[70] GL, Gibbs papers, Ms 11,036/3, H.H. Gibbs private letter book, to W. Hope, 16 October 1865.

[71] HUL, IC, 9 November 1865 and IB, 23 November 1865.

[72] GL, Gibbs Papers, Ms 11,036/7, H.H. Gibbs private letter book, to W. Gibbs, 24 November 1865.

[73] HUL, IB, 22 February 1866.

Consequently, in February 1866 a compromise was reached with Metropolis Sewage, although one indicating that International retained the upper hand in the company's affairs. It had been agreed that

> if after the completion of the first 3½ miles of Culvert, the company should determine to carry out the scheme as proposed then the International Financial Society should consent to register themselves but that in the contrary event the Sewage Co. should release this Society from any obligation so to register themselves.[74]

Within three weeks of this compact, in order to increase their control International and Gibbs began jointly to buy out smaller shareholders in Metropolis Sewage.[75] This was formalized with a more general offer that would become effective should Metropolis Sewage relinquish its concession after the completion of the scheme's experimental phase. International offered to find

> parties prepared to take a transfer of the shares now on the Register of the Company (irrespective of those shares registered in our names or in the name of our nominees) in the event of the holders of such shares desiring to transfer them for a nominal consideration so as to separate themselves entirely from the company.[76]

The Hope party were irritants who could only exert effective pressure upon International and Gibbs by a threat of adverse publicity, such as that arising from a legal action. However, although holding a majority interest in Metropolis Sewage, International and Gibbs only had two seats on the company's board. The Hope party had the loudest voice within its management but International and Gibbs could appeal to the company's General Meeting, where their jointly held shares provided the necessary voting power.

The failure of Metropolis Sewage's flotation raised further and particular problems for International. As the London market went through the prologue to the 1866 crisis, the finance company's holding of Metropolis Sewage shares rendered part of its capital illiquid, thereby weakening it. These problems accompanied others of an equally serious nature since a gulf rapidly opened between International's directors and their general manger, Hope, as a result of continued friction over the realization of Metropolis Sewage's objectives. This conflict resulted in Hope leaving International at the end of 1867, although with a retainer with respect to Metropolis Sewage.

---

[74] HUL, IB, 1 March 1866.
[75] HUL, IB, 22 March 1866.
[76] HUL, IB, 22 and 29 March 1866.

Experiments

If Metropolis Sewage's prospects had been blighted by the failure of its share issue in midsummer 1865, they were almost totally extinguished in May 1866 by the crisis that erupted with the failure of Overend, Gurney and rocked the City's very foundations. International was badly affected by the resultant locking up of its assets and, in turn, this severely circumscribed its management's ability to finance further Metropolis Sewage's development. Gibbs was also in straitened circumstances, the house having incurred a small loss in 1865 but then experiencing much greater ones in 1866 and 1867 of the order of £66 000 per annum.[77] Consequently, for Metropolis Sewage economy became retrenchment after May 1866. International's directors made a site visit in June, following which they decided to press for civil engineering work to be halted.[78] The only exception came to be the siphon at Barking Creek, required to raise sewage and water for the projected trans-Essex culvert.[79] With their total reliance upon International for funds, Metropolis Sewage's board could only but agree, although this involved paying a penalty of £30 000 to their contractor.[80]

The November 1866 decision to abandon construction meant that one of Metropolis Sewage's major objectives – land reclamation at the mouth of the Thames – was lost. However, the resulting penalty paid to its contractor had to be set against £1.5 million, the now estimated cost of completing the whole scheme and which in the conditions of late 1866 could only be met by a greatly debilitated International and its partner, Gibbs.[81] In the mean time, Metropolis Sewage's management concentrated upon supplying sewage fertilizer immediately around Barking. However, it was discovered that the price had been set too high, while neither landlords nor farmers were willing to shoulder the costs of preparing their holdings for sewage irrigation.

During spring 1866 Metropolis Sewage had acquired John Morton's Lodge Farm at Barking, which Mechi had praised two decades earlier for its utilization of London's effluent.[82] From autumn 1866, it was used both to pursue further research into sewage as a fertilizer and to generate publicity. A Wiltshire water meadow surveyor prepared the land for

---

[77] Mathew, *House of Gibbs*, Appendix III, p. 249.
[78] HUL, IB, 21 June 1866.
[79] HUL, IB, 15 November 1866.
[80] HUL, IB, 22 November 1866.
[81] International Financial Society, *Circular, 23 February 1871, to the Shareholders of the International Financial Society Ltd: Report of the Directors*.
[82] Booker, *Essex*, p. 181.

sewage irrigation through the laying of five-foot and seven-foot drains so that fertilization was combined with effluent filtration to purify the run off.[83] Under the supervision of Metropolis Sewage's farm committee, the holding was initially managed by John Chalmers Morton, who had continued his father's work and, by the mid-1860s, was also an inspector under the Land Commissioners, commanding great respect amongst landowners.[84] When Chalmers Morton joined the reconstituted River Pollution Commission in spring 1868, his place at Lodge Farm was taken by, first, the Hon. H.W. Petre, a director of Metropolis Sewage and a Deputy Lieutenant for Essex, and, then, John Morgan, the company's secretary.[85]

The farm experiments were substantial. Initially, they involved trials on both a 30-inch bed of sand brought from Maplin to the contractor's yard and 200 acres of light, gravelly soil at Lodge Farm. The first major crop was Italian rye grass.[86] During 1868–9, 0.36 million tons of sewage were distributed over 120 acres for test crops of beans, cabbages, carrots, cereals, onions, potatoes, strawberries and sugar beet.[87] Morgan kept the project in the public eye by letters to *The Times*. One in summer 1870 included an appraisal by William Beadel, who thought that the vegetable crops were 'startling' and the cereals were 'above average'.[88] Members of the River Pollution Commission and Mechi also viewed the farm.[89]

On his own initiative, Hope set up Dairy Reform Co. to sell milk from Lodge Farm, but the venture lost money and ended in a dispute between him and Metropolis Sewage.[90] There is every sign that Hope was committed to achieving success with sewage irrigation. He had some differences of opinion over the methods used at Lodge Farm and so, in

---

[83] *The Times*, 9 November 1870, p. 4e. On the methods used at Lodge Farm, see also 26 October 1870 p. 12d and 2 November 1870, p. 4d.

[84] Breeze, *River Pollution*, p. 81.

[85] H.W. Petre, *Report for the Year Ending 31 August, 1868 upon the Lodge Farm*; and International Financial Society, *Directors' Report*, 5 April 1871. Petre was the second son of William, 11th Lord Petre. For the River Commissioners, see BPP, XLVIII (1865), Commission issued to inquire into the best means of remedying the pollution of rivers; XXXIII (1874), Royal Commission to inquire into best means of preventing pollution of rivers, *6th Report*, c.1112; Luckin, *Pollution and Control*, pp. 40, 91, 151–2, 158, 162, 163, 168, 173; and Breeze, *River Pollution*.

[86] Letter, H.J. Morgan, secretary, Metropolis Sewage, *The Times*, 22 May 1867, p. 10e; and letter, J. Chalmers Morton, *The Times*, 3 December 1867, p. 9a.

[87] Howson, *Brief History*, p. 10 and Oxley, 'Barking and Ilford', p. 216.

[88] *The Times*, 24 August 1870, p. 5f.

[89] *The Times*, 8 August 1871, p. 11b.

[90] See PRO, BT 31/1591/5277, Dairy Reform Co.

1870, personally acquired Britton's Farm, Hornchurch.[91] On this holding, which he had under-drained and levelled into rectilinear beds, he applied Romford's sewage, drawn through an 18-inch iron pipe by an eight horse-power centrifugal pump. Mechi praised the results, pointing not only to the variety of crops grown and the frequency of harvesting – every two to three months – but also the resultant increase in employment. Hope had a work force of 35 to 40 together with 16 horses, as opposed to the three men and two boys who had previously worked the farm.[92] A further visit by Mechi caused his astonishment over the raising of a crop of French beans on 'pure gravel'.[93]

However, the various experiments conducted by Metropolis Sewage during the late 1860s had a negative impact on the locality. Without the conduit, they involved the movement of muck through Barking, which it was thought resulted in a local typhoid outbreak.[94] The matter went to the House of Commons but the Metropolitan Board of Works took comfort in Islington West and Sydenham experiencing greater mortality, while firmly laying the blame for the Barking incident at the door of Napier and Hope.[95] The Northern Main Outfall Sewer's discharges into the Thames caused other difficulties.

The Board became embroiled with the inhabitants of Barking, led by their vicar, who in January 1869 presented a memorial over the Outfall Sewer's pollution and obstruction of the town's creek. The matter was investigated by Rawlinson, an established engineer and tetchy member of the first River Pollution Commission. He found the complaints groundless, although querying whether the outfall had been sited too close to the metropolis for effluent to be effectively carried away by the ebb tide.[96] His investigation also became enmeshed with complaints from the Thames Conservators, who maintained that the discharges at both Barking and Crossness were threatening the Thames' safe navigation. In 1870 the Conservators gained an act that made the Metropolitan Board of Works responsible for ensuring that sewage did not impede traffic on London's river. Mechi used the clash between these two bodies to

[91] ECRO, D/DB/361, Lease, Romford Local Board of Health to W. Hope, Brittons/Bretons Farm, 16 May 1870.
[92] *The Times*, 11 October 1870, p. 4e.
[93] *The Times*, 19 June 1871, p. 11e.
[94] T. Clifford, *Barking and Dagenham Buildings Past and Present* (Barking, 1992), p. 53.
[95] *The Times*, 10 July 1869, p. 12d. See also BPP, XL (1870), Royal Commission upon inquiry as to pollution of Thames at Barking, *Report*, c. 7.
[96] PRO, HO 45/8308. Thames pollution by discharge of sewage . . .; enquiry by Mr Rawlinson in consequence of complaints . . ., 1869–1870; Owen, *Government of Victorian London*, pp. 65–6; and Luckin, *Pollution and Control*, 146.

emphasize once more that London's effluent was being wasted when allowed merely to flow into the Thames. He argued that the Board should employ at least some as a fertilizer.[97] Mechi could keep on promoting sewage utilization but Lodge Farm continued to be regarded as a local nuisance, blamed again in 1873 for a further typhoid outbreak in Barking.[98]

Metropolis Sewage's experiments occurred in tandem with those undertaken by the River Pollution Commission. At Leicester they were substantial, undertaken to improve the water quality of the river Soar, and took place along with smaller trials at Tottenham, in part caused by concern over the state of the river Lea. In each case, the objective was to reduce pollution caused by sewage but the processes tested also yielded manure as a by-product, with claims for its ammonia and phosphate content.[99] Official investigations were accompanied by further commercial attempts to transform sewage into fertilizer. One was made by Liverpool Sewage Utilization Co. By autumn 1869, successful results were being reported but the company lacked capital and its objective of gaining a 20 per cent profit from selling sewage at 3d. a ton had still to be achieved.[100] Possibly, the greatest headway was made at Banbury, where the Local Board of Health had forced the adoption of sewage irrigation in order to reduce the town's pollution of the river Cherwell. The scheme had commenced in 1867 and, initially, as at Lodge Farm, the principal crop was Italian rye grass. Oats, parsnip and sprouts were also tried in 1868, followed in 1869 by cabbages and much praised mangold wurzels.[101]

The growing pressures exerted by the River Pollution Commission also caused larger, industrial towns to have to develop plans for sewage irrigation. During March 1870, both Blackburn and Reading gained necessary private acts, although in the teeth of violent opposition.[102] With the requisite powers to raise £200–300 000, Blackburn embarked upon a major programme of works.[103] A year later, Birmingham

---

[97] *The Times*, 4 August 1870, p. 12c.

[98] ECRO, D/P81/28/16, Report of Dr. Buchanan on enteric fever at Barking; its relation to sewage irrigation at Lodge Farm.

[99] 'Sewage experiments at Leicester', *The Times*, 4 August 1868, p. 4c. See also 6 August 1868, p. 6f, 7 August 1868, p. 8f; and 25 August 1868, p. 9d. For the context of the Tottenham trials, see Luckin, *Pollution and Control*, p. 161 and Breeze, *River Pollution*, pp. 51, 52.

[100] *The Times*, 12 August 1868, p. 10d; and 15 September 1869, p. 10b.

[101] *The Times*, 17 August 1869, p. 9d. For context, see Luckin, *Pollution and Control*, pp. 159–60.

[102] *The Times*, 30 March 1870, p. 11e.

[103] *The Times*, 23 September 1871, p. 4f.

obtained an act giving powers to mortgage land for 75 years in order to establish a sewage farm.[104] As these projects commenced, a commercially based trial works at Leamington was acquired by Lord Warwick to provide sewage for his estate, assisted by the Local Board raising a £14 000 loan in order to provide a pumping station.[105] There were comparable developments at Bishop's Stortford and Cambridge.[106] One culmination of these various schemes was the session devoted to sewage irrigation at the 1870 meeting of the British Association for the Advancement of Science. Hope was one of a number that gave lectures. The Society of Arts also considered the problem in May 1872.[107]

Further possible resolutions

Apart from its experiments at Lodge Farm, Metropolis Sewage was to all intents and purposes in limbo during the second half of the 1860s. Its original overall scheme became unviable once International's management, who had expended £120 030 on it by 1870, refused to employ any more of their now scant resources.[108] Hope appears to have bombarded International's directors with ideas and suggestions but none had any substance. A more promising possibility had arisen in October 1869, when Hope put International into contact with Messrs Easton, Amos & Sons, an engineering firm whose partners were considering undertaking the sewage scheme on an amended basis. They proposed a conduit to Canvey Island, at 25 miles distance, somewhat closer to Barking than Dengie.[109] Easton, Amos were prepared to obtain the necessary parliamentary powers, while International with Antony Gibbs & Sons were ready to assign all their interests for £25 000 in cash, representing the caution money, and £27 500 in stock. However, despite some initial progress, these arrangements never reached fruition.[110]

---

[104] *The Times*, 8 August 1871, p. 11b. For context, see E.P. Hennock, *Fit and Proper Persons: Ideal and Reality in Nineteenth Century Urban Government* (London, 1973), pp. 107–11 and Breeze, *River Pollution*, pp. 149–51.

[105] *The Times*, 7 September 1871, p. 5f.

[106] *The Times*, 11 September 1871, p. 8b.

[107] W. Hope, *Sewage Irrigation: A Lecture* ... (London, 1871) and *The Times*, 9 November 1870 and 15 May 1872, p. 11f. Hope sustained his propaganda for sewage as a manure, see W. Hope, *Food Manufacture Versus River Pollution: A Letter addressed to the Newspaper Press of England* (London, 1875).

[108] International Financial Society, *Directors' Report*, 5 April 1871.

[109] See ECRO, Q/RUM 2/210, Deposited plan section and book of reference of Metropolis Sewage, including plan of Canvey Island, 1870.

[110] International Financial Society, *Directors' Report*, 5 April 1871.

Metropolis Sewage's position was nearly altered radically in autumn 1870, when the Metropolitan Board of Works introduced a bill both to abrogate its concession and to forfeit its caution money.[111] The Board had tired of the company's efforts, the first public marker of this being its decision in early 1870 to let the remainder of the land at Barking Creek.[112] Metropolis Sewage countered with its own bill during the 1870–71 session. This sought to continue its scheme but on an amended basis, for which the necessary capital was to be raised either through the Metropolitan Board of Works or with its guarantee.[113] When brought to the attention of International's shareholders, the dispute caused a revolt that went as far as an attempt to bring about the finance company's own voluntary liquidation.[114] Hope led the opposition and was successful to the extent of forcing the calling of an Extraordinary General Meeting in April 1871. However, the motion to empower a shareholders committee 'to conclude a transfer of the interest of the International in the Metropolis Sewage Company' failed.[115] Nonetheless, International's board, as they informed Hope, remained prepared to deal with any party interested in acquiring the sewage utilization scheme.[116] International had retained this power since both parliamentary bills – that of the Metropolitan Board of Works and that of Metropolis Sewage – had been thrown out by the committee of the House of Commons.[117]

During the early 1870s, there was also a considerable flurry of prospectuses for companies that aimed commercially both to deal with water pollution caused by sewage and to turn the effluent into manure.[118] To some, their very number was almost reminiscent of the railway mania of the 1840s. International took an interest in Native Guano Co., Phosphate Guano Co. and Phosphate Sewage Co.,[119] but none ultimately provided a way out of the dilemma posed by Metropolis Sewage for its directors.

Of the three, only Native Guano enjoyed some experimental success,

---

[111] *The Times*, 19 November 1870, p. 7c.

[112] *The Times*, 26 January 1870, p. 10b.

[113] International Financial Society, *Directors' Report*, 5 April 1871.

[114] International Financial Society, Minutes of General Meetings (hereafter IG), 27 January 1871.

[115] IG, 5 April 1871.

[116] HUL, IB, 13 April 1871.

[117] HUL, IB, 1 June 1871.

[118] For one example – Sewage Disinfecting & Manure Co. – see *The Times*, 23 February 1872, p. 10c. From 1844 until the mid-1870s, at least 32 such concerns had been registered as joint-stock companies, 15 between 1870 and 1875. For one, see A.J. Moore, *The Hastings Sewage Manure Company Limited* (St. Leonards-on-Sea, 1993).

[119] HUL, IC, 29 August 1871 and 26 February 1872.

its management finding that London sewage mixed with alum, blood and clay resulted in an effective yet too costly manure.[120] The company had previously developed experimental works at Leamington and Hastings, and then employed the results to gain a foothold at Barking from the Metropolitan Board of Works.[121] However, its first formal agreement with the Board was for works at Crossness to develop further the 'ABC' process – to treat 0.5 million gallons of sewage daily – but, initially, the company failed to proceed.[122] The plant was only ready for inspection in June 1872, by when its concession was due to expire. Furthermore, the company had given the impression of a very close connection with the Metropolitan Board of Works, which, although boosting its shares, invoked the anger of Board members.[123] As to the others, Metropolis Sewage's secretary wrote to International in October 1872: 'I am not very hopeful as to the results of the experiments now being made by the Phosphate Sewage Company at Barking.'[124] Although Phosphate Sewage began to be wound up in 1877 under a court order, Native Guano survived until 1926.[125]

Hope continued to harry International over Metropolis Sewage until 1881. In 1876, he brought an action over a contract between him and International relating to the company's formation in 1865, but it was dismissed.[126] His hostility grew to embrace International in general, on a number of occasions attempting, like other disaffected shareholders, to prevent a reduction of its capital.[127] International's investment in Metropolis Sewage had been written down to £5000 by 1877 and was finally written off during the early 1880s.[128] The various attempts to employ London's sewage as a fertilizer on a large scale only came to an end five years later, after the Metropolitan Board of Works found that farmers would not even take sewage sludge when offered it free of charge. Consequently, special vessels were constructed to ship the sludge

---

[120] Owen, *Government of Victorian London*, p. 65.

[121] *The Sewage Question settled, by the Purification of the Water and the Manufacture from Town Sewage of a Dry and Portable manure . . . as effected by the 'Native Guano Company Limited.'* . . . (London, 1870) and *The Times*, 19 April 1870, p. 10f.

[122] *The Times*, 7 April 1871, pp. 4a, 9a; and 2 March 1872, p. 5e.

[123] *The Times*, 3 June 1872, p. 9d.

[124] *The Times*, 25 November 1871, pp. 6c-d and HUL, IB, 10 October 1872.

[125] See PRO, BT31/14409/4348, Native Guano Co., BT31/1555/5016, Phosphate Guano Co. and BT 31/1607/5412 with C 26/499, Phosphate Sewage Co. and A.F.B. Cooke (ed.), *Register of Defunct and Other Companies 1955* (London, 1955), pp. 320, 365.

[126] HUL, IB, 20 July and 8 November 1876, and IG, 24 August 1876.

[127] IG, 24 August 1876, 29 September 1879 and 1 March 1883.

[128] IG, 26 January 1877.

from the recently constructed precipitation works at Barking and Crossness for disposal at sea.[129]

Conclusions

Metropolis Sewage & Essex Reclamation Co. might be regarded as another folly, another wild expression of the expansionist spirit of the mid-Victorian age. However, it had a foundation in Chadwickian views that were carried forward particularly by *The Times* during the mid-century sewage mania. Apart from Barings or Rothschilds, the company had probably the best of available midwives for its birth. The International was well connected throughout the City, while Antony Gibbs & Sons had specialist knowledge of the fertilizer market. When the company was put before the investing public at the same time as the publication of the Sewage Commissioners' Rugby trials, its time had appeared to come. It even had an aura of a royal imprimatur, applied by the vote of the Prince of Wales for its private act in the Lords. Yet, despite all the efforts made by the company's promoters immediately following the publication of its prospectus, investors were not swayed. The new issue market was beginning to turn sour during summer 1865, and the failure of the flotation of Metropolis Sewage was a first marker of this change in investor sentiment.

Metropolis Sewage cannot be taken as a general marker of whether London's financial institutions serviced the needs of the City and its environs. The company was promoted as a result of very particular personal contacts between its concessionaires and one of the issuing houses that became responsible for putting it before the public – International. Even so, its flotation was only undertaken after considerable discussion amongst International's directors and, then, subsequent modifications of the basic agreement with its concessionaires. What is more notable is that the issuing houses stood behind the venture after the failure to raise its capital – to the extent of at least keeping its sewage fertilizer scheme 'ticking over' until the early 1870s.

Perhaps most striking is the continuity, including personal continuity, from the mid-1840s until the early 1870s – from Chadwick's conception of a 'unified scheme' to the plans of Napier and Hope and then Hope alone. That continuity had a few lasting results through Metropolis Sewage's Lodge Farm becoming a further experiment in the development of sewage irrigation, adding to those of the Rivers Commission and

---

[129] Owen, *Government of Victorian London*, p. 72.

Hope himself. However, the greater use from the late 1860s of the terms 'Sewage Farm' and 'Sewage Grass' (Italian rye grass) was primarily due to municipal enterprise, albeit largely forced by the conclusions and recommendations of the Rivers Pollution Commission. Consequently, it was urban bodies and authorities – local boards of health and corporations – that raised the funds required to address the problem posed by urban effluent, leading to only a limited use of sewage as a fertilizer.[130] Sir Edward Frankland, working as a member of the Second Rivers Pollution Commission, had found in 1870 that sewage would be oxidized if allowed to percolate through a sufficient depth of soil. His technical work on biological treatment was developed during the early 1880s by R. Warrington and W. Santo Crimp. The latter's experiments for the Croydon Rural Sanitary Authority involved the raising of vegetables on underdrained land, using somewhat comparable methods to those that had been employed by both Metropolis Sewage and Hope at Brittons farm. However, the advantages of a biological filter were not fully established until the turn of the century with the experiments of the Royal Commission on Sewage Disposal. These had a major consequence, leading to the introduction of artificial filters, so obviating the requirement under the Rivers Pollution Prevention Acts that sewage was initially passed through land. This major stipulation had led the Local Government Board during the late nineteenth century to sanction local authority loans for sewage disposal only if the proposed schemes involved land treatment. As a result, sanitary authorities had had to face the considerable problems of either land costs or locating suitable areas of land.[131]

---

[130] See in general, J.F. Wilson, 'The Finance of Municipal Capital Expenditure in England and Wales, 1870–1914', *Financial History Review*, 4 (1997), pp. 32–6.

[131] See H.H. Stanbridge, 'History of Sewage Treatment in Britain', 6, 'Biological Filtration (1)', mimeo, Institute of Water Pollution Control, Maidstone, 1976, pp. 22–37.

CHAPTER FIVE

The Sheffield Democrats' critique of criminal justice in the 1850s[1]

Chris A. Williams

The nineteenth century saw the basis of urban governance in Britain change markedly. This chapter deals with the issue of the legitimacy of the criminal justice system, as seen in the context of an attempt to create an alternative basis for local government in the city. It assesses the attempt by the Sheffield Democrats to take control of the institutions of local government in 1851, through an examination of their statements and activity regarding urban police power and the criminal justice system. This was another manifestation of what David Reeder has described as 'the general reaction in the mid-Victorian period against centralised bureaucratic models and continental precedents'.[2] The political basis for this challenge was the collapse of the national political stage provided by Chartism; the ideological framework was the ultra-localist analysis of English liberty provided by Joshua Toulmin Smith. The Democrats utilized a specifically urban variant of 'Norman yoke' theory to justify a bottom-up democracy, which was offered as an alternative to a centralizing and professionalizing tendency. Their challenge was driven as much by expediency as by theory, and it reveals the limits to political action and the extent to which the Democrats were consciously excluded from police power by the town's Liberal ruling group.

This chapter discusses the underlying ideology of the Democrats, how they fitted into the national context and the reasons for their ultimate failure. In addition, it analyses the extent to which they took Toulmin Smith's rhetoric and applied it to the demands of political organization

---

[1] This chapter benefits from feedback given at the University College Northampton History Department Seminar, the Leicester University Economic and Social History Seminar, the GERN/CESDIP 'Policing Matters' Seminar and the University of Sheffield Nineteenth Century Studies Seminar. Thanks are due to Clive Emsley, Peter King, Rosemary Sweet, Janet Smith, Lucy Faire, Richard Rodger, Rob Colls and John Salt for especially useful suggestions.

[2] D. Reeder, 'Introduction' in D. Reeder (ed.), *Educating our Masters* (Leicester: Leicester University Press, 1980), pp. 1–43, at p. 3.

in local areas. It provides a further example of what Reeder pointed out concerning 'radicalism' within the history of education, that there are many 'varieties of radicalism within the left and the right, and each of these bear a complex relation to what might be regarded as "liberal" and "libertarian" tendencies'.[3] It also demonstrates that a firm adherence to 'respectability' among the working class and lower middle class need not necessarily lead to support for the political order and its police institutions. The final section uses these events to comment on the central place that the 'politics of language' has taken in understanding working-class politics in the nineteenth century.

Central to any consideration of these changes in governance is the issue of legitimacy. To what extent were these new forms of state power and authority – and the new classes that were wielding them – accepted by those over whom power was exercised? One of the key changes in the nature of state power was in policing practices – the 'new' police were able to control the streets via patrols and via military-style discipline to defeat large-scale protest. But did the working classes accept them, and if so, on what terms?[4] Evidence suggests that during the early 1850s, in one of the few areas where there was sufficient political space, there was widespread popular support among the working class for a relatively sophisticated analysis that firmly rejected the legitimacy of the new police. I recognize the limits of local urban studies, but plead in mitigation that they are best placed to study idiosyncratic localism in depth.[5] The post-Chartist era saw a fragmentation of the national movement as local adherents carried on their political activity in many different ways: generalizations at the national level are thus limited in their applicability.

Policing and the justice system need to be recognized as an important component of the way that the nineteenth-century city developed and governed itself. Policing has a specifically urban content to it, given the special demands for the close regulation of space that are exerted by towns and cities. 'Police' power, of course, is not limited to the application of the criminal law. The traditional meaning of the word, as used in the eighteenth century by Adam Smith, was the close regulation by

---

[3] D. Reeder and A. Rattansi, 'Introduction', in Reeder and Rattansi (eds), *Rethinking Radical Education: Essays in Honour of Brian Simon* (London: Lawrence and Wishart, 1992), p. 1.

[4] Storch speaks of the new police being 'well implanted by the early 1840s' in several large industrial towns: R.D. Storch, 'The Plague of the Blue Locusts: Police Reform and Popular Resistance in Northern England, 1840–57', *International Review of Social History*, 20 (1975), pp. 61–89, at p. 76.

[5] For the problems of studies such as this, see R.J. Morris, 'Introduction', in R.J. Morris (ed.), *Class, Power and Social Structure in British Nineteenth-century Towns* (Leicester: Leicester University Press, 1986), pp. 11–12.

governmental authority of the physical environment.⁶ The 'new' police did not merely consolidate the enforcement of the criminal law into the hands of a bureaucratically organized and disciplined body of men. They also (in a process that has been discussed far less by historians than have their roles vis-à-vis crime and crowds) concentrated the enforcement of a variety of urban civil and administrative regulations, many of which were contained in local improvement acts as well as in general statutes.⁷ Many of these issues were universal in that they applied to inhabitants of all classes, but a number applied chiefly to those engaged in economic or social activity that might impinge on public space. Police in Sheffield were responsible for identifying obstructed footpaths, smoky chimneys and unsafe walls, cellars and middens.⁸ The monthly meetings of the Improvement Commission saw appeals from individuals, debates over priorities and contested interpretations of its statutory powers: regulation was an important and contentious part of its job.⁹

The traditional view of the good old 'bobby' was that after a very few years of opposition, orchestrated by men who were either fools or knaves, Englishman of all classes rallied behind him.¹⁰ Yet from the 1970s, 'revisionist' historians of the police such as Bob Storch and David Philips charted a sustained antipathy to the police in defence of working-class values of public order, against which the police were operating as 'domestic missionaries'.¹¹ The police were imposing an alien level of

---

⁶ A. Smith, *Lectures on Justice, Police, Revenue and Arms* (New York: Kelley & Millman, 1956), p. 154.

⁷ R.J. Morris and R. Rodger, 'An Introduction to British Urban History, 1820–1914', in R.J. Morris and R. Rodger (eds), *The Victorian City: A Reader in British Urban History, 1820–1914* (Harlow: Longman, 1993), pp. 1–42, at p. 34. Winstanley has shown how the process of regulation was also a key element in the powers of the police in Oldham: M. Winstanley, 'Preventive Policing in Oldham, c.1826–56', *Transactions of the Lancashire and Cheshire Antiquarian Society*, 96 (1990), pp. 17–35, at p. 20.

⁸ Sheffield Improvement Act (58 Geo. II c. 54), ss. 40, 42, 45.

⁹ *Sheffield Iris*, July 1818; *Sheffield Independent*, 9 June, 1833, 5 April and 10 May 1834, 10 June 1837 and 6 June 1840.

¹⁰ C. Reith, *British Police and the Democratic Ideal* (London: Oxford University Press, 1943), pp. 16–17; C. Reith, *The Police Idea* (London: Oxford University Press, 1938), p. 252; T.A. Critchley, *A History of Police in England and Wales* (London: Constable, 1978), pp. 54–5; J.J. Tobias *Crime and Police in England* (Dublin: Gill and Macmillan, 1979), pp. 88–9; C.D. Robinson, 'Ideology as History: A Look at the Way in which some English Police Historians look at the Police', *Police Studies*, 2(2) (1979), pp. 35–49.

¹¹ This opposition has been widely recorded. See, for instance, C. Emsley, *The English Police: A Political and Social History* (Harlow: Longman, 1996), p. 40; S.H. Palmer, *Police and Protest in England and Ireland, 1780–1850* (Cambridge: Cambridge University Press, 1988), p. 447; Storch, 'Blue Locusts',

public order upon an unwilling and recalcitrant working class. More recently, David Taylor has revisited the issue in a less revisionist tone: 'The crucial distinction is between a dislike of (and even a violent response to) a specific police action and a general rejection of the legitimacy of the police *per se*.'[12] This chapter will consider a broad-based working-class movement whose opposition to the police was the other way round: the specific activity of the police and the new standard of order they represented were not opposed, rather the 'legitimacy of the police *per se*' was the target.

Sheffield and the Democrats

In 1851 Sheffield had a population of 135 000, which was growing at a rate of about 20 per cent per decade. Its economic foundation was the steel industry, both in the traditionally organized light trades and the more capital-intensive heavy steel sector. The grinding trades relied on the town's unique skills base, and most firms were small: many workers were semi-independent and hired their own power and light. In the heavy steel sector, companies were a lot larger and relied more on subcontractors and labour gangs. In both, though, there was a real prospect of economic mobility: to 'little mester' status in the grinding trades or to well paid skilled work in the heavy trades. Yet mobility worked both ways; the economy also threatened to proletarianize the artisan.[13] Thus, respectability and a certain degree of deference and

---

pp. 66–7; R.D. Storch, 'The Policeman as Domestic Missionary: Urban Discipline and Popular Culture in Northern England, 1850–1880', *Journal of Social History*, 9(4) (1976), pp. 481–509, at p. 481; J. Foster, *Class Struggle and the Industrial Revolution: Early Industrial Capitalism in Three English Towns* (London: Weidenfeld and Nicolson, 1974), p. 51; B. Weinberger, 'The Police and the Public in Nineteenth-century Warwickshire', in V. Bailey (ed.), *Policing and Punishment in Nineteenth-century Britain* (London: Croom Helm, 1981), pp. 67–93, at p. 65. There were many disturbances elsewhere – for instance in Leicester in 1842 a Chartist was arrested for making a speech in which he described the police as 'blue vampires': (*Leicester Chronicle*, 3 September, 1842).

[12] D. Taylor, *The New Police in Nineteenth Century England: Crime, Conflict and Control* (Manchester: Manchester University Press, 1997), p. 82.

[13] S. Pollard, *A History of Labour in Sheffield* (Liverpool: Liverpool University Press 1959), pp. 125–6, 159, 170; D. Smith, *Conflict and Compromise* (London: Routledge, 1982), pp. 256–7; C. Reid, 'Middle Class Values and Working Class Culture in Nineteenth Century Sheffield: The Pursuit of Respectability', in C. Holmes and S. Pollard (eds), *Essays in the Economic and Social History of South Yorkshire* (Barnsley: South Yorkshire County Council, 1976), pp. 275–95, at p. 281; I. Inkster, 'Social Class and Popularised Culture in Sheffield during the 1840s', *Transactions of the Hunter Archaeological Society*, 12

ambition co-existed uneasily with perceptions of economic and social vulnerability.

Sheffield incorporated as a self-governing borough in 1843. The town council was elected on a ratepayer franchise, with a further property qualification for councillors. Its only mandatory task was to provide a police force for the borough. It took over the old watch force, which had been created in 1818 and was extensively reformed in 1836. This was under the control of Superintendent Thomas Raynor, who had started as a shopkeeper and street commissioner before taking over the police in 1834. He reported to the borough Watch Committee, a group of councillors who met weekly. In 1850, there were about 120 police in the force.[14] Despite the liberal and reformed nature of the town's government, its structure of authority was as likely to be based on appeals to paternalism as to utilitarianism. The ruling group were keen to be seen as dealing in English fair play – just as they were also keen that subordinates should defer to those set up in authority above them.[15]

The Sheffield Democrats were an offshoot of the Chartist and Owenite movements. When Chartism nationally collapsed in 1848, the local organization in Sheffield remained intact. Its main orientation, inherited from battles over the 'Whig betrayal' and incorporation, as well as the People's Charter, was against the town's liberal establishment.[16] The renamed 'Democrats' came close to controlling a majority on the borough council. In the late 1840s they began to run slates of candidates in borough council elections. Some of these men were themselves active members of the Democratic Association – others were radicals or independents who agreed to support the Charter.[17]

They were closely – perhaps too closely – led by Isaac Ironside, an accountant whose political involvement spanned that whole spectrum of nineteenth-century radicalism. Ironside moved through Whiggism, Owenism, Chartism, ultra-localism and Urquartite conspiracy theory to

---

(1983), pp. 82–7; A. White, '"... we never knew what price we were going to have til we got the warehouse": Nineteenth-century Sheffield and the Industrial District Debate', *Social History*, 22(3) (1997), pp. 307–17, at p. 315.

[14] C. Williams, 'Police and Crime in Nineteenth-Century Sheffield', Ph.D. thesis, University of Sheffield, 1998, pp. 128–132.

[15] Mayor Wilkinson to the Council, *Independent*, 8 May, 1847.

[16] B. Barber, 'Sheffield Borough Council, 1843–1893' in C. Binfield et al. (eds), *The History of the City of Sheffield 1843–1993*, vol. I: *Politics* (Sheffield: Sheffield Academic Press, 1993), pp. 25–52.

[17] Barber, 'Sheffield Borough Council', p. 34; J. Salt, 'Local Manifestations of the Urquhartite Movement', *International Review of Social History*, 13 (1968), pp. 350–65, at p. 358.

die a rich and apolitical businessman.[18] He was 'possessed of an irrepressible ego protected by a convenient absence of self-awareness'.[19] His preferred tactic was to combine a *cause célèbre* with a radical social theory and local direct action.[20] He followed this pattern over the issue of criminal justice. Cases were taken up, anti-authoritarian rhetoric was produced, and a skeletal attempt was made to create an alternative local government. The Democrats attempted to challenge the structure of local authority by appropriating both the moral and the organizational functions of the paternalist rulers into the collective institutions of the local working class.

From the start, the Democrats had a history of intervening in the politics of criminal justice. In 1847 they joined in a public campaign against Wilson Overend, a magistrate accused of anti-trade union bias.[21] Later that year, Ironside forced the town council to carry out an inquiry into the case of ex-PC George Bakewell, who was sacked from the police and banished from the town by Superintendent Thomas Raynor, after an affair involving a pair of allegedly stolen trousers.[22] Alongside Ironside's public agitation, prominent Liberals supported the inquiry on the grounds that the Watch Committee had been irregularly bypassed.[23]

---

[18] Ironside's move from respectable radical to agitator began in 1839, when he was forced out of his position as Secretary of the Mechanics' Library for introducing books on socialism. A. Mersons, *The Free Press 1851–1866* (Sheffield Local Studies Library, n.d.), vol. 50/8, p. 1. Ironside's subsequent political career has been chronicled by John Salt: see J. Salt, 'Isaac Ironside and the Hollow Meadows Farm Experiment', *Yorkshire Bulletin of Economic and Social Research*, 12(1) (1960), pp. 45–50; Salt, 'Urquhartite Movement'; J. Salt, 'Experiments in Anarchism, 1850–1854', *Transactions of the Hunter Archaeological Society*, 10 (1979), pp. 37–54; J. Salt 'Isaac Ironside 1808–1870: The Motivation of a Radical Educationist', *British Journal of Educational Studies*, XIX (1971), pp. 183–201; and D.K. Jones in 'Isaac Ironside, Democracy, and the Education of the Poor', *Transactions of the Hunter Archaeological Society*, 11 (1981), pp. 28–38. Claeys has examined the influence of European revolutionary republicanism upon the Democrats' politics: J. Claeys, 'Mazzini, Kossuth and British Radicalism, 1848–1854', *Journal of British Studies*, 28 (1989), pp. 225–61. The rise of the Democrats is also considered in Barber, 'Sheffield Borough Council'. Ironside's biographical entry in Stainton's *The making of Sheffield* almost ignores his Chartism and looks at him only as a self-made businessman: J.H. Stainton, *The Making of Sheffield 1865–1914* (Sheffield, 1924), p. 230.

[19] Jones, 'Isaac Ironside', p. 35.

[20] So, for example, the Democrats used a threefold strategy to oppose the Poor Law. See Salt, 'Hollow Meadows'.

[21] *Sheffield Independent*, 8 May 1846.

[22] Sheffield Town Council Minutes, (Sheffield City Record Office), 9 June 1847.

[23] Alderman Lowe, a previous chair of the Watch Committee, appeared disgruntled when he commented: 'As for the Watch Committee . . . the case had

From 1848 onwards, the Democrats devoted much organization to fighting the borough elections by making sure that working-class tenants paid their rates directly, rather than through middle-class landlords. They created efficient party organizations in most of the town's wards. At the start of 1851, Democrats held between 22 and 13 of the 50 seats in the council.[24] In the course of the year they gained more. When the *Sheffield Free Press* was started in January 1851 as Ironside's mouthpiece, they were given a weekly platform.[25] The Democratic experiment, therefore, allows us a glimpse of how the criminal justice system was seen by one group of working-class radicals – a group whose substantial degree of popular support means that they cannot be written off as marginal. Most of the following analysis is based on a critical reading of the information contained in the *Free Press* and published in 1851 and 1852, when the Democrats were at the apogee of their influence.

Ultra-localism

Around 1849, Ironside had fallen heavily under the influence of the work of Joshua Toulmin Smith, a protagonist of the doctrine of popular Saxon-style sovereignty expressed via local units of government justified by 'a deduction of English constitutional principles from the national records'.[26] Smith's work was 'the most elaborate theoretical defence of

---

not come before them at all. Until Thursday night, they knew nothing of it', Sheffield Town Council Minutes, 9 June 1847, p. 178.

[24] The conservative estimate of 13 is derived from the voting record from the *Sheffield Free Press*, (hereafter *Free Press*) of 17 May, 1851, which recorded the way the councillors voted on the question of who were to be Aldermen. Those who voted for Ironside, or for more than three of the candidates that he himself voted for, are counted as members of the Democrat group. Seven other councillors voted for one or two of Ironside's preferences. Salt puts the number of Democrats in 1849 at 22: Salt, 'Urquhartite Movement', p. 355.

[25] The *Free Press* was started by some compositors from the *Sheffield Independent*. Isaac Ironside soon became the official proprietor of the newspaper, as well as the moving spirit: Mersons, *Free Press*, pp. 2–3.

[26] J.T. Smith, *Local Self-government and Centralization: The Characteristics of Each, and its Practical Tendencies . . . including . . . Outlines of the English Constitution* (London: J. Chapman, 1851); *Dictionary of National Biography*, vol. 53 (London, 1898), pp. 94–5. In 1852, Ironside invited him to stand for election in Sheffield, but he declined the invitation. In 1854 he formed the 'Anti-Centralisation Union' and wrote all 13 papers issued by this society in its three-year life. He devoted the remainder of his life to reporting and commenting on the business of Parliament in his 'Parliamentary Remembrancer', before his health failed him and he died relatively young in 1869.

local independence that has ever been produced in Great Britain'.[27] His panacea was the 'folk-motes': monthly meetings of all the ward's inhabitants.[28] Smith's version of the old Saxon constitution was notable for its urban nature: Smith lived in London, and the basic unit that he talked about was not an idyllic rural parish of yeoman farmers, but an urban one composed of artisan householders. His original espousal of rationalist radicalism grew from his interest in phrenology, which he interpreted as a body of knowledge which demanded social mobility.[29] He had been spurred to apply himself to politics by heavy-handed attention from local excisemen, and the local response to the 1847 cholera outbreak in London: the arrival of the disease and the reactions to it probed and revealed existing political and ideological divisions.[30] Toulmin Smith was drawing on his experience as a resident of the United States, where he had lived for five years, and a tradition of vigorous individualism in local affairs by men who were self-directing and social, a view of the good society which had been advocated by Adam Ferguson, the originator of the phrase 'civil society'.[31] The view of national history that he put forward was a subversive re-reading of a widespread and long-held establishment view that located the uniqueness and legitimacy of English institutions in the unbroken thread of continuity that allegedly stretched back to the Witan of the kingdom of Wessex.[32]

Through the *Free Press*, each 'burgher' in the ward was invited to attend the mote.[33] Use of the phrase 'burghers' was not just an irrelevant archaism, but also an attempt to define the respectable yet radical Sheffield skilled working class as members of an urban 'middling sort'.

---

[27] W.H. Greenleaf, 'Toulmin Smith and the British Political Tradition', *Public Administration*, 53 (1975), pp. 25–44, at p. 25. See also the assessment of Toulmin Smith's central role in many campaigns against centralization in the 1850s: W.C. Lubenow, *The Politics of Government Growth: Early Victorian Attitudes Toward State Intervention, 1833–1848* (Newton Abbot: David and Charles, 1971), pp. 86–94.

[28] This is Smith's term. Ironside called them 'Ward-motes': Smith, *Local Self-government*, p. 80.

[29] Reeder has taken up this theme: see *Educating our Masters*, p. 15.

[30] Greenleaf, 'Toulmin Smith', pp. 27, 40; R.J. Morris, *Cholera 1832: The Social Response to an Epidemic* (London: Croom Helm, 1976), pp. 96–101.

[31] *Dictionary of National Biography*, vol. 53 (London, 1898), pp. 94–5; R.J. Morris, 'Civil Society and the Nature of Urbanism: Britain 1750–1850', *Urban History* 25(3) (1998), pp. 289–301, at p. 291.

[32] M. Oergel, 'The Redeeming Teuton: Nineteenth-century Notions of the "Germanic" in England and Germany' in G. Cubbutt (ed.), *Imagining Nations* (Manchester: Manchester University Press, 1998), pp. 75–91, pp. 82–5; J. Greenberg, *The Radical Face of the Ancient Constitution: St. Edward's 'Laws' in Early Modern Political Thought* (New York: Cambridge University Press, 2001).

[33] *Free Press*, 4 January and 25 January 1851.

Their political claims to influence and the right to discuss every topic that impinged on the life or attention of a free-born Englishman was an act of presumption. What it presumed was that they too had the social stature to make public policy directly on these issues. The power they claimed for themselves could be seen as analogous to that of the members of the town council, and this was a constant refrain in the ridiculing of Ironside's project. The Democrats' pretensions to be 'burghers' were an extension of a classic Chartist political tactic, that of colonizing the public political space traditionally occupied by the urban middle classes.[34]

Insofar as the idea of the 'burgher' was an attempt to tap into a specifically local form of consciousness, it was not too far removed from the political mainstream of the early nineteenth century; Ironside was not attempting to turn the clock back too far. In 1818, Sheffield's influential radical newspaper editor James Montgomery had written in his paper, the *Iris*, of the layered forms taken by individual identity. First was the 'insulated individual', then the man 'in the bosom of his family', who understands

> That he is resident in a neighbourhood, where all the inhabitants, besides their peculiar and domestic concerns, have certain local interests, in which he must take a part and bear a burthen for the sake of the benefits, which result to himself and his connection from their due administration.[35]

So far this is highly congruent with Toulmin Smith's view, yet it was extended by Montgomery to another political level, the political nation, where the archetypical individual 'is the subject of a civil government which has the power to enforce universal allegiance throughout its jurisdiction, that it may have the power to secure private liberty, and national independence'. In crude terms, the professionalizing and centralizing measures of the 1830s and 1840s stressed the latter identification at the expense of the former: both Ironside and Toulmin Smith were attempting to restore the household and neighbourhood as the true focus for public political involvement. It is worth remarking that Ironside also took a far less gendered view of the autonomous citizen than Montgomery had: he supported moves to bring women into the political system. At a council debate bemoaning the offence felt by women at disorderly youths on footpaths, Ironside recommended that they be given the franchise so that they could wield the law as far as necessary in their own defence.[36] The *Free Press* also reported with approval the case of a

---

[34] R.J. Morris, *Class, Sect and Party: The Making of the British Middle Class, Leeds 1820–1850* (Manchester: Manchester University Press, 1990), p. 191.
[35] *Sheffield Iris*, 24 February 1818.
[36] *Free Press*, 15 March 1851.

Sheffield woman who was withholding her rates in protest at her exclusion from the franchise.[37]

The ward-motes themselves were significant more for what they were attempting than for what they achieved: certainly they were not remotely as indicative of support for the Democrats as were their high votes in municipal elections. They were begun in December 1850, when Ironside took advantage of a council mandate that public meetings should be held in the wards to discuss free public libraries: he used these to begin and justify a scheme whereby the inhabitants of each ward should meet every month. Beginning in March 1851, by the end of the year they were meeting regularly in four wards, and they continued to do so until the end of 1853. Attendance was variously estimated at between 20 and 40 by their friends and less than that by their enemies.[38] Like the settlement movement described by Reeder, ward-motes formed an attempt to make 'communities out of neighbourhoods'.[39] Even so, for the Democrats, the mundane demands of political power came first: one of the key tasks that Ironside set for Sheffield's ward-motes was to prepare a list of well-disposed voters: it is significant that the ward-motes' boundaries were electoral rather than following those of Sheffield's six existing townships and their vestries.[40] In addition, they were to debate all possible political questions: from the state of the French government to the state of the parish pump. Once a number of ward-motes had been created, they sent delegates to the town's Central Democratic Association.

The agenda of the ward-motes demonstrated that the Democrats were not arguing for any tolerance of 'traditional' disorder.[41] Rather, they stressed their orderliness, and the meetings demanded a higher level of order. In February 1851 the Nether Hallam meeting mandated its committee, among other things, to prevent the congregation of children on footpaths.[42] The May meeting resolved to issue a placard enjoining Sabbath observance on the population at large.[43] In order to pre-figure

---

[37] *Free Press*, 25 October 1851.

[38] Salt, 'Experiments in Anarchism' p. 43; *Sheffield Times*, 13 December 1851, 'A Visit to a Wardmote'.

[39] Reeder, *Educating our Masters*, p. 31.

[40] See, for instance, the report of the Park ward-mote. *Free Press*, August 2, 1851.

[41] For examples of 'traditional' disorder see Davey on Horncastle in the 1830s, where 5 November was marked by both symbolic and real disruption: B. Davey, *Lawless and Immoral: Policing a Country Town 1838–1857* (Leicester: Leicester University Press, 1983), p. 61; R.D. Storch 'Domestic Missionary', p. 481.

[42] *Free Press*, 8 February 1851.

[43] *Free Press*, 3 May 1851. This provides a contrast to the situation in Leeds, where anti-Sabbatarianism was a key part of the assault on an autono-

the ideal society, the Democrats attempted to present an alternative as well as merely criticizing the status quo. The practical interventions into the criminal justice system taken by the ward-motes were a result of a holistic approach to local government. Problems of crime and public disorder were among many possible issues these local groups were asked to raise. Ironside, speaking to the ward meeting at Nether Hallam in July 1851, called upon those present to

> turn his attention to the subject [local self-government] and see where, in his own neighbourhood, there was any nuisance, or bad footpath, or destruction of water courses, or anything, in fact, detrimental to the public good, and come to the ward mote and name it.[44]

As well as public order problems, they were also keen on close regulation of the human physical environment – a key police power. A ward-mote complained about nuisances caused by smoky chimneys and blocked watercourses, while the *Free Press* declared that 'We abhor false weights and measures.'[45]

Most significantly, the Democrats attempted to actively intervene in criminal cases. Ironside, in the chair at a ward meeting, named five youths he had caught disturbing the peace on a Sunday. The meeting resolved to write to their parents or guardians, asking them to attend the next monthly meeting, and if they did not, to take out summonses.[46] One of the boys attended the next meeting with his mother. He was let off as a first offender, after Ironside assured him that he was lucky not to have been taken before the magistrates and fined 40 shillings.[47]

This case demonstrates how the ward-mote, under Ironside's direct guidance, attempted to arrogate to itself a share in the all-important decision to prosecute or compromise: a decision that was a source of great social power.[48] In addition, by requesting that the culprits' parents

---

mous working-class culture: M. Hewitt, *The Emergence of Stability in the Industrial City: Manchester, 1832–67* (Aldershot: Scolar Press, 1996), pp. 178–81.

[44] *Free Press*, 12 July 1851.

[45] *Free Press*, 11 October and 15 November 1851.

[46] *Free Press*, 15 November 1851.

[47] 'A Visit to a Wardmote', *Sheffield Times*, 13 December 1851.

[48] Hay has written that the power to prosecute or not: 'was in the hands of the gentlemen who went to law to evoke that gratitude as well as fear in maintenance of deference'. The significance of this process of decision-making survives the cogent criticisms of Hay by King, which call into question the precise social location of the decision-makers: D. Hay, 'Property, Authority and the Criminal Law, in D. Hay, P. Linebaugh and E.P. Thompson (eds), *Albion's Fatal Tree* (London: Allen Lane, 1976), pp. 17–64. at p. 41; P. King, 'Decision-makers and Decision-making in the English Criminal Law', *Historical Journal*, 27(1) (1984), pp. 25–58.

appear, it was also adopting the role of community mediator, and attempting to create a new arena in which the politicized local community could exercise quasi-state power. As well as this grass-roots action, the Democrats also called for the democratization and localization of other regulatory police functions: Inspectors of Weights and Measures should be elected from each ward and confirmed at the local feudal court, the Court Leet.[49] The newspaper advised its readers to send the county-appointed inspector 'about his business. Don't allow him to meddle and interfere.'[50]

The Democrats were in favour of public order, but against the standard solution for this problem: increased powers for the police. In January the *Free Press* printed a letter which gave an account of a woman running from a pub and pointing out to a passing constable 'a brute in human form' who had hit her when she refused to serve him.[51] The policeman replied that he could not arrest the man since he had not witnessed the assault: her proper course of action was to take out a summons against her attacker. The correspondent thought that the policeman *should* have arrested the man but the editorial reply to the letter disagreed. It ran:

> ['A Ratepayer' is wrong in supposing that the officer in question neglected his duty ... An extension of the powers of the police should be very carefully set about.] – Ed.

The Democrats' view of the criminal justice system was more complex than any simple populism. They had doubts about entrusting the preservation of order to a bureaucratic institution. Instead they described the police as 'a body irresponsibly appointed, and with practically irresponsible powers'.[52] Ironside attempted to use the ward meetings to develop a critique of the police based on Smith's work. To the first Ecclesall meeting, he read aloud from Smith's *Local Self-government*:

> our police force is merely superficial, and dependent upon its physical power; ... The only police system that can ever be really efficient, morally and truly, instead of merely physically and superficially, must be one which is founded on mutual confidence and immediate local responsibility.[53]

As well as moral condemnation, the Democrats were keen to make political capital out of alleged abuses of police power. In May and June

---

[49] *Free Press*, 2 August 1851.
[50] Ibid.
[51] *Free Press*, 25 January 1851.
[52] 'Justice's Justice and Truncheon Law', *Free Press*, 7 June 1851.
[53] *Free Press*, 22 November 1851.

1851, they printed and publicized a petition – under the title 'Justice's Justice and Truncheon Law' – from an Irish labourer named Luke Clark, who claimed to have been robbed by members of the Bradford police force.[54] Subsequent comment in the *Free Press* sought to draw general conclusions from this issue: 'under our present police system, such cases are daily occurring'.[55] They blamed the 'crown-appointed justices and other irresponsible creatures which form parts of the system of a centralised police'.[56]

Throughout 1851, the *Free Press* was keen to point out the failures of Sheffield's police. It provided a platform for a Watch Committee member to complain that the police guarding an anti-Catholic meeting had been paid for by the ratepayers. It printed another letter on wrongful arrest which called Superintendent Raynor 'The Truncheon Chief'. It reported the theft of a watch from a prisoner by a policeman. When Nether Hallam ward-mote discussed improvement, those present cited 'several cases of meddling interference by the police' – including wrongful arrest and surveillance of a known trade unionist.[57]

The Democrats' suggested alternatives were twofold. The first was to return to the situation before the watch was improved in 1818. Ironside

> remembered the time when Sheffield had only two or three constables and only half a dozen watchmen . . . and the town was not burned down then.[58]

The second alternative was to appeal to a revived version of the mutual pledge, or a continually sitting jury.[59] This was explored by Smith himself in a speech at Sheffield, during which he stated as axiomatic that 'the

---

[54] *Free Press*, in news of 31 May, editorials of 7 June and 14 June 1851, and letters of 21 June 1851, 17 February and 27 March 1852. Clark claimed that he was stopped on suspicion in Bradford, and before release robbed of 'a gold watch, seal, and key, two common keys, two half-crowns, one shirt, one pair of stockings, and two handkerchiefs'.
[55] *Free Press*, 7 June 1851.
[56] Ibid.
[57] 'Police at Private Meetings' – letter from Samuel Sanderson in *Free Press*, 18 January 1851. This letter demonstrates that the newspaper was not merely a mouthpiece for Ironside, who had welcomed the use of police at the meeting, in order to prevent an anti-Catholic riot: *Sheffield Independent*, 14 December 1850. *Free Press*, 1 February 1851, Letter from 'TGP'. *Free Press*, 8 February 1851, report of the Watch Committee, *Free Press*, 14 February 1852.
[58] *Sheffield Times*, 13 December 1851.
[59] The 'Whig' police historian T.A. Critchley sees this system of 'frankpledge' as the original institution from which the traditional English system of police emerged: T.A. Critchley, *A History of Police in England and Wales: 900–1966* (London: Constable, 1967), p. 2.

law must be administered by the freemen among themselves'.[60] Going further, he cleverly turned the preventative principle from an argument in favour of the new police to an argument against them:

> The present system leads man to rely on the watchman, whilst all that the thief thinks of is, how can he 'dodge' the policeman. (Laughter.) But if the thief knows that in every house in every street, every man is on the alert, because every man is responsible, he will know that there is little chance of his committing a theft without being found out.

The *Free Press* was not entirely negative about police forces. In May 1852, it reprinted an article from 'Household Words' which was a laudatory account of a night spent on duty with the Metropolitan Police.[61] Indeed, the ward-mote system also provided an opportunity for the police force to defend itself. One of the auditors of the Ecclesall ward-mote defended the level of Raynor's salary when it came up for debate since he held a 'very unpleasant' office.[62] Later, one councillor got a chance to express his total support for Raynor before the same meeting, and to collect some names of hitherto successful watch-rate defaulters from their resentful neighbours.[63]

The radical critique of the legal system

The Democrats' critique of the criminal justice system was not confined to the police, but extended to the magistrates' courts as well. From the very first issue, the *Free Press* sought to make the case that the law was being devalued by corrupt, lawyerly [sic] practices. An article entitled 'Law and Morals' criticized lawyers for cooperating in immoral and scheming defences of obviously guilty clients.[64] For the Democrats the evil was contained in a system symbolized by 'the Sheffield SHALLOWS', un-elected justices. Appointed magistrates were 'crown-appointed justices and other irresponsible creatures which form the parts of a system of a centralised police' while a stipendary magistrate was 'paid out of public funds, without the public having an opportunity of

---

[60] *Free Press*, 21 February 1852, Toulmin Smith to public meeting.

[61] 'The Metropolitan Protective' – reprinted from 'Household Words', *Free Press*, 3 May 1851.

[62] *Free Press*, 22 November 1851, Mr Wilson to Ecclesall Ward-mote.

[63] '[T]hey would all be aware of the impossibility of a policeman being popular . . . He had never seen a public officer in his life (not even excepting Mr. Bramley) who conducted himself better [than Raynor]': *Free Press*, 10 January 1852, Mr Alcock to Ecclesall Ward-mote.

[64] *Free Press*, 4 January 1851.

questioning his fitness' and ex officio magistrates, although elected, were 'a novelty', 'statute-born only' and crown-appointed – 'unknown to common law'.[65] All were too ready to listen to the double-talk of lawyers, and eager to trap unwary free Englishmen into condemning themselves. The police were complicit:

> Every one knows what the police are in the habit of doing in this respect; and how they are, practically, encouraged in doing it by magistrates. They worm out of the frightened prisoner something in the way of confession or excuse, which they afterwards manage to convert into evidence against him.[66]

Magistrates and state functionaries generally assumed the guilt of the accused, rather than his innocence, and for party motives were ready to bend the law in order to act against trade unions.[67] Their justice was characterized as summary, centralizing, despotic and foreign.[68] Counterpoised to the existing practice was the idea of the 'local responsible tribunal'.[69] This consisted of the peers of the accused, operating under common law and via common sense.[70] Their ignorance of 'legal quibbling' and desire to throw aside 'the technical tortuousities of law' were seen as assets.[71] This of course, is not new: since the seventeenth century English radicals had been calling for simple common law to be used as an alternative to over-mighty lawyers.

The *Free Press* was ever ready to connect live issues and disputes in the town to larger questions of political ideology. One such case was the dispute in 1851 between the coroner, Thomas Badger and the magistrate

---

[65] *Free Press*, 14 June 1851; 7 June 1851; 2 August 1851; 14 June 1851; 24 May 1851.

[66] *Free Press*, 14 June 1851, editorial.

[67] 'The rule of all alike is to assume the guilt of every man as a first principle': *Free Press*, in 'Justice's Justice and Truncheon Law', 7 June 1851. Specific reference was made to Wilson Overend's activity in the 1840s: 'No jury can ever show itself so ignorant of law as did a certain Sheffield justice who, in his eagerness to crush the artizans, passed judgement on many of them under the Combination Act': *Free Press*, 14 June 1851, editorial.

[68] Summary jurisdiction is condemned in the editorial in *Free Press*, 14 June 1851. Reference is made to 'the foreign and degrading system of summary jurisdiction' in *Free Press*, 21 June 1851.

[69] *Free Press*, 7 June 1851. The phrase appears in a discussion of the complaint of Luke Clark: 'under such, a wrong like this could never have been perpetrated'.

[70] 'Trial by peers or Summary Jurisdiction?' was the title of the *Sheffield Free Press*'s editorial on 14 June 1851; 'The people, the only administrators of the law among each other': *Free Press*, 21 June 1851; 'Common Law': *Free Press*, 7 June 1851; '[C]ommon sense juries': *Free Press*, 2 August 1851.

[71] *Free Press*, 14 June 1851, editorial.

Wilson Overend, over the former's ability to subpoena witnesses who might later face criminal proceedings. The coroner's court was extolled as the last vestige of democracy: a survival from the Saxon era when magistrates were all elected and merely presided over the real arbiters of justice, the assembled freemen. Its authority, stemming from common law not statute, was seen as purer, even though by 1851 the office was formally in the hands of the borough corporation. This attitude was not a local aberration: in 1830 the office was elsewhere referred to as that of the 'People's Judge'.[72]

The Democrats were ready to point out the class inequalities in the law. When the Home Secretary suggested that Luke Clark sue Bradford for damages, the *Free Press* was scathing:

> A poor, though honest man, is told to go to law with policemen and magistrates, having a 'borough fund' at command.[73]

They recognized that the law was not class-blind. Institutional hegemony was easier to preserve, than the rights of the individual. As the *Free Press* noted:

> Jurists tell us that the laws were instituted for the protection of the poor and weak against the oppression of the rich and powerful; but experience shows that in practice, the reverse of this is their general effect, and that the poor 'Have nothing to do with the laws but obey them.'[74]

The Democrats were against crime, but did not see the criminal law as absolute. Their views on criminals included a special category of 'political crime': seen as an inevitable response to economic and social conditions, not a moral lapse. One ward-mote, called for the pardon of all those imprisoned for rioting in Ireland in 1848 and 1849, as well as for Frost, Williams and Jones, 'and all other political offenders whatsoever'.[75]

Furthermore, they were also aware of the social mitigating circumstances that were produced by an imperfect society. When the ward-mote attempted to try the four unruly boys, the social context of the crime was noted, but discounted owing to the seriousness of the offence:

> Several ... regretted that our boasted civilisation does not provide healthful recreation for the youthful portion of the population, who, after a week's application to business, very naturally sought the

---

[72] G.H.H. Glasgow, 'The Election of County Coroners in England and Wales *circa* 1800–1888', *Legal History*, 20(3) (1999), pp. 75–108, at p. 76.
[73] *Free Press*, 6 September 1851.
[74] *Free Press*, 16 August 1851, editorial on 'Capital v. Labour'.
[75] *Free Press*, 11 October 1851. The Ecclesall Ward-mote passed a similar motion in January 1852: *Free Press*, 10 January 1852.

suburbs for recreation on the Sunday. Nevertheless, the obscene language and riotous conduct of the youths were intolerable, and no one could pass near them without being insulted.

This attitude could be summed up as tough on crime, yet tough on the cause of crime. It was only articulated in an essentially oppositional setting, and thus the extent to which those holding it favoured one or the other part of the equation remained unknown.

Limitations of the radical strategy

The Democrats wanted the respectable citizen to take autonomous action and set up institutions that would usurp power from the existing ones. Toulmin Smith's version of the libertarian ideal of the freeborn Englishman was harnessed to this end, yet the Democrats were unable to escape the contradictions that it contained. A tension ran through their rhetoric: they were respectable and therefore wished to see crime punished, even by the current imperfect system. The ward-mote's action against Sabbath breakers only went as far as invoking the self-same state power which they often castigated as flawed. As a reformist organization they needed sometimes to call upon the existing institutions to make the changes they desired. In the case of the 'centralizing' inspector of weights and measures, for example, they advised people to 'sue him in the County Court, before a jury for damages'.[76] By 1851, the County Court was one of the newest innovations in a modernized legal system (which professional lawyers were in the process of taking over).[77] One of the main planks of Luke Clark's case was a certificate from Superintendent Raynor, proving that, contrary to the allegations levelled at him in Bradford, he had never made malicious accusations involving the Sheffield police. The concept of the 'honest' magistrate necessarily involved a tension present in their activity. They did not attack local serving magistrates by name. Indeed, the opposite was the case when they reported the death of W.J. Bagshawe in June 1851. The obituary they carried was highly complimentary, making reference to his long years of service to the town.[78]

On the one hand, the tactical demands of a day-to-day critique meant

---

[76] *Free Press*, 2 August 1851. In 1852, an article appeared in the *Free Press* on the antiquity, democracy and legitimacy of the Court Leet: *Free Press*, 24 February 1852.

[77] H.W. Arthurs, *Without the Law: Administrative Justice and Legal Pluralism in Nineteenth-century England* (Toronto: University of Toronto Press, 1985), pp. 42–4.

[78] *Free Press*, 7 June 1851.

that the Sheffield Democrats used some 'legitimate' public institutions to attack other 'illegitimate' ones. On the other, the ideological demands of their strategy sought to create a new basis for all power. As part of its polemic in favour of the powers of the coroner the *Free Press* once more revealed that it was not above using one police jurisdiction against another. It called upon the coroner to 'have one of the county constabulary in attendance' to carry out any order from the jury to commit anyone (that is, the local justices) who refused to produce a witness.[79] The Democrats' antipathy to centralization thus created a tension between a need to harness demands for reform of social conditions, and an antipathy to new powers being given to 'undemocratic' institutions. Their support was mobilized on the basis of grievances that were difficult or impossible to tackle while they clung to their ultra-localist ideology. This contradiction was at the heart of the fiasco over the Sheffield Improvement Bill of 1851. Initially supported by radical sentiment, it was defeated at a public meeting when Ironside and the Democrats turned against it on the grounds that *inter alia* it would 'place immense power in the hands of policemen and magistrates'.[80] It was the sudden about-turn of the Democrats on this issue that helped to destroy their credibility, and from then on, their prestige and numbers sank.

Much of the Democrats' activity was reactive. The *Free Press* and their tactics were intended to put their own interpretations on the live issues of the moment rather than follow any ideologically prescriptive pattern. Yet despite Ironside's pragmatism, theoretical patterns underlying these reactions can be discerned and closely related to the doctrines of Smith. These can be expressed as acceptance of responsibility by individuals for their own actions, opposition to '[f]unctionaries, paid out of the people's money' and a conviction of 'the value and ubiquity of primitive Saxon democracy'.[81]

At one point, Ironside showed that he could be motivated more by short-term politics than by any real adherence to Smith's views. In March 1852 he proposed that the council consider appointing a public prosecutor.[82] This was his response to a recent scandal involving Super-

---

[79] *Free Press*, 2 August 1851. The *Free Press* carried a letter from Toulmin Smith himself setting out the antiquity and democratic nature of the office of coroner, in the issue of 28 February 1852.

[80] Ironside to Nether Hallam ward-mote: *Free Press*, 6 December 1851. Barber also describes these events: 'Sheffield Borough Council', p. 34. Ironside hailed the victory with an editorial entitled 'Municipal Centralisation Defeated': *Free Press*, 6 December 1851.

[81] *Free Press*, 21 June 1851; Greenleaf, 'Toulmin Smith', p. 36.

[82] *Free Press*, 13 March 1852.

intendent Raynor, who stood accused of having mishandled a case which he was dealing with in his position as de facto public prosecutor. Clearly, Ironside considered scoring points off the failings of the new police to be more important than advocating decentralization. Significantly, the grass-roots organization did not consistently follow him: Nether Hallam ward-mote approved the plan, but that of St. George's reserved judgement. The ward-motes, therefore, were not merely pliant tools of Ironside's will: some of the people involved in them were convinced of the logic of local self-government, whether by exposure to Smith's work, previous ideological commitments or personal conviction. Despite this lapse, Ironside might have largely believed Toulmin Smith's philosophy. His close ally Richard Otley certainly did not, but it did not stop him from supporting the Democrat's political project. In 1839 Otley had detailed and crushingly rejected the 'Norman yoke' theory in *The wrongs of Englishmen and the rights of freemen, being a comparison between the pretended English and the real American constitutions*. Yet in November 1851 he hailed the success of the Central Democratic Association's activity.[83]

The concern of the ward-motes to add regulation of watercourses and weights and measures to their powers can also be seen as a desire to exercise the power to regulate nuisances as well as the power to prosecute the disorderly. Furthermore, it located them as contesting power in an area that was as crucial to the activity of the self-employed artisan as it was to the more established trader: the right to obstruct the streets in order to carry out lawful business presupposed an agency charged with arbitrating what was 'lawful'. But in this particular context, a second limit on the ability of the ward-motes to offer a concrete alternative – technical considerations – can be seen. The city inevitably threw up problems of organization and prioritization of land use, services and sanitation.[84] Most responses to this situation contained an element of 'domination and social control', but the problems themselves were real and needed to be dealt with one way or another.[85] Houses needed numbering, rights of way needed defining and preserving, nuisances

---

[83] R. Otley, *The Wrongs of Englishmen and the Rights of Freemen, being a Comparison between the Pretended English and the Real American Constitutions* (Sheffield, 1839) Sheffield Local Studies Library vol. 5/9a; *Free Press*, 8 November 1851.

[84] Greenleaf, 'Toulmin Smith', p. 40.

[85] P. Fraile, 'Putting Order into the Cities: The Evolution of "Policy Science" in Eighteenth-century Spain', *Urban History* 25(1) (1998), pp. 22–35, at p. 34; J.M. Ellis, *The Georgian Town, 1680–1840* (Basingstoke: Palgrave, 2001), pp. 87–93.

needed proscribing and traffic needed regulating.[86] The creation and management of complex and necessarily universal schemes of regulation in order to allow the city to trade with and live with itself had successively pre-occupied Sheffield's Town Trustees, Improvement Commission and Municipal Corporation. Regulation in most of these cases had to be preceded and underpinned by a process of legitimization of the regulating agency. The attempt by the Democrats to put the ward-motes at the centre of urban regulation threw up a host of potential problems which they were in no shape to solve without a mass base of active support. Yet they conspicuously lacked this, even though they retained passive support.

Opposition to the radical strategy

The Democrats failed in their bid to establish alternative institutions that could deliver the real benefits of state power. Effective action to solve local problems backed up by state power inevitably meant accepting the legitimacy of some of the very institutions – the appointed magistracy and statute law – which they wished to undermine. Without any support for a 'dual power' situation, the ward-motes never looked capable of effectively taking over the multifarious functions of local government.[87] They continued to see their dominant task as being a party to register and deliver votes in local elections.

The Democrats also failed in their attempts to overthrow the existing police institutions. This latter failure was caused less by their own failings and more through the active opposition of the town's ruling elite. In November 1851, the Central Democratic Association drew up a number of slates designed to 'secure the election of some radical councillors on the committees'.[88] The week before the first meeting of the new council the *Free Press* printed the slates for the Watch, Health, General Purpose and Finance Committees.[89] In each of these lists, about 40 per cent of the candidates were Democrats. In the event, the Democrats were only

---

[86] For numbering, see *Sheffield Independent* 19 May 1821, 7 October 1837 and 8 March 1838. For obstructions, 29 August 1829 and 5 February 1842.

[87] The phrase 'dual power' was best defined by Leon Trotsky as a 'split [in] the state superstructure. It arises when the hostile classes are already each relying upon essentially incompatible governmental organisations': L. Trotsky, *The History of the Russian Revolution*, vol. 1: *The Overthrow of Czarism* (London: Gollancz, 1932), pp. 221–2.

[88] *Free Press*, 8 November 1851.

[89] The Watch Committee was invariably placed first in any list of Council committees.

Table 5.1 The relative successes of the Democrat slates in Sheffield in 1851

Committee	No. on c'ttee	No. of Dems on slate	No. of slate members (Dems + others) on actual c'ttee	No. of Dems on actual c'ttee
Watch	14	5	6	2
Health	14	6	10	4
General Purposes	9	3	5	2
Finance	9	3	4	2

able to secure token representation on the committees.[90] Table 5.1 sums up the position. It is clear from these figures that the Democrats, and those Liberals whom the Central Democratic Association felt were acceptable, were excluded most of all from control of the Watch Committee: the centre of executive control over the police and hence an institution of great power within the town.[91]

Ironside's campaign against the town's police force had been simmering for four years.[92] A climax was reached in November 1851, when he attempted to reduce the watch rate and claimed in the council that 'Unless the police force be put on a different footing to that at present, it would be impossible to maintain order in the town.'[93] His proposal was ruled out of order, although a more technical call for 'economy in local government' was successful. Yet those in control of the Watch Committee fought a successful rearguard action, stating that 'the safety of the borough would not allow a diminution of the number of the force'. Ironside could not win arguments about disbanding the force altogether.

The other problem was that the Democrat councillors resisted becoming mere delegates of the ward-motes. The experience of being installed in the council, and of having responsibility for controlling the town's institutions, led some of them to 'jump ship' and adopt the role of reforming liberal. This had been predicted by one of the delegates to the

---

[90] *Sheffield Independent*, 15 November 1851.
[91] C. Steedman, *Policing the Victorian Community: The Formation of English Provincial Police Forces, 1856–80* (London: Routledge & Kegan Paul, 1984), p. 67.
[92] The *Sheffield Times* opined that he had been 'nibbling' at the watch rate for this long: *Sheffield Times*, 29 November 1851.
[93] *Free Press*, 15 November 1851, report of Town Council Meeting.

Democrat Association in 1851, who complained that, with the exception of Ironside and 'the late Mr. Briggs', all the Democrat councillors were 'half-hearted Whigs'.[94]

Wider conclusions

Was the ideology of the Democrats too exceptional for us to base wider conclusions about opposition to the criminal justice system on them? This was not the case. If we examine opposition to the growing state in general and to the new police in particular, we can see that Smith's rhetoric, and Ironside's attempt to expound it, were expressions, albeit extreme expressions, of a solid and widespread political tradition. 'Backward-looking' radical localism with its ability to evoke a 'language of feeling' had a wide emotional appeal in the 1840s.[95] Chartist leader Bronterre O'Brien extolled Saxon institutions since 'they allowed every parish, and every tithing and every county to legislate exclusively for its own internal affairs . . . This is genuine democracy.'[96] As well as its more general application, it was explicitly referred to in the opposition to the new police forces that surfaced between 1829 and 1856. Barbara Weinberger wrote of Warwickshire:

> In the 1830s and 1840s, opposition to the new police was part of a 'rejectionist' front ranging from Tory gentry to working-class radicals against an increasing number of government measures seeking to regulate and control more and more aspects of productive and social life.[97]

In 1829 the initial response by *The Times* to the Metropolitan Police was to suggest that its power be devolved back down to the parishes.[98] In 1839 the Chartist Convention saw the rural police as an unprecedented threat to the nation's rights.[99] In Sheffield, a Chartist meeting of 1839 had heard the virtues of the 'courts of frankpledge' and their mutual

---

[94] *Free Press*, 6 September 1851.
[95] Lubenow, *Government Growth*, pp. 50, 90; P. Joyce, *Visions of the People: Industrial England and the question of Class, 1848–1914* (Cambridge: Cambridge University Press, 1991), p. 34.
[96] R.G. Hall, 'Creating a People's History: Political Identity and History in Chartism, 1832–1848' in O. Ashton, R. Fyson and S. Roberts (eds), *The Chartist Legacy* (Woodbridge: Merlin Press, 1999), pp. 232–54, at p. 246; J. Vernon, *Politics and the People: A Study in English Political Culture, c.1815–1867* (Cambridge: Cambridge University Press, 1993).
[97] Weinberger, 'Police and the Public', p. 66.
[98] Reith, *British Police*, p. 51.
[99] Emsley, *English Police*, p. 40.

responsibility spelt out.[100] Opposition to the new police that looked to the past as the haven of freedom was a general phenomenon. Explicit appeal to tradition was not confined to any one political extreme or even to the political extremes themselves. The Democrats were appropriating a radical version of traditional constitutionalism which had been used to justify the right to remove authority from the state. In 1851 the Clerk to Sheffield Magistrates, Albert Smith, said of a case of wrongful arrest that 'Englishmen do not like to feel the hand of the constable on them.'[101]

The second problem is whether or not the Democrats were unrepresentative of their society. The evidence suggests they were not. Thousands of Sheffield's working men and lower middle classes voted for Democrat candidates at the height of the 'ward-mote' experiment. The highest estimate is that they had 22 out of 50 councillors in 1851: a very conservative count puts the number at 13. Either way, it was significant. The ward-motes were undoubtedly advancing the agenda of an exceptional individual – but at the same time they were successfully mobilizing people to fight borough elections. They cannot have totally disconnected from the opinions of a substantial fraction of the people. It took positive action on the part of the town's elite to keep them out: active enforcement of the property qualification in the case of Richard Otley, and exclusion from the key committees.

On the issue of working-class opposition to the police, the Democrats, and their many supporters, certainly aimed at rejecting the legitimacy of the police per se. Even so, they supported a new, respectable, standard of order and regulation. The ward-motes' love of public order calls into question interpretations that see the new police as there to impose an alien standard of order on a wilfully unruly working class. Conversely, it strengthens the case for police unpopularity: if the order they brought was not the problem, the demonstrable unpopularity of the police themselves must have stemmed from what they were rather than what they were trying to do.[102]

The Democrats stand out as one of several documented examples of oppositional popular justice. At the time of their political challenge, Sheffield was already host to another form of alternative justice, in the shape of the illegal intimidatory practices of the trade societies.[103] The 1840s also saw the last big outbreak of 'Whiteboyism' – the often brutal

---

[100] Rev. Mr Thornton of Bradford to Chartist Meeting: *Sheffield Mercury*, 11 August 1839.

[101] *Free Press*, 11 October 1851.

[102] Storch, 'Domestic Missionary'; and 'Blue Locusts'.

[103] S. Pollard, 'The Ethics of the Sheffield Outrages', *Transactions of the Hunter Archaeological Society*, 8 (1957), pp. 118–39, at p. 131.

enforcement of non-market traditions designed to defend the interests of the smallest landholders – in parts of Ireland. But the Whiteboys were enforcing strongly and widely held community norms that went against the law of the sovereign state, and thus differed from the Democrats, for whom a closer (far more successful) historical parallel was in the Civil Guard in 1940s/1950s Johannesburg: enforcing the existing law and the (ostensible) 'public' and state standard of values, while opposing, for wider political reasons, the activity of the state's police.[104]

Examining the tactics and the impact of the Democrats also brings out some general conclusions relevant to the current debate over the nature of social history that has often been carried on in studies of British Victorian radicalism. The debate over the nature and basis of plebeian activity in the nineteenth century is useful and generally necessary. Yet – partly because the focus of this controversy is on the significance of the 'linguistic turn' – the politics of discourse and the discourse of politics tend to get placed in the foreground and the politics of action is forgotten.[105] Texts are definite even though their meaning and significance can be debated. For the historian, action lies at a further remove. The Democrats tried to do things. They were partially successful with poor relief, in which arena they successfully supported a municipal version of the Chartist land scheme at Hollow Meadows.[106] Ironside failed with the ward-motes and the wholesale attempt to apply Toulmin Smith's prescriptions to Sheffield: later he succeeded on a less ambitious attempt to take control of the local Boards of Highways in order to (illegally) provide the town with adequate sewers.[107]

Toulmin Smith's ideology of localism was a 'political discourse', yet its application in Sheffield was contingent on agency and political will. In 1850, it fitted the political need of the Democrats for a mobilizing ideology, so it was taken up by them and put to use in an attempt to forge a popular revolutionary constitutionalism. This ideology was, if anything, a result of political circumstances rather than a cause of them. The basic need it filled was to maintain a political force that could materially improve the condition of its supporters through allowing them

---

[104] M. Beames, *Peasants and Power: The Whiteboy Movements and their Control in Pre-famine Ireland* (Brighton: Harvester, 1983), pp. 124–6; D. Goodhew, 'The People's Police-Force: Communal Policing Initiatives in the Western Areas of Johannesberg, circa 1930–62', *Journal of Southern African Studies*, 19(3) (1993), pp. 447–470.

[105] For a summary of this controversy, see M.W. Steinberg, 'Culturally Speaking: Finding a Commons Between Post-structuralism and the Thompsonian Perspective', *Social History*, 21 (1996), pp. 191–214.

[106] Salt, 'Isaac Ironside', pp. 45–50.

[107] Salt, 'Experiments in Anarchism', pp. 42, 44.

a measure of control over the multiplying institutions that regulated their lives, by capturing and exercising elements of state power. But the rhetoric was not merely a passive tool. Ironside's political tactics over the public prosecutor were undermined because his supporters took rhetoric seriously. Toulmin Smith was fond of the maxim that 'Parliament was a result, not a source': for his follower, Ironside, ideology was also a result as well as a source.[108]

---

[108] *Free Press*, 21 February 1852.

CHAPTER SIX

A year in the public life of the British bourgeoisie

R.J. Morris

The year 1829 was an ordinary year in the history of the commercial and industrial town of Leeds. There was no slump, no major strikes, epidemics, riots, political campaigns or reforms. For that reason it is well suited to the purpose of this chapter, which is to examine the nature and meaning of certain social forms that had been developing in British urban society for at least a hundred years. Central to this enquiry was a series of meetings which were recorded in the local newspaper press. Each was to some degree 'public' and transparent. Each was linked to some form of organization, state, commercial or voluntary. Each displayed evidence of the customs, rules and rituals which characterized 'the meeting'. Many were linked to the voluntary society with its constituent elements, the committee, the annual general meeting, the public meeting, the subscription, the published subscription, the printed notice, the annual report and the rules and regulations. These elements were those of the subscriber democracies which had grown in influence and number since the 1780s but they were shared in varying degrees by local government, commercial organizations, property owning trusts and other non profit service providers like the Friendly Societies.[1]

By their nature, the commercial and industrial cities of Europe involved a variety of disparate interests. Economic and cultural position, class, status, ethnicity, language and religion all defined these interests. The inhabitants, especially the elite and policy-makers of urban places, had always had powerful motives for negotiating and regulating such interests to achieve cooperation, to guide and reduce the costs of interaction between those with complex and varied objectives. Population growth, the expansion of world trade, the changes in industrial tech-

---

[1] R.J. Morris, 'Voluntary Societies and British Urban Elites, 1780–1870: An Analysis', *The Historical Journal*, 24 (1982), pp. 95–118; R.J. Morris, 'Associations', in F.M.L. Thompson (ed.), *Cambridge Social History of Britain, 1750–1950*, vol. 3: *Social Agencies and Institutions* (Cambridge, 1990), pp. 395–443.

nology and organization and the growing intensity of the capitalist environment increased such motivations and potential gains. For the purpose of this argument capitalism requires a simple definition. It is a system of economic and social relations characterized by private ownership of property, the organization of exchange through cash and the market, and the search for profit and accumulation of property rights as the major motive for economic decisions.[2] It was and is a powerful and effective means of organizing human interaction but expressed in this way the tension between the individuality of this system and the gains to be made from cooperation become clear. Such gains were not unique to the urban place but were increased by such an environment. Thus this account of meetings and organization needs to be set in a wider context of a debate, which has run since at least the early eighteenth century, around the tension between the individuality of commercial and capitalist systems and the clear gains to be made from cooperation and trust in human interaction.[3]

The urban historian may approach this in a number of ways. Weber gives a central place to issues of authority and domination in his account of the Fort and the Market. Wirth's account of 'the urban way of life' as a response to an environment of size, density and complexity accepts too easily the ecological metaphor of the individual decision maker, although some attention was given to the voluntary association.[4] More recently theorists have recognized the importance in the urban context of the creation of collective capital, of the creation of positive externalities and the reduction and control of negative ones.[5] Above all there has been a revival of interest in the historical processes that created a 'public sphere' as a key component in the organization of order which despite the potential for conflict through the variety of interests, and despite frequent and usually temporary breakdowns of order, has been the historical achievement of the inhabitants of most urban places.[6]

---

[2] Anthony Giddens, *Capitalism and Modern Social Theory: An Analysis of the Writings of Marx, Durkheim and Max Weber* (Cambridge, 1971).

[3] Adam Ferguson, *An Essay on the History of Civil Society*, ed. F. Oz-Salzberger (Cambridge, 1995); Anthony Giddens, *The Consequences of Modernity* (Stanford, 1990).

[4] Max Weber, *Economy and Society*, ed. Guenther Roth and Claus Wittich (Berkeley, 1978), vol. II, pp. 941–1006; L. Wirth, 'Urbanism as a Way of Life', in L. Wirth, *On Cities and Social Life*, ed. A.J. Reiss (Chicago, 1964), pp. 71 and 82. The essay itself was first published in 1938.

[5] David Harvey, *Social Justice and The City*, (London, 1973), p. 58; R.J. Morris, 'Externalities, the Market, Power Structures and the Urban Agenda', *Urban History Yearbook*, 17 (1990), pp. 99–109.

[6] Craig Calhoun (ed.), *Habermas and the Public Sphere* (Cambridge, Mass., 1994); Jurgen Habermas, *The Structural Transformation of the Public Sphere: An*

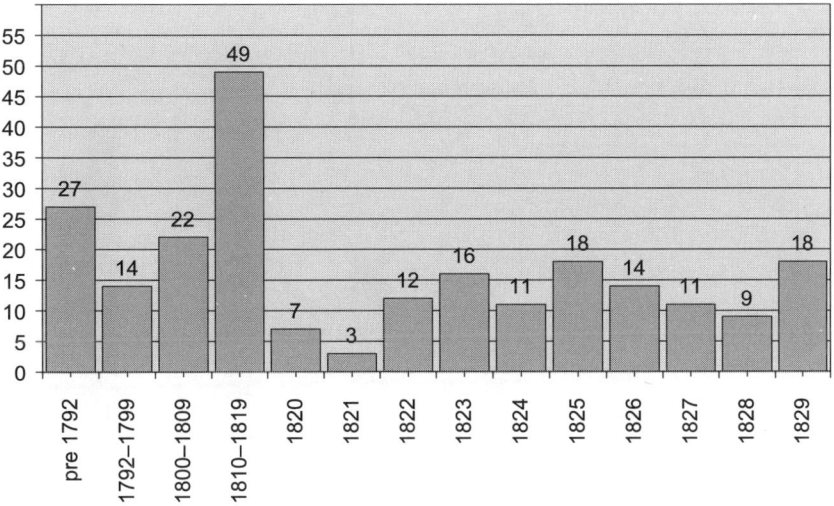

6.1 Steam engines erected in Leeds up to 1829

In 1829, the borough of Leeds was approaching the end of a decade of rapid population growth. A population of 84 000 in 1821 was to reach 123 000 in 1831 with considerable social and environmental stress. At the same time, this growth was an indicator of a period of major economic growth. The figures for investment in steam engines published in the local newspaper were another indicator (Figure 6.1). Leeds had grown in the eighteenth century as a major regional commercial, service and finishing centre for the woollen cloth industry of the West Riding of Yorkshire. The first 50 years of the nineteenth century saw a rapid expansion of factory production in woollens and flax as well as the growth of chemical and machine-making industries. Problems were created by changes in working relations, by the declining wage of groups such as the hand loom weavers of the Bank in east Leeds and by the need to represent local interests on the national political stage.[7] This was represented by the manner in which a rather hesitant language of class developed to express these claims and explore the new relationships.[8]

As with so many towns, the middle classes of Leeds as measured by

---

Inquiry into a Category of Bourgeois Society, trans. Thomas Burger (Cambridge, Mass., 1989).

[7] R.J. Morris, *Class, Sect and Party: The Making of the British Middle Class: Leeds, 1820–50* (Manchester, 1990); Derek Fraser (ed.), *A History of Modern Leeds* (Manchester, 1980).

[8] Dror Wahrman, *Imagining the Middle Class: The Political Representation of Class in Britain, c.1780–1840* (Cambridge, 1995).

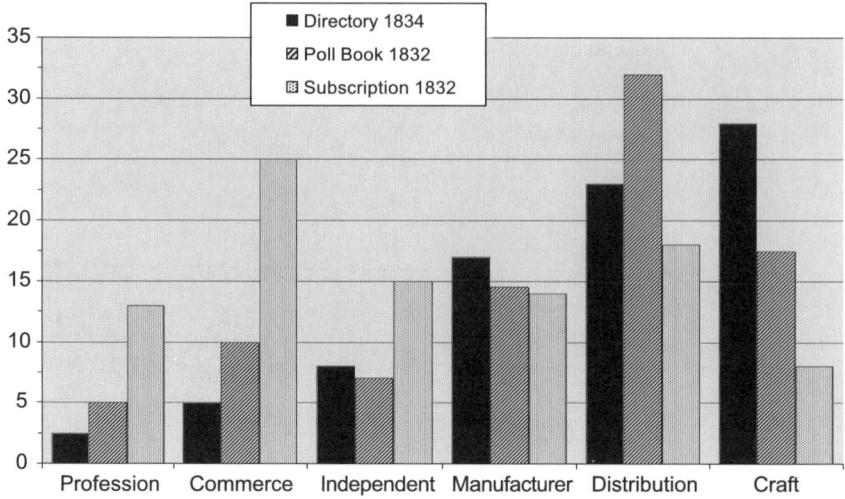

6.2 The subscribers of Leeds 1832

entries in the commercial directory were dominated by retailers and owners of small craft workshops. As a whole the middle classes of Leeds made up some 15 to 25 per cent of the adult male population. The proportion depends on the indicator used – appearance in the commercial directory or appearance in the parliamentary poll book – but in any case the boundary was neither sharp nor precise. The range of economic and social status within the middle classes was considerable. If the middle classes are examined in terms of their social status and willingness to participate in the public sphere – here measured by participation in a voluntary subscription for the relief of the poor in 1832 – then the dominance and leadership of a relatively small number of professional and commercial men becomes clear (Figure 6.2).[9]

In 1829, there were 143 meetings of various sorts reported in the *Leeds Mercury*. The *Mercury* was a whig-liberal dissenting newspaper which supported the reform of parliament. Hence it was likely to be in sympathy with the diversification, ethic and ideology of an active, open and dynamic public sphere through which the elite and middle classes of the towns and cities of Britain increasingly related to the identities and spaces of the urban.[10]

---

[9] R.J. Morris, *Class, Sect and Party*, p. 326; R.J. Morris, 'Occupational Coding: Principles and Examples', *Historical Social Research/Historische Sozialforschung*, 15 (1990), pp. 3–29.

[10] Clyde Binfield, *So Down to Prayers: Studies in English Nonconformity, 1780–1920* (London, 1977), pp. 54–99.

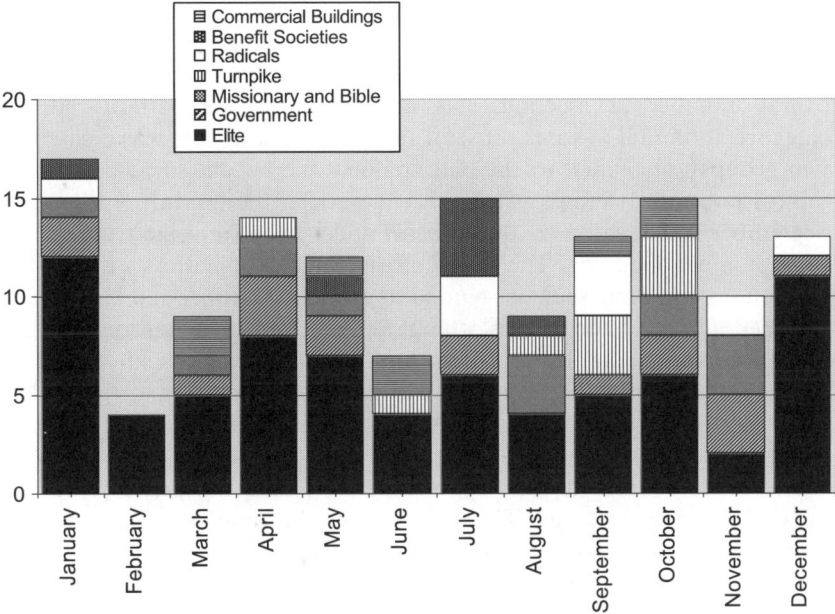

6.3 Meetings in Leeds 1829

The dedicated participant in the public life of Leeds had a variety of events from which to choose. The bulk of those reported in the *Mercury* concerned elite activities, subscription concerts, joint-stock companies and the major voluntary associations, but equally important were lower status groups that met in public houses or the radical meetings held in the open air. For purposes of analysis, six specialized groups have been identified in addition to the elite voluntary element. One set of meetings was related to the Commercial Buildings, opened in 1829 and intended as a commercial exchange on the lines of Liverpool, but in fact acting as a meeting place and subscription newspaper room. The next two categories were meetings of the benefit societies and the radical political meetings. The turnpike trusts which financed and benefited from the toll road system also met in a formal manner. The missionary and bible societies were distinct not only in their religious identity but also for their link to national associations. Lastly there were the wide range of meetings related to local government and vestry such as workhouse and highways boards.

There were several patterns of seasonality with a peak around December and January related to the annual general meetings of the voluntary associations and local joint-stock organizations such as the Oil Gas Light Company and Leeds and Hull Railroad (Figure 6.3). There was a minor peak in April and May around Easter and Whitsuntide, which did include some formal voluntary associations but also had a seasonal element with two flower shows and a nearly defunct race meeting. The overall number of meetings has a more confusing pattern but the categorization makes some sense of this. The peak in July was created by two groups not related to the elite, namely the benefit societies and the radical political meetings. An apparent peak in the unhealthy month of September was created by the radicals and by the turnpike trust season of September–October. The latter mostly met in solicitor's offices. The missionary and bible societies tended to group in October and November. October also saw the nearest thing to the start of a 'season' for the industrial-commercial town. The Amateur Musicians held their first meeting and lectures began at the Mechanics Institution and the Philosophy and Literature Society. There was also a new series of subscription concerts.

Social status, identity and space were all linked together in a variety of ways by the meetings. The first was in the practice of naming the groups which took part in each meeting. Many were simply functional. There were 'subscribers and friends' in the Lancastrian School, and 'shareholders' in the Oil Gas Light Company. A meeting of 'the inhabitants of the town and neighbourhood of Leeds' was called to fix the Improvement Rate and 'a meeting of merchants, manufacturers and others interested in the prosperity of Leeds' was called to link up with other commercial towns and petition parliament.[11] On many occasions the description of participants asserted their high social status, 'opulent individuals' for the West Riding Medical Charitable Society, 'highly respectable and numerous' at the Auxiliary Bible. These societies embodied the public social actions of the high status members of the middle classes. This was linked to a double language of 'Leeds and its neighbourhood', and 'respectable and opulent' merged the identity of the high status leadership of Leeds with that of the socio-geographic community of Leeds, thus giving reality and asserting legitimacy to the leadership and authority of that high status group over the whole community. They spoke for Leeds in a way that no other social group could.

The second link between space and status was in the choice of meeting place. Of the 134 meetings for which a place of meeting can be clearly identified the most commonly used was the Court House (Table 6.1). Many of the others were held in either a chapel or a public house. Many organizations, such as the medical institutions and the infant school used their own buildings. The figures for the Philosophical and Literary

---

[11] *Leeds Mercury*, 9 May 1829.

Table 6.1 Public meetings in Leeds 1829: meeting places

Court House	30
Chapels	28
Public houses	17
Medical institutions	11
Vestry of parish church	9
Commercial Buildings	8
Music Hall	5
Mechanics Institution	5
Phil and Lit	3
Woodhouse, Hunslet and Leeds Moor	6
Bank and solicitors offices	4
Workhouse	2
Assembly Rooms	1
Street procession	1
Coloured Cloth Hall	1
Leeds Central Market	1
Leeds Infant School	1
Hunslet vestry	1

Source: *Leeds Mercury*, 1829.

Society and the Mechanics Institution were underestimates as the newspapers tended only to record opening meetings in each season. There was a clear shortage of meeting places that were not identified with local government, the denominational loyalties of the chapel or the culture of a public house. This question of identity through meeting place worried the Benevolent or Stranger's Friend Society in January. They had met for years in the committee room adjoining the Old Methodist Chapel. This probably had not mattered when the sectarian awareness of the Wesleyan Methodist Church in the north of England had been relatively light, but during the 1820s the spreading influence of Jabez Bunting and his followers meant that the Methodists had gained an increasingly aggressive sectarian identity, just as the Stranger's Friend Society was developing ambitions to become a town not a sectional society.[12] Thus the annual general meeting of 1829 discussed the possibility of moving next year to the Court House for their annual general meeting. The opening of the Commercial Buildings in 1829 created a high prestige

---

[12] Robert Currie, *Methodism Divide: A Study in the Sociology of Ecumenicalism* (London, 1969); W.R. Ward, *Religion and Society in England, 1790–1850* (London, 1972).

meeting place free of party and sectarian identity. One feature of the record for 1829 was the identity of open air meetings with low status and the lack of street processions. Some of this may have been the *Mercury*'s whig-liberal view of what public life constituted, but mostly it was a reflection of the care taken to hold meetings which were bounded and ordered. The confident use of the street and the open park had to await the mid-century.

These meetings were part of a larger process of the ordering of order in the growing commercial and industrial town. Some of the operations of these meetings and organizations were directly concerned with influencing ideological perceptions and understandings. When the Leeds Auxiliary Bible Society met in October, the Revd George Walker, curate of Trinity Church, told them,

> There was a person in Leeds within a week who supposed that he had a remedy for all evils – he contended that men were merely the creatures of circumstances and might be made exactly what they pleased – that the reason why there was so much evil in the world was, men had not been taught that every person, instead of seeking his own good should seek the common welfare.

When that parody of the Owenite and radical utilitarian ideas sponsored by James Mann, the radical bookseller, had been dismissed, he turned to the utilitarian ideas which lurked in the minds of many of the elite, including the flax spinning Marshalls. To combat 'the fallacy of this pernicious view, it was desirable that the sacred scriptures should be put into everyone's hand'.[13] The Lancastrian School claimed that it was making its pupils ready for useful places in the economy.

> The committee have the satisfaction to state that of that number those leaving two thirds are known to have been placed in situation of usefulness to which the rudiments of knowledge which they have obtained in this school have rendered them eligible.[14]

The Benevolent or Stranger's Friend Society related its activities directly to the needs of the growing Leeds economy for in migration, a need which the poor laws with their settlement laws were ill equipped to serve. Mr Cawood, the treasurer, told the annual general meeting

> that description of distress which has least claim to local relief has, in a higher degree, claims on special benevolence: for the stranger is unaided by those ties of family connections, and those kind attentions of neighbourly feeling, which are engendered by long residence. At the same time, a town like Leeds which depends for its prosperity on the talents and genius of every country is bound . . . to display an

---

[13] *Leeds Mercury*, 17 October 1829.
[14] *Leeds Mercury*, 21 February 1829.

active sensibility in relieving the occasional wants of such persons
... Policy, public spirit, humanity and all the Christian virtues call
therefore, for liberal support.[15]

Much of the impact of the meetings and societies was through implicit rather than explicit structuring of perceptions. Selected sets of relationships were acted out and affirmed. The organizing committee of any society always found itself turned two ways. It turned towards potential subscribers and members to gain confidence and support. Hence the panic amongst the trustees of the Leeds Public Dispensary in July. The organization was already running short of funds, and was clearly preparing for an appeal. In June 1825 'afflicted objects' had been turned away and many applications for help were unsuccessful. The Dispensary, said the *Mercury*, combining the traditional appeal of interest and duty,

not only brings into exercise the best feelings of humanity, but materially tends to check the progress of disease.[16]

Then in August, the apothecary of the Dispensary was accused of neglecting to go to a child who had been badly scalded. The child had been left for six hours including an extra hour whilst the apothecary had his tea. The *Mercury* demanded an enquiry by the trustees, or 'public odium will attach to the institution', which was a nice way of saying it would lose subscriptions. The enquiry managed to pass blame from an over-worked apothecary to an inarticulate weaver, the boy's father, and the issue was dropped.[17]

The other direction in which organizers always had to face was towards the 'objects' of charity. Care had to be taken that only the 'deserving' were helped. Dr Williamson, the physician to the Leeds General Infirmary, was concerned that

persons were admitted residing at a distance, who were able to pay for themselves at home; for the purpose of receiving what they considered superior treatment... [He wanted] ... 'whom I believe to be an object of charity' to be printed on the form of recommendation.[18]

The disciplining and distancing language of 'objects' was coupled with the idealistic hope for a direct, personal, face-to-face relationship between the subscribers and the poor. The recommendation form and the visiting were part of this. So also was the religious Tract Society's belief in the

---

[15] *Leeds Mercury*, 3 January 1829.
[16] *Leeds Mercury*, 27 June 1829.
[17] *Leeds Mercury*, 29 August and 5 September 1829.
[18] *Leeds Mercury*, 3 January 1829.

importance of the personal distribution of tracts.[19] This relationship, whether face to face or not was an important part of the middle classes' definition of themselves, hence their shock when it was discovered that the Leeds General Infirmary was running out of cash.[20] The *Mercury* was confident that the 'disgrace of closing part of the house would never be incurred.

One set of relationships that was structured by action within the societies was with the 'ladies'. They were almost totally excluded from public life. Even when required they failed to appear. Hence the rather coy plea of the gentlemen amateurs of the Leeds Amateur Musical Society. They 'wish us to hint that they would esteem themselves highly honoured if our fair townswomen would kindly contribute a share of their musical acquirements on these occasions'.[21] Even when the title of an event might create an expectation of active female participation little was evident. When the Leeds Ladies Auxiliary Society for the Promotion of Christianity amongst the Jews held their annual meeting in the Music Hall, the chairman was T.S.B. Reade, merchant, and the report was read by Revd Miles Jackson, minister of the Anglican Church of St Paul's in fashionable Park Square. The public event for the 'ladies' was the bazaar. When the Dispensary moved into new premises in February comment was made

> To the ladies of Leeds and its vicinity, it will be peculiarly gratifying to perceive so substantial a monument of their successful exertions in connexion with the bazaar of 1826.[22]

When the General Infirmary lurched towards one of its periodic financial crises later in the year, the bazaar was anticipated as an obvious solution. No bazaar was held in Leeds that year but the Yorkshire Bazaar held in York for the County Hospital well illustrates the ritual of prestigious display, economic triviality and oppressive competitiveness that was generated by these occasions.

> For months past the ladies of the principal families . . . have been engaged in preparing drawings, paintings, work boxes, baskets and various objects of fancy and elegance for this bazaar. Several of the ladies were appointed as saleswomen at the bazaar, and all their influence was of course exerted to obtain contributions to the object.

As a stimulus to their exertions the newspapers published not only the total receipts from the bazaar, but the individual daily totals of each stall

---

[19] *Leeds Mercury*, 21 November 1829.
[20] *Leeds Mercury*, 5 December 1829.
[21] *Leeds Mercury*, 28 November 1829.
[22] *Leeds Mercury*, 21 February 1829.

with the names of the ladies responsible, so we can still trace the fluctuating fortunes of Miss Atkinson, Miss Champney, Lady Milner and Mrs Wake as they exerted themselves for the 'object', and wonder if Lady Petre really did run out of things to sell when her returns slumped from 40 on the first day to 8 on the last.[23]

Central to the annual round of the voluntary societies was the annual general meeting. This was a ritualistic occasion on which the leaders of the society affirmed its identity, aims and structure. Notice of the meeting was printed in the local press, together with the names of the leading organizers. Some societies had a patron whose name was also added. The Leeds Auxiliary Bible Society patron was Lord Harewood, indicating approval sought and gained from the local Tory aristocracy. Merely to print such a name indicated acceptance of the hierarchical Anglican authority represented by the Tory landowners. The meetings of the major societies were held in one of the buildings which indicated a claim for status on a town wide basis. The chair was taken by a leading official of the society, president or treasurer. The chairman's opening address usually stated and justified the aims of the society. The *Mercury* summed up the introduction of William Wilks, stuff merchant, in the chair for the Church Missionary Society, 'the object of which was to excite the zeal of the public in favour of the institution'.[24] The introduction was followed by the secretary reading the report. The report which was later printed was the basis of the committee's accountability to members. It gave a summary of the society's activities and a financial account. Often this was followed by a series of motions which gave leading members a chance to speak in support of the society. This structure created an illusion of openness and rational debate based upon information. The rituals and practice of transparency and rational debate were one basis of the claim for legitimacy and authority made by participants in these meetings.

Usually the whole operation was so smooth that no one reflected on its nature or had to justify what was happening. Something of the nature of the high status middle class view of the legitimate way to run a society was revealed by comments Baines made on the Radical Reformers during 1829. Meetings should be called through open publicity by a committee which had clearly derived authority, usually from a previous open meeting. A meeting to discuss unemployment, held on Woodhouse Moor in mid-July, was derided thus:

---

[23] *Leeds Mercury*, 19 December 1829.
[24] *Leeds Mercury*, 24 October 1829.

> The meeting appears to have been convened in consequence of messages communicated to the workpeople in each mill by certain individuals claiming to act as a committee.[25]

By September, the radical leaders of the working class had turned their attention to parliamentary reform. They called and ran a meeting in a manner which the *Mercury* found equally distasteful.

> The notice being anonymous did not unite, as all public meetings on this vitally important subject ought to do, all classes ... The arrangements were defective. Some resolutions had it seemed been prepared, but there was no body to propose them, and the bald way in which the penny a week subscription was proposed, gave to the meeting an idea, which they did not fail freely to express, that the object was to extract a few pence from the pockets of the labouring classes to be placed in the hands of no-body knew whom, neither treasurer, nor secretary, nor any other responsible person being named.[26]

The Baines were delighted by the row that blew up about the collection of pence by the Radical Reformers. They quoted with glee speeches made by Smithson and Cunliffe. These two had fallen out with James Mann, who was trying to collect the money. The reports of their speeches may include words put into their mouths at sub-editing stage but the result was a clear statement of the middle-class elite view of the ideology of a public meeting. The main elements were open publicity and accountability. Smithson stated that 'every penny taken from the people by an unauthorized committee is robbery'. Cunliffe rejected private meetings as they destroyed unity.

> what has the private system done, but to entrap the unwary, by which means our ranks were cut open and our enemies could take advantage of us (hear, hear) ... Their (the reformers) number would be greatly increased by a union on a public, liberal and consistent plan. That must be done by a requisition formed respectfully, a public meeting called, subjects discussed; and if expense is incurred let those pound gentlemen come forward and I will subscribe mine ... Let the thing come openly before the public ... I cannot join an object, when I know not what it is founded on or intended for.

He proposed a requisition for a public meeting which Smithson seconded. Their views exposed a contradiction in the radicals' situation. If they accepted the public form of meeting with the expenses involved for publicity (James Mann wanted most of the pence for printing), then they needed to accept the hegemony of 'the pound gentlemen' whom Baines called 'respectable'. As the *Mercury* editorial said, the Radical Reformers

---

[25] *Leeds Mercury*, 11 July 1829.
[26] *Leeds Mercury*, 19 September 1829.

have 'wisely . . . called upon those in the wealthy classes . . . to take steps to petition for this important measure'. Smithson was more precise in stating the terms on which he acknowledged the authority of the upper middle classes: 'In this country . . . influential men are looked up to by the people, and when they conduct themselves with propriety towards the working classes, it is proper they should be.'[27]

This was an excellent statement of conditional deference. The freely acknowledged authority of those of higher social status was a third element in the ideology of public meetings revealed by the discussion. This commentary on the chaotic proceedings of the Radical Reformers showed something of the theory which lay behind the sedate proceedings of the Mechanics Institution and the Church Missionary Society.

The Leeds Commercial Buildings were built between 1826 and 1829. They were financed by a joint-stock company. As an investment the return to the shareholders was slim, but as an amenity the Commercial Buildings were important. The Commercial Buildings were an item of collective consumption designed to increase the efficiency with which capital circulated.[28] In reality, their major impact was to facilitate the development of the practice and ideology of the 'meeting' outlined in this chapter. They were built at the south end of Park Row, easy of access for the wealthy of the west end and the hills to the north-west. They were on the edge of the growing commercial area of Leeds. The banks of Commercial Street and Bond Street, the warehouses of Basinghall Street and the Coloured Cloth Hall were all within 300 yards of the Buildings. There were 400 to 500 subscribers who were, said the *Mercury*, 'a large proportion of the bankers, merchants, manufacturers and principal traders of the town'. Allowing for exaggeration, this was an excellent descriptive definition of the middle class of Leeds. The trust deed of the Commercial Buildings showed that there were only 155 shareholders with a total of 542 shares.[29] Only 8 per cent of the shareholders came from outside Leeds. Most were men likely to use its facilities. Authority rested with a committee of subscribers. This authority again derived from a general meeting. Thus the rules were not fixed until a general meeting has been held with due publicity. The detail of these rules fixed the social identity of the subscribers to the Buildings with great care. In February, the *Mercury* announced

> The principal of admission will be on the most liberal plan; all subscribers to the coffee room and the Leeds Commercial Newsroom

---

[27] *Leeds Mercury*, 26 September 1829.
[28] Manuel Castells, *The Urban Question*, (London, 1977), pp. 454–60.
[29] Kevin Grady, 'The Georgian Buildings of Leeds and the West Riding, *Publications of the Thoresby Society*, LXII(133) (Leeds, 1987).

> without exception will be eligible to become subscribers to this room, without any introduction and other subscribers will require only the introduction of one member without any ballot. The annual subscription cannot be fixed till the Rules and Regulations have received the sanction of a general meeting; but a guinea and a half is proposed for gentlemen resident in the town, and a guinea for non resident members.

The rules of this proto bureaucracy were duly approved. They dealt with choosing a committee, paying subscriptions, admitting strangers and the conduct of annual meetings. They regulated the use of newspapers under the watchful eye of Mr Atkinson, superindentent of the newsroom. The initial list of newspapers reflected the geographical world of the Leeds middle class. Leeds and London papers dominated just as Leeds and London news dominated the pages of the *Mercury* and *Intelligencer*. Then came Liverpool, Manchester, York and Hull, with two papers from each, and then one from Birmingham, Sheffield, Nottingham, Bristol, Norwich, Newcastle, Oxford, Cambridge, Edinburgh, Glasgow and Dublin. This list represented the trade and family links of the men who subscribed to the rooms. Wool came from Norwich, Hull and London; cotton and cousins from Manchester and Liverpool. County society was in York. Anglicans were educated in Oxford and Cambridge; nonconformists at Edinburgh. Wives, customers and cousins came from all these places. The newspaper list was a mental map of the world of the Leeds middle classes.

The rule for the admission of new subscribers was an important part of this structure.

> The principle of admission is to the highest degree liberal and the union of men of all parties meeting at a place of common resort is calculated to introduce and maintain in the town and neighbourhood the best possible feeling.[30]

The form the entrance rules took had a deliberate and important effect on the social composition of the membership of the rooms. Ostensibly many societies were as open as the market place. Pay a subscription and join. This was part of the practice that legitimized authority, but in fact a high level of subscription excluded all individuals of low status. The Commercial Buildings required an introduction which eliminated those who were total strangers and anyone who was so personally undesirable that no one would sponsor them. This meant that the rooms were socially open to all sections of the high status middle class. Other entrance rules had very different results. If members had been balloted for, then minorities like the Unitarians could have been excluded. If a

---

[30] *Leeds Mercury*, 1 May 1829.

system of black balling members had been in force, then uniformity would have been imposed on the membership, as some suspected was happening in the Leeds Library through the exclusion of nonconformists. Thus the choice of rules was important for determining the future identity of the subscribers to the Buildings.

The affirmation and search for unity was not an idle one. Leeds, like other urban centres, was recovering from bitter local disputes over the Catholic Emancipation Acts of 1828. The Pitt Club and the Brunswick Club had campaigned actively and viciously against the bill. The nonconformist readers of the *Mercury* identified closely with the Catholics for they suffered a range of legal disabilities over church rates and burials, and were only protected from more serious disabilities by annual acts of indemnity. The Pitt Club, with the mayor in the chair, was a 'fruitful source of faction' and Alderman Hall was condemned for 'fanning the expiring flames of religious bigotry and political exclusion against Catholics'.[31] Sectarian identity was never far from many aspects of social life in Leeds. Advertisements for servants preferred a woman of 'the Methodist connexion'; another was required 'in a dissenting family'.[32]

The need for unity was made clear by the threats to the power and prosperity of the high status middle classes. As the Commercial Buildings came near to completion, the papers reported the summer riots of 1829 coming close to Leeds. Violence from weavers of all kinds spread from Bolton to Manchester. It was reported in Spitalfields and then Barnsley. The unemployed met near Huddersfield and were addressed by William Ashton from Barnsley 'in a very intemperate and inflammatory harangue'.[33] The *Mercury* was glad to be informed 'by the persons who took the lead in this business, that this intemperate address was as unexpected as it was unwelcomed to them'. When the Leeds unemployed began meeting in July, care was always taken to report that 'the meeting quietly separated'. From the newspaper reading drawing rooms of the middle classes, the working classes presented a double mood of aggression and deference. The mood could change with bewildering rapidity. Within days of rioting the weavers of Barnsley were marching to Wentworth Woodhouse to beg for funds from Earl Fitzwilliam and received his help with hearty cheers. Unity amongst the middle class elite was essential if they were to respond to working class needs and encourage the stability of these moods.

This sense of unity was to be built around the commercial activities of

---

[31] *Leeds Mercury*, 14 March 1829.
[32] *Leeds Mercury*, advertisements from 1829.
[33] *Leeds Mercury*, 20 June 1829.

Leeds. At the end of September, the subscribers met to fix a time for a daily exchange

> there is less occasion for an exchange here than in Liverpool, Manchester, Bristol and several other places, (but) great convenience will arise from a certain hour of day being fixed for persons in trade to congregate and meet their friends at a place of public resort. The exchange will, we understand, be held at the principal entrance to the buildings and in the vestibule leading to the grand staircase.[34]

The subscribers pledged 'regular attendance, and using their influence with others to regular attendance'.[35] The idea of an exchange was hard to get across to the Leeds merchants and later reports suggest that it was ill attended. The Buildings had a greater success as a place for public meetings. As soon as the Buildings opened several voluntary societies chose the large room for their annual general meetings. Even the sectarian based societies were aware that by meeting here they were sharing in a town identity and not just asserting that of their own religious section. When Edward Baines, jr addressed the Bible Society meeting he claimed 'the hall they were met in would probably in future be used for many different purposes – for purposes of harmony, of commerce, of politics, of religion'.[36]

The act of opening the Buildings was an act of ceremonial and ritual. Events began on Monday, 12 October when the proprietors of the Buildings gathered outside and went in procession to the principal entrance. The 'doors were thrown open' by the architect, who presented them with the keys. The chairman of the committee, Lepton Dobson, hoped that the Commercial Buildings would be

> an ornament to this wealthy and populous town; ... as a public edifice, there is nothing superior to them in the north of England except perhaps the Liverpool exchange ... they afforded ample and even splendid accommodation [for] the free intercourse and cordial communication amongst the merchants, manufacturers, professional gentlemen and traders in the town.[37]

Once inside the proprietors took some 'wine and refreshments'. The sharing of food and drink was the oldest of all human expressions of unity and friendship. It was also a way of affirming class divisions in the creation of the Buildings. At four o'clock, the workmen of the buildings were furnished with 'cheese and bread and strong beer'. Capital drank wine and labour drank beer. The main event was a public dinner held in

---

[34] *Leeds Mercury*, 26 September 1829.
[35] *Leeds Mercury*, 3 October 1829.
[36] *Leeds Mercury*, 17 October 1829.
[37] Ibid.

the large room of the Buildings on Wednesday, 27 October. It was a festival of the unity and power of the middle classes of Leeds and their friendly relationships with other sources of power in the county. The symbolism and organization of this event deserves careful analysis as a major exemplar of urban practice. The four county MPs were invited, to the delight of the *Mercury*:

> this is one of those occasions in which both they and all mercantile and trading classes may meet with great cordiality and propriety, on the general and public ground of advancing the commercial prosperity of the town, without any admixture of party politics.

One hundred and ninety, people bought their 15/- tickets, which included a bottle of port wine. In addition there were 20 specially invited guests. Much of the evening was entertainment. The guests arrived at five o'clock. Dinner was announced at twenty to six. The guests withdrew at midnight, although hardier spirits prolonged things until three in the morning. Much time was spent eating, drinking, listening to songs and glees and cheering speeches. What mattered was the manner in which men chose to entertain themselves and the ceremony with which that entertainment was surrounded. It would be wrong to dismiss this dinner as just a good night out. The room was decorated with laurel and illuminated with gaslight. The guests were marshalled by stewards who carried white staves. The laurels were symbols of triumph taken straight from the culture of classical literature which most of the guests would share and understand. The staves were symbols of authority which again came from Rome. Gaslight was not only practical but had become in 10 years one of the symbols of social and economic progress. Gaslight enabled streets to be better lit and law and order to be better maintained.[38] Gaslight enabled factories to be run during darkness, making fuller use of capital; 'the blazing evidence of their midnight manufactories' was evidence of the prosperity of the West Riding.[39] None of this would be lost upon the guests. The layout of the room represented the power structure of the Leeds middle class. The top table was raised so that it could be seen. Even the food had meaning beyond the satisfaction of appetites. The head of the middle table was crowned by 'a baron of beef (worthy of its noble rank) ... stores of venison and game [had come] from the parks of Wentworth and Duncombe'. Despite the anti-landlord remarks which Baines made when commenting on the Corn Laws, the layout and ceremonies of the dinner had feudal echoes of

---

[38] Morris Berman, *Social Change and Scientific Organization: The Royal Institution 1799–1844* (London 1978), pp. 146–91.

[39] *Leeds Mercury*, 14 November 1829.

power. The top table represented all major centres of power in the borough. The chairman was Christopher Beckett, mayor, banker and important member of the Tory Anglican power group which dominated the legitimate agencies of state power in Leeds. Balance was maintained by Thomas William Tottie, vice chairman, solicitor, leading Whig and local agent for Earl Fitzwilliam. Also on the high table were Viscount Milton, MP, the Hon. William Duncombe, MP, and John Marshall, MP, representing county parliamentary authority which was a delicate balance of landowners and manufacturers.[40] The major manufacturing families, the Marshalls and the Gotts, were both present. Leading members of the corporation included Henry Hall, with his divisive efforts at the Brunswick Club all forgotten. Colonel Townsend of the 14th Light Dragoons, then stationed in Leeds barracks, was there, whilst his regimental band played in the gallery. This band frequently played on public occasions, a reminder of the manner in which military power contributed to the security of the Leeds middle class. Finally, in one corner was Revd John Urquart, AM, curate at the parish church, representing the vicar as he so often did on public occasions.

If this tableful represented the local power structure then the toasts were a simple celebration of the national and local power structures.

> The King
> The Duke of Clarence and the rest of the Royal Family
> The King's Ministers
> The County Members
> The Mayor
> The Mayor and Corporation
> The Vicar of Leeds
> The Magistrates of the West Riding
> The 14th Light Dragoons
> The Yorkshire Hussars

It would be hard to give a better account of the official structure of power in that part of the West Riding in 1829. Even the agencies of main force state power were given a proper but subordinate mention. The speakers from the top table did not forget the commercial ethic. They toasted the prosperity of the borough. They praised the architect for keeping within the cost estimates he had made back in 1826. When glasses were raised to the manufacturers it was Gervas Walker, one of the senior trustees of the White Cloth Hall, who replied. They drank the health of the bankers of Leeds, especially Beckett. They drank with some feeling remembering the crisis of 1826.

---

[40] F.M.L. Thompson, 'Whigs and Liberals in the West Riding, 1830–60', *English Historical Review*, 74 (1959).

bankers cannot exist without merchants, any more than merchants can exist without manufacturers – it is a branch of commerce which is able to return the benefit of all pre-existing branches. (Lord Milton)

T.W. Tottie extended this sense of the interconnected economic activities of the elite.

> in the days of peril you know what was done for the commercial people of Leeds by the bankers of Leeds who stood their ground, and afforded their liberal aid and assistance in times of the greatest need.

The ability to supply credit in times of crisis such as 1826 explains the quiet authority of the successful banking families of Leeds.

In the speeches two themes dominated. The first was the manner in which Leeds as a community sought and received status. Public buildings like the Commercial Buildings were part of this claim for status. Henry Hall, alderman and merchant, stated

> In most of your recollections, the town of Leeds, though celebrated as the favoured seat of manufactures and commerce, presented little in her exterior to attract the attention of the passing visitor, or to denote our advance in arts and sciences. But gentlemen when we consider the public buildings which in the course of the last ten years, the piety, benevolence, and public spirit of our inhabitants have established in the town, we shall also be of the opinion that our advance in Arts has been equal to our extension of commerce.

A central concept in their self-esteem was that of 'improvements'. Benjamin Dealtry, a West Riding Magistrate, praised the street widening as well as the new buildings. He praised the new markets which had been built in the 1820s. Lepton Dobson, merchant and chairman of the subscribers, saw the search for further improvements as part of their identity as an elite. He suggested action to improve the supply of pure water,

> of more real service and value to the inhabitants of the town, but more especially to the middle and lower classes, than any improvements that have yet taken place.

For John Marshall, the elderly and supremely successful flax manufacturer, now Member of Parliament for the county, the recently created voluntary societies were also part of this claim.

> But gentlemen, as merchants and manufacturers are not merely plodders and getters of money, the town has had the spirit, not only to obtain wealth but to employ it most creditably to itself in a variety of modes (cheers). We possess charitable institutions of every description. This town has taken the lead not only in works of charity, but

> in institutions of literature and science, and I believe Leeds took the head of the county of York in the establishment of a Philosophical and Literary Society – (Cheers). I trust that the spirit of improvement will always be felt in our town.

When the bottle of port was well down the company could even laugh at that central but equivocal agent of 'improvement', the steam engine. Replying to a toast to his father, Earl Fitzwilliam, Lord Milton said,

> He came into life at a period when that native smoke which the worthy Alderman has alluded to, when that native smoke had not been wrought for the purpose of generating steam, into the black, and I will say sometimes beautiful curls they are.

But it was Milton who was cheered for giving them the recognition of status they sought: 'I see assembled in this room such a manifestation of the wealth, the intelligence and the public spirit of this place.'

The other major theme was unity. Lord Milton, the Hon. William Duncombe and John Marshall all commented upon it. Marshall insisted that he was able to represent the agricultural as well as the manufacturing interests. The speech by T.W. Tottie, the Whig solicitor, was class formation in the making and the Commercial Buildings the material embodiment.

> The present occasion, I cannot let pass without expressing the sincere gratification that I feel at the harmony of this meeting (Applause). Gentlemen, if divisions prevail amongst us, they are weakness. Union is strength . . . The corner stone of this building was laid in union . . . Let the meeting we have now be an anticipation of our union in the future . . .

Class formation required not just the experience and potential of conflict, but the incidents and ceremonial which affirmed identity and unity, and which taught ideology in the widest sense. This dinner was just such an incident. The elements of middle-class ideology taught over the port were pride in a prosperity and improvement which included commerce, manufactures and cultural and charitable action. The speeches sought an open relationship with the aristocracy and a desire for their approval. The ideology sought a caring relationship with the lower classes, and a responsibility by the high status members of the middle classes for the lower status members of that class. The dinner was not a full account of middle class formation, but it was an account of the idealized perception which the Leeds elite had of their own actions.

The variety and very different aims of these events should not hide the importance of the common general social structures which were involved – the meeting, the annual report, the printed notice in the newspapers, the public dinners and breakfasts, the committees and subscriptions. There was an element of ceremony and ritual in all these social forms. By these activities the middle class acted out and affirmed key social relationships. The individual subscriber was related to 'Leeds and neighbourhood' as one of the 'respectable and opulent inhabitants'. And as one of the high status strata of Leeds society, the subscriber took part in class relationships with 'objects' of charity and with other members of his social class, especially the high status leaders. In this last relationship deference was only given in return for open accountability. Much of the ritual of the meetings and reports was designed to serve the need to combine these two elements. In the societies, members took part in relationships with other high status communities which were both local and national in scope. They also took part in national international links, usually with cultures they regarded as morally inferior. The meetings, the dinners, the public buildings and the subscriptions gave a reality to key elements in middle-class ideology, and gave legitimacy to that ideology and to the power and wealth with which it was associated. The elements most clearly revealed were 'improvement', a relationship of disciplined and humane superiority with the poor, and a relationship of deference and open accountability with those of higher status.

The ritual and practice of the meeting, the dinner, the speeches and associated publications in newspaper press and handbill had evolved over several generations. They were well understood by participants. At one level this understanding simply defined the group, the 'inhabitants of Leeds' and excluded others, the 'workmen' who met on Woodhouse Moor who did not know the rules. At another level such ritual and practice defined, structured and affirmed key social relationships. The relationship of 'subscribers' to 'objects' was one of conditional deference which was a selected aspect of the inequalities of labour and employer as exemplified in the hand loom weaver disputes. The naming of groups and of organizations affirmed the relationship of elite and middle classes to place, to Leeds and neighbourhood. There were occasional references to a county grouping with its base in York and to a sense of a combined interest of commercial towns, but the vast bulk of claims were to the place and space of Leeds. For the most part these rituals operated in a manner which was inward looking and self-affirming. They structured a group which as yet was uneasy about its name, the middle classes, the opulent and respectable . . .

The meetings were bounded in the sense that the bulk took place in enclosed buildings or spaces with clear entry rituals of price and often membership, but one aspect of the group's self-image was the illusion of boundarylessness. They were the inhabitants, the public, tickets were on sale, meetings were open to all who joined. The ideology of these occasions was about overcoming divisions of politics, religion and ideology. The key rituals were about disciplining the negative and disruptive aspects of individuality. The key feature was transparency. Accounts were published. Meetings were announced in advance and speeches printed in the local press afterwards. This openness was one basis of building trust between individuals and the disparate interest groups of politics, economy and religion. The participants in these meetings also sought legitimacy from the meeting itself with its illusion of openness. Such legitimacy might come by acclaimation and display as it did in the opening dinner of the Commercial Buildings, or through the ideology of open informed debate, of hearing both sides of the argument displayed in the meetings of the 'subscriber democracies'.

The generation of 1829 needs to be placed in the long-term development of the ordering of order in British towns. Several key features of eighteenth-century order have been identified. Borsay has shown that the eighteenth-century town was rebuilt in a more ordered, integrated and comfortable manner. This included a variety of public buildings and public spaces, new guild halls and court houses, assemblies, theatres and public walks. Many were financed and sponsored by Municipal Corporations and other public bodies.[41] They were objects of display and places of display, but in their form, ideology and regulation they were places of separation. There was no illusion of openness in John Wood's account of the public square in Bath:

> But yet I preferred an inclosed Square to an open one, to make this as useful as possible: For the intention of a Square in a City is for People to assemble together; and the Spot whereon they meet, ought to be separated from the Ground common to Men and Beasts, and even to Mankind in General, if Decency and good order are necessary to be observed in such Places.[42]

Clark has demonstrated the rapid and massive increase of associational life in the eighteenth-century town. Although precursors of the subscriber democracies were evident, especially in the general hospitals of the midcentury, this associational cultural was dominated by clubs and societies meeting in the closed rooms of public houses and inns with a focus on feasting and sociability.[43] Sennett has outlined the ordered openness of the coffee house culture in the creation of a public, especially in London, whilst Smail has shown that in the manufacturing town of Halifax, by

---

[41] Peter Borsay, *The English Urban Renaissance: Culture and Society in the Provincial Town, 1660–1770* (Oxford, 1989).

[42] John Wood, *Essay Towards a Description of Bath* (Bath, 1742), p. 345 quoted by Ron Neale, *Bath: A Social History, 1680–1850, or A Valley of Pleasure, yet a Sink of Iniquity* (London, 1981) p. 171.

[43] Peter Clark, *British Clubs and Societies, 1580–1800: The Origins of an Associational World*. (Oxford, 2000).

mid-century, the family and household was withdrawing from the public arena and being replaced by public meetings devoted to a wide variety of objectives from local government to political petitioning and the financing of local utilities and roads.[44] There were many continuities with the situations of 1829, but the eighteenth century sustained a clear ideology of closure both in the physical forms of the square and the entrance rituals of the club and the lodge. Order was sustained by boundaries with little ambition for the illusion of being all inclusive. One context for this drawing of boundaries was indicated in Tilly's study of 'contentious gatherings'. In 1780, some 74 per cent were violent and none linked to associations, whilst in 1829, some 20 per cent were still violent but 23 per cent were organized by associations and another 25 per cent were ordered public meetings. The only constant was the 20% in both years which were authorized by the local authority.[45] Although Tilly was dependent upon the newspaper press and other public records for his count, the order of magnitude of change was so great that it must be taken as a clear indicator of a qualitative change in the manner in which contending interests negotiated and organized in British towns. By the second part of the nineteenth century, a new rebuilding of public infrastructure based upon the municipal and the commercial supplied grand town halls, wider, improved streets, concert halls and art galleries. This was the base for meetings, music and above all street processions. The department store, sports ground and new club land provided more ordered and gendered space for a local elite-led middle class to display its assured local identity and dominance.[46] The behaviour patters of 1829 were more than a transition. In 1829, the dynamic elements of public life were in the voluntary sector and included the notion of debate, transparency and freedom from the compulsion of the state and of the family. In short there was a period of reliance on the forms of 'civil society' as a means of overcoming division amongst those with power and countering the tensions of individual and collective needs.[47]

---

[44] Richard Sennett, *The Fall of Public Man* (London, 1986), pp. 80–84; John Smail, *The Origins of Middle Class Culture: Halifax, Yorkshire, 1660–1780*, (Ithaca, NY, 1994).

[45] Charles Tilly, *Popular Contention in Great Britain, 1758–1834* (Cambridge, Mass. Press, 1995), pp. 342–3.

[46] Simon Gunn, *The Public Culture of the Victorian Middle Class: Ritual and Authority in the English Industrial City, 1840–1914* (Manchester, 2000).

[47] R.J. Morris, 'Civil Society, Subscriber Democracies and Parliamentary Government in Great Britain', in Nancy Bermeo and Philip Nord (eds), *Civil Society before Democracy: Lessons from Nineteenth Century Europe* (New York, 2000); J. Hall (ed.), *Civil Society: Theory, History, Comparison* (Cambridge, 1995); E. Gellner, *Conditions of Liberty: Civil Society and its Rivals* (London, 1994.)

CHAPTER SEVEN

The 'common good' and civic promotion: Edinburgh 1860–1914

Richard Rodger

> the commoun gud of all our Souerane lords burrowis within the realme (is) to be spendit in commoun and necessare things of the burgh be the avise of the consule of the toun for the tyme.
>
> Act of 1491, James IV c. 19

On 7 July 1898 the Austrian training ship *Donau* anchored off Edinburgh in the Leith Roads. The senior officer, Captain Mendelin, led a party of officers ashore and, together with the Austrian Vice-Consul, assembled at the Edinburgh City Chambers. They were met by the Lord Provost to whom they 'paid their respects'.[1] The party crossed the High Street from the City Chambers, visited St Giles Cathedral and, 'having had various objects of interest in the interior explained to them', entered carriages rented by the Council and spent a few hours viewing the principal sights of the city. They visited Edinburgh Castle, the University's newly completed McEwan Hall, Holyrood Palace and then, at one o'clock, the Lord Provost presided over lunch at the Balmoral Hotel. The toasts – 'the Queen' and 'the Austrian Emperor' – were given from the chair and 'fittingly honoured'.[2] The Austrian captain replied toasting 'the health of the Corporation'; the Lord Provost responded by toasting 'the health of the officers' and that of Mr John Holmes, Trade Commissioner from New Zealand, who was also present. Councillor Cranston proposed the health of Colonel Morgan Puyler, commanding officer of the 1st Battalion Royal Scots, stationed at the Castle, and Bailie Sloan concluded proceedings by proposing a vote of thanks to the Lord Provost. The officers returned to their ship and, later in the afternoon, the Lord Provost and other municipal officers accompanied by the Town Clerk paid a return visit to the *Donau*. Judged by the number of toasts and the

---

[1] *The Scotsman*, 8 July 1898, p. 5, col. a.
[2] *The Scotsman*, 8 July 1898.

reciprocal visit, it was a convivial occasion. Lunch cost a total £152 – or £9435 in 2002 prices.[3]

Nor was the *Donau* the only foreign warship to which the hospitality of the city of Edinburgh was extended. In May 1894, the Edinburgh town council had organized a ball in the Waterloo Rooms for officers from several ships during the extended visit of the German Imperial Navy; naval ratings were entertained separately in the Music Hall.[4] The total cost to the public purse on this occasion was £692, equivalent to £43 000 in 2002 prices. Officers of the Russian warship *Djiguit* were given lunch in 1895 (cost £47), and officers and ratings of the American warship *Minneapolis* treated to dinner in 1896 (cost £162).[5] Perhaps international tension and the search for diplomatic alliances in the 1890s and early 1900s lay behind these naval missions but, for whatever reason, the pattern of visits picked up pace and the town council of Edinburgh picked up the tab. The US training ship *Hartford* and the French ship *Ibis* both made two visits in the first three years of the new century. In 1903, officers and men of another Austrian warship, *Szigetvar*, and the Italian warship *Amerigo Vespucci* visited the city. The French navy sent the frigate *Lavoisier* in 1907 and their cruiser *Bougainville* in 1910; Edinburgh town council sent lunch. In 1903, 1907, 1910 and 1911 it was the turn of the German warships *Moltke*, *Charlotte* and *Hanza* (twice) to sail into the Firth of Forth and for their crews to be entertained at the expense of the citizens of Edinburgh. Nor was the Swedish navy spurned: in 1899 the officers and men of the corvette *Freja* and, in 1912, officers of the *Oscar II* were entertained. All told, between 1894 and 1912, foreign navies cost Edinburgh citizens £1966 or about £120 000 in 2002 prices.

For the officers and men of the British channel squadron who also found themselves anchored off Edinburgh on several occasions between 1862 and 1907, the town council was even more generous. In four visits – 1887, 1895, 1903 and 1907 – the cost of hospitality and entertainment to the Edinburgh town council was £1960, an amount identical to the expenses associated with all the visiting foreign warships in the quarter century before the First World War.

The naval visits were not unplanned, of course, and the town council

---

[3] Edinburgh City Archives (ECA) City Ledger no. 9, 1895–1901. Perhaps the councillors should have been informed of the risks they ran in boarding the *Donau* since in 1883, 1885 and 1895 there had been fires on board sufficiently serious to warrant coverage in *The Times* (9 January 1883, p. 6 col. b; 10 January 1883, p. 7 col. f; 31 December 1885, p. 10, col. a; 20 March 1895, p. 10 col. d).

[4] ECA SL35/27, Abstract of Accounts, 1895, Appendix, pp. 25.

[5] T. Hunter and R. Paton, *Report of the Common Good of the City of Edinburgh* (Edinburgh, 1905), pp. 88, 92.

had some notice of them. Even so, the arrival of a warship was determined by the decision of a foreign ministry and the city was obliged to respond. In practical terms it did so in a manner that might seem more typical of the twenty-first century, by appointing an 'event-manager' who booked venues and musicians and organized the logistics of visits by hiring carriages as necessary. In financial terms, naval visits were an irregular charge on the civic purse and were paid for from the 'Common Good' fund, a source of revenue derived largely from property owned by the town council. This fund was, therefore, entirely separate from the rates, which were paid mainly by house owners, tenants and, on a reduced level, businesses, and which sustained the town council's day-to-day activities in respect of the gasworks, tramways, voter registration, lighting and cleansing, cemeteries, parks and a multitude of responsibilities either imposed or assumed as control during the nineteenth century.

When the officers of the *Donau* were entertained in 1898 there was no need to provide any justification for the disbursement of public funds. As the act of 1491 stated, the common good was to be spent on what the council deemed 'commoun and necessare things'. This virtually unrestricted power was reaffirmed in 1593 when the common good, referred to as 'patrimonie', was to be annually disbursed 'at the sicht of the magistrates and counsel ... to the doing of the commoun effayres allanerlie' [exclusively].[6] If civility and contemporary standards of etiquette towards the Austrians were insufficient reasons in 1898, a precedent had been established in the 1860s when delegations of Edinburgh officials' expenses had been paid from the Common Good fund to attend meetings in an unashamed effort to bring major national conferences and exhibitions to the city. For example, in 1862 and 1863 approaches were made to the National Association for the Promotion of Social Science to host their next annual meeting in Edinburgh; in 1868 and 1869 representatives were similarly despatched to Norwich and Exeter to encourage the British Association for the Advancement of Science (BAAS) to follow suit. In addition, an offer to underwrite the costs of the BAAS meeting with a £300 'donation' proved appealing, and was repeated in 1892 when a trip to Cardiff with a further £300 on the table again achieved the desired result.

Business lunches and corporate hospitality are not recent inventions. In entertaining the Directors of the North British Railway Company in 1869 and members of the Board of Trade team inspecting tramway routes in 1900, Edinburgh town council had first obtained information

---

[6] Act of 1593, James VI c.39.

about the agendas of these organizations. Providing lunch to a deputation from the Municipal Council of Paris and the General Council of the Seine in 1908 was part of a wider strategy of understanding how municipalities outside Britain dealt with their urban problems.[7] To look beyond England to a European city with multi-storey tenements and socio-spatial patterns akin to Edinburgh was both logical and cost-effective. These meetings, and others like them, established good working relations and business etiquette in an age when courtesy and hospitality were highly valued; not to have entertained would have been potentially damaging to Edinburgh's capital city status and its reliance on banking, insurance and head office locations.

The civic message was unequivocal: Edinburgh was an important location in which to develop scientific, technological and professional activities. It was a city of standing, a national capital, and even if the Scottish Office, newly created in 1885, remained in London then the International Exhibition of Industry, Science and Art in 1886 confirmed Edinburgh's status in the international firmament of world cities. By the last quarter of the nineteenth century the city was already firmly positioned on the conference circuit, as Table 7.1 shows. Indeed, this 'urban entrepreneurialism', as Harvey[8] described a more recent version of civic self-promotion, was adopted in an increasingly extensive and sophisticated manner by Edinburgh town council in the last third of the nineteenth century. Considerable public sums were spent in these years to develop good public relations with the national and international committees of many organizations. These included freemasons, various Christian denominations, educationalists, the police, societies of industrial chemists, iron and steel manufacturers, mechanical engineers, the TUC, retail federations in the bakery and meat trades, and the commercial travellers' association. There is a real need, therefore, to counter both the limited view of 'selling places' and the romantic version of identity based on recycled renderings of Walter Scott's Scotland, the highland myth and Queen Victoria, and to accord a more prominent place to the promotional efforts of Edinburgh and other burghs in the years before 1914.[9]

---

[7] The Town Council had also printed and published a book by J.C.A. Pollard, *A Study of Municipal Government: The Corporation of Berlin* (Edinburgh, 1893).

[8] D. Harvey, *The Urban Experience* (Oxford, 1989); D. Harvey, *The Condition of Post-Modernity: An Enquiry into the Origins of Cultural Change* (Oxford, 1989).

[9] S.V. Ward, *Selling Places: The Marketing and Promotion of Towns and Cities 1850–2000* (London, 1998), p. 2; J.R. Gold and M.M. Gold, *Imagining Scotland: Tradition, Representation and Promotion in Scottish Tourism since 1750*

Table 7.1 Promoting the city: civic receptions in Edinburgh 1879–1913*

Year	Reception for	Cost (£)	Year	Reception for	Cost (£)
1905	American Society of Chemical Industry	45	1882	International Fisheries Exhibition	291
1901	Baptist Union of Great Britain	231	1904	International Home Relief Congress	211
1892	British Association for Advancement of Science	256	1879	International Telegraph Conference	37
1913	British Carriage Manufacturers	48	1888	Iron and Steel Institute	211
1895	British Dental Association	111	1905	Municipal Electrical Association	56
1893	British Institute of Public Health	226	1889	National Association for the Advancement of Art and its Application to Industry	227
1898	British Medical Association	586	1910	National Association of Consumption and other forms of TB	180
1913	British National Conference of YWCA	147	1911	National Conference of Friendly Societies	39
1908	British Order of Free Gardeners	10	1912	National Federation of Meat Traders	51
1909	British Women's Temperance Association	117	1903	National Independent Order of Oddfellows	18
1905	Canadian Manufacturers' Association	48	1894	Opthalmological Society	11
1902	Charities Association	18	1907	Pan Celtic Congress	49
1904	Church of Scotland Congress	34	1908	Pan Congregational Church	57
1907	Council of the Boys' Brigade	14	1908	Prussian Botanical Society	5
1908	Council of the Tonic Sol-Fa College	32	1895	Registered Plumbers Congress	68
1894	Educational Institute of Scotland	180	1907	Royal Institute of British Architects	59
1907	Esperanto Congress	49	1912	Scottish Association of Master Bakers	120
1912	Federation of Master Printers of the UK	37	1894	Society of Chemical Industry	185
1897	Franco Scottish Society	480	1911	Tercentenary of the Society of High Constables	153
1898	Free Gardeners' Society	18	1896	Trade Union Congress	245
1907	Incorporated Phonographic Society	6	1911	Triennial Conference Reformatory and Refuge Union	113
1896	Incorporated Society of Musicians	242	1899	UK Commercial Travellers' Association	455
1899	Independent Order of Good Templars	233	1897	United Presbyterian Church	405
1897	Independent Order of Rechabites	227	1913	World Conference of YMCA	204
1904	Institute of International Law	167	1900	World Women's Christian Temperance Union	283
1892	Institute of Journalists	172	1910	World's Missionary Conference	323
1887	Institute of Mechanical Engineers	191	1892	YMCA Annual Conference	168
1907	International Conference of Teachers of the Deaf	42	1894	Young Men's Guild	19
1905	International Conference on the Blind	38			

Note: *This is a select list of receptions chosen to show the variety of organizations hosted by the town council.
Sources: Edinburgh City Archives, Abstract of Accounts, Statements of Casual Expenditure, SL35/1 (1869), SL35/7 (1875), SL35/17 (1885), SL35/27 (1895), SL35/30 (1898) and SL35/46 (1914); City of Edinburgh, *Report on the Common Good* (Edinburgh, 1905).

No doubt the lavishness of the reception reflected, in part at least, the power of the organization itself and, as with the BAAS in 1868–9, the town council recognized that sweeteners were needed. An index of institutional status was implicitly applied to determine the quality of the wine, food and entertainment at the conference reception. To secure the International Exhibition of Electrical Engineering, General Inventions and Industries Conference for Edinburgh in 1890, the town council paid £1000 from its Common Good account into the association's special guarantee fund.[10] To lure the powerful and influential British Medical Association's annual meeting to Edinburgh in July 1898 required more financial support than for infant professional organizations such as the Municipal Electrical Association or the International Telegraph Conference, whose receptions cost less than 10 per cent of those provided for the BMA meeting.

The symbolic exercise of municipal power through receptions, international conferences and, in 1886, by hosting the International Exhibition of Industry, Science and Art, for which Edinburgh officials had lobbied over many years, was simply a logical step in the construction of civic identity.[11] By applying over £12 000 of the Common Good fund to attract prominent organizations between 1880 and 1914 the common good was itself advanced since this promoted the city to targeted, influential groups. Citizens, it could be claimed, participated in the collective benefits of place promotion.[12]

(Aldershot 1995); D. McCrone, A. Morris and R. Kiely, *Scotland the Brand: The Making of Scottish of Heritage* (Edinburgh, 1995).

[10] ECA SL35/23, Abstract of Accounts, 1890–91, Appendix, p. 18.

[11] For an examination of Scottish international exhibitions and their civic significance, see E. Rembold, 'Negotiating Scottish Identity: The Glasgow History Exhibition 1911', *National Identities*, 1 (1999), pp. 265–85 and P. Kinchin and J. Kinchin, *Glasgow's Great Exhibition's 1888, 1901, 1911, 1938, 1988* (Wendlebury, 1988). The earliest of the Edinburgh International Exhibitions was the International Forestry Exhibition in 1884, held at Donaldson's Hospital, Edinburgh.

[12] See M. Barke and K. Harrop, 'Selling the Industrial Town: Identity, Image and Illusion', in J.R. Gold and S.V. Ward (eds), *Place Promotion: The Use of Publicity and Marketing to Sell Towns and Regions* (Chichester, 1994), pp. 93–114. See also D. Reeder and R. Rodger, 'Industrialisation and the City Economy', in M.J. Daunton, (ed.), *Cambridge Urban History of Britain*, vol. III: *1840–1950* (Cambridge, 2000), esp pp. 585–92, for a discussion of civic self-promotion. See also D.N. Cannadine, 'The Transformation of Civic Ritual in Modern Britain: The Colchester Oyster Feast', *Past and Present*, 94 (1982), pp. 107–30, for a similar view of discretionary public patronage. However, Cannadine's claim that these were akin to 'a private party' appears less appropriate in relation to Edinburgh town council who at least proclaimed the 'commoun and necessare' nature of their discretionary expenditure.

Symbol and pageant

The exercise of civic-sponsored sociability provided continuity and symbolic legitimacy for the town council itself. In the promotion of the city, naval visits and conference receptions alike combined both the 'dignified' and the 'efficient' in Bagehot's description of the ceremonial and daily administrative functions of government.[13] Receptions added dignity to the local state while at the same time raising its commercial and cultural profile. So, resplendent in their naval dress uniforms, the officers of the *Donau* were received by town councillors wearing civic chains of glinting modernity minted less than five years previously and part of a carefully constructed civic identity.[14] These civic robes and regalia were costly replacements commissioned in the 1890s for an earlier issue, ordered in the 1870s and also paid for out of the Common Good fund.[15] Civic ceremonies and urban pageants became more frequent in the 1870s and 1880s in many British towns though recently it has been suggested that for English cities the civic procession was in retreat towards the end of Victoria's reign.[16] If this was so, then Edinburgh was not like English provincial cities since civil and royal ceremonies in the 'capital of North Britain'[17] became more common in the 1880s and 1890s.

The Freedom of the City was a ceremony at which councillors paraded in civic regalia. If they lived long enough, as some councillors did, there were over 50 opportunities between 1863 and 1912 to wear robes for this purpose; 39 of these occasions took place after 1880 (Table 7.2). Recipients were mostly hereditary Scots peers, members of the royal family and

---

[13] W. Bagehot, *The English Constitution* (London 1964), p. 61. See also R. Colls, 'The Constitution of the English', *History Workshop Journal*, 46 (1998), pp. 97–127, for a perspective on the adaptable nature of 'efficient' government.

[14] ECA SL35/25, Abstracts of Accounts (1893) and SL35/29 (1897).

[15] ECA SL35/3, Abstracts of Accounts (1871) and SL35/6 (1874), SL35/25 (1893), SL35/29 (1897), SL35/31 (1899). The cost of the robes and liveries ordered in the 1870s was £200; by the 1890s this had risen to £1590 or the equivalent of £98 000.

[16] D.N. Cannadine, 'The Context, Performance and Meaning of Ritual: The British Monarchy and the Invention of Tradition c.1820–1977', in E. Hobsbawm and T. Ranger (eds), *The Invention of Tradition* (Cambridge, 1984); S. Gunn, 'Ritual and Civic Culture in the English Industrial City c.1835–1914', in R.J. Morris and R.H. Trainor (eds), *Urban Governance: Britain and Beyond since 1750* (Aldershot, 2000), pp. 226–41; S. Gunn, *The Public Culture of the Victorian Middle Classes: Ritual and Authority in the English Industrial City 1840–1914* (Manchester, 2000);

[17] The phrase 'Plan of the Streets and Squares intended for the Capital of North Britain' was inscribed on James Craig's Plan, 1767, for the Edinburgh New Town.

Table 7.2 Presentations of the Freedom of the City: Edinburgh 1863–1912

Year	Freedom of the City to	Year	Freedom of the City to
1863	Viscount Palmerston	1898	Lord Lister
1864	General Guiseppe Garibaldi*	1898	Lord Kitchener of Khartoum and Aspall
1866	HRH Prince Alfred*		
1867	William Lloyd Garrison*	1898	Marquis of Dufferin and Ava
1867	Benjamin Disraeli	1899	HRH Prince of Wales
1868	Lord Napier of Magdala	1902	Colonial Premiers[1]
1868	John Bright	1903	Lord Balfour of Burleigh
1869	Professor James Y. Simpson*	1903	Lord Strathcona
1874	Baroness Burdett Coutts	1904	Mr J.H. Choate, American Ambassador
1875	William Edward Forster		
1875	Earl of Derby	1905	HRH Duke of Connaught and Strathearn
1877	Willeneral Ulysses S. Grant		
1878	Lord Shaftesbury	1905	A.J. Balfour
1882	Marquis of Salisbury	1905	Field Marshal Sir George Stuart White
1883	Earl of Rosebery		
1885	Earl of Aberdeen	1905	Lord Reay
1887	Andrew Carnegie	1905	Lord Young
1887	Marquis of Lothian	1905	Miss Flora Stevenson
1889	Charles Stewart Parnell+	1907	Colonial Premiers[2]
1890	Henry Morton Stanley	1907	Sir Henry Campbell Bannerman
1891	Sir Daniel Wilson	1909	Sir William Turner
1893	Earl of Elgin and Kincardine	1909	Rev Alexander Whyte
1893	HRH Duke and Duchess of York	1910	H.H. Asquith PM
1893	Lord Roberts of Kandahar	1911	Earl of Minto
1895	Earl of Hopetoun	1911	Colonial Premiers[3]
1896	John Ritchie Findlay	1912	Lord Pentland
1897	William McEwan	1912	Viscount Haldane
1898	Lord Viscount Wolseley	1912	Lord Dunedin

Notes:
* These investitures were not funded by the Common Good
+ This investiture was not identified in C.J. Cousland, *Honoured in Scotland's Capital*
[1] Premiers of Canada, Australia, New Zealand, Natal and Newfoundland
[2] Premiers of Australia, New Zealand, Cape Colony and Transvaal
[3] Premiers of Australia and Newfoundland

Sources: Edinburgh City Archives, Abstract of Accounts, Statements of Casual Expenditure, SL35/1 (1869), SL35/7 (1875), SL35/17 (1885), SL35/27 (1895), SL35/30 (1898) and SL35/46 (1914); City of Edinburgh, *Report on the Common Good* (Edinburgh 1905); C.J. Cousland, *Honoured in Scotland's Capital: Freemen or 'burgesses and gild-brethren gratis' of the City of Edinburgh* (Edinburgh, 1946), pp. 37–40.

British prime ministers; two-thirds had titles and only two women were honoured. While in the early years of the twentieth century 11 colonial premiers were also made freemen of the city, again reflecting strong Scottish connections with the Empire and its self-belief as an international city, noticeable by their absence were a caste of industrialists and financiers. Their capacity to influence policy decisions in Westminster was considered marginal and only the Scottish-born American steel baron Andrew Carnegie and the brewer William McEwan were honoured with Freedom of the City status. In effect, the civic honours system showered recognition upon political figures and representatives of titled families whom the town council believed offered access to the London establishment. In making frequent depositions to select committees and investigations initiated by parliament, Edinburgh town council lobbied vigorously in support of civic interests, and according the Freedom of the City to prominent figures offered a political route by which the interests of the city and those of the state could be mediated.[18] Furthermore, the 'flag-saluting, foreigner-hating and peer-respecting'[19] side of working-class culture and its interest in pomp and civic ceremony delivered a measure of popular support for such public spectacles as the Freedom of the City and royal visits.[20]

Full regalia, pomp and ceremony, hierarchy and heraldry were in evidence during the Freedom of the City ceremony. These were seasonal events, normally held in the autumn or winter when indoor venues were available, though as the awards became more frequent two or even three ceremonies in a year were required, with some held in the spring. The inscribed peroration and receptions reflected the elaboration of civic ritual, each of which cost on average £109 or about £6500 in 2002 prices. Civic funerals came cheap, by contrast, each costing on average just over £17 to the public purse or just one-sixth of the Freedom rituals.[21] This was because they were essentially private family affairs and the principal expenses charged to the Common Good were the cost of flowers and either the hire of carriages to convey councillors to the church and cemetery, or a rail fare to London or some other destination to represent the City. Thus, there was no long-run increase in the complexity and

---

[18] The complexion of this honours system and the networks of influence that it represented warrants further investigation in other cities, as does the award of honorary degrees.

[19] G.F.A. Best, 'The Making of the English Working Class', *Historical Journal*, 8 (1965), p. 278.

[20] D.N. Cannadine, *Lords and Landlords: The Aristocracy and the Towns 1774–1967* (Leicester, 1980), pp. 29–40.

[21] This figure excludes the exceptional expenses associated with the deaths of Queen Victoria, Viscount Palmerston and W.E. Gladstone.

nominal cost of funerals for former councillors and the 'centipedic funeral' with extravagant processions for municipal notables described as the 'English way of death' and reaching a 'golden age' in the 1890s seems not to have been reproduced in Edinburgh.[22]

Some developments, the start or completion of a new civic building for example, warranted the attendance of councillors and their chains of office as the Lord Provost cut the first sod, laid the foundation stone or declared a municipal project open. Such ceremonial events included the opening of West Princes Street Gardens (1876), the Braid Hills (1889), Inverleith Park (1891) and later parks at Portobello (1901) and Saughton (1905), thus continuing a tradition of public access to open spaces long fought over by the citizenry of Edinburgh.[23] The Common Good fund was used also to finance commemorative events associated with the opening of the Fishmarket (1876), Central Library (1890), North Bridge redevelopment (1896), Shrubhill Tramway Cable Power Station (1890), Electricity Generation Station (1899), Central Fire Station (1900), City Chambers (1901), slaughter-market (1910), and opening of the main concert arena, the Usher Hall (1914).[24]

Contrasted with these high profile ceremonies were others of more modest proportions but which nonetheless made significant improvements to daily lives in working class neighbourhoods. The ceremonies on 4 June 1896 that marked the opening of the 'Walker Bridge', 'Russell Road' and 'Telfer Sub-way' were of this type, linking as they did the neighbourhoods of Polwarth and Ardmillan, Dalry and Roseburn, Fountainbridge and Dalry. These modest capital projects represented quantum improvements in the circulation of local people and traffic and, just for

---

[22] J. Litten, *The English Way of Death: The Common Funeral Since 1450* (Cambridge, 1991), p. 170; Gunn, 'Ritual and Civic Culture', p. 234; ECA SL35/1–46, Abstracts of Accounts, 1859–1914. Based on an analysis of expenses paid by Edinburgh Town Council in connection with the funerals of former Lord Provosts, bailies and councillors. Expenses in connection with the funerals of those who had been granted freedom of the city or royal family members have been excluded.

[23] ECA Princes Street Sederunt Book, vol. 1, 1816–19, ff. 51–119; 7 and 8 Geo. IV c.76 and 1 and 2 Will. IV c.45. See also R. Rodger, *The Transformation of Edinburgh in the Nineteenth Century: Land, Property and Trust* (Cambridge, 2001), p. 96, for a survey of contested amenity and A.J. Youngson, *The Making of Classical Edinburgh* (Edinburgh, 1966), pp. 86–91.

[24] Some events were celebrated twice! According to the Common Good Accounts, Saughton Park was opened on 14 June 1905 and 11 June 1910. Laying the foundation stone of the Usher Hall was commemorated on 19 July 1911 and the opening on 6 March 1914. See ECA SL35/37, 43, 44, 46, Extraordinary Expenditure under the Common Good, 1905, 1910, 1911, 1914.

good measure, on the same day the foundation stone for the earliest council houses in the city was laid at Tynecastle.[25]

Significantly, opening ceremonies for large-scale civic projects were scattered throughout the city. Indeed, land-hungry civic activities – parks, slaughter-market, fever hospital, docks – were by their very nature on the fringes of the city.[26] From the Braid Hills in the south to Leith Docks in the north, and from Portobello baths in the east to the Gorgie corn, cattle and slaughter-markets in the west, conspicuous public buildings were visible in almost every one of the 35 square miles in the Edinburgh quadrilateral. From the 1870s, power and administrative authority were increasingly distributed, literally, throughout the city in the form of police and fire sub-stations, parks, cemeteries, schools and poor law hospitals. As the platform parties assembled for the ceremonial openings of these diverse public buildings and open spaces, councillors basked in the image of civic progress, even if the municipality was not always the initiator of the building to be opened. Increasingly, the civic gospel and municipal empire had real meaning and physical presence throughout the city and the attendance of officials decked out in civic regalia was intended to attach respect and recognition for the initiatives undertaken in the name of the citizens.

As suburbanization developed – rather later in Scottish burghs compared to their English counterparts – so, logically, did the tentacles of municipal administrative responsibility with all that implied in relation to 'watching' over private and public property, and persons. Yet unlike Newcastle, Liverpool, Leeds, Glasgow, Birmingham, Bradford and many other major cities, no new civic complex was carved out in central Edinburgh.[27] Scarred by financial problems associated with civic

---

[25] ECA SL35/28, Extraordinary Expenditure under the Common Good, 4 June 1896.

[26] J.W.R. Whitehand, 'The Building Cycle and the Urban Fringe in Victorian Cities: A Reply', *Journal of Historical Geography*, 4, (1978), pp. 79–96; and *The Changing Face of Cities: A Study of Development Cycles and Urban Form* (Oxford, 1987), p. 26–9, 36–44, 76–94; T.A. Markus, 'Buildings for the Sad, the Bad and the Mad in Urban Scotland 1780–1830', in T.A. Markus, (ed.), *Order in Space and Society: Architectural Form and its Context in the Scottish Enlightenment* (Edinburgh, 1982), pp. 25–113.

[27] See, for example, T. Faulkner, 'Architecture in Newcastle' in R. Colls and B. Lancaster (eds), *Newcastle upon Tyne: A Modern History* (Chichester, 2001), pp. 222–5; F.A. Walker, 'Glasgow's New Towns', in P. Reed, (ed.), *Glasgow: The Forming of the City* (Edinburgh, 1999), pp. 31–40; Q. Hughes, *Seaport* (London, 1969), pp. 95–105; J.J. Parkinson-Bailey, *Manchester: An Architectural History* (Manchester, 2000), pp. 96–125; G. Tyack, 'The Public Face', in P.J. Waller (ed.), *The English Urban Landscape* (Oxford, 2000), pp. 290–310.

7.1 Ceremony of laying the foundation stone, General Post Office, Edinburgh 1861

improvements at the end of the eighteenth century and scared by the design and logistical problems of a new office building, Edinburgh councillors procrastinated.[28] As a result, Edinburgh civic ceremonies were less focused on the town hall square than elsewhere and though the theatrical backdrop of castle and palace presented a possible stage-set for official ceremonies, these were symbols of church and state, not of civitas, and were generally avoided as the locus of public ceremonies.

Some civic projects were of such significance as to merit royalty to open them. Robes and regalia were required. On such ceremonial occasions as the laying of the Post Office foundation stone (1861) (see Figure 7.1) and that of the Royal Infirmary by the Prince of Wales (1870), urban pageant assumed a different scale and complexity. This was also the case when the new Edinburgh Dock in Leith was opened by the Duke of Edinburgh (1881) and the New College of Art by the Prince of Wales (1907). The significance of these royal occasions was that the council turned out in force, duly robed and chained, and in strict order of seniority. It was a public display with a social logic that included other notable individuals – ministers, magistrates and county dignitaries – and

---

[28] I. Maver, *Glasgow* (Edinburgh, 2000), pp. 153–7; Gunn, 'Ritual and Civic Culture', p. 231.

promoted civic solidarity on the occasion of the royal visit itself. As has been noted, they were also occasions that brokered relations between the city and the state, and between county and city.[29]

Like many cities in the kingdom, Edinburgh sent its ritualistic expressions of fealty and fawning addresses whenever a royal birth, death or marriage took place. It mattered little that His or Her Royal Highness was far removed from the accession. Jubilees and coronations came in quick succession between 1887 and 1911 and on each state occasion the city lavished money from the Common Good fund on the entertainment of the commoners, as well as on the civic elite. Bells, banquets and bonfires marked the life cycle stages of the royals and the sights, sounds and spectacles that accompanied them enlivened Edinburgh life, however temporarily. In July 1893, for example, the city presented Prince George Frederick of Wales, Duke of York, and Princess Victoria Mary of Teck with a gold rosewater dish costing £360 as a wedding gift and paid £83 for a delegation to deliver it to Windsor together with a congratulatory address and casket costing £106 to accompany the gift.[30] On the wedding day, public rejoicing involved a military review in Holyrood Park (£21), a banquet, reception and ball given by the magistrates and council in the Music Hall (£361), music in the public parks (£79), street decorations (£38) and dinner for 6000 'poor persons' in the principal exhibition space in the city, Waverley market (£407). With miscellaneous expenses, £1481 was the cost to the civic purse.

An indication of the direct cost of the monarchy to the city of Edinburgh can be obtained from the visit of King George V and Queen Mary in July 1911. Just one month after their coronation, the new King and Queen visited Edinburgh to lay the foundation stone for the new concert hall endowed by the brewer Andrew Usher and described subsequently as 'a notable Beaux-Arts performance'.[31] The grandstand and platform for the opening ceremony, coins for the foundation stone, lunch, advertising and a pendant for Queen Mary totalled £1728 and was charged to the Common Good. It was, however, just part of a triple bill since in the preceding four weeks the city had spent £2234 on expenses associated with the coronation and £3808 on the visit of the new King and Queen to the city. Combined, the sum of £7771 was equivalent to almost £0.5 million in 2002 prices (see Table 7.3).

If Edinburgh shared with other places a wish to express sympathy and

---

[29] Gunn, *The Public Culture of the Victorian Middle Class*, pp. 168–71.

[30] ECA SL35/25, Abstract of Accounts, 1893, Appendix II, p. 20.

[31] J. Gifford, C. McWilliam and D. Walker, *The Buildings of Scotland: Edinburgh* (Harmondsworth 1984), pp. 261–2. The architect was J. Stockdale Harrison, Leicester and the cost of the hall was £100 000.

Table 7.3 Royal ceremonies and public entertainments, Edinburgh 1911

Coronation expenses June 1911	£	Royal visit July 1911	£
Dinners to poor persons	412	Presentation of address to HM King	70
Fetes for school children, various parks	607	Bouquets and decoration of royal train	54
Coronation mugs to children	425	Decoration of streets	2669
Highland games, Saughton park	245	Decoration of Corporation buildings	508
Music in public parks	165	Parade of School children Holyrood Park	366
Procession through streets	67		
Ringing church bells	13		
Public service in St. Giles	40	Luncheon in City Chambers	56
Luncheon in the City Chambers	38	Coach hire for town council	70
		Miscellaneous expenses	17
Expenses of representatives to London for coronation	131		
Miscellaneous expenses	89		
Total	2234	Total	3808
		Usher Hall foundation stone ceremony	
		Expenses	19
		July 1911	1728

Note: Figures are rounded to the nearest £.
Source: Edinburgh City Archives SL35/44, Statement of Extraordinary Expenditure under the Common Good, 1911–12, p. 262.

joy with the royal family, from the mid-nineteenth century it was also a city more engaged with them than most. There were 24 royal visits between 1861 and 1911, eight by the reigning monarch. In addition, members of foreign royal families were also drawn to Edinburgh, including King Kalakua of the Hawaiian Islands (1881), the King of Persia (1889), the Emperor and Empress of Russia (1896), the King of Siam and two Indian Princes (all in 1897), and Prince Fushimi of Japan (1907). To receive and entertain royal visitors in such numbers and style, as well as to send official messages of congratulation and condolence on over 20 state accessions, coronations, jubilees and funerals involved Edinburgh town council in considerable expense. Indeed, in stark contrast to the period 1688 to 1822 when no reigning British monarch visited Edinburgh, over the half-century 1861 to 1911 the direct cost of the monarchy to the

Edinburgh citizenry was £27 000, or equivalent to £1.8 million in 2002 prices. It was a considerable sum, funded from the Common Good, and was never a direct charge on the general rate-paying property-owning middle classes. Equally as important, it was an irregular charge, since royal births, deaths and marriages were only marginally more controllable than those of their subjects.

Royal celebrations embraced the citizenry. The street decorations and triumphal arches (see Figure 7.2) were inescapable, and the public banquets for the poor involved large numbers. Bonfires on hills surrounding the city were highly visible, and fireworks heightened the sense of spectacle that accompanied royal visits. Contemporary photographs show packed vantage points along the processional route of George V and Queen Mary in 1911 and there were instances of shopkeepers disputing the ownership of balconies to which they wished to give access to family and friends.[32] Crowd control concerned the police who were unable to obtain assistance from the Glasgow force due to a seamen's strike there in 1911, and Winston Churchill prohibited flights within a four mile radius of the city given the casualties that would result from an airship or plane crash in such congested circumstances. If, after 23 previous royal visits, the citizens of Edinburgh turned up in such numbers in 1911 there is little evidence for the view that by the end of Victoria's reign processions had paled as a spectacle, devalued by the frequency of political rallies and labour demonstrations.[33] This hardly seems likely in Edinburgh where the level of civic funding offered entertainment and excitement, souvenirs and suppers, and in so doing developed an inclusivity consistent with the term 'Common Good' from which fund these were financed. Rituals, then, are 'far more than drapery; they play an altogether different and more substantial role in political affairs.'[34]

City and state

Tension and suspicion have characterized relations between local and central government to such an extent that the political culture of early nineteenth-century Britain has been described as 'inimical to central

---

[32] T.E.R. Yerbury and M. Cant, *Yerbury: A Photographic Collection 1850–1993* (Edinburgh, 1993), pp. 114–27.

[33] Gunn, *The Public Culture of the Victorian Middle Classes*, p. 178; P. Joyce, *Work, Society and Politics* (Brighton, 1980), pp. 331–42.

[34] Q. Skinner, 'The World as a Stage', *New York Review of Books*, 16 April 1981, reviewing C. Geertz, *Negara: The Theatre State in Nineteenth Century Bali* (Princeton, 1980).

7.2 The royal panorama, Edinburgh 19 July 1911

The photograph shows the royal procession approaching the west end of Princes Street and turning back to the site of the Usher Hall.

government intervention in aid of local problems'.[35] At its core, the issue was one of local autonomy versus central authority, and the permissiveness of Victorian social legislation can be viewed as a nineteenth-century version of 'subsidiarity' whereby a national administrative template allowed a considerable measure of local variation.[36] Local byelaws in effect were opt-outs within a framework of minimum national standards with the socio-political character of each town or city determining the particular character of the opt-out.[37] To some extent technological developments in gas and water engineering, tramway operation and electricity power generation produced common features in many towns and cities that in turn induced a degree of administrative convergence. Civic ceremonies and the processional culture associated with them have also been viewed as part of a process by which the urban elite repositioned itself in line with national priorities. Closer fiscal relations between local and central government in the form of block grants to town councils from the Treasury accelerated this trend towards local conformity.[38]

However, as the relationship between Edinburgh and central government reveals, this was no easy onward march towards a uniform national British agenda. Local councillors persisted certainly into the mid-1890s with priorities forged in Edinburgh and were in vigorous dispute with Westminster virtually throughout the entire period.[39] The town council

---

[35] R. Millward, 'Urban Government, Finance and Public Health in Victorian Britain', in Morris and Trainor, *Urban Governance*, p. 47; R. Millward, 'The Political Economy of Public Utilities', in Daunton, *Cambridge Urban History of Britain*, vol. III, pp. 339–44, on the discussion of the erosion of local control. See also E.P. Hennock, 'Finance and Politics in Urban Local Government in England 1835–1900', *Historical Journal*, 6 (1963), pp. 212–25; E.P. Hennock, 'Central–Local Government Relations in England: An Outline 1850–1914', *Urban History Yearbook*, (1982), pp. 38–49.

[36] For a review of the financial relationships between city and state, see M.J. Daunton, *Trusting Leviathan: The Politics of Taxation in Britain 1799–1914* (Cambridge, 2001), pp. 256–301.

[37] See, for example, S.M. Gaskell, *Building Control: National Legislation and the Introduction of Local Byelaws in Victorian England* (London, 1983); R. Millward, 'The Emergence of Gas and Water Monopolies in Nineteenth Century Britain', in J. Foreman-Peck (ed.), *New Perspectives on the Late Victorian Economy* (Cambridge, 1991), pp. 96–124; C. Bellamy, *Administering Central–Local Relations 1871–1939* (Manchester, 1988).

[38] A. Offer, *Property and Politics 1870–1914: Landownership, Law, Ideology and Urban Development in England* (Cambridge, 1981) pp. 184–206; Daunton, *Trusting Leviathan*.

[39] *Nicol* v. *The Magistrates of Aberdeen*, 20 December 1870, 9 Macpherson 306. Lord President Inglis ruled in the Court of Session that the town council had not exceeded its powers under the Common Good when it acquired property in the name of the burgh. The implications for the independent authority of the

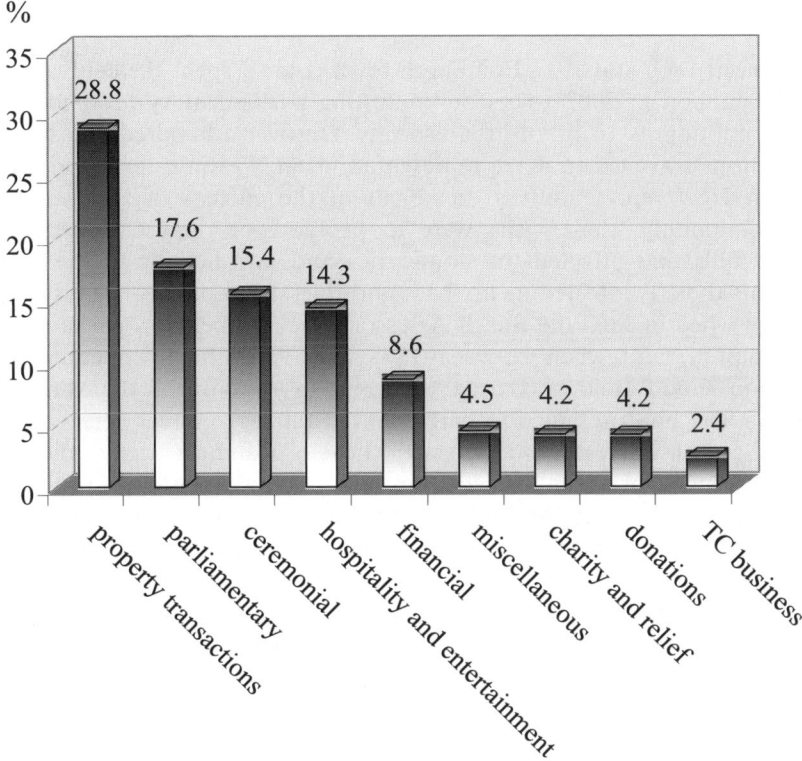

7.3 Public expenditure and civil priorities, Edinburgh 1860–1914

was, therefore, no mere agent of the nation state.[40] So protracted and bitter were the disputes that, despite its heavy expenditure on hospitality and public ceremonies and apart from expenditure on property (Figure 7.3), the town council spent more of its discretionary revenue on sending delegations and depositions to London in an effort to influence legislation than on any other single activity. Nor can antagonism between Edinburgh and London be explained as an expression of some emergent Scottish nationalist fervour. Although thistle and saltire were carved on public buildings and an imagined Scots architectural style gained a

---

town council in revenue and expenditure matters was reaffirmed for Scottish burghs generally.

[40] For a discussion of inter-governmental relations see R.A.W. Rhodes, *Control and Power in Central Local Government Relations* (Aldershot, 1981), pp. 71–8; R.A.W. Rhodes, *Understanding Governance: Policy Networks, Governance, Reflexivity and Accountability* (Buckingham, 1997).

momentum, Edinburgh continued to relish its imperial and international status.[41]

Between 1860 and 1914 Edinburgh town council spent the equivalent of £2.7 million in 2002 prices on contesting parliamentary proceedings and promoting its vision of urban society. On over a hundred occasions deputations travelled to make representations at Westminster or briefed London legal representatives on behalf of the citizens of Edinburgh. Most commonly, these visits were to promote or oppose clauses in specific bills that affected the boundaries and jurisdictions of the city since this directly affected its tax base and thus its autonomy.[42] This was the case when in 1865 the Burgh Assessor appeared before a parliamentary enquiry, and when between 1868 and 1870 the town council's Common Good fund was used to lobby in support of the various Annuity Tax bills presented to parliament. Taking a broader perspective where Scottish interests coincided with those of Edinburgh, city officials met the Chancellor of the Exchequer in 1891 to discuss the 'appropriation of Scotland's share of the budget surplus'.[43] The 'common good' was held in these cases in common with other municipalities and was not narrowly defined as bills promoted or opposed specifically by Edinburgh town council. In 1865 a deputation sought clarification on the jurisdiction of the magistrates and constabulary of Edinburgh, and pressed for an extended jurisdiction in 1868 over the oyster beds in the Forth estuary that were the basis of some of the revenue generated for the Common Good fund itself.[44] Not surprisingly there were more narrowly defined interests that were supported in this parliamentary lobbying activity but even when Edinburgh officials set off to press for a royal charter for the Dick Veterinary College they were effectively splaying the territory for veterinary education in the city by seeking a royal imprimatur for this

---

[41] M. Glendinning et al., *A History of Scottish Architecture from the Renaissance to the Present Day* (Edinburgh, 1996), pp. 243–53; ECA SL35/1, Abstract of Accounts for 1863–4 and 1864–5. For comparisons with Glasgow, see J. Schmiechen, 'Glasgow of the Imagination: Architecture, Townscape and Society', in W.H. Fraser and I. Maver (eds), *Glasgow*, vol. II: *1830–1912* (Manchester, 1996), pp. 486–518.

[42] Some of the most extensive, and expensive, lobbying concerned the Edinburgh Municipal and Police Bill 1882; Edinburgh Municipal Buildings Bill, 1887; representation to the Secretary of State for Scotland in relation to the Unification of the Parishes within Edinburgh under the Local Government (Scotland) Act 1894.

[43] Hunter and Paton, *Report of the Common Good*, p. 87. There were actually two visits to the Board of Trade, one in December 1894 and another in January 1895.

[44] ECA SL35/1, Abstract of Accounts, 1864–5 and 1868–9.

esteemed Edinburgh institution.[45] In a different though related form, the promotional nature of civic interests was present in these endeavours, as it was in seeking counsel and indeed going to the Privy Council over the matter of Edinburgh's precedence over Dublin in processions and state occasions generally.[46]

To advance the case of Edinburgh interests or to defend it from encroachment, then, was the central concern of this lobbying activity. Far the most persistent lobbying was undertaken in opposition to railway companies' interests. Time and again proposed mergers and operational changes were opposed on the grounds that they infringed civic amenities and affected land use and zoning in the city. Though this was not the language used, the implications for the public were defended vigorously by city officials in their opposition to the several railway rationalization proposals presented by the North British, Caledonian, Edinburgh and Glasgow, Scottish Central Railway and even the Forth and Clyde Navigation Company as it attempted to merge with the Caledonian Railway Company.[47] No less important, therefore, was the issue of power and accountability in the city, with the council implicitly taking the view that it was their elected responsibility to take decisions on behalf of the electorate and that only they had a mandate to do so. Corporation power was thus ranged against corporate power in a protracted conflict fought out over half a century and financed by the Common Good fund.[48]

Constructing civil society

Far from being seen as a municipal machine with its tentacles of power extending steadily into the suburbs, it is important to acknowledge that a humanistic civic society also existed, and touched the everyday lives of Edinburgh citizens. Between the ideological opposites of municipal provision on the one hand and laissez-faire capitalism on the other were constellations of private organizations and clubs to which the town council made donations in order to encourage them. Just as clubs and associations were crucial contributors to the rich diversity of eighteenth

---

[45] ECA SL35/1, Abstract of Accounts, 1867–8.

[46] ECA SL35/1, Abstract of Accounts, 1863–6; see also Abstract of Accounts, 1869, Appendix II, p. 15.

[47] ECA SL35/1, Abstract of Accounts, 1859–61 and 1867–8; ECA SL35/44–45, Abstract of Accounts, 1911–13.

[48] There were 24 occasions between 1860 and 1914 when parliamentary lobbying against the railway companies was financed by the Common Good fund at a cost of over £17 000.

and early nineteenth century urban life[49] donations to encourage, among others, chrysanthemum growers, dog breeders and bird watchers carried on that club tradition well into the twentieth century. However, members of the literary and philosophical, fine art, antiquarian and 'high' cultural societies received no discretionary payments from the council from the Common Good fund (Table 7.4).

Clubs and associations, through their constitutional procedures, minute-taking and book-keeping not only 'empowered' office-bearers but required them to deal with new forms of power and authority in the form of the town council, even if this was only in a letter seeking an annual donation to engrave the champion cup or award a prize. Edinburgh town council was sensitive to requests for small sums of money to enrich private activities, but also confident enough to support pressure groups such as an early footpaths association and a private group formed to oppose railway amalgamations.[50]

Publicly funded prizes sponsored agricultural and highland societies' activities and in so doing simultaneously promoted national consciousness and cultural identity. Compared to cultural activities, however, the civic purse was four times more generous in providing silverware for the annual artillery and rifle competitions common amongst the many volunteer corps raised in Edinburgh.[51] Significantly, it was army units, not naval ones, whose competitions were supported, no doubt in recognition of their developing presence in the city between 1890 and 1914 both in terms of property and personnel.[52] The 1st battalion of the Queen's Own Cameron Highlanders were garrisoned in the Castle, the Royal Artillery at Leith Fort, and the 1st Brigade RFA were based at Piershill in east Edinburgh.[53] In addition, there were 19 other units of the

---

[49] P.A. Clark, *British Clubs and Societies 1580–1800: The Origins of an Associational World* (Oxford, 2000); R.J. Morris, 'Clubs, Societies and Associations', in F.M.L. Thompson (ed.), *Cambridge Social History of Britain 1750–1950*, vol. 3: *Social Agencies and Institutions* (Cambridge, 1990), pp. 395–443.

[50] ECA SL35/28, Abstract of Accounts, 1895–6, Fund for the Improvement and Safety of Access and Pathways, Colinton Dell, donation 10 guineas, and ECA SL35/44, 1911–12, again 10 guineas; ECA SL35/1 Opposition to the Caledonian Railway and Forth and Clyde Navigation Companies Amalgamation Bill 1867, donation 20 guineas.

[51] The weighted average donation for military-related activities was £47 and for hobbies and cultural pursuits £12.

[52] The challenge cup or quaich was often the prize, not a cash sum, for which the Common Good fund was used.

[53] The construction of Redford Barracks, Colinton in 1915 at the city boundary was partly a response to this fragmentation in the military organization

Table 7.4 Town council donations to clubs and societies, Edinburgh 1860–1914

	Years in which donations made	Average donations (£)
Hobbies and Cultural Activities		
Edinburgh Working Men's Flower Show	1885–1914	11
Royal Caledonian Horticultural Society Show	1874–1914	16
Royal Scottish Horticultural Association: prize fund	1912–14	25
Scottish Horticultural Association (Chrysanthemum Exhibition)	1889–1912	25
Portobello Horticultural and Industrial Society	1896–1903	2
Edinburgh Ornithological Open Society	1893–1914	5
Scottish Metropolitan Ornithological Association	1890–1902	5
Caledonian Canine Society: prize fund	1913–14	5
Edinburgh Kennel Club	1899–1907	5
Scottish Kennel Club	1906–14	5
Scottish Toy Dog Club and Edinburgh Kennel Club joint show	1911–12	5
Portobello Brass Band	1896–97	21
Sports		
Forth Swimming Club and Humane Society	1875–88	11
Lorne Swimming Club and Humane Society	1880–87	10
Corporation's Swimming trophy at public baths	1892–3	35
Edinburgh Burgess Golfing Society	1893–4	22
Highland related		
Highland and Agricultural Society of Scotland	1869–70; 1883–4; 1892–3; 1898–9; 1907–8	105
Highland Association	1898–9; 1910–11	14
Highland Society of Edinburgh	1887–99	11
Shooting and army		
Edinburgh and Midlothian Rifle Association Prize Fund	1861; 1868–1914	25
First Edinburgh City Volunteer Artillery Corps	1888–9; 1893–9;	50
First Edinburgh City Royal Garrison Artillery Volunteers	1902–7	25
Rifle and Artillery Competition Prizes	1863–1907	80
Artisan Volunteers Competition Prizes	1896–1904	85
Edinburgh Territorial Forces – artisan prizes for shooting	1908–14	53
Edinburgh Territorial Forces – athletic and mounted sports fund	1910–14	21
Scottish National Artillery Association	1889–1904	10
Scottish Volunteer Review	1860–61	77
Agricultural related interests		
Edinburgh Agricultural Association Prize Fund	1880–1914	50
Edinburgh and Leith Dairymen's Association Prize Fund	1910–14	5
Edinburgh Christmas Poultry Club	1881–6	10
National Fat Stock Club	1897–8	11
National Rifle Club of Scotland	1897–8	21
Pressure groups		
Association of Scottish Objectors to Proposed Railway and Canal Traffic Rates	1889–90	300
Free Importation of Canadian Cattle Trade Association	1905–6	5
Society for the Improvement and Safety of Access and Pathways, Colinton Dell	1895–6	11
Scottish National Toll Abolition Association	1872–3	20

Source: Edinburgh City Archives SL35/1–46, Abstract of Accounts, 1859–1914.

Territorial Army who drilled regularly in halls and parade grounds scattered around the city.⁵⁴ Locally, the symbolism that this military presence represented for Edinburgh people was captured in Robert Burns' 'Address to Edinburgh':

> There, watching high the least alarms,
> Thy rough, rude fortress gleams afar;
> Like some bold vet'ran, grey in arms,
> And marked with many a seamy scar.⁵⁵

With the Castle brooding over the city the town council was not likely to lose sight of the military contribution to the local economy and, with 300 senior officers commanding the volunteer corps and 2 per cent of the male population employed in the army and navy, their social and political significance was not lost on the council.⁵⁶

Civic sensitivity extended into areas of social welfare, too. To those victims of fires, floods and famines around the world the Edinburgh town council showed its increased international credentials by making contributions towards disaster relief funds. For those made homeless by fires in Quebec (1866), Chicago (1871) and Saint John, New Brunswick (1877), as for hurricanes victims in the West Indies (1871) and French flood victims (1875) as well as for famine relief in India (1877, 1897–9) and Ireland (1879, 1897) the city coffers were used to contribute to rescue and relief efforts.⁵⁷ Nearer to home, for the miners' families affected by pit disasters at High Blantyre (1877) and Penicuik (1889), the fisher-folk in Shetland (1881) and Sutherland (1890) made destitute by shipwrecks, and those affected by economic disaster in the Hebrides (1882) and in Lancashire during the cotton famine (1862–3), Edinburgh town council

---

in the city. See also *Edinburgh and Leith Post Office Directory*, various years, for details of the meeting halls in the city.

⁵⁴ These included the 4th, 5th, 6th, 7th, and 9th Battalions of the Royal Scots who drilled at Forrest Road, Gilmore Place; Dalmeny Street, and East Claremont Street; 1st and 3rd Lowland Brigades who drilled at Grindlay Street, Easter Road and McDonald Road; 4th, 5th, 6th, 7th and 8th Battalions of the Lothian Infantry; Lowland ; Royal Engineers based at Bellevue Terrace Drill Hall, the Army Service Corps, including the mounted Brigade Transport, based at Brandon Terrace; and various medical units and Field Ambulance Corps based at High School Yards, Easter Road and Lindsay Place. For further details, see *Edinburgh and Leith Post Office Directory*, 1913–14 (Edinburgh, 1914), pp. 1194–1201.

⁵⁵ R. Burns, 'Address to Edinburgh' in *Poems and Songs* (London, 1930), Everyman, pp. 167–8.

⁵⁶ *PP 1913 LXXX*, Census of Scotland 1911, Cd. 6896, vol. II, p. 446.

⁵⁷ I am grateful to Anne Colling for information relating to the fire in Quebec, 14 October 1866, and to the French floods in 1875.

responded to their suffering and made contributions to alleviate poverty, averaging about £100 per disaster or £6000 in present day values.[58]

Then as now, disaster struck a chord in the minds of the public, and the public conscience could be assuaged by the public purse. This was the case with a disaster at Ibrox Park in Glasgow (1902) and the tragic incident in which Herbert Spilling and Samuel Langmaid lost their own lives while attempting to save those of five boys adrift in a boat at Portobello (1911).[59] This compassionate dimension to civic relief was evident not just in the context of collective loss in the high profile disasters across the globe but also in cases of individual loss, particularly where death was unexpected or encountered in the service of the city. Thus, prior to the limited introduction of the state pension in 1908 or the existence of occupational pensions, the city's 'gratuity' often paid over many years to the widows of its loyal servants was a lifeline to them and their families and was charged to the Common Good.[60] The Common Good fund was also used increasingly to support children. Troublesome youngsters were assisted in reformatory and industrial schools both in Edinburgh and when relocated to other burghs, and the town council made contributions to assist with these expenses as they did for day nurseries, holiday outings and orphanages, such as those organized by the *Courant* newspaper and the Amalgamated Society of Railway Servants. Children's refuges for both boys and girls were funded both in Edinburgh and elsewhere and the social reformer Flora Stevenson's Committee for Feeding and Clothing Destitute Schoolchildren also received small annual sums, as did the Scottish branch of the National Association for the Prevention of Cruelty to Children. By these diverse means, support for the child accounted for just over a quarter (25.8 per cent) of charitable and welfare contributions by the town council, with sums paid often on a regular basis to the voluntary committees and resident staff who organized them (Table 7.5).

The town council assigned significant and rising sums to the welfare of the poor generally. Soup kitchens were the largest single element (17.9 per cent) of the council's charitable expenditure and with contributions (15.0 per cent) distributed amongst the Night Asylum, several rescue shelters, a Breakfast Mission and to various homes[61] scattered around

---

[58] ECA SL35/1–46, Abstract of Accounts, 1859–1914.

[59] ECA SL35/34 and SL35/43, Abstract of Accounts, 1901–2 and 1910–11. The Ibrox disaster was on 5 April 1902.

[60] ECA SL35/26–8, Abstract of Accounts, 1893–5, for example, recorded gratuities paid in respect of accidents at the Lochrin Sewer, North Bridge, St Leonard's Hill and Waverley Market.

[61] For example, at Minto Street, Springwell Street and Simon Square.

Table 7.5 Charitable and relief payments by Edinburgh Town Council 1860–1914

Type of expenditure	%
Disaster relief	20.2
Soup kitchens	17.9
Children's homes, orphanages, nurseries,	15.1
Asylums, rescue shelters, and refuges for poor and aged	15.0
Pensions, gratuities	13.2
Industrial schools	10.7
Medical related	2.7
Miscellaneous	5.2
Total	100.0

Source: Edinburgh City Archives SL35/1–46, Abstracts of Accounts, 1859–1914.

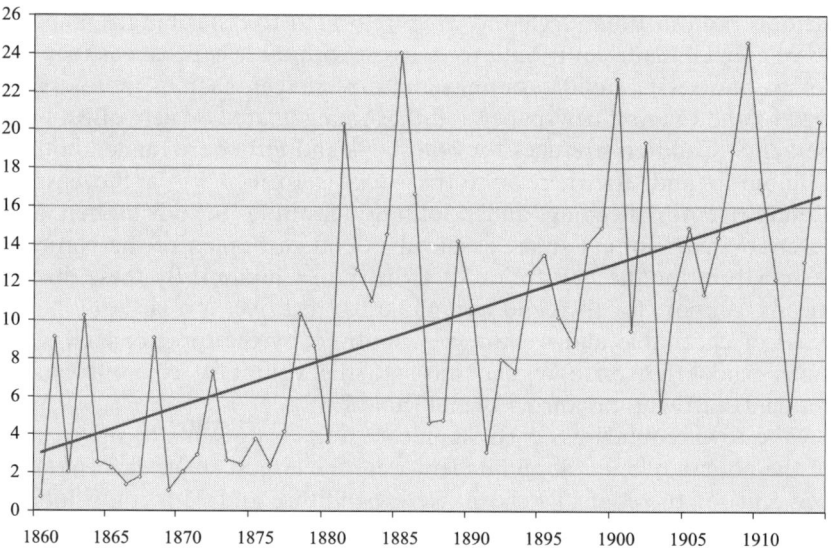

7.4 Charitable relief and donations in Edinburgh 1860–1914 (%)

Source: Edinburgh City Archive, SL35/1–46, Abstract of Accounts, 1859–1914.

the city specifically for fallen women, sailors and the aged, the town council increasingly targeted the disadvantaged in the years 1880–1914 (Figure 7.4). As well as these specifically local initiatives the town council also contributed to the Edinburgh branches of national organizations whose agendas coincided with their own – the Charity Organisation

Society, the Association for Improving the Condition of the Poor and the Social and Sanitary Society, for example.

It is highly unlikely that the level of council contributions to relieve poverty and social distress did more than encourage willing volunteers to continue in their worthy efforts since the average amount from the council to such organizations was just over £21 or about £1375 in 2002 prices – well below the average level of support for visiting naval officers or Freedom of the City ceremonies, though on a par with Common Good expenditure associated with the funerals of former town councillors. Certainly, after 1880 the level of financial contribution was on the increase (Figure 7.4) but compared to the municipal sums spent on pressurizing parliament or developing the property portfolio, the caring council spent just over 4 per cent of its discretionary Common Good fund on the distressed citizens of the burgh and the same proportion on encouraging private organizations by means of donations (Figure 7.3).

The property portfolio

The Corporation of Edinburgh held its territory and privileges from the sovereign. In the twelfth century, under charters granted between 1143 and 1147 by David I, burgesses paid the king 5d per annum per rood of land. Burgesses were individually responsible for this payment, though from 1329 the royal burgh was recognized as the Crown vassal and the bailiffs or bailies of the burghs acted as Crown stewards and were responsible for collecting and forwarding payments to the king.[62] Burgesses then discontinued their payments to the 'Common Fund', that is, to the account held in common to pay the annual levy made by the Crown, and subsequently they held their property 'in free burgage' in return for their services to the burgh.[63] Crown land and revenues were also assigned by David I to the abbey and convent of Holyrood based on an area between the abbey and the burgh of Edwinesburgh, later known as the Canongate burgh. In addition to lands held by burgesses from the Crown, the Scottish kings had also granted lands for the use of the community and it was these that formed the 'Common Good' of the burgh. Until the late fifteenth century common land was let to tenants

---

[62] ECA Charters. Hunter and Paton, *Report of the Common Good*, pp. 6–10, list 34 different charters between 1143 and 1725 and the principal areas and subjects affected by these.

[63] These burgage holdings were not subject to 'feu-duties' or 'casualties' and this meant that the nature of their redevelopment in the nineteenth century was not subject to the same intensity as elsewhere in Edinburgh.

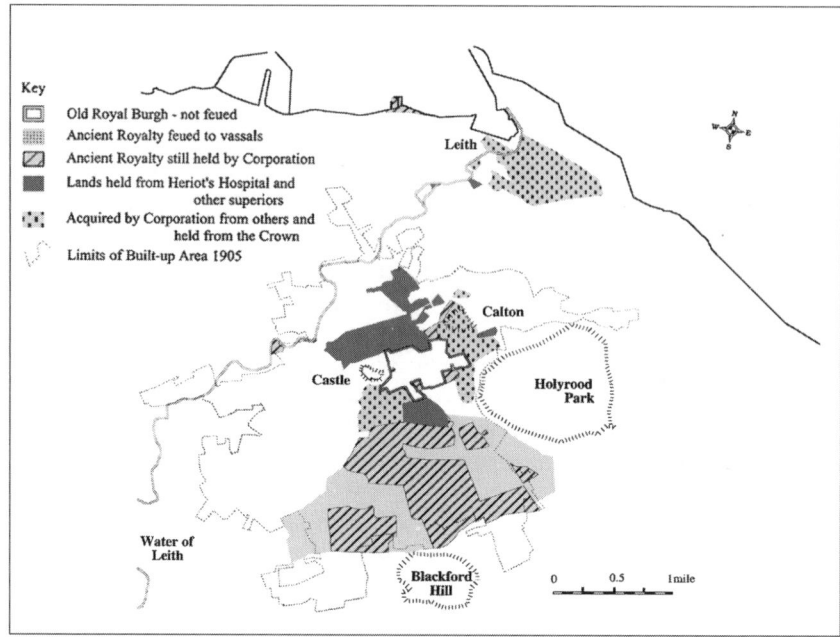

7.5 The basis of the Common Good fund: lands and properties held by the city of Edinburgh 1905

ron short leases but, in the belief that more revenue would accrue to the burgh, from 1508 the Edinburgh magistrates increasingly transferred property titles to individuals in return for an annual payment or 'feu-duty', fixed in perpetuity.[64] The exact extent of the lands held by the Corporation from the Crown is unclear but based on 34 charters granted between 1143 and 1725 and on titles and 'superiorities' conveyed from the sixteenth century, a reasonably accurate assessment can be made (Figure 7.5).

The shaded part of this map shows a significant area of the burgh, as well as areas of the nearby burgh and port of Leith held by Edinburgh town council. In a census of property owners in 1872, it was the Corporation that was shown to be the third largest landowner in the city, exceeded only by Heriot's Hospital and the Crown, the latter by virtue of its ownership of the royal park of Holyrood.[65] Between 1645 and 1913 over 1400 property transactions were recorded whereby the

---

[64] For an explanation of feuing and its long-run significance for urban development, see Rodger, *The Transformation of Edinburgh*, pp. 53–76.

[65] *PP 1874 LXXII*, pt. III, Owners of Lands and Heritages, 1872–3.

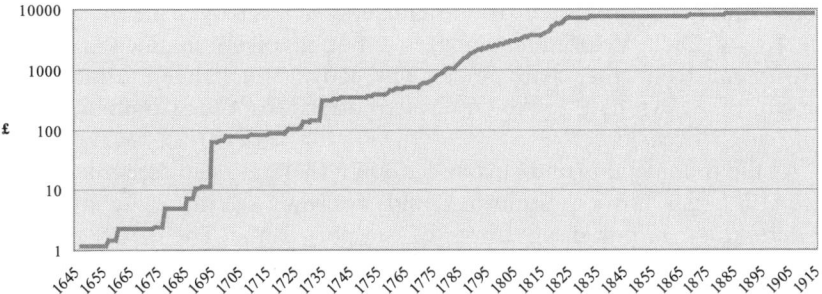

7.6 Annual revenue available to the Common Good fund, Edinburgh 1644–1914 (logarithmic scale)

Corporation transferred titles to individuals while for the most part still retaining feudal superiority and the right to receive an annual 'feu-duty' from their 'vassals'.[66] These duties formed the basis of the Common Good fund so that in the years 1895 to 1904 an average of 57 per cent of the fund was derived directly from property-based sources and a further 40 per cent from dues payable at the town council's market.[67]

Extensive tracts of land were held by the city either directly from the Crown or from Heriot's Hospital and other major landowners in the city (Figure 7.5). Urban development and particularly suburban extensions in the nineteenth century engulfed acreages controlled either directly by the Council or indirectly in that it had relinquished immediate control over the property but still received an annual feu-duty payment. This annual income stream from urban development (Figure 7.6) shows the significant sums from this source available for the purposes of the Common Good.[68] Of course, with interests on this scale, the property portfolio required constant attention, and in the half-century before the First World War, the costs of property additions, alterations and maintenance constituted the heaviest drain on the Common Good fund (see Figure 7.3). In the final quarter of the nineteenth century civic involvement in the property market was concerned with slum clearance and housing improvement and the Common Good funded such initiatives. There were other high profile projects – major contributions to educa-

---

[66] ECA, Roll of Superiorities, 1914–15.
[67] Hunter and Paton, *Report of the Common Good*, pp. 68–71.
[68] The semi-logarithmic graph shows the rate of growth of revenues accruing to the Common Good fund, principally from the expansion of property levies and customs and market dues associated with economic growth in the city. From a very low base, there is a tenfold increase from 1645 to 1695, from 1695 to 1705, from 1705 to 1790 and finally a further ten-fold increase in revenues in the course of the nineteenth century.

tional initiatives promoted by the University, the Royal Infirmary, and the Royal Dick Veterinary College – that involved significant capital investment from the civic purse. The Royal Exchange, Edinburgh's version of a town hall, soaked up contributions from the Common Good fund on 22 occasions.[69]

As the municipal agenda expanded after 1870 into the construction of reservoirs, gas works, tramways and housing, so the scale of these undertakings required an army of support staff. The town council recognized the importance of administrative efficiency and took steps to simplify procedures. In the Town Clerk's legal department, for example, labyrinthine research was undertaken in the Register of Sasines to clarify titles to properties and thus to expedite compensation and hasten urban improvements. While documentary research clarified the legal complexities of ownership no less important were the five detailed surveys of the city commissioned from the embryonic Ordnance Survey office between 1875 and 1880. These provided a sound survey base to the engineering works that became the hallmark of civic expenditure in the areas of gas, water, tramway and electricity operations in a city that expanded its acreage several fold by means of boundary extensions in the final two decades of the century. Though much less demonstrative than capital projects opened with fanfares and civic ceremonies, these infrastructural investments delivered productivity that was no less real. The Common Good fund provided an indispensable financial mechanism by which municipal property revenues circulated. By investing and holding long-term interests in property, the Corporation participated in the accumulation of capital values that are normally considered the preserve of the private property developer and building speculator. In so doing, the benefits that accrued provided both a pool of funds for reinvestment in property itself and a reservoir from which to support initiatives deemed to be 'commoun and necessare'.[70]

In short, accounts of municipal excursions into gas and water provision, the cultural agenda as presented in the development of public libraries, galleries and museums, analyses of civic ritual and ceremony, the emergence of direct labour departments and the onward march of municipal socialism all miss some of the less spectacular yet vital contributions made from the public purse to support private initiatives.[71]

---

[69] This was equivalent to almost £1 million in 2002 prices. For references to the numerous proposals for extensions to the Edinburgh Royal Exchange, see Rodger, *The Transformation of Edinburgh*, p. 489, n.12.

[70] Act of 1491, James IV c. 19.

[71] C. Hamlin, 'Muddling in Bumbledom: On the Enormity of Large Sanitary Improvements in Four British Towns 1855–85', *Victorian Studies* 33

The Common Good accounts were entirely separate from the burgh rates. In the nineteenth century, rates were levied by the town council on the full annual value of lands and buildings and were spent in the prosecution of statutory responsibilities and local byelaws in relation to lighting, cleansing, watching and the multiplicity of functions associated with municipal trading (water, gas and tramways) and a developing cultural or civilizing agenda (museums, galleries and libraries). By contrast, revenue accrued to the Common Good fund from property owned by the city and from which it obtained market and custom dues, rents and 'feu-duties'.[72] Unlike the rates, these funds were not earmarked. This gave the town council room for manoeuvre and their decisions reveal the priorities and preferences underlying municipal thinking in a way that was not possible under the rating system. Lobbying, raising the international profile of the city by means of place-promotion and sponsoring private clubs and welfare organizations each formed part of the 'Common Good' as defined by the town council. In an age of increasing financial transparency, independent action was not extinguished, either in Edinburgh or in the 58 burghs where similar funds were managed by the town council.[73]

(1988–9), pp. 57–91; R. Millward and S. Sheard, 'The Urban Fiscal Problem 1870–1914: Government Expenditure and Finances in England and Wales', *Economic History Review*, 48 (1995), pp. 501–35; D. Matthews, 'Laissez-faire and the London Gas Industry in the Nineteenth Century: Another Look', *Economic History Review*, 39 (1986), pp. 244–63; R.J. Morris, 'Governance: Two Centuries of Urban Growth', in Morris and Trainor, *Urban Governance*, pp. 1–14; W.H. Fraser, 'Municipal Socialism and Social Policy', in R.J. Morris and R. Rodger (eds), *The Victorian City* (London, 1993), pp. 258–80.

[72] For a description, see ECA SL35/46, City of Edinburgh Accounts, pp. iii–vii; Hunter and Paton, *Report of the Common Good*.

[73] National Archives of Scotland, E 82 Common Good Accounts. Royal burghs were required under the Act of 1535 to produce accounts. The 58 burghs, together with the date of their first Common Good accounts are Aberdeen 1574; Annan 1619; Anstruther Easter 1634; Anstruther Wester 1627; Arbroath 1621; Ayr 1627; Banff 1612; Brechin 1660; Burntisland 1612; Crail 1574; Cromarty 1634; Cullen 1628; Culross 1667; Cupar 1574; Dingwall 1577; Dumbarton 1577; Dumfries 1590; Dunbar 1574; Dundee 1574; Dunfermline 1628; Dysart 1628; Earlsferry 1663; Elgin 1622; Forfar 1576; Forres 1627; Glasgow 1621; Haddington 1557; Inverbervie 1576; Inverkeithing 1576; Inverness 1575; Inverurie 1576; Irvine 1627; Jedburgh 1591; Kinghorn 1575; Kintore 1628; Kirkcaldy 1664; Kirkcudbright 1579; Lanark 1576; Lauder 1575; Linlithgow 1575; Montrose 1664; Nairn 1665; North Berwick 1580; Peebles 1608; Perth 1575; Pittenweem 1634; Queensferry, South 1664; Renfrew 1576; Rothesay 1619; Rutherglen 1587; St Andrews 1626; Sanquhar 1612; Selkirk 1606; Stirling 1575; Tain 1620; Wick 1578; Wigtown 1578.

Conclusions

When in 1898 the Austrian naval officers boarded their carriages to tour Edinburgh they were treated to a tableau of the town's history. As they passed through areas of civic improvement and architectural distinction visual signals were selected to convey images of solidity, continuity and progress. The subliminal message was that the city was itself closely identified with its municipal history and if councillors took great care to emphasize their concern for historical continuity to their Austrian guests, they were no less concerned to construct the past for their own citizens. They achieved this by using funds from the Common Good to publish several volumes of municipal history, by transcribing historical records and by conserving the burgh charters.[74] This archival initiative gained momentum from 1867 and then ceased between 1876 and 1890, only to be recommenced on an annual basis until again suspended in 1907.[75] The town council also constructed the civic past by commissioning paintings and engravings to represent significant events in the public history of Edinburgh.[76] These included 'The Unveiling Ceremony of the Market Cross by William Ewart Gladstone in 1885' by Thomas Sawers (1891), the acquisition of 'The Parliament Close and Public Characters of Edinburgh', a painting venerating important civic representatives of the 1820s and 1830s, and a series of watercolours of former Edinburgh buildings demolished under the City Improvement Scheme in 1893. Local heroes (no heroines) were memorialized in statues, busts and tablets, all financed by the Common Good fund and, if the construction of memory faltered, there were always eminent Scots that could be adopted, notably Andrew Carnegie, David Livingston and James Simpson, to create links to the past. The landscape of civic memory, therefore, was addressed in a number of ways and at a total cost spread over 40 years not far short of £0.5 million in 2002 prices.

The physical landscape constructed during Edinburgh's age of civic

---

[74] J. Colston, *The Guildry of Edinburgh* (Edinburgh, 1887); J. Colston, *The Incorporated Trades of Edinburgh* (Edinburgh, 1891); J. Colston, *The History of Trinity College*, 2 vols (Edinburgh, 1896); J. Colston, *The Town and Port of Leith* (Edinburgh, 1892); W. Skinner (ed.), *The Society of Trained Bands of Edinburgh* (Edinburgh, 1889); R. Miller, *The Municipal Buildings of Edinburgh* (Edinburgh, 1892); S. Frank, *Bits of Old Edinburgh* (Edinburgh, 1885); J. Pollard, *A Study of Municipal Government* (Edinburgh, 1893).

[75] All told, £6000 was assigned for archival purposes, equivalent to approximately £385 000 in 2002 prices.

[76] Glasgow Town Council spent £44 500 from the Common Good fund on works of art in an effort to make the city a 'model municipality', see I. Maver, *Glasgow* (Edinburgh, 2000), p. 79.

improvement unambiguously romanticized the past. Almost a third of the housing stock in the Old Town was demolished, mostly between 1867 and 1875, and replaced by newer versions with turrets, battlements and roof lines in an imagined Scots baronial style spuriously associated with an earlier Scottish history of strife and resistance.[77] Romanticized in Walter Scott's novels and represented by Scott's home at Abbotsford, the town council's version of this building style was so pervasive that by 1908 its actions were considered those of 'the house-wrecking Philistine' since only one in three buildings in the ancient burgh retained any historical authenticity.[78] Under the banner of modernity the town council managed its historic past using the Common Good fund to acquire properties, simplify legal titles and then authorize rebuilding consistent with their architects' imagined Scots style.

Symbol and substance were intermingled, therefore, through the activities financed from the Common Good fund. Though self-promotional activities were a feature of the city of Edinburgh long before 'spin' and 'logos' had entered the vocabulary, achievements were also real. While sustaining the gospel of municipal intervention at the end of the nineteenth century the council also fostered private clubs and organizations. By offering succour to the homeless and relief to the disaster-stricken, the council gave practical assistance and demonstrated the Christian gospel in action. Ceremonials were constructed to observe protocols and massage civic egos, but care was taken also to provide dinners for the poor. Decorated streets and public parades provided a celebration of civic amenity to all citizens. Fireworks lit up the sky but they also illuminated a dreich (drab) day. So, too, did the programmes of summer music in the public parks and gardens.[79] These, of course, were cosmetic and occasional promotions, though many became a permanent feature of relief provided by the council in the 30 years or so before 1914.[80] The construction of the city and the accumulation of its physical and social capital is a recurrent theme in the work of David Reeder.[81]

---

[77] P.J. Smith, 'Slum Clearance as an Instrument of Sanitary Reform: The Flawed Vision of Edinburgh's First Slum Clearance Scheme', *Planning Perspectives*, 9 (1994), pp. 1–27; F. Walker, 'National Romanticism and the Architecture of the City', in G. Gordon (ed.), *Perspectives of the Scottish City* (Aberdeen, 1985), pp. 125–59.

[78] Anon., 'Provisional List of Old Houses remaining in the High Street and Canongate of Edinburgh', *Book of the Old Edinburgh Club*, 1 (1908), p. 1.

[79] Begun in 1875, these entertainments were initially provided by regimental bands and enlivened summer afternoons and evenings throughout the city.

[80] ECA SL35/8–46, Abstract of Accounts, 1876–1914. The total expenditure of over £1.1 million was incurred for the years 1876 to 1914.

[81] See, for example, D. Reeder, 'Predicaments of City Children: Late

At no stage in Edinburgh was there a presumption that the Common Good fund would be dispensed in equal measure to the inhabitants of the capital. By promoting the city and by providing tangible if modest benefits, citizens of all classes became 'stakeholders' in urban society. The council discharged its statutory obligation under the act of 1535 to spend on 'commoun and necessare' items and avoided overtly generous expenditure on sectional interests. As a result, the claims of one individual or group were mediated by the legitimate claims of others; collective interests were nurtured. Edinburgh's age of enlightenment permeated far beyond the late eighteenth and early nineteenth centuries, therefore, and the Common Good fund was instrumental in that achievement. How 'commoun' and 'necessare' were interpreted in practical terms did not imply that all sections of the citizenry shared equally in the actions of the local state, nor that ordinary citizens themselves had more than a rudimentary view of the common good based on natural justice since, as T.H. Green noted, they were more concerned that wages be paid and access to the law be commonly available to all, whether as neighbours or workmates.[82] Like any slush fund, the town council raided the revenues of the Common Good in a pragmatic way to address immediate crises and pressing political issues, while also approving, year after year, sums of money for clubs, disasters and welfare organizations. What can be identified from an analysis of the municipal accounts, however, is that the property portfolio acquired over centuries by the Corporation of Edinburgh delivered a social dividend and promoted a spectrum of private activities and public interests.

The common good disbursements, then, were not thought out systematically and never reviewed objectively. The town council's decisions were largely pragmatic, and rarely was the public interest discussed in public. This was the very essence of the Scottish Enlightenment, a civil society whereby intuitively and without annual special pleading, the citizenry acknowledged the legitimate claims of all members of the public, individually and collectively, on a basis equivalent to their own. Participation in the disbursements of the Common Good fund was not interpreted as sectional since benefits could indirectly accrue to all citizens through diversity and tolerance. Civil society, thus, was constructed in

---

Victorian and Edwardian Perspectives on Education and Social Policy', in D. Reeder (ed.), *Urban Education in the Nineteenth Century* (London, 1977), pp. 73–94; D. Reeder, *Suburbanity and the Victorian City* (Leicester 1980); D. Reeder (with H.J. Dyos), 'Slums and Suburbs', in H.J. Dyos and M. Wolff (eds), *The Victorian City: Images and Realities* (London 1973), vol. I, pp. 369–87; D.A. Reeder and H.A. Diederiks (eds), *Cities of Finance* (Amsterdam, 1996).

[82] T.H. Green, *Principles of Political Obligation* (London, 1895) p. 121.

both intellectual and practical terms, and sustained throughout the nineteenth and into the twentieth century partly through the activities of the Common Good fund. Edinburgh, at the epicentre of the Scottish Enlightenment, gloried in the co-existence of polite, liberal culture in the form of artistic and literary ideas alongside the rejuvenation of folklore, ballads and applied science. Rational discourse obliged the toleration of alternative ideas and so, too, the parallel identities of the British state and Scottish nationality were equally legitimate, founded, as elsewhere, on mutual benefit and peaceful co-existence. To do otherwise, reasoned Green, was to render the individual part of the 'dangerous classes ... virtually outlawed by himself' since he lacked any sense of an interest shared with others.[83] The claims of the individual on the due process of the law and on civic amenities were conditional on recognizing those of others and it was this principle that underpinned the common good. Mutual interest and tolerance at the level of the local state were values that Adam Smith had previously claimed for the nation-state since

> erecting and maintaining those public institutions and those public works which, though they may be in the highest degree advantageous to a great society, are however of such a nature that the profit could never repay the expense to any individual or small number of individuals.[84]

By promoting the city and lobbying parliament, by contributing to the social welfare of the disadvantaged, and by supporting the hobbies and leisure pursuits of clubs and organizations, the Edinburgh town council sought to improve the urban environment, both moral and physical, and thereby to construct a civil society. The administration of the Common Good fund was a step in that direction.

---

[83] Ibid.
[84] Adam Smith, *The Wealth of Nations* (1776; Harmondsworth, 1974), book 5, 1, p. 325.

CHAPTER EIGHT

David Reeder's 'alternative system': the school boards in the 1890s

Brian Simon

'The mass of the English people have never yet evolved genuine schools of their own', Fred Clarke concluded in *Education and the Social Order* (1940), on the eve of wartime moves to open up education opportunity. 'Schools have always been provided for them from above, in a form and with a content of studies that suited the ruling interests.'[1] Sir Fred Clarke, as he became, had passed much of his professional life in the dominions before taking up the post of Director of the London University Institute of Education; he was also a supporter of the then influential Christian News Letter group, which pressed for reform on various fronts.

An incomer of this order was forcibly struck by the ingrained conservatism of prevailing education thought and practice. Nevertheless, half a century or so earlier, there had been a notable breakout from the standard pattern which still remained relatively unnoticed. From the elementary base of the school system, consolidated under the 1870 Education Act, a strong, and altogether unexpected, upthrust of popular demand was met and consolidated by local achievement. So well grounded did the new forms of organization become, on an administrative basis not at all intended for the purpose, and so threatening did this effective meeting of popular demand for education seem to the established order – that, in 1902, an act of parliament was forced through to re-impose the standard restrictive pattern. Thereby, with the local administrative base that had serviced reform deliberately eliminated, new initiatives were successfully extinguished all along the line. This chapter sets out to place on record afresh the advances achieved, with the aid of recent research which, in underlining the level of development gained, brings to light the nature of the opportunities lost.

It was the elected school boards, erected during the closing years of the nineteenth century, which created what became an effective 'alterna-

---

[1] Fred Clarke, *Education and Social Change* (London, 1940), p. 30.

tive system', in David Reeder's phrase.[2] Democratically controlled, and responsive to popular pressure, school boards, particularly in the cities of the Midlands and the north, began to introduce a popular, non-selective, modernized system, witnesses to a vibrant energy backed by efficient organization. Separate elements, ranging from infant school level up to that of the new civic universities, began to be brought into fruitful relationship. One step led to another. The establishment, alongside the elementary school, of a higher grade school was the main, most important step. But there were two other related initiatives.

At that time two distinct levels of education were recognized. One, the elementary, for the majority, led nowhere. The 'higher' level, in due course called 'secondary', for the few, selected in terms of payment of fees charged, was provided by unevenly distributed endowed grammar schools, rooted in past educational practice. In response to popular pressure, locally elected school boards brought into being a set of higher grade schools of the elementary system. These introduced the teaching of science and technology in a modernized scheme of studies and, as a result, retained pupils well beyond the low recognized leaving age.

In parallel was another initiative, the establishment of the pupil-teacher centre to provide, by a new method, teachers suitable to the needs of elementary schools generally, including the new higher grade types. By 1900 several purpose-built centres had come into existence. These provided what amounted to secondary schooling offering a new way into the teaching profession. A great expansion in this area was also underway by 1900.

The third initiative was the promotion of evening continuation schools (ECSs) from the basis of 'night' schools which had developed alongside the elementary schools earlier in the century. With the day school system brought systematically into being from 1870, it was open to the evening schools to offer a more diverse array of lifelong learning activities. What became known as evening continuation schools spread with great rapidity, especially in the 1890s.

Each of these developments, in response to a clamorous demand from below for more and varied education, was fostered and presided over by the school boards, which, consequently, were strongly attacked in some quarters for exceeding the limits of the programme assigned to them. Educational historians, in particular, have tended to accept the validity of criticisms by, for instance, Sir John Gorst, 'Minister of Education' in

---

[2] For the 'alternative system', see David Reeder, 'The Reconstruction of Secondary Education in England, 1869–1920', in Detlef K. Müller, Fritz Ringer and Brian Simon (eds), *The Rise of the Modern Educational System, Structural Change and Social Reproduction, 1870–1920* (Cambridge, 1987).

the early 1900s. A long-standing and inveterate enemy of the boards, Gorst saw them as a powerful influence, dangerous to the stability of the social order.

The main function of the school boards, it had been laid down in 1870, was to provide elementary schooling for the mass of the nation's children, not yet effectively provided for in the voluntary schools. On this score, it must be said, they did a magnificent job, in particular by ensuring the erection, and staff, of substantial, modernized buildings catering for, by 1900, some two million children. Then, as the elementary school bedded down, as parents and children began to look for a longer school life, school boards exercised powers accorded to them (though ambiguously) to meet these wishes. During the 1890s, permission was sought to raise the leaving age to 12, even 14, as facilities became available. The local school board was the administrative base for launching both the higher grade schools and the pupil-teacher centres provided locally to meet immediate needs for staff. With these developments came a demand for evening continuation classes to provide both older pupils and mature students with an opportunity for post-school experience. By responding to popular demand, elected school boards not only presided over a breakout from the intended pattern of elementary-only schooling, but came to administer an alternative, well-grounded, educational system capable of general development.

On the eve of the hotly contested 1902 Act, the grand old man of the state educational system declared his view. One time principal of a leading training college, then for some 30 years a distinguished inspector of schools, Sir Joshua Fitch had serviced several commissions and enquiries. It was absolutely clear to him where 'the future destiny of English primary education mainly' rested – 'on the School Boards', to which 'the nation owes all the best educational enterprise of the last few years' whether in terms of equipment, 'rational and effective experiments' in organization or 'better teaching'. It was 'to measures which will improve the constitution of the boards, and invest them with new powers and responsibilities', that 'the best friends of education' looked; that is, for the adapting of machinery to changing circumstances to further 'the intellectual and social advancement of the nation in the coming century'. For Fitch, there were two sorts of people who sought to discredit the school boards – Tories 'who believe that any further advance in the education of the 'lower classes' will imperil the social order', and those who sought to increase religious teaching in schools – that is, the Church of England.[3]

---

[3] The article cited was reprinted, from the *19th Century Review*, in *Social Democrat*, VI (January 1902), the theoretical journal of the Social Democratic

It is past time for historians to make a reassessment of the school boards, and there could hardly be a more suitable moment to learn from than the example set in the 1890s. It has become apparent that the school board was an astonishingly democratic institution. The mode of election was an advanced form of proportional representation enabling minorities to find their due place. Size of board depended on population so that small parishes might have a five-member board as against 15-member boards in cities, with the London School Board, the exception, numbering 45 members. Election was for a three-year term. Both men and women could stand for election; neither a property nor a residential qualification was required. The ballot was secret. All ratepayers had the right to vote. Each voter commanded the same number of votes as there were places to be filled. Votes could be distributed as wished. The voter could give more than one to a single candidate, indeed 'plump' all votes on one candidate only; another means of ensuring minority representation. Here was a democratic system and transparently so, seen to be so by all observers, including a labour movement gaining in power and prestige towards the end of the century. All this derived from the 1870 Act.

This chapter seeks to bring home the significance of the movement from below 'to evolve genuine schools of their own', to use Fred Clarke's phrase, in an attempt to consolidate an alternative and democratic system of schooling for the nation. One way of going about this is to recreate the situation as developments took place. In fact it will not be the first time the argument has been restated with the aid of Joshua Fitch. But his argument that England in the 1890s enjoyed the elements of a forward-looking and forward-moving educational programme with an administrative system to back it up needs restating. It remains common form to acclaim the 1902 Act – intended to quench and eliminate this alternative system – as a necessary 'tidying up', even a progressive move.[4]

A good reason for returning to this controversy is the recent completion of some penetrating research relating to the three main areas at issue. A doctoral thesis by Meriel Vlaeminke offers a close and scholarly study of the higher grade school movement, which has never before been attempted. Another thesis, by Wendy Robinson, very effectively excavates the entire 'lost' system of pupil-teacher centres. Finally, evening continuation schools have also found their historian in W.A. Devereux. His study is confined to London, certainly the largest provider of these

---

Federation; see Brian Simon, *Education and the Labour Movement, 1870–1920* (London, 1965), p. 214.

[4] In *Education and the Labour Movement*, I argued that the 1902 Act should be seen as a disaster whose effect has yet to be outgrown.

new opportunities. Taken together these studies throw a whole new light on developments in the 1890s, and on the true significance of the 1902 Act, which prematurely brought these promising initiatives to a juddering halt.[5]

The role of the school boards, defined as 'the most democratically constituted of all elected bodies of local government',[6] is now, therefore, open to radical revision. In an attempt to reconstruct the situation anew in the light of the three contributions above, I propose to draw heavily on their works. One of these dissertations, that by Vlaeminke, was guided by David Reeder at Leicester. The task set may perhaps be accepted as an acknowledgement of his pioneering work in the field. This he approached uniquely, both as an *urban* and an *educational* historian.

Higher grade schools

In the mid-1890s the new higher grade schools in the Midlands and the north of England were certainly making an impact. In 1894 A.P. Laurie, Assistant Commissioner to the Bryce Commission then investigating secondary education, visited the Leeds higher grade school and was mightily impressed. 'It is impossible to convey', he reported, 'the impression which this school makes upon one of efficiency, energy and vitality', adding that no one who had spent some time inside it could fail to realize 'that we are here in the presence of a new educational force which has already developed into a vigorous and lusty youth'. 'It is impossible to say', he went on, 'what may be the limits of its growth', or how soon 'the organisation which was originally devised for the elementary education of the country, passing with great strides across the realms of secondary education, may soon be battering at the doors of the

---

[5] See Meriel Vlaeminke, *The English Higher Grade Schools: A Lost Opportunity* (London, 2000), based on her thesis. Wendy Robinson, 'The Pupil-Teacher Centre in England and Wales in the Late Nineteenth and Early Twentieth Centuries, Policy, Practice and Promise', Ph.D. thesis, University of Cambridge, 1997; W.A. Devereux, *Adult Education in Inner London, 1870–1980* (ILEA, 1982), especially ch. 2, 'The School Board for London 1870–1904'. For an acute analysis of the dramatic events surrounding the Education Act 1902, see Eric Eaglesham, *From School Board to Local Authority* (London, 1957). This remains the most perceptive study to date. A more recent contribution is Neil Dalgish, *Education Policy-making in England and Wales: The Crucible Years, 1895–1911* (London, 1996).

[6] J.S. Hurt, *Elementary Schooling and the Working Classes, 1860–1918* (London, 1979), p. 75.

ancient universities themselves'. This higher grade school, he concluded, 'represents a new educational movement from below, and a demand from new classes of the population for secondary education which has sprung up in a few years'.[7]

The Leeds school was by no means unique. A few years earlier, in 1892, several such schools had been visited by members of the Royal Commission on Technical Instruction. 'The first and most remarkable' of the two higher grade schools the Commission gave as examples was the Central School in Manchester, taken over by the school board in 1880. The headmaster, James Scotson, became a leading statesman of this whole movement. The Commission's visitors were particularly impressed by the teaching of science (sound, light, heat, magnetism and electricity), mathematics, physical geography, French and other subjects to some 300 boys who had passed Standard VI. 'The commissioners', they recorded, 'were impressed by the high character of the teaching and the enthusiasm which animated both teachers and scholars'. A second higher grade school at Manchester, Ducie Avenue, was also commended in the main report and the school board warmly congratulated on its achievement.[8]

Higher grade schools first emerged as a natural product of the elementary system established in 1870. By the early 1880s a marked tendency for children to stay longer at school had emerged. By 1893–4, 75 per cent of children aged 12–13 were on the registers, while those staying beyond that age also increased, some staying to 14 and even beyond that. So higher level work did develop, encouraged by modification of the Code of Regulations which had widened the scope of education beyond the original 'standard' subjects, the three Rs plus needlework. Grants for such 'specific' subjects were now available from the Education Department.[9]

The more progressive school boards now began to take the logical step of centralizing the higher grades into a single institution, bringing together from a number of schools the older and more advanced pupils whose parents wished them to stay to 13, 14, 15 years and beyond (no upper age limit was then imposed). These were sometimes called Central Schools. In some of these schools the pupils' education could be taken beyond Standard VII, the top standard, financed under the regulations of the Science and Art Department and sometimes known as 'Organised

---

[7] *Report of the Royal Commission on Secondary Education* (Bryce Commission, London, 1895), vol. VII, pp. 162–3.

[8] *Report of the Royal Commission on Technical Instruction* (Samuelson Commission, London, 1884), vol. 1, p. 425.

[9] Simon, *Education and the Labour Movement*, pp. 176ff.

Science Schools'. 'The movement', as the civil servant R.L. Morant pointed out in a memorandum written in 1897, 'was mainly in the great industrial and manufacturing towns of the North'.[10] The first higher grade school of the central type was opened in Sheffield, but Bradford, Nottingham, Halifax, Manchester, Leeds and Birmingham were not far behind.

This movement had popular support, a matter which we will refer to again shortly. By the close of the century, for instance, Bradford had six higher grade schools offering teaching beyond the normal elementary grades – the direct result of continuous pressure from local inhabitants. These schools were now entering over 1000 candidates for Science and Art Department examinations annually. Manchester had nearly 2000 candidates in 10 schools with over 1000 more in other institutions. It was the same elsewhere. The Bryce Commission on secondary education (1895) found 65 higher grade schools in existence – that is, schools taking students beyond Standard VII, the top standard, and so categorized by the school boards themselves. Four years later the National Union of Teachers claimed 80 schools while many school boards were planning to establish more. The momentum was developing 'and the enthusiasm it engendered was to be found all over the country', writes Vlaeminke. One can only wonder, she adds, 'what might have been achieved if this forerunner of the comprehensive school had been allowed to flourish'.[11]

One point that stands out from the surviving evidence is the extreme popularity of these schools among local people. This emerges from the evidence gathered by Vlaeminke, and not only in connection with the three Bristol schools of which she makes a special study. One example given is the Manchester Central School whose first 'at home' attracted 1000 visitors. The Bradford schools, as we have seen, were the direct result of popular demand, each varying the curriculum to provide certain specialities. Two were designated as centres for art and commercial subjects, one for boys and one for girls, while others focused on science.

---

[10] Looseness in the working of the financial clauses of the 1870 Act, and in the precise definition of 'elementary education', meant that the financing of higher grade schools, pupil-teacher centres and evening continuation schools became a grey area, much contested. For a full and detailed analysis, see Eaglesham, *From School Board*. The main source of income for the school boards was the Education Department, established in 1839, supplemented by monies raised from the rates (and fees). The Science and Art Department, established in 1853 to support teaching in these areas (science and art), became an additional crucial source of income for advanced work by the school boards towards the end of the century.

[11] Vlaeminke, *English Higher Grade Schools*, pp. 50–51.

These schools, flexibly organized and well staffed, set out to meet local needs and were clearly, for the most part, highly successful.[12]

The contrast between these vigorous new schools and the bulk of the surviving local endowed grammar schools was by now becoming quite striking. The latter, of course, charged fees beyond the means of working-class parents, but were also constricted by adherence to an outmoded curriculum still based on classical learning. They were mostly small institutions with from about 30 to 80 pupils, and not well equipped. Surveying grammar schools in Lancashire, for instance, the Bryce commissioner F.E. Kitchener found 'a very unsatisfactory state of affairs in many instances', concluding that 'either the existing grammar schools must be provided with proper staff and teaching equipment or they had better be swept away and replaced by higher grade board schools'. Under existing circumstances, 'the competition between the two is as unequal as that between Nelson's *Victory* and an ironclad'.[13] It was prognostications of this kind that struck terror into the hearts of the upholders of the established order.

The fact is that these new schools appealed strongly to new sections of the population anxious to extend their qualifications to meet new opportunities. This applied particularly to working and lower middle class people. Evidence from surveys done at the time indicates very clearly that the great bulk of the pupils shared this social origin. Vlaeminke cites an analysis of 316 parents of pupils at a Birmingham higher grade ('VII Standard') school in 1892–3 where 67 per cent were skilled or semi-skilled workers, clerks and in other white-collar occupations. Another 9 per cent came from the unskilled working class, indicating that three-quarters (76 per cent) of all pupils came from the working and lower middle classes. The remaining quarter (24 per cent) were the children of semi-professionals, merchants and traders, while 5 per cent were from professional backgrounds. There was here a healthy mixture of classes, the bulk of the pupils, however, coming from the more deprived section of the population.[14]

Ten years later a larger survey covering some 30 schools was carried out by the National Education Association (NEA). This indicated that 40 per cent of male pupils in these schools had working-class parents (both skilled and unskilled), while another 34 per cent may be categorized as lower middle class (retail tradesmen, commercial travellers, shop assistants, clerks, book-keepers and 'subordinate officials'), the rest (17 per cent) being children of teachers, professional men, manufacturers,

---

[12] Ibid., p. 40.
[13] Quoted in Simon, *Education and the Labour Movement*, p. 181, n. 1.
[14] Vlaeminke, *English Higher Grade Schools*, pp. 50–51.

managers and farmers. The Association drew the conclusion that 'the higher grade school is the school of the people'.[15] Further confirmation comes from an official return made in 1897. For higher grade schools, 91.2 per cent of their pupils entered from state elementary schools compared with 48.9 per cent of grammar school pupils, while children of skilled and unskilled manual workers formed 34.1 per cent of their pupils but only 6.8 per cent of grammar school pupils.[16] It seems that the NEA's claim – that these were 'the schools of the people' – was correct.

Evidence of the class origin of pupils in these schools is stressed because it brings out the extent of working-class support and participation. Here was an educational initiative that really sparked enthusiasm among the excluded sections of the population – an issue which, a hundred years later, still dogs the nation's schools, as all are now very well aware.[17]

For a full, and striking analysis of all this the reader is referred to Meriel Vlaeminke's fine book *The English Higher Grade Schools: A Lost Opportunity*. Particular emphasis is put on the modernized and varied curriculum made available, in spite of constrictions. This she evaluates as 'commendably balanced and "modern"'. Contemporary criticisms of its supposed 'narrowness' should be treated with caution. Staffing was at a level higher than at normal schools. Teachers generally had good academic qualifications and professional competence. This was, indeed, a new breed of teachers who increasingly 'had been educated in a higher grade school, pupil-teacher centre and training or university college', in all of which significant pedagogical advances were being made.

The purpose-built higher grade schools, mostly erected in the 1890s, were generally large, as Vlaeminke says, 'even by today's standards'. The Fairfield Road School in Bristol, for instance, was designed for 1000 pupils; the main Sheffield higher grade school provided for 1200, and the Leeds Central school for as many as 2600 'of whom 1000 were in Standard VII or above'. These schools were 'better equipped and more spaciously laid out' than ordinary elementary schools.[18]

Vlaeminke concludes that the pupils in these schools generally worked hard. Attendance was excellent. Discipline was light. The whole movement was fuelled by the pedagogic optimism of the period which loaned

---

[15] Kevin Manton, 'Socialism and Education in Britain, 1883–1902', Ph.D. thesis, University of London, 1999.

[16] Olive Banks, *Parity and Prestige in English Secondary Education* (London, 1955), p. 29.

[17] For further evidence of labour movement support for higher grade schools, see Manton, 'Socialism and Education'.

[18] Vlaeminke, *English Higher Grade Schools*, p. 46.

purpose to the teachers' activity. The tendency in the 1890s was for the age of entry to move up towards 12 while an increasing proportion now stayed on to the age of 17 or 18. To cope successfully with such large schools, usually for both girls and boys, was no mean achievement. Although these schools were self-selected in terms of their student intake, they approximated to genuinely comprehensive schools in the modern sense.

All this was achieved on the most tenuous foundations. The 1870 Act permitted expenditure only on elementary education, though looseness in drafting of the legislation allowed scope for those prepared to undertake bold initiatives. Rate expenditure on projects of this kind was constantly challenged – survival depended on gaining the support of the civil servants and bureaucrats and sometimes the political head of the department. But in the mid-1890s, with a Liberal government in power (1892–5) and Acland at the helm (a committed educationist) the wind stayed fair. Progressive school boards in the main cities took their opportunity and in so doing created a model for the future, and showed how to make it work. Odd though it may seem, there was no central planning; the Education Department did not see itself as a policy-making department.[19] So, without necessarily intending it, advanced school boards were themselves showing the way to the future, creating the building blocks of a cohesive 'alternative system'. Nor were these the only initiatives which now took root. In parallel with the higher grade school movement new developments of the utmost significance were also taking place elsewhere.

---

[19] In her meticulously researched *Policy-Making in Elementary Education, 1870–1895* (Oxford, 1973), pp. 42–3, Gillian Sutherland makes this absolutely clear. On the leading civil servants (known as 'Examiners') she refers to the literary pursuits of several of these, which 'bred detachment from, if not boredom with, the concerns of elementary school children and teachers', quoting a well-known passage from a civil servant's autobiography: 'The staff of distinguished and aristocratic scholars from the Universities treated elementary education and elementary teachers with contempt. Their cherished creed was that no education mattered or was of any real value except classics and mathematics ... They had no use for village Hampdens, nor any idea that a child from the "lower" classes might, after all, possess a modicum of brains. A ploughman's son was "destined to be a ploughman as his father was"'. This quotation is from Sir W.G. Kekewich, *The Education Department and After* (London, 1920), p. 10. Kekewich was Permanent Secretary to the Education Department in the late 1890s. He was a strong supporter of higher grade schools but was elbowed aside by Robert Morant in 1902.

Pupil-teacher centres

David Reeder's 'alternative system' was grounded in the school boards and was the product of the thrust upwards of the elementary system erected by the 1870 Act. Among the new institutions involved were the 'lost' system of pupil-teacher centres (or later, colleges) which flourished especially in the 1890s before being ruthlessly destroyed in the period 1900–1910. Having been, to all intents and purposes, ignored by historians for almost a full century, these have been expertly excavated by Wendy Robinson, who delineates the emergence and the characteristics of these institutions with sympathy and expertise. Her account will be drawn on liberally in this analysis.[20]

Robinson has identified a total of 361 pupil-teacher centres run by school boards, together with a further 95 under the aegis of voluntary bodies, mostly Church of England, in 1905, when growth achieved its maximum. Indeed since this was very much a school board initiative, official statistics covering the country as a whole were only first published in this year, by which time official policy had determined their demise. A database of over 300 teachers in these centres was also established by Robinson, enabling her to reconstruct the essence of the movement, and to make a fresh assessment of its overall significance. The deliberate destruction of this system she regards as a disaster of the first magnitude. Here was another educational initiative which emerged from below, grounded, like the higher grade schools, in the elementary system, only to be laid low by the statutory and administrative measures embodied in the 1902 Education Act.

The initiative to establish pupil-teacher centres came originally, and interestingly, from teachers in elementary schools determined to raise the level of the teaching profession and therefore its training. In the mid-nineteenth century the pupil-teacher system, essentially an apprenticeship system in origin, provided the main source for the recruitment of trained teachers. Pupil-teachers, as they were called, were apprenticed to a particular school or headteacher, both to teach in the school and to receive instruction in academic and pedagogical matters from the head in sessions supposed to take place before or after the school day.

By mid to late century the inefficiencies of this system were becoming apparent, especially to the more forward-looking and skilled teachers within the elementary system generally. To bring pupil-teachers together for tuition and education seemed a clear improvement, especially in urban areas. Proposals from leading teachers to this effect, following the

---

[20] See footnote 5.

establishment of school boards after 1870, received support and the first such centres were established in Liverpool, London and other major cities. These brought pupil-teachers together for joint instruction in the early evening but later, as the scheme developed, during the school day too – the students combining attendance as teachers in the schools and, as students, at the centres. Expenses were initially covered by the school boards who pre-empted their expenditure from the rates.[21]

In the early 1870s, when the new system was first established, the pupil-teacher system was itself in a state of crisis. By 1850 there were already some 15 000 pupil-teachers in England and Wales, but the draconian measures introduced by the Revised Code (1863) administered a severe blow to the whole system. However, after the passage of the 1870 Act, elementary school teachers were suddenly in great demand. School boards all over the country were getting their first schools off the ground, providing places for thousands of pupils. It was, therefore, an auspicious moment to start this new initiative and this partially accounts for its success over the next 30 years.[22]

Pupil-teacher centres spread rapidly, having strong teacher backing and gaining widespread support from school boards concerned to recruit qualified and motivated teachers. There was no clear central policy relating to these initiatives. The Education Department in London in general simply reacted passively to proposals involving finance. Robinson refers to the 'unchecked growth' of the centres which received support from sympathetic Education Department officials. The result was a rapid increase in centres, especially during the 1890s. The net outcome was the surprisingly large figure of existing and functioning centres eventually discovered later in 1905. By this time, well-designed purpose built centres were in operation, most of them established in the mid to late 1890s. Here was another example of creative interpretation by school boards of their powers under the 1870 Act, originally intended to propagate and support *elementary* education, but now pushing beyond.

What was the character of these new institutions? Together with the higher grade schools they represented 'the pride and hope' of the larger school boards. By this time evening tuition had been altogether abandoned and the half-time system instituted, so that they offered a systematic education to pupils aged 14–18, some divided into junior and senior sections with a break at 16. In close cooperation with a network of local elementary schools, where the students spent the other half of their time, they both enhanced their students' academic education and inducted

---

[21] For the historical development of the pupil-teacher system, see Robinson, 'Pupil-Teacher Centre', ch. 2.

[22] Ibid., pp. 31ff.

them into the theory and practice of teaching. Indeed, the unification of theory and practice was their great strength. Further, as an indigenous growth from within the elementary school system, their students were recruited largely from the upper working and lower middle class – a strong contrast with university educated graduates who tended to staff the training colleges and the new university education departments. By the late 1890s, students from pupil-teacher centres were successfully taking bachelor degrees and even doctorates. So the centres, an organic growth from the elementary system, were now establishing close links with local universities and higher education generally, from elementary to degree level, and the lineaments of David Reeder's 'alternative system' were coming into being.[23]

In the large cities in particular this pattern of development was becoming common. Robinson outlines variants. In several cases the new centres shared premises 'with the newly-emerging higher grade schools and Schools of Science'. The Leeds centre, for instance, shared accommodation with the Leeds higher grade school. Later, the new purpose-built 'College', created at the turn of the century, adjoined a new higher grade school. The same is true of Sheffield where a new purpose-built centre also shared with a higher grade school. Robinson refers to many other instances of connections with Science and Art schools, or local technical colleges – for instance at Nottingham and Worcester.[24]

This kind of development became general. While, in the 1890s, many centres continued to make use of makeshift accommodation made available by local school boards (the offices of the board, space in local schools and technical institutions), there now developed 'a concerted effort' by a large number of boards to erect purpose-built buildings. These plans, comments Robinson, might be interpreted 'as representing, at the local level a tangible manifestation of school board enthusiasm for all that the pupil-teacher centres symbolised', not only in terms of their contribution to initial training, 'but also in the progress and success of the school boards themselves'.[25]

In this new phase of the movement, London led the way with its purpose-built centre at Battersea in 1892, followed by others at Southwark (1894) and Finsbury (1901). The Battersea centre comprised three storeys, a hall, seven classrooms, a chemistry laboratory, art room, teachers' room, common room and roof-top playground. In October 1898 Sheffield opened its new four-storey building containing several fully equipped classrooms, laboratories and a library. In 1899 Liverpool

---

[23] Ibid., ch. 3, 'Pupil-teacher Centres at work', pp. 53ff.
[24] Ibid., pp. 62–3.
[25] Ibid., p. 64.

opened 'its huge, purpose-built, buff, terracotta and pink brick pupil-teacher 'college''. This included a principal's residence, classrooms for 570 students, chemistry laboratory, lecture and preparation room, art room, dining room, recreation hall and cloakroom. In 1901 the Leeds Pupil-Teacher 'College', also very well equipped, was opened, while in 1903 Bolton's three-storey building, embodying physics and chemistry laboratories, science lecture room and other modern facilities was opened. By the end of the century, apart from those at London, Sheffield, Bolton and Leeds (as mentioned above), similar centres also existed at Birkenhead, Bristol, Cardiff, Coventry, Newcastle, Leicester and Worcester.[26]

It is evident that here was a movement that had developed considerable power and strong support from local democratically elected school boards. Finance, of course, was always a problem and here the role of the Science and Art Department was crucial, particularly so since the grants offered for approved courses could be gained by the students. Indeed the whole 'alternative system' – including higher grade schools, schools of science and evening continuation classes – gained crucial marginal financial support from this source in the 1890s. This supplemented funding from the rates (via school boards), and Department of Education grants and fees (where charged), so rendering these new institutions solvent. But they all operated 'at that ambiguous and ultimately perilous edge of what counted for elementary provision', as under the 1870 Act.[27]

It was partly the momentum of the pupil-teacher centres movement at the turn of the century – 'the growing confidence of the school boards to provide bigger and better equipped centres' – that now attracted the interest of the new Board of Education (1899) 'and consequently acted as a powerful catalyst' to changing attitudes and policies. Through the 1890s several school boards had made successful applications for loans to build the new centres, but in 1900 this relaxed attitude 'suddenly altered'. Policy makers in the Board of Education now held that such grants 'should never have been allowed'. The new centres proposed were 'far too grand'. And, just at this moment, the so-called Cockerton judgement ruled that money from the rates should not be spent in such ways. The issue arose from a ratepayer's complaint relating to the funding of a new centre in London, Hilldrop Road in Islington. It was this judgement, and succeeding events relating to a School of Art in London, that sparked the whole legislative and administrative assault on the school boards and their activities, which culminated in the Education

---

[26] Ibid., pp. 64–5.
[27] Ibid., p. 72.

Act of 1902 which both destroyed the boards and set educational development on a new course.[28]

It is interesting to note that, in an early draft of his 1903 regulations, R.L. Morant specifically stressed that, like the higher grade schools and evening continuation classes, the pupil-teacher centres 'had grown up as a response to local initiative'. He described these as offering forms of 'pseudo-higher education' from within the elementary sector and castigated the Education Department 'for neglecting to take control of this initiative from its early stages'. He suggested that hundreds of thousands of pounds of Treasury money had been 'scattered across the country in ad hoc payments to school boards for their new centres, while no serious attempt had been made to increase grants or to finance the centre movement adequately.[29] By a particular conjuncture of events, it seems, space and money had been found by school boards to unleash an educational movement from below which not only had some significance, but was now increasingly perceived as being dangerously subversive of traditional educational norms. Robinson summarizes this movement in the following words:

> Behind the development of pupil-teacher centres in the 1880s and 1890s was a progressive impetus focused upon the betterment of opportunities and facilities for pupil-teachers. Through their commitment to providing as many stimulating and up to the mark educations facilities as possible, the centres had built into them the potential to offer pupil-teachers an exciting and inspiring learning environment, the appeal of which extended beyond the immediate, functional requirements of academic work.[30]

It is worth drawing attention to one of the main aspects which assured the success of the new centres. We have seen that they originated through a teacher led initiative. The main source of recruitment, according to Robinson, was the steady employment of high quality male and female teachers drawn from the elementary sector. Through the 1880s, the new centres 'appealed to the cream of the elementary teaching profession'. These were often 'highly ambitious, career minded and committed to their personal education and professional development'. Robinson's database shows that 93 per cent passed through the traditional route to elementary school teaching: they had been pupil-teachers themselves, then moved on to training college and so to teaching in elementary schools. Many gained high positions in the Queen's scholarship exams and so were allotted three years at college (instead of the usual two),

---

[28] Ibid., p. 67.
[29] Ibid., p. 73.
[30] Ibid., p. 82.

thus gaining certificated status. At a time when the teachers in elementary schools were widely attacked for the narrowness of their outlook and the limitations of their skills, they 'like their colleagues in the parallel higher grade school movement', demonstrated both 'an impressive professional command and commitment to the acquisition of further academic qualifications', so challenging 'prevailing negative stereotypes of their profession'.[31]

This is confirmed in HMI reports which, after 1899, 'were unanimous in their celebration of the superior quality of teachers employed in the centres'. The early centres had recruited many successful local heads whose experience assured their success. As indicated earlier, several studied for and were awarded university degrees.[32] Centres also offered a stimulating cultural experience for their students, as several biographies attest. Ellen Wilkinson, for instance, writes enthusiastically of her Manchester centre where her principal encouraged her to write, to participate in drama groups, to speak in public at debating societies as well as supporting and encouraging her political development. D.H. Lawrence found his days at the Ilkeston centre particularly enjoyable. 'I wish they could be repeated', he wrote later to one of this teachers.[33]

Generally, Robinson concludes that, as far as academic work was concerned, the centres 'undoubtedly injected a more rigorous and systematic structure into pupil teaching' providing their students with 'a unique and specialised learning environment'. They offered a balanced programme involving both 'a systematic and practical acquaintance with school work' and 'an extended personal education'. Their success was undoubtedly largely owing to the high quality staff employed at the centres.[34]

Pupil-teacher centres, it must be remembered, operated within the 'pedagogy of optimism' (as I expressed it elsewhere) which also inspired teaching in the higher grade schools. This was already an important ingredient of their success, lending purpose and conviction to their work. As well as providing an academic education, the centres also inducted their students into classroom management and the theory and practice of teaching. Here, Robinson notes, centre lecturers avoided conflict with head teachers in the schools where their students were employed, usually either confining themselves to broad principles or covering a variety of

---

[31] Ibid., p. 84.

[32] Ibid., pp. 85–6.

[33] See the chapter by Ellen Wilkinson in *Myself When Young*, ed., Countess of Oxford and Asquith (London, 1938), and John Worthen, *D.H. Lawrence: The Early Years 1885–1912* (Cambridge, 1991), p. 115.

[34] Robinson, 'Pupil-Teacher Centre', pp. 177–8.

teaching methods considered appropriate, while recommending and making use of the growing range of textbooks becoming available. The general ethos of these books might be termed 'progressive'; encouraging innovation in pedagogical approaches. These tied in with the pedagogy of optimism characteristic of many books beginning to be published on teaching and school management – for instance that by A.H. Garlick, principal of London's Woolwich Centre which reached a fifth edition in 1901. 'If centre teachers were at the cutting edge of pedagogical development in terms of its dissemination and application in the centres', writes Robinson, then it follows that the centres were 'potential breeding grounds for the new types of teachers envisaged in these new conceptions of pedagogy'. Practical guidance for teachers came from within the elementary school profession 'and was not imposed on elementary practitioners by the universities or central government'. In this lay the strength of the whole movement.[35]

Pupil-teacher centres, or 'colleges' as they were now becoming known, were a direct product of local teacher initiatives which won warm support from the leading school boards. They were solid evidence of what this alliance could achieve when given its head with resources made available. The deliberate destruction of this indigenous growth and its supersession by a system based on segregation and elitism, condemned teacher education to decades of uncertainty and division for which the country paid dear throughout the century following 1902. The key problem of the relation between theory and practice in teacher education, which the centres were on the way to solving, remains with us to this day.

Evening continuation schools

One of the most strikingly successful school board initiatives was the development of what came be known as evening continuation schools. By 1900 6154 of these had been brought into being with 509 251 scholars. At this point, half of their students were over the age of 16. Indeed expansion over the last few years of the century had been tempestuous – from 4347 to 6154 schools between 1896–7 and 1900–1901.[36]

This development, like the higher grade schools and pupil-teacher colleges, was never centrally planned. It took place in response to the school boards and the people they served. What was originally conceived as simply a night school offering only the most basic elementary edu-

---

[35] Ibid., pp. 135–6. For the 'pedagogy of optimism', see Brian Simon, *Does Education Matter?* (London, 1985), pp. 32–53.
[36] Board of Education *Reports*, 1899–1900 and 1900–1901.

cation became transformed into what were in fact multi-disciplinary colleges offering a very wide range of subjects and activities taught to a relatively high level to mature students.

The origin of this unique movement lay in the growing demand for literacy and numeracy in the mid-nineteenth century. In 1855 finance to assist night schools, whose curriculum simply replicated that of day schools for young children, was first made available by the Privy Council. Grants were now offered for proficiency in the three Rs to scholars who, after leaving day school (or not having attended one at all), regularly attended a recognized evening school. But there were early difficulties. One problem was to find teachers, especially since the elementary code of regulations forbade a teacher to teach in both a day and an evening school. By 1862 only 317 such schools existed in England and Wales.[37]

The Revised Code of 1862–3, however, proved unexpectedly helpful to this initiative. It both removed the restriction on day school teachers, allowing them to take evening classes, and abolished Education Department grants for day scholars over the age of 12 – an action very typical of the penny-pinching approach of the time. The unexpected outcome, however, was to give new life to the night schools which could now recruit day school teachers for the increased number of young children wishing to attend. Quite rapidly the night school became, in H.C. Dent's words, 'a national institution, in places rivalling the elementary day school'. For some 30 years these schools in fact did the same work as the day schools, often at the lower levels (to Standard II).[38]

At about this time, in the early 1860s, the Science and Art Department began to offer grants on the results of examinations in a variety of subjects, including the three Rs.[39] Here was a new source of income for enterprising night schools, which otherwise depended on the limited support available from the Education Department. Science and Art Department grants stimulated the study of subjects beyond the three Rs 'and kept many a deserving educational establishment alive'.[40]

But it was in the 1880s that the situation began to be really transformed. By this time the school boards had bedded down and were beginning to respond to the growing local demand for advanced education, and to take note of the recommendations of both the Samuelson

---

[37] H.C. Dent, *Part-time Education in Great Britain: An Historical Outline* (London, 1949), ch. 2, 'The Night School'.

[38] Ibid., pp. 15–16.

[39] The Science and Art Department at South Kensington, established in 1853, was first part of the Board of Trade, but transferred to act as a separate department under the Education Department in 1857. See footnote 10.

[40] Dent, *Part-time Education*, 16–17.

Commission on Technical Education, which reported in 1882 and 1884, and, later, of the Cross Commission on Elementary Education, reporting in 1887 and 1888. The outcome was a transformation of technical education and of the function of the night school. The Cross Commission, for instance, noted that, with the rapid development of elementary education following the 1870 Act, the need for night schools concentrating specifically on the three Rs, as then required by the code, had diminished. It hoped that existing night schools could all be developed as 'continuation schools' leading to 'institute classes, science and art classes, and university extension lectures'. The Commission also stressed the potential civilizing influence of ECSs which should offer both moral and physical education.[41]

The situation was again transformed in 1889. This time new legislation was motivated by increasing pressure for enhanced facilities for technical education. The Technical Instruction Act empowered the newly established county councils, brought into being as a result of the Local Government Act 1888, and the urban sanitary authorities to devote a one penny rate to providing and aiding technical education. Both authorities started to establish local technical education boards with powers in this area. A year later this modest initiative was supplemented by a windfall, the allocation of surplus funds from Customs and Excise duties – the so-called 'whisky money' – which could be used for technical education or rate relief.

Substantial sums suddenly became available – over £470 000 in 1892–3 rising to over £860 000 by 1900–1901. These sums greatly exceeded what was available from the rates. Some of this money was spent on secondary education, but facilities for technical education 'expanded enormously' between 1892 and 1900.[42] Some of it found its way into the ECSs. The technical education boards in both cities and counties benefited greatly and were responsible for bringing into being some striking new technical colleges and institutions operating alongside the school boards' higher grade schools and pupil-teacher centres. In this way a whole new system was being brought into being under local control.

According to Dent, the 'lower reaches' of evening school work were also 'revolutionised' by the implementation of Cross Commission recommendations which did not require legislation. A new Code of Regulations issued in 1890 allowed the ECSs to teach (and so earn grants from) foreign languages, science, art and domestic work. The results, comments Dent characteristically, were 'yet another astonishing illustration of the

---

[41] Ibid., p. 20.
[42] Ibid., p. 21.

desire and determination of the English People to gain knowledge and skill, at their own expense and in their own time'. Within 12 years the number of students attending evening school had increased sixfold. By 1902–3, as we have seen, it reached over half a million.[43]

The significance and extent of this whole movement is clearly brought out by W.A. Devereux in his reconstruction of the situation in London in the period 1870–1904.[44] Noting that while the 1870 Act did not in fact empower school boards to provide evening schools, it did not prevent it, Devereux records that from its early days the London School Board went ahead vigorously on this front despite both legal and financial difficulties (and widespread criticism of 'lavish expenditure').[45]

The situation eased in the early 1880s. Already in 1879 the London School Board had resolved radically to extend the basic provision for elementary education. This involved both establishing higher grade schools and, further, night schools and classes offering a wide variety of courses relating to the City and Guilds of London Institute, recently established. The cost of these initiatives was to be met by fees, government grants and voluntary assistance. It was from this point that things took off. In that year, 1879, 83 new evening schools opened with 9000 students. These were purely elementary schools, paralleling the day schools, but including some classes in the new 'specific subjects' now allowed.[46]

The evening schools were encouraged to extend their scope. In 1883–4 1300 London students sat the Science and Art Department exams. Many of these new students were teachers enhancing their qualifications, especially in science and modern languages. Such classes were organized voluntarily and depended on student fees for their support. This move had strong support from the London Trades Council which, in 1885, asked the school board to provide both recreative and practical subjects in their evening schools (singing, drawing, modelling, carving and so on). The London School Board agreed. The Recreative Evening Schools Association was now formed which, from this time, gave a powerful impetus to evening schools and, by breaking the stranglehold of the Education Department's codes, made a lasting impression on this work.[47]

In the mid-1880s the number of students in London ECSs continued to rise by up to 5000 students annually. The London School Board now

---

[43] Ibid., pp. 21–2.
[44] Devereux, *Adult Education*, ch. 2, 'The School Board for London, 1870–1904'.
[45] Ibid., pp. 21–3.
[46] Ibid., p. 23–4.
[47] Ibid., p. 25.

took two progressive decisions, first, that *attendances* of students on courses should be recognized for grant, rather than exam results and, second, that students above Standard IV, rather than VII, should be allowed to take 'additional' subjects which allowed scope for more varied courses. As part of their pressure to push upwards, the boards in 1889 urged the Prime Minister that evening continuation schools should be recognized as an integral part of elementary education – as a preparation for life activities in general.[48]

Attendance continued to increase – a further 4000 in 1889–90 included a marked growth in those studying French. Indeed, classes generally were now showing such vitality that courses ending at Easter were continued over the early summer to July. In 1889, as we have seen, the Technical Instruction Act was passed authorizing county councils to raise a penny rate for technical instruction. Evening schools now experienced 'a period of development and intensive growth'. The London School Board pressurized the government to modify, or liberalize, the Code governing their functions, and made a number of positive proposals based on the Cross Commission's recommendations. A year later, in 1890, the government responded, the Code was amended as suggested. Indeed 'so radical were the changes in the Code' that a Bill had to be rushed through parliament to legitimize them.[49]

This was clearly a period of great development, in London as elsewhere. The Act allowed a raft of new subjects to be taught, for instance German, shorthand, Science and Art Department courses, manual training and physical education – though no grant was allowed from the Education Department for these. As a result, the London School Board itself now took responsibility for advanced classes. There followed 'a dramatic increase' in student attendance – 12 000 in a single year.[50]

During the 1890s the advance accelerated. In 1893 a separate Code of Regulations was issued for 'Evening Continuation Schools'. This allowed a wide choice of subjects, some very popular, for instance typewriting and needlework. The era of advanced work 'had now really begun'. Science classes increased in number and gradually grew into science 'schools'; commercial subjects became popular; wood carving, laundry work and vocal music were taken up with considerable enthusiasm. Specially equipped centres also came into being for the study of history, literature, gymnastics and citizenship, all staffed by qualified teachers. The early pessimism as to the educability of these students now gave way to an enthusiastic optimism. Much of this teaching was innovative.

---

[48] Ibid., p. 26.
[49] Ibid., pp. 27–8.
[50] Ibid., p. 36.

Access was deliberately extended in the 1898–9 session when the London School Board abolished all fees at ECSs. Student numbers rose dramatically – from 57 586 in 1897–8 to nearly double that number a year later (109 121). At the same time, a shift to older age groups also marked an important change – the proportion of students over 21 increasing. Between 1901 and 1904 many new science and art and commercial schools were established in London and elsewhere.[51]

There was also a rapid extension of the number of subjects on offer, reaching as many as 46 by 1898. This 'illustrates vividly the tremendous development' which had taken place. The reports of the London School Board and its committees at this time 'reflect the pride and excitement' at the progress made. The ECSs were now seen as the yardstick measuring the educability of the people generally. The gloomy, pessimistic forecasts of the early night school years, when many doubted whether more than a very few pupils in elementary schools would ever reach and pass Standard VII, now 'gave way to the excitement of the more advanced classes in commercial, science and art subjects'.[52]

London's ECSs now began to be divided by age. With students aged from 12 to 80, juniors (under 18) were taught separately from seniors (18 and over). No restrictions were imposed as to the upper age level. Grants were available from the Education Department only for those attending over the compulsory school age. The proportion aged under 14 now fell rapidly to only 7 per cent in 1898–9, while that of those over 21 rose steadily.[53]

ECSs normally opened three evenings a week, from 7.30 to 9.30, though science and art schools met four or five times a week. These schools were housed in the ordinary elementary school buildings (for adults, children's desks presented a small problem). As with the ordinary day schools, log books were kept by the teacher in charge and bear abundant testimony to the social side of the schools' activities, detailing combined staff and student social committees, various forms of entertainment, sports, dramatic activities and the like. 'Many poor hard-working factory girls openly say that some of the happiest hours of their lives have had their source in the evening continuation schools of the board.'[54]

In 1899, over 1000 students in these London schools took Society of Arts exams in French, German, Spanish, Portuguese, book-keeping and shorthand. There were no tests of nationality – all could attend freely.

---

[51] Ibid., pp. 29–30.
[52] Ibid., p. 30.
[53] Ibid., p. 31.
[54] Quoted by S.E. Bray, *The Work of the London School Board* (n.d.), p. 260.

The teaching, by experienced teachers, was generally of high quality. There were now over 100 000 students from a total London population of four million. This may seem a small proportion, writes Devereux, but it gave promise for the future. Further analysis indicates a significant trend. An increasing proportion of school leavers aged 14–15 in London were enrolling in evening classes. In 1902 the figure reached 60 per cent. Enrolment of students aged 15–16 in that year also increased, indicating that half of all school leavers in London continued their education in ECSs for a least a further two years.[55]

In 1899–1900 the London School Board 'was at the height of its power'. There were now nearly 400 ECSs in existence, with nearly 150 000 students offered a 'wide and varied' curriculum. From 1893 more subjects were added, especially in the commercial area and that of science and art. Several of these continuation schools were located 'in rougher areas'. No fees were charged. The curriculum covered gymnastics, swimming, history, geography, drawing, first aid, metalwork, elementary science and the three Rs. Students (Devereux refers to males only) included labourers, stablemen, costermongers, bricklayers, watermen, car men, milk boys, street orderly boys, boys in telegraph works, soapworks and candleworks, boys on barges and errand boys.[56]

London set up its Technical Education Board in 1892–3. Agreement as to the division of the curriculum was reached in 1899 when the school board withdrew from most of the advanced work.

One of the most popular subjects was music, both singing and instrumental, where the number of students expanded enormously around the turn of the century. Drama classes also expanded rapidly, but the most popular activity of all was physical education with over 20 000 students attending – the majority boys from local factories and offices. In that year a further 12 000 were involved in swimming classes.[57]

The day schools were anxious to support the ECSs, seeing them as the natural continuation of their work. They took their duties seriously, the teachers frequently visited the schools giving strong support. Local employers also helped, as did local men and women, and trade union representatives.[58]

An ECS with an average attendance of 65 students had three teachers; one with 140 had six. In 1898 the London School Board abolished all fees. Classes remained free until 1902–3. In 1901–2, as a result of the Cockerton judgement, the South Kensington branch of the Board of

---

[55] Devereux, *Adult Education*, pp. 32–3.
[56] Ibid., pp. 38–9.
[57] Ibid., p. 40.
[58] Ibid., pp. 42–3.

Education took over the administration of ECSs. They insisted on fees in general, but were prepared to consider individual cases. In 1902–3, 289 ECSs charged fees, 76 did not.[59] In 1903–4 the London County Council assumed responsibility for ECSs.

A serious analytical study of evening continuation schools covering England and Wales remains to be written. By 1904–5 over 700 000 students attended 'at any time during the year'. Nearly 550 000 of them paid fees. Board of Education grants were paid for 487 699 students. The system as a whole was flourishing.[60] In 1908 Michael Sadler, leading educational statesman of the period and then Professor of the History and Administration of Education at Manchester University, published his massive survey *Continuation Schools in England and Elsewhere: Their Place in the Educational System of an Industrial and Commercial State*. Nearly 800 pages in length, this includes a mass of material on the whole development of continuing education covering especially the main urban centres of Lancashire, several rural counties and related areas. This rich material, as far as I know, has never been mined by educational historians, but for any assessment of school board initiatives it is essential reading. At the time of its publication, part-time education seemed to many to provide a crucial way forward. It may be remembered that compulsory attendance at continuation schools features as a major clause in the Fisher Act of 1918, and again in the Butler Act of 1944. In neither case were the clauses implemented. These provide another 'might have been' in the sombre history of British education. For our purposes, however, this whole movement, with all its promise, must rate as essentially a school board initiative – like the higher grade schools and pupil-teacher centres. They were each a key element in David Reeder's 'alternative system'.

The demise of the 'alternative system'

School boards have had a bad press. Sir John Gorst's intemperate objurgations during the passage of the 1902 Act have stuck; since that Act passed through parliament successfully and is still regarded by many as a progressive measure, his critique has generally been accepted. But the evidence points in a different direction. What now seems clear is that many school boards were successful not only in carrying out their

---

[59] Ibid., pp. 44–6.
[60] Michael Sadler, *Continuation Schools in England and Elsewhere: Their Place in the Educational System of an Industrial and Commercial State* (Manchester 1908), p. 111.

original brief, but also in pushing well beyond it into new areas of activity. Indeed so popular were their initiatives that the most 'radical' solution was chosen. The school boards had to be suppressed.

'The story is one of rapid and continuous development', writes Stuart Maclure, historian of London education. 'In its first heroic 34 years the London school board – a body which it is only possible to hold in the highest admiration – established the main lines of an elementary system',[61] but it did more than this, seizing opportunities to establish new institutions teaching well beyond the elementary sphere. Nor was London alone in this.

But let us look at two examples briefly, Bradford and Manchester, the first under the aegis of an admittedly unusually progressive school board, the other under a board that, throughout its existence, was dominated by the church and voluntary bodies. The fact that *both* were developing new, advanced institutions is itself significant. They were responding to a secular trend more powerful than contemporary religious or even political, division.

A useful source is the last annual report of the Science and Art Department (46th report, 1899), since this lists and categorizes every institution earning grants from this source, and therefore covers all advanced day and evening students in every local institution. At this date the largest centre in Bradford was the technical college with nearly 1000 students (day and evening) earning a grant of nearly £2000. This was not, itself, a school board responsibility, but the board schools of course were – and these indicate considerable vitality. The Belle Vue board school, which included a School of Science, earned the second highest grant in the city, of £1283 (including 70 day students studying for science exams). But the school also came alive in the evening, when 458 students earned grants for science with another 100 studying arts subjects – a total of 558. The school must have hummed with life day and night. In addition, the Hanson higher grade school, earning a grant of £716, which also embodied a School of Science, could boast 251 students. These would be students at the upper end of the school. This school also provided evening classes in both science (172 students) and art (57 students), giving a total of students studying advanced subjects of nearly 500. The total grant earned was £807.

These, then, were the three main centres of advanced work in science and art in Bradford, catering for about 2500 students. A total of 17 institutions are listed as earning Science and Art grants. These include the six higher grade schools mentioned earlier, seven board schools with

---

[61] Stuart Maclure, *One Hundred Years of London Education, 1870–1970* (Harmondsworth, 1970), pp. 9–10.

both day and evening classes, four Schools of Science, a 'junior teachers centre' (with nearly 200 students studying science and 180 studying art), two 'Schools of Science and Art' with day and evening students and the local grammar school whose pupils followed Science and Art courses. Not all these were school board initiatives but the bulk were: they convey an atmosphere of considerable energy.[62]

Manchester, of course, was a larger city with a greater population. The burgeoning educational institutions, mostly under the school board, reflected this. In 1899 Manchester could claim five functioning higher grade schools, including the central high school, seven Schools of Science located in board schools and three pupil-teacher centres. Many board schools also hosted evening classes – for instance I note with interest that two of the Manchester schools I taught at in the late 1940s (Abbott Street and Varna Street) had once offered this facility though by my time they did not. The Birley Road school, admittedly one of the most successful, catered for 337 studying science and 60 studying arts subjects as well as providing School of Science facilities for 103 day students. The largest grant was earned by Manchester's central board school – £2293.5s.10d. earned by 410 scholars.[63] All this was in response to local demand.

To Bradford and Manchester a third example may be added, Nottingham. By 1898 this city had established as many as 10 higher grade schools including three Schools of Science together with a central School of Science and Art having four attached branches in different areas. Hull, a smaller but still vibrant city, had three higher grade schools each embodying a School of Science, together with the Municipal School of Science and Art and two 'technical schools'. Sheffield concentrated resources on its large Central Higher Grade Board School, a Technical School and another School of Science and Art. All over the country similar developments were taking place. In the 1890s especially, new forms of 'higher' education were being established. Who could tell what the future might bring? Some of these institutions were now administered by Technical Education Boards, but the school boards' initiatives were striking.[64] And so one could go on.

This flourishing system was brought to a juddering halt by the 1902 Act and its related legislation and administrative measures. The process

---

[62] *Forty-sixth Report of the Department of Science and Art* (HMSO, 1899), pp. 143–4.

[63] Ibid., pp. 95–7.

[64] Ibid., pp. 124, 147, 151. For the Sheffield Central Higher School, see J.H. Bingham, *The Sheffield School Board* (Sheffield, 1945), ch. viii, pp. 174–98. The Board of Education's finally successful attempt, under Morant, to destroy Nottingham's flourishing system after 1902 is vividly recounted in Vlaeminke, *English Higher Grade Schools*, pp. 167–71.

by which this was achieved and the sharp and bitter conflicts it evoked, cannot be entered into here. The Act abolished the school boards, put the voluntary schools on the rates, so evading their demise, and established an elitist and selective system of secondary education parallel to the elementary system but charging fees, catering essentially for the middle and lower middle class.[65]

But the damage done was even greater than that. New regulations made it impossible for the higher grade schools to survive. In their place the public was offered a new category of 'higher elementary schools' so restricted in their scope that few ever got off the ground. Those that survived met their demise when the category was finally abolished a few years later. A Consultative Committee report on higher elementary schools in 1906, 'riddled with class prejudice'[66] made clear the government's intention of ensuring rigid control, thus allowing no scope for creative development. Its purpose was unmistakable – that the elementary school system should be firmly battened down allowing no possibility of a renewed breakout as had occurred in the 1890s.[67]

This action was reinforced by parallel measures now taken against pupil-teacher centres. These, over 400 of them, were the next target. All intending teachers, it was laid down, must attend the new secondary ('grammar') schools. A new 'bursary' system was evolved to ease the transition, but these measures implied, and very successfully brought about, the eventual demise of the whole pupil-teacher system.[68]

Both sets of actions, against higher grade schools and pupil-teacher centres, were strongly opposed in the decade 1900–1910, both by the

---

[65] The sharp battles over the contested demise of the higher grade schools are charted in Vlaeminke, *English Higher Grade Schools*, ch. 5. It is a sombre and almost unbelievable story. See also ch. 6. The parallel process involving the extirpation of pupil-teacher centres is chronicled in Robinson, 'Pupil-teacher Centre', ch. 8. See also Wendy Robinson, 'In Search of a 'Plain Tale': Rediscovering the Champions of the Pupil-teacher Centres 1900–1910', *History of Education*, 28, (1) (1999), pp. 53–71. For an overview of official policy relating to both sets of institutions, though written earlier than these recent publications (1965), see Simon, *Education and the Labour Movement*, pp. 235–46, 'The Aftermath – the Board of Education under Morant'.

[66] Vlaeminke, *English Higher Grade Schools*, p. 171.

[67] Manton, 'Social and Education', pp. 162–3. This fine thesis is essential reading for anyone wishing to understand the dynamics of educational change in the period covered (1883–1902).

[68] Simon, *Education and the Labour Movement*, p. 223. A massive demonstration on Woodhouse Moor against the Bill attracted from 70 000 to 100 000, the procession taking two hours to pass through the city of Leeds. Sixteen MPs were present, speaking from six platforms, the resolutions being carried unanimously at the sound of the bugle.

main teacher union (National Union of Teachers) and the labour movement generally, who combined together in a campaign against the Board of Education, accusing it of a conspiracy to close down opportunities for the working class. But they were fighting a losing battle, the cards being now heavily stacked against them especially with the abolition of their main support, the school boards. At the same time, a selective system of secondary education was being carefully constructed. It had two main elements: the remnants of the endowed grammar schools inherited from the past and the new 'county secondary' schools established by new local authorities now permitted to finance them to the extent of a twopenny rate. To the latter category should be added those higher grade schools and pupil-teacher centres which were permitted to qualify for grant as 'secondary' schools.

These two institutions now went through a process of close monitoring by the Board of Education and its (classical and literary minded) inspectors. The object was to wean them away from the popular educational culture they had adopted and transform them into poor replicas of public schools, whose ethos the HMI's and Board officials saw as the ideal type to which all secondary schools should conform.

Struggles on all these matters between the new local authorities and the Board of Education continued throughout the first decade of the century. Large and powerful urban authorities, for instance Leeds, Manchester and others, resisted the more heavy-handed of these top-down changes with some effect. In 1911, R.L. Morant, chief state architect of these countermeasures, was transferred from the Board of Education to the new Ministry of Health after a particularly tactless intervention had exacerbated relations all round. But the damage had been done. Two of the three main streams of the 'alternative system', were blocked. The third, evening continuation schools, was permitted to continue, though here new regulations after 1900 also caused difficulties.

The crucial step was, of course, the actual abolition of the school boards. Directly elected, transparently democratic, clearly committed to serving local communities, their end was also the end of the higher grade schools and pupil-teacher centres which they had produced and which they had effectively nurtured. From now on, with the establishment of committees of city or county councils, local control of education was to be distanced from local populations. As Manton has argued, this created a new situation by which educational policy making and its day-to-day administration shifted away from the control of the population these committees served.[69]

---

[69] Manton, 'Socialism and Education'.

In *Education and the Labour Movement* I evaluated this shift as a disaster. Recent research has revealed the true dimensions of the loss. Much of the succeeding century has been spent in the attempt to overcome the weaknesses and divisions in the system now created. A great opportunity was missed – indeed was deliberately stamped out.

Let us suppose, if we may make a dart into virtual history, that R.L. Morant, effective architect of the 1902 Act, had fallen under a bus in the summer of 1901 and that, sadly, Sidney Webb, ideologist of that measure, had at the same time suffered a stroke (too much brain work). Where would the government have been, and how could they have cobbled together such a piece of legislation? And just suppose, at roughly the same time, that massive demonstrations in Yorkshire, where the nonconformists proclaimed their total and undying opposition to the Act (bill), had convinced the Tory government that it would be madness to drive the measure through and that all this had led to the withdrawal of the bill. Then what?

It is a possible scenario. The Liberal landslide of 1906 was certainly at least partially due to the massive opposition of the nonconformists and the organized labour movement. That is well known and generally accepted. Morant saw the religious clauses of the 1902 Act, by which voluntary (church) schools were subsidized from the rates, as providing the crucial motive power for the passage of the Act as a whole – and especially for the abolition of the school boards. To withdraw the bill might have made sensible politics.

School boards persisted in Scotland until 1928. In the USA they are still the means by which local systems are financed, administered and controlled. With some modifications, perhaps, it might still have been the case here, at least in the main cities and population centres. The 'alternative system' they nurtured – non-selective and popular – might have grown, matured and fructified. How different the scene might then have looked from the selective and crystallized structure which came to dominate our public system of education through at least the first 60 years of the twentieth century. For this act of vandalism the country has paid a heavy price.

CHAPTER NINE

Futures from the past: the rise and fall of university liberal adult education

Bill Williamson

> A cloistered and secluded refinement, intolerant of the heat and dust of creative effort, is the note, not of civilization, but of the epochs that have despaired of it – which have seen, in one form or another, the triumph of the barbarian, and have sought compensation for defeat in writing cultured footnotes to the masterpieces they are incapable of producing.
>
> R.H. Tawney (*Equality* 1931)

I would like to begin, as many sessions in extra-mural history courses did, on a personal note. One of my favourite places used to be the Library of the Department of Adult and Continuing Education, in the University of Durham. On the upstairs of an elegant old building on Old Elvet, one of Durham's finest streets, it looked out on both Durham Cathedral and Durham Prison. From the window of this building extramural staff could watch the annual procession of the Durham Miners' Gala as lodge banners followed by their brass bands and families from villages all over the County paraded to the racecourse.

I liked to be there in the afternoon light. The cathedral has a unique historical presence; its architecture expresses the highest ideals of humanity. Even with my secular outlook, it still symbolizes for me the best that human beings are capable of. And for over one hundred years, the Miners' Gala has been an expression of community and solidarity and struggle that in its own way captures the highest hopes of most of the people of this country.

In the framed light of this window, all of the things that have interested me as a social scientist and educator were present. Among them were debates about the foundations of values and beliefs, structures of power, social control and ignorance and the ways in which experience – in this case of hard work under harsh conditions – was refashioned into hopes and demands for a better world. The words on the lodge banners that paraded past this window expressed those hopes: for peace, solidarity, freedom, decent homes and education, including the telling assertion for all educators to think about: 'Knowledge is Power'. The message in all this was also clear: the way to build the new society was through democratic politics, learning and education. The banner of the Mechanics' Lodge of the National Union of Mineworkers has inscribed on it the words 'The Past We Inherit, The Future We Build'. It remains a key task to understand that past so that the best of it can inform our future. It was always good to be reminded of these principles.

The library itself was not part of the university library. It had been built up separately because its students were not full time students of the university and for much of its history it was staffed by volunteers. Its users were extra-mural students. The stock represented a compromise between tutors' expert advice on what students should read, student demand for books of their choice and, unknown to both, the Zeitgeist that governs intellectual fashions and defines the meaning and nature of academic subjects. The tutorial staff, who from 1947, when the department was reconstituted after the war, developed the library, did so out of a love of learning and a passion to provide opportunities for everyone to continue to learn. The best that has been written in the English language lined its walls. Here was Shakespeare, George Eliot, Auden and Orwell. In translation there was Chekov, Dostoevsky, Pushkin, Goethe. Students could read Seamus Heaney and Toni Morrison. The history shelves were stacked with G.M. Trevelyan, Christopher Hill and E.P. Thompson. The social science shelves covered Marx and Hayek, Tawney and Talcott Parsons. Philosophy acquisitions covered the full stretch from Plato to Wittgenstein. From art to astrophysics, geology and archaeology to atomic particles, it was all there.

As Director of Continuing Education in the University of Durham from 1986 to 1996, I often visited that library and drew inspiration from it. During one rather wistful afternoon looking out onto the street, a photograph of Sid Chaplin, Durham's novelist, came to mind for in the picture he is walking immediately in front of the department and at the time, during the 1950s he was probably one of our students. Chaplin wrote very eloquently of that period in his book of stories *A Tree With Rosy Apples* (1969), describing how he 'plumped for any available subject, sailing down rivers of divinity, plodding through a jungle of economics or gasping for dear life on the lower slopes of Everests of psychology and philosophy'.[1]

---

[1] S. Chaplin, *A Tree with Rosy Apples* (Newcastle upon Tyne, 1969), p. 87.

His memory conjured up others: of students we had taught who had gone on to become regional politicians, trade union leaders, artists and writers and teachers. This moment of reflection led me to a deeper realization that the future of departments like this one depended more on the support of a wider and informed public, than on that of university Vice-Chancellors and the bureaucrats who controlled the purse strings in funding councils. I told my own Vice-Chancellor, Sir Fred Holliday, a man who actively supported our work, that I would not feel happy until such times as, faced with yet more cuts to the funding of the university, the people of Durham would march along Old Elvet with banners shouting 'Save Our Universities' with the same commitment that moved them in the Gala of 1984/5 to shout 'Save Our Pits, Save Our Communities'. They would not do so, however, I explained, because at bottom they did not think the university was theirs.

In another conversation, Sir Fred asked me how it would all be paid for. I told him, inspired again from a visit to the library – and I later wrote this into one of my annual reports – that it had been paid for already. People who had died for democracy on the Somme, at El-Alamein, in Italy, in Burma – had paid for it with their lives. They had died for a better world in which, among other things, people would have access to education throughout their lives.

On one of my last visits to the library, following the effective closure of the department by the university under the leadership of Professor Holliday's successor, Professor Evelyn Ebsworth, I checked out the acquisitions ledger. The results of this little piece of impromptu historical research were telling. They highlighted that it was more than funding shortfalls and intellectual myopia among senior academics that was at fault for the ending of university adult education in Durham.

We need to look deeper. Inadequate funds, incompetence and elitism are widespread but not sufficient in themselves to explain the ending of a tradition or the different forms that ending took in different English universities. In fact, adult education survived all three during much of the twentieth century. In the department library, I recorded the first and the last group of ten books ordered by our librarians. The results are shown in Table 9.1.

The shift is from history and international affairs to the study of psychology and management. Books in English literature were still being bought but they were not the ones dominating the purchasing list. That ledger is a record of changing fashions in adult education, a mirror in which to see a changing world. It records the decline of the great tradition of liberal adult education and the rise of a new kind of society and of the educational values that sustain and inform it.

Older colleagues in the department often recalled for me the 1950s

Table 9.1 Extra-mural library acquisitions, Durham University 1950 and 1998

The first ten (1950)

Ensor, R.K.C. (1936)	England, 1870–1914
Macmillan, W.M. (1949)	Africa Emergent
Collingwood, R.G. and Myers, J.N.L (1936)	Roman Britain and the English Settlement
Crump, G.C. and Jacob E.F. (1926)	The Legacy of the Middle Ages
Bailey, C. (ed.) (1923)	The Legacy of Rome
Ashley, S.W. (1949)	The Economic Organisation of England
Trevelyan, G.M. (1949)	English Social History
Spoon, E. (1949)	The Growth of English Society
Hammond, J.L. and B. (1947)	The Bleak Age
Hill, C. (1947)	Lenin and the Russian Revolution

The Last Ten (1998)

Woolfe, V. (1964)	To the Lighthouse
Ondaatje, M. (1992)	The English Patient
Girouard, M. (1978)	Life in the English Country House
DfEE (1998)	Recruitment and Induction
Lawson, K.H. (1988)	Philosophical Issues in the Education of Adults
King, Z. (1998)	The IPD Guide to Career Management
Earnshaw, J. (1996)	Stress and Employer Liability
Patterson, M.G. (1997)	Impact of People Management
Clutterbuck, D. (1991)	Everyone Needs a Mentor
Hardingham, A. (1998)	Psychology for Trainers

when they ran Saturday lecture courses in economics in Durham mining villages and attracted audiences of 200 people. Many of our courses during the 1980s ran with minimum numbers of 12 people and the values that inspired our students – many of whom were elderly – had little to do with the social emancipation of the working class and were much more concerned with their own creative recreation, love of literature or family history. Courses in art and counselling psychology were oversubscribed.

The impression was inescapable. By the 1990s we were caught up in a larger moment of change in society itself. It was too close for us to comprehend properly and too complex to simplify into the actions of a few guilty people – though I did have a long list of them. In Durham University, in the Department of Education and in the Universities Council for Adult and Continuing Education (UACE) were people, I believed, who should have been more effective in defending our work. They should have been less willing to collaborate with the state's Treasury-led agenda – itself a concession to the lobbying of the former polytechnics for a share of liberal adult education money – of funding only those courses that carried accreditation.

In 1996, following changes in funding arrangements that steadily withdrew financial support for non-award bearing courses to favour the growth of accredited courses, the University of Durham lurched through a series of committees into a set of decisions that effectively closed the Department of Adult and Continuing Education. Like a phoenix from the ashes, 'lifelong learning' became the new institutional commitment, but it required the closure of a department that had been in existence since the end of the nineteenth century and, at several points in its history, had taught more students than the university as a whole.

There were no street demonstrations and there were no feelings of regret or guilt among senior officers of the university. These were practical people, doing what they believed they had to do in the light of government policies for higher education. That mighty abstraction in their minds – 'The University' – no longer carried for them even the residual connotations of part-time modes of study pursued for its own sake by adult students from the region. There had been a subtle but telling shift in their vocabulary for discussing these issues. 'Adult education' had metamorphosed into 'lifelong learning' or 'professional development' or even, as one senior academic in Durham used to describe it, 'work-based training'.

Words like culture and democracy had dropped surreptitiously from the registers of their speech to be replaced by a manager's language of quality assurance and assessment and audit. Courses had become 'modules' and essays 'units of assessment'. Education programmes had to 'generate income'. They could only imagine what the university could do in terms of what its principal paymasters would fund.

There was no longer a critical language of education; there was no talk of values or social purpose in learning. It had all been replaced by a dead language of necessity and by strategic metaphors that were used uncritically to describe the aims and objectives of courses. There was no sense of a common culture, or any hint of that essential distance from mainstream political discourse that any university course worth the name should nurture.

The library could no longer remain my safe haven of hope, however. As the Department of Adult and Continuing Education was closed down, the library was Balkanized and finally sold off in what some said was the best second-hand book sale Durham had ever seen.

In at least 10 other universities in England a similar story could be told. The details, of course, vary, but the story is the same, including the story at David Reeder's own University of Leicester in the Department of Adult Education where he did some of his greatest teaching. In all of these universities, however, liberal adult education came to an end in England just over a century after its birth. Those university departments that still exist – and the best of them are among the most innovative of their host institutions – do so on the basis of providing award bearing courses or part-time degrees that are justified primarily in terms of the new policy language of widening participation in higher education. The work they do *reproduces* rather than *challenges* the mainstream undergraduate work of their universities. The problem of maintaining the equivalence of academic standards in their courses with those of the undergraduate university has been finally solved. The universities have colonized adult education and the language in which it exists.

Unlike Shakespeare's Caliban, who used the foreign language he had been taught to curse his oppressor, members of the community of practice that was once adult education have been as supine as their more conventional colleagues in embracing the new language to cooperate with current policies in higher education. The needs that universities meet most effectively are those of the already educationally privileged – the business community, the organized professions and the state itself. Those who gain access to higher education through the non-traditional routes have good reasons to be proud of their achievements and grateful for their opportunities. They should not be deceived into the belief, however, that the quality of their education is anything like as good as it should or could be.

From experience to analysis

Why did liberal adult education end? Could anything have been done to prevent it? Should we care? Was it not a tradition that had in many ways outlived its usefulness? Is it the case that the values that this tradition once represented have been taken on within new agendas that seek to open the doors of universities to all who wish to attend? These questions need to be asked for they touch upon what we mean by higher education.

Those who have searched for explanations in the politics and philosophy of liberal adult education have focused on only one part of the problem. Just as curious as the decline of the liberal tradition is the expansion and differentiation of a higher education system within what remains a fairly stable set of old-fashioned ideas about the nature of the university itself.

Power is the issue to consider. The provision of education is shaped by political decisions. Since all systems of education reflect pre-suppositions about how social life should be organized and what values should prevail in society, we need to explore what kind of society is being nurtured within our current frameworks of education. We need to understand how our society has changed and how the changes that have occurred have been refracted through our universities and in different ways in different universities. We need to know this in order to have the chance to conceive of different futures to those currently on offer.

Why, then, did the tradition come to an end? I want to propose four arguments that together help us answer the question. Each needs further careful historical research and wide, open debate.

The first is that, despite the eloquence of its advocates and against the grain of what many adult educators would like to believe, liberal adult education never really struck deep roots in the life of British society. Had it done so, there would have been much more protest about its demise. It would have been politically inconceivable to kill it off.

Second, the link between universities and adult education from the end of the nineteenth century onwards benefited the universities themselves rather more than it did the cause of adult education. Those who worked to make adult education an integral part of the life of a university and to develop adult work to the same standards of undergraduate education did adult education a disservice. They tied it to the intellectual values and structures of institutions that were themselves in need of radical reform. By seeking to extend and duplicate what universities offered as education, adult educators unintentionally headed off legitimate criticism of their host institutions.

Third, the extra-mural movement in British higher education never really built upon or analysed carefully its own achievements as a basis upon which to transform its host institutions. It succumbed too easily and uncritically to the curriculum of the universities, accepting their definitions of subjects and standards as the measure of its own. The adult education movement was too prepared to accept as part of its own practice a model of expert, didactic teaching backed up by modes of assessment resting on a highly individualistic model of learning and a deeply hierarchical view of different levels of achievement.

Fourth, the community of practice that became adult education in British universities was too slow to respond to the profound social changes that coursed through this society during the second half, but particularly the last quarter of the twentieth century. The result was that when the final attack on its funding base came, there was no community of resistance and no coherent alternative vision for its future.

These are contentious propositions. Each one can be contradicted and all must be qualified. For example, adult educators in British universities and their partners in the Workers' Educational Association (WEA) maintained throughout the twentieth century lively debates among themselves about the purpose of their work and as a group have always been critical of their own practice. Roger Fieldhouse, author of one of the most important histories of adult education in the recent past, commented in his Albert Mansbridge Memorial Lecture at the University of Leeds, that adult educationists have always been robustly self-critical in their aims and objectives.[2] S.G. Raybould, a giant among this country's adult educators, observed also that the WEA was failing to attract manual workers to its courses and therefore risked not contributing to the education of responsible citizens in a country that had just acquired a welfare state.[3] In 1955, having chaired an enquiry into it, Eric Ashby described adult education as pathological because the impetus behind it came from universities themselves and not from the needs and interests of students and potential students.[4] For 40 years the professional journals of adult education have been filled with critical assessments of what has and is being achieved in this important field.

Such commentary, and there is a great deal of it, is hardly evidence of a movement uncritical of its own work. But the critique was in many ways misdirected and the model of education it sought to develop was too narrow. It was certainly not robust enough to defend itself against the changes that eventually overwhelmed it. The roots of Sid Chaplin's *Tree With Rosy Apples* were not struck deeply enough into the nurturing soil of a wider society.

Proposition one: that university adult education had shallow roots

The nineteenth-century university extension movement that gave birth to twentieth-century liberal adult education was as much a response to the needs of universities to reposition themselves in a fast-changing, modern society in which they were in danger of being perceived as elitist and

---

[2] R. Fieldhouse, 'Adult Education History: Why Rake up the Past?', University of Leeds, Sixteenth Albert Mansbridge Memorial Lecture.

[3] S.G. Raybould, *The WEA: The Next Phase* (London, 1949).

[4] E. Ashby, *The Pathology of Adult Education: William Harvey Memorial Lecture* (Belfast, 1955).

irrelevant, as it was a response to meeting the needs of new constituencies of learners. University extension in any case offered an opportunity to some remarkable men and women, such as Dr R.D. Roberts of Cambridge and London University and James Stuart of Trinity College Cambridge, Arthur Acland of Balliol College Oxford and Josephine Butler, to develop public careers in higher education.[5]

The interplay of personal ambition and a social commitment to extend the benefits of education to people, especially women (many of whom were pupil-teachers), previously denied a higher education cannot be lightly dismissed as an important thrust of change behind the development of university extension lectures. Stuart Marriot has shown convincingly, however, that the politics of maintaining the hegemony of Cambridge and Oxford during a time of reform in universities and the growth of competition in higher education was also decisive.[6] The older universities were keen to hold the high ground of higher learning, fending off the 'vulgarity of purely mercantile communities' and their universities which, as Jowett of Oxford saw them, were places 'exclusively confined to the needs of business'.[7] Liberal values had to be defended as a way of defending the national position of Cambridge and Oxford themselves.

These tensions in the origins of the extension movement left their mark in the development of extra-mural programmes throughout the twentieth century and in the politics and philosophy of adult education. While the extra-mural tradition struggled with issues of values, standards and competition among providers the root question, never properly answered, was this: was adult education an integral part of the university or was it something separate, something, literally, 'beyond the walls' of the academy? The Final Report of the Adult Education Committee of the Ministry of Reconstruction in 1919, which recommended the setting up of extra-mural departments, was very clear about this. The report insisted that adult education was not a luxury for the few but a 'permanent national necessity, an inseparable aspect of citizenship, and therefore should be both universal and lifelong'.[8] The report was clear in its advice to government about the role of universities in this field: it was a duty of universities to the nation – their contribution to the development of active citizenship – to promote this kind of learning. The

---

[5] T. Kelly, *A History of Adult Edcuation in Great Britain from the Middle Ages to the Twentieth Century* (Liverpool, 1962).

[6] S. Marriott, *Extra-Mural Empires: Services and Self-interest in English University Adult Education* (Nottingham, 1984).

[7] Quoted in Marriott, *Extra-Mural Empires*, p. 25.

[8] Ministry of Reconstruction, *Final Report of the Adult Education Committee* (London, 1919).

Table 9.2 Tutorial classes and enrolments 1910–1950, Great Britain

Year	Number of classes	Students
1910	72	1829
1920	298	5528
1930	638	10942
1940	548	7055
1950	938	13912

Source: Adapted from the annual reports of the Central Joint Advisory Committee on Tutorial Classes.

mistake, in retrospect, was to leave it to the universities to make their own decisions to support this work or not. Nevertheless, after the First World War, extra-mural work did grow and became an important part of university educational provision in this country. It was always, however, something additional to what universities considered to be their main responsibility, which was to teach undergraduates and to pursue their scholarly ambitions.

We should not overestimate the significance of the development of extra-mural liberal adult education. As late as 1913–14 the term 'adult education' was not well understood and there were only in any case 110 university tutorial classes in receipt of grant aid from the Board of Education.[9] Courses increased in number after the First World War but growth was slow throughout the 1920s. Extension classes increased during the 1930s, reduced in number during the Second World War and increased significantly after it. The numbers of students enrolled were not, however, large, as Table 9.2 shows.

University tutorial classes certainly declined during this period as a proportion of the total volume of adult education taking place under the auspices of bodies like the WEA, the Educational Settlements Association, the local authorities and a range of voluntary bodies including the Young Mens' Christian Association (YMCA) and the National Adult School Union. In 1927, for instance, there were over 3800 Women's Institutes with a membership of 230 000 holding monthly meetings of a social and educational character. In that same year, the Royal Arsenal Co-operative Society, a member of the Co-operative Union, conducted 100 classes for adults in conjunction with the London County Council.[10]

---

[9] Adult Education Committee, *Pioneer Work and Other Developments in Adult Education: A Report by the Adult Education Committee of the Board of Education being paper No 9 of the Committee* (London, 1927).
[10] Ibid.

At this time the London Working Men's College was active and successful in recruiting working men to its courses and London County Council promoted a vigorous programme of literary institutes.

Of the 3627 students enrolled in university tutorial classes in 1927 (of whom 2426 were men), the largest single group of students were teachers (619) followed by clerks and draughtsmen. The social class make-up of students varied between the north and south of the country – with more industrial workers in the north. Students from a working-class background were thought predominantly to come from the skilled working class and women students were primarily teachers. Demand and supply are not independent of one another, however. What is offered and the manner of its offering, particular in the suppositions made about the nature of the students' abilities, is likely to shape demand itself.

The reports of the Adult Education Committee are deeply revealing of the attitudes towards students that prevailed among providers. Two deserve to be highlighted. The first was that a proper university education is a disciplining experience that leads to the development of a trained mind. In its report for 1930, the Adult Education Committee took great pains to highlight that this was no easy task, not one to be entered into lightly, and not at all one to be pursued for utilitarian reasons of improving job prospects. Nor was it available to everyone:

> Academic studies, as pursued by those who have not only received a long preparation in school and university, but are also able to devote the large part of a life-time to their special pursuits, are impossible to those who have neither the same equipment nor the leisure for long and arduous application.[11]

At that time, such assumptions were the stock in trade of educated people. Twenty years earlier, C.F.G. Masterman had charted the social contours of Edwardian society and noted that 'The rich despise the working people, the middle classes fear them.'[12] In Thomas Hardy's *Jude the Obscure* (1895) the beliefs that kept Jude the stonemason out of the university – that he was inadequately prepared for such an education because of his class – remained intact for at least another half century.

In fact, the Board of Education Adult Education Committee (of which R.H. Tawney was a member, along with Albert Mansbridge, founder of the WEA) argued that these stern requirements of academic study should not constrain the development of a more diverse framework of adult education. It was, in fact, a committee that argued for pioneer work in communities and through the work of voluntary organizations to pro-

---

[11] Adult Education Committee, *The Scope and Practice of Adult Education, Paper no. 10* (London, 1930), p. 46.

[12] C.F.G. Masterman, *The Condition of England* (London, 1911), p. 66.

mote an education not constrained by the requirements of universities. In retrospect it is now easier to see that it might have been better if adult education had gone its own way and resisted those requirements altogether.

A second, telling assumption of the period, which shaped expectations about how courses should be provided, concerned the students even more directly. A report by a joint committee of the British Institute of Adult Education and the Tutors' Association in 1928 (which included prominent people from the universities and the WEA) noted important differences between undergraduate students and extra-mural students. These differences were such that the report argued that the two groups should not be brought together.

> The most obvious contrast between the internal and the extra-mural student or adult student is, that while the former has (in various degrees) a trained mind but an immature experience, the adult student often has a wide experience of men and things, but an untrained intellect.[13]

This distinction justified keeping their two worlds apart so as not to disadvantage extra-mural students or restrict the essential flexibility of the courses needed to hold their interest. Accordingly, it was a document that argued strongly for the development of a professional, university-based adult education 'staff tutor' and its recommendations directly strengthened the development of extra-mural departments in British universities after 1945. But the distinction led inexorably to the argument that different provision was needed for the extra-mural student. The basic idea that universities should be primarily for the (immature) young with their (trained) minds was taken as something so obvious it needed no further justification.

One consequence of this was that university extension lectures proved more attractive to the already well educated than they did to the growing constituencies of urban workers. They proved attractive also to women, especially pupil teachers who had few opportunities to enter higher education.

The working-class majority of the adult population were never the majority student group within university extra-mural provision. Despite its location in the centre of a great coalfield, the social composition of students of the Durham Extra-Mural Department in the period 1949–51 was predominantly white collar. A Ministry of Education report on provision in Durham showed that for 1949–50 only 22.4 per cent of the

---

[13] British Institute for Adult Education and the Tutors' Association, *The Tutor in Adult Education: An Enquiry into Problems of Supply and Training. A Report of a Joint Committee* (Dunfermline, 1928), p. 95.

total number of students (1163) were manual workers, while 27 per cent were teachers and 20% were classified as clerks and shopkeepers.[14] John McIlroy has noted that surveys of extra-mural students in the 1950s and 1960s confirm that only 8 per cent of them came from the lowest socio-economic groups.[15] Even the WEA had difficulty in recruiting and retaining manual workers during this period. The record shows, too, important differences in patterns of enrolments between different parts of the country, and between men and women. In 1951 the Central Joint Advisory Committee on Tutorial Classes published an analysis of the student body. It is clear from the data that in all major centres (Birmingham, Bristol, Newcastle, Leeds, Southampton, Cardiff and Leicester) white-collar workers outnumbered those from a manual working-class background. Only in Leeds and Cardiff did the proportion of manual workers exceed that of clerks, but even in these two mining dominated centres, manual workers comprised less than 30 per cent of enrolments.[16]

The expansion of enrolments in the 1950s and early 1960s did little to alter this balance. A study was carried out in Leeds by Ian Hanna into the composition of the extra-mural student body. His survey showed them to be a group significantly different from that of the city and its region. They were on average younger, better educated and from groups with high social status who came from the better off parts of the city – the 'well-to-do areas' – as Hanna put it.[17] Leeds local education authority ran a number of evening institutes for adults that in 1963 enrolled over 8000 students, significantly more than the university extra-mural department. A similar pattern was detected.

In the 1980s liberal adult education in universities continued to be criticized for its failure to engage people from a working class background. Paradoxically, success during the 1970s and 1980s in the development of courses in industrial studies or special access courses for other excluded groups, such as working-class women and ethnic minorities, merely highlighted the historical failures of the great tradition itself. The conclusion is inescapable: by and large university adult education benefited those who were already well off in educational terms. Its role throughout much of the twentieth century, especially after 1945, was to

---

[14] Ministry of Education, *Report by H.M. Inspectors on a Survey of Adult Education Provided by Durham University* (London, 1951).

[15] J. McIlroy, 'Trade Union Education for a Change', in B. Simon (ed.), *The Search for Enlightenment: The Working Class and Adult Education in the Twentieth Century* (London, 1990).

[16] J.M. Cameron, *The Teaching of Philosophy to Adult Students* (London, 1951).

[17] I Hanna, 'Adult Education Students', in *Rewley House Papers* (Oxford, 1966), p. 23.

provide a semblance of a university education to groups denied the real thing.

Proposition two: that the universities, not local communities, were the prime beneficiaries

The work of university adult education departments continued to expand throughout the 1960s, right up to their demise in the late 1990s. In the 1980s enrolments exceeded a quarter of a million annually in courses that could be classified as liberal, and there were over half a million enrolments on other kinds of courses, particularly short courses with vocational relevance. From this perspective the extra-mural world was something of a parallel universe; it accommodated more students (albeit part-time ones) than the universities themselves.

From the mid-1970s onwards, however, the annual reports of the Universities Association for Continuing Education were dominated by concerns about state funding and local authority support funding. The theme of the UACE annual conference in Edinburgh for 1979–80 was 'Adult Education in the New Austerity'.

Despite the new austerity, extra-mural departments continued to innovate and grow and build on some of their earlier pioneer work. They developed innovative courses for new constituencies of students, for example New Opportunities for Women (NOW). They stretched their provision to reach outwards to the unemployed. The UACE annual report for 1980–81 noted that 'Most departments see extra-mural work in relation to the unemployed as a crucial new development and in a number of cases special courses or other initiatives are on record.'[18] There were pre-retirement courses, return to study courses, the development of award-bearing certificate courses and, as will be seen, key steps were taken towards the development of part-time degrees. These developments were possible because funding for liberal adult education provided the basis upon which they could be built.

Universities had benefited from liberal adult education in several different ways. The work attracted significant funding. It provided them with excellent public relations and a flow of good students. The best extra-mural departments were among the most innovative academic departments in the whole system of universities. Extra-mural staff engaged with the communities. They developed strong vocational links

---

[18] UACE, Annual Report and Yearbook (1981), p. 6.

with the professions, and they pioneered the new agenda of continuing professional development.

Throughout the period after the Robbins enquiry into higher education (1963), universities in the United Kingdom increased both in number and in size. Growth in size, however, did not result in a significant alteration in the form of the institution. Universities remained wedded to the three year undergraduate degree designed for 18 year olds offered by departments committed primarily to scholarship within strong disciplinary and research boundaries. They remained committed also to methods of student selection based on school examinations, which disguised what was really academic rationing with a rhetoric of legitimate competition for places. Extra-mural work eased the consciences of elites. It fostered the impression that the university served all groups in society when, in fact, they attended most closely to the needs of those from educationally privileged backgrounds. The community of practice that was liberal adult education was never strong enough to challenge this hegemony, and indeed, it could be argued that it replicated the same academic values in it own curricula. It failed to develop a coherent challenge to the dominant orthodoxies of higher education. Certainly, many of the pioneers of adult education in universities after 1945 established creditable academic careers and deservedly came to take up senior positions in universities. They were innovators in many fields of enquiry such as cultural studies – where the work of Raymond Williams and Richard Hoggart remains seminal – and social history, literary studies and social science. Although they broke the academic moulds of their subjects, they were far less successful in reshaping the institutions in which they worked.

Extra-mural work was always marginal to the mainstream work of the universities and often was managed through committees and structures that were separate from those that managed the internal departments. When the time came for the limb to be amputated, it was easy for university managers to do it. In the late 1990s many extra-mural staff moved easily from reorganized departments to 'mainstream' subject departments in order to teach undergraduates and develop more conventional university careers. Many who had once been pioneers of new methods of teaching in higher education or articulate advocates of the learning needs of the socially excluded and oppressed slipped effortlessly into the mainstream of academic culture unable any longer to overcome or expose its limitations.

Proposition three: that adult education theory and practice was too uncritical

Throughout the twentieth century, university adult education reflected the mainstream curriculum of the undergraduate programme. There had, of course, been challenges to the system, most noticeably in the 1920s. Before the First World War the WEA had been formed in part to overcome the weaknesses of university extension in bringing serious studies to the working class. During this period, the University of Oxford had attempted to establish closer links with Ruskin College in a move rejected by some of the more radical students of the college who organized themselves into the Plebs League to fight for *independent* working-class education. These conflicts led to the setting up of the Central Labour College to connect adult education much more directly to the needs of the labour movement. After 1918, the conflict over the nature of adult education escalated. The Plebs League, the Central Labour College and the WEA fought it out, as Brian Simon has explained,[19] drawing heavily on support from within the universities. In the 1920s, with considerable trade union support, this movement for independent working-class education was consolidated in the National Council for Labour Colleges. This body fell victim, however, to the industrial defeats of 1926, when it could no longer rely on trade union funds, and was closed in 1928.

During the same period, the links between the universities and the WEA strengthened, as did state support for universities to set up extra-mural departments ('responsible bodies') to promote higher education. The tutorial classes associated with this work expanded considerably both in the universities and in the WEA. The focus of the work, aided by university tutors, was the tutorial class with its carefully prepared syllabus and its programme requiring students to write critical, reflective essays. The 'tutorial class' was a tradition of teaching and learning that had developed under the watchful eye of Ministry of Education inspectors who were sensitive to the need to oppose politically motivated teaching or methods of teaching that were deemed too informal.[20] In the period of the Cold War during the 1950s the same imperatives prevailed, but for a different reason: the need, as government saw it, to protect the 'free world' from Soviet or Communist propaganda.

University extra-mural work developed around the 'tutorial class'.

---

[19] B. Simon, 'The Struggle for Hegemony, 1920–1926', in Simon, *The Search for Enlightenment*.

[20] R. Fieldhouse, *Adult Education and the Cold War: Liberal Values under Siege 1946–1951* (Leeds, 1985).

This became the academic gold standard of the tradition. Debates within this tradition from the 1940s onwards were dominated by questions about standards. Were tutorial classes of the same standard as undergraduate study? Were adult students as capable?

If they were not generally thought of as inferior, they were often conceived of as being different. In 1951 J.M. Cameron, a lecturer in philosophy at the University of Leeds, where, under the influence of Raybould, the university's Director of Adult Education, the issue of standards was keenly discussed, noted a key difference. Adult students turn to philosophy for guidance on the serious problems of life. 'In this', he writes, 'they differ from most undergraduates; and they have a background of experience much richer than that of undergraduates.'[21] 'What they lack', he went on, 'is an extensive background of formal knowledge and some of the rudimentary techniques of learning.'[22] He went on to suggest that 'they have more within them than they can express' so the inescapable conclusion was that tutors needed great skill in teaching them and courses had to be at least three years in length. This was a time when there was active discussion about the relative standards of university and extra-mural work and in the field of literature, in particular, there was an active debate about the values that should inform literary studies.

Some extra mural tutors rejected such comparisons of extra-mural work with mainstream university studies, and questioned the ideological character of those studies. E.P. Thompson was an adult tutor in English and History with Leeds University in the late 1940s and all through the 1950s. Sometimes he despaired of working men who showed little interest in poetry. But in 1950, as Andy Croft has explained,[23] Thompson wrote a polemic against what he took to be the stifling role of the universities and their narrow 'standards'. He saw the tutorial class movement's insistence on tolerance and objectivity as a form of class indoctrination promoting 'intellectual numbness'.[24] The better tutorial classes displayed, Thompson felt, a 'sturdy independence' not seen in the university-based classes that were considered to be of a higher academic standard.

There was another aspect to this, not so clear at the time. It concerns access to learning. Roger Fieldhouse, reflecting on the history of the

---

[21] Cameron, *The Teaching of Philosophy*, p. 3.
[22] Ibid.
[23] A. Croft, 'Walthamstow, Little Gidding and Middlesbrough: Edward Thompson the Literature Tutor', in R. Taylor (ed.), *Beyond the Walls: 50 Years of Adult and Continuing Education at the University of Leeds 1946–1996* (Leeds, 1996).
[24] Ibid., p. 151.

extra-mural department of Leeds University, noted that the debate about academic standards can now be seen as something alien to adult education practice. '"Standards"', he writes, 'became a way of promoting quality by exclusion – excluding those who would not commit themselves in advance to regular attendance, written work and private study over a three year period – without giving due recognition and credit for the wide range of experience and achievement which adult learners bring with them to a class.'[25]

During the heyday of university adult education, between 1950 and 1980, much innovative curriculum development took place both within and alongside the core-funded provision founded on the tutorial class. A full account of this would include work in the field of industrial studies carried out with the cooperation of trade unions. All the universities in mining districts have a proud record of such work with miners.[26] In the 1980s, extra-mural departments developed a range of certificate and diploma courses for different groups of professionals such as social workers and community workers. They developed short course programmes of professional updating, summer schools, study tours and some of the first part-time degree programmes outside Birkbeck and the Open University. They developed also innovative methods of teaching. Long before the professionalization of archaeology, extra-mural students in this subject carried out excavations. Local history became a popular subject in liberal adult education, as did environmental studies and geology, and there is an archive of pamphlets in every British university with Responsible Body status of local research that continues to inform scholarship in these fields. Literature courses in creative writing added significantly to the cultural life of local communities. Pioneer work with the socially disadvantaged and educationally excluded laid the foundation for new kinds of community development and still informs policies to combat social exclusion. The 1970 study by Ken Coates and Richard Silburn, *Poverty, The Forgotten Englishmen*, based in the district of St Anne's, Nottingham, was carried out by extra-mural and WEA students.[27] It is a sociological classic.

It was not really until the 1970s and 1980s that serious attempts were

---

[25] R. Fieldhouse, 'Raybould, Sedgwick and the Early Department', in Taylor, *Beyond the Walls*, p. 21.

[26] See G. Mitchell, *Responsible Body: The Story of Fifty Years of Adult Education in the University of Sheffield* (Sheffield, 2000); R. Dyson, 'Educating Industrial Workers 1954–1974: Growth and Achievement within the Raybould Formula', in Taylor, *Beyond the Walls* and J. McIlroy, 'The Triumph of Technical Training?' in Simon, *The Search for Enlightenment*.

[27] K. Coates and R. Silburn, *Poverty: The Forgotten Englishmen* (Harmondsworth, 1970).

made to place curriculum development in this field on a sound theoretical basis. To his credit, Raybould at Leeds was always clear about the importance of professionalizing the adult tutor and establishing adult education as a serious topic of study in its own right.[28] In Nottingham, too, there has been a long-standing interest in research in this field. Some writers, such as Jane Thompson, Tom Lovett, Sallie Westwood, Peter Jarvis and others, through journals like *Studies in the Education of Adults* or the *International Journal of Lifelong Education* have contributed to clarifying the theoretical rationale for different forms of adult education practice.[29] For many extra-mural staff, however, and certainly for all of the subject specialists from internal departments who in the early postwar years until the early 1980s were willing to take tutorial classes, it was *subject knowledge* that mattered more than the theory of adult education itself. It was not until the early 1990s that the funding of adult education research was seriously discussed, but by then it was too late.

At a time when the adult education community needed to articulate a new vision for its work in the altered circumstances of the world, it clung to what Alistair Crombie had identified earlier as a 'dynamic conservatism' which fought 'to remain the same, in a radically different world'.[30] The tradition clung to the epistemological assumptions of their host institutions with their accompanying, old-fashioned models of teacher–learner relationships and subject divisions, and highly individualized ideas about learning and the creation of knowledge. It was not a good basis on which to develop their own work or, more importantly, to challenge the socially exclusive pedagogy of universities themselves.

When the challenge to extra-mural departments became intense, their response was to seek to become more useful to their host institutions. They pioneered the access programmes, developed the continuing education portfolio and they sought in many other ways – through certificates and credits and part-time degrees and pioneering work in what is now called 'lifelong learning' – to make universities more accessible. It

---

[28] M. Zukas, 'Researching the Education of Adults', in Taylor, *Beyond the Walls*.

[29] J. Thompson, (ed.), *Adult Education for a Change* (London, 1980); T. Lovett, *Adult Education, Community Development and the Working Class*, (London, 1975); S. Westwood and J.E. Thomas, *Radical Agendas and the Politics of Adult Edcuation* (Leicester, 1991); S. Westwood (ed.), *Border Country: Raymond Williams and Adult Education* (Leicester, 1993); P. Jarvis, *The Sociology of Adult and Continuing Education* (London, 1985); and P. Jarvis, *Adult and Continuing Education: Theory and Practice* (London, 1995).

[30] A.D. Crombie and G. Harries-Jenkins, *The Demise of the Liberal Tradition: Two Essays on the Future of British University Adult Education* (Leeds, 1983).

might have been better to go down fighting the host institutions than to have been absorbed by them.

Proposition four: not reading the runes

Nevertheless, university liberal adult education remained a community of practice that sustained some educational debate about the aims and purposes of education. From the late 1920s onwards there prevailed in this community a strong sense of the distinctiveness of its work, the training needs of its tutors and a more sensitive reading of the educational needs of adults and society more generally. The report of the Advisory Council for Adult and Continuing Education (1982) is an outstanding, and prescient, expression of this, providing a close reading of the technological, demographic and social changes that required new forms of educational provision for adults in successful, democratic societies. Under its Chair, Professor Richard Hoggart, it argued convincingly for a comprehensive adult education service funded by the state, perhaps through hypothecated taxation and organized coherently by regional planning bodies integrating the work of a range of providers. 'Can Britain afford to create a comprehensive system of continuing education?' the report asked. It then supplied its own answer: 'The question is more pertinent in reverse: can the country afford not to?'[31]

We know with hindsight that the country could well afford not to. So what was wrong with the prevailing perception in the period just before the Thatcher revolution? Like many other public sector communities of practice, the adult education community underestimated a right wing government's determination to hold back public expenditure and insinuate a market logic into the public sphere. In addition, and this remains the case, there was a collective failure properly to understand the social and cultural changes of the 'new times' and to assess the significance of new forms of social differentiation and popular culture. Nor was the liberal adult education community alert enough to realize the significance of growing demands for continuing vocational education, for qualifications, or to assess the impact of a growth in opportunities for new learning that were not confined to formal education.

The key failure, however, lay in the academic naivety of what remained of the liberal tradition in universities. This tradition, whose members were so proud of their positions in higher education, had not

---

[31] Advisory Council for Adult and Continuing Education, Continuing Education: From Policies to Practice: A Report on the Future Development of a System of Continuing Education in England and Wales (Leicester, 1982), p. 16.

assessed properly the radical changes that were taking place in their host institutions or even, for that matter, within their own profession. There was a strong body of opinion within the extra-mural world that liberal adult education had outlived its usefulness and had little to contribute to the more dynamic agendas of income generating 'continuing education.'[32] Throughout the 1980s, Conservative governments expanded university education enrolments, lowered the unit of resource for doing so and injected market logic into the funding of higher education. The ending of the binary divide between universities and polytechnics in 1992 opened up a key question: if the former polytechnics had, as was often claimed, extended learning opportunities without ever receiving liberal adult education funding, what was the justification for continuing this funding in the older universities?

Sadly, there was no convincing answer to that question. The historical failure to define a unique, widely supported, successfully operational, research-based, densely networked role in both the university and the communities they served was the undoing of liberal adult education. That failure reflected a more profound one: a failure to challenge the prevailing model of the university itself and the pressures that were giving it its decisive modern shape. In the cultural markets of higher education, the decisive actors were the business community and the organized professions, including university staff themselves. Socially mobile parents from the new middle class looked for university education for their children. The research communities, driven hard by both the state and the logic of a changing economy, looked to the universities to play a more significant role in knowledge development, technology transfer and economic regeneration. Liberal adult education had no place on the agendas of these groups.

The constituencies that were still supportive of liberal adult education included local authorities, voluntary bodies like the WEA, and community groups that had benefited from pioneer work and the wide range of new opportunities that had become available through the extra-mural departments. They were not, however, groups with political power. The socially disadvantaged and the oppressed had in any case received more help from local authority educational provision and from politically inspired new social movements than they had had from liberal adult education provision. When the funding finally dried up, there was little to be done.

---

[32] See, for example, Crombie and Harries-Jenkins, *The Demise of the Liberal Tradition*.

The future

What, then, of the future? Roger Fieldhouse has argued that adult educators should be tackling with renewed vigour the old problems of inequality, democracy and social justice, but in new ways. They should work with new social movements and voluntary sector institutions to overcome the limitations of 'institutionalized adult education'.[33] But he adds darkly that the historical record shows that voluntary effort is not enough. What he looks forward to is a reformed WEA building on people's knowledge, participation and collective, collaborative learning. He urged his audience, quoting Wilson and Melichar to 'critique the present so that we can attain the not yet in the future'.[34]

This task is daunting. Modern British society is clearly affluent. The perception is widespread that people are now materially far better off than their parents and grandparents. Despite this, there is much in modern society that is illiberal, materialist, individualist and driven by commercial values that threaten to corrode a culture of learning. The sociological accounts of modern society outline an underlying order to our experience that is global, driven by the logic of free trade, producing an international order that is unequal, unstable and faced with risks that are unmanageable. It describes civil societies that are fragmented and individual lives that are scarred by uncertainty, the absence of trust and of obligations of mutuality based on extremely fragile platforms for self-respect. Individualism in this context is less a philosophy of the morally autonomous individual and much more a desperate search for a personal identity through the social conformity of consuming.[35] The political culture of postmodernity is apathetic, a culture, as Galbraith tellingly described it, of contentment.[36] Modern democracies are deeply complacent about the corroded state of their political foundations. Young people do not vote in elections and electoral turnouts everywhere are low.

There are problems here for which our current educational language and policies are inadequate. There is a need to rebuild a critical democracy within a society that is just and fair and tolerant of differences. Such

---

[33] Fieldhouse, 'Adult Education History', p. 19.

[34] Ibid., quoting A.L. Wilson and K.E. Melichar, 'A "Rhetoric of Disruption" by Way of Attaining the not yet in the Future: Re-membering the Past by way of challenging our Present Educational Practices', *International Journal of Lifelong Education*, 14 (6) (1995), pp. 422–33.

[35] Z. Bauman, *Life in Fragments: Essays in Postmodern Morality* (Oxford, 1995).

[36] J.K. Galbraith, *The Culture of Contentment* (London, 1992).

a society has to be an efficient producer of wealth and therefore needs people with highly developed skills and competencies.

Who can doubt that society requires people – active citizens – with an intellectual capacity to recover some important connections between experience and politics, themselves and others, their own society and a wider world. In this respect the past has much to teach us. There were people engaged in adult education in the 1930s, surveyed by Williams and Heath, who valued adult education not only for its capacity to enrich the personality, but because they believed it to be 'the redemptive force of this disordered world'.[37] There were adult students from Britain in the late 1940s who attended summer programmes of the International People's College in Denmark to study alongside German, French, Czech and Scandinavian fellow students to explore the ways they could live together and reconstruct a continent based on peace and democracy.[38] There was a commitment here to politics and internationalism that remains relevant to contemporary Europe and the threats we all face in the risk society[39] of the global, informational economy with its terrifying new political and ideological divisions.[40]

There is an international dimension to adult education. The professional bodies of the discipline have been thoroughly internationalized and engage in each other's conferences. The idea of lifelong learning that has become so important to educational discussions in bodies like UNESCO, the OECD and the European Union has been a stimulus to some innovative thinking.[41] Historians of the future will have to judge whether this work is inspired by an internationalism capable of building a better, safer world, or whether it is an expression of a new kind of professional academic identity that leaves the old world nicely intact.

What kind of institutions could facilitate the kind of continuous, critical and creative learning that would enable us, in the words of Matthias Finger, to 'learn our way out' of these problems?[42] A key educational challenge for the twenty-first century is to transform the

---

[37] W.E. Williams and A.E. Heath, *Learn to Live: The Consumer's View of Adult Education* (London, 1936), p. 3.

[38] International People's College, *Adult Education in the Struggle for Peace* (Copenhagen, 1949).

[39] U. Beck, *Risk Society: Towards a New Modernity* (London, 1992).

[40] M. Castells, *The Rise of the Network Society* (Oxford, 1996), vol. I.

[41] J. Field, *Lifelong Learning and the New Educational Order* (London, 2000); F. Coffield, *Differing Visions of the Learning Society: Research Findings* (Bristol, 2000).

[42] M. Finger, 'Adult Education and Society Today', *International Journal of Lifelong Education*, 14 (2) (March–April 1995), pp. 110–19.

relationship between educational institutions, particularly universities, and society.

Adult education may have failed to transform the institution that spawned it but modern universities are not immune to change. There are clear voices calling for them to become more attuned to the needs of adults,[43] to develop new structures to cope with the new production of knowledge[44] and the cultural conditions of *supercomplexity*.[45] The discussion of the political and educational themes of citizenship, empowerment, inclusion and globalization – all features of the radical edges of contemporary discourse – have provided ample recent opportunities to restate some of the values of an adult education that is both liberal and radical and expresses a common purpose between educators and those in the global economy who are silenced and excluded.[46] There are still grounds for hope. The voices for change within universities must engage with others in a new kind of global civil society to challenge prevailing values and social structures. The promotion of active citizenship through lifelong learning was an important goal in this country after the First World War and it was seen as central to the work of universities. We have to be imaginative enough to envisage new forms of citizenship for a new kind of civil society and to build support for it through new kinds of lifelong learning. The history of adult education shows that this can be done. The best that has been achieved in this tradition is still something to be proud of and to learn from.

---

[43] E. Bourgeois, C. Duke, J.-L. Guyot and B. Merrill, *The Adult University* (Buckingham, 1999).

[44] M. Gibbons et al., *The New Production of Knowledge: The Dynamics of Science and Research in Contemporary Societies* (London, 1994).

[45] R. Barnett, *Realizing the University in an Age of Supercomplexity* (Buckingham, 2000).

[46] J. Thompson, M. Shaw and L. Bane (eds), *Reclaiming Common Purpose* (Nottingham, 2000).

CHAPTER TEN

Women and citizenship: gender and the built environment in British cities 1870–1939

Helen Meller

There are many ways of approaching the theme of women and citizenship. When the great 'umbrella' campaigning society for female suffrage changed its name in the wake of partial female suffrage in 1918 from the National Union of Women's Suffrage Societies, it called itself the National Union of Societies for Equal Citizenship.[1] The name embodied the idea that alongside the rights of women went responsibilities, especially moral responsibilities. What role should women play now that they had a chance to operate in the mainstream of national life?[2] For most women though, the question was academic. Family ties, education and job opportunities kept women close to home. This had been true before women got the vote and remained so for most of the inter-war period. The scope for women's action remained their immediate neighbourhood and the city to which it belonged.[3] Thus for many over the whole period from the 1870s to the Second World War and even beyond, citizenship was not a theoretical concept but a practical issue of commitment to locality. There were many outlets for such commitment: in philanthropy, local government, socio-religious activities and the support of women's organizations, the political and non-political, feminist and non-feminist.[4] The element

---

[1] Brian Harrison comments that Eleanor Rathbone, President of NUSEC, made her major contribution to British feminism in this organization: B. Harrison, *Prudent Revolutionaries: Portraits of British Feminists Between the Wars* (Oxford, 1987), p. 103; see also M. Pugh, *Women and the Women's Movement* (2nd edn, Basingstoke, 2000).

[2] H.L. Smith (ed.) *British Feminism in the Twentieth Century* (Aldershot, 1990).

[3] Norbert Elias offers sophisticated insights into the forces creating modern civilization but he excludes a feminist perspective: N. Elias, *Power and Civilization* (New York, 1984).

[4] For a discussion of this, see C. Beaumont, 'The Women's Movement, Politics and Citizenship 1918–1950s', in I. Zweiniger-Bargielowska (ed.), *Women*

that I want to explore is the contribution women made, out of a sense of citizenship, to improving the quality of the urban environment for those less fortunate than themselves. They provided ideas, organizations and voluntary labour to improve the quality of the physical environment of the poor and promoted a whole range of cultural activities for leisure and pleasure. Their contributions in this respect have largely been ignored.

In recent years, partially as a consequence of the development of women's history, historians have begun to explore in different ways the contribution of women to the building of the welfare state.[5] In this chapter, I would like to take up a parallel theme: the way in which a focus on women's history can develop a new interpretation of women's responses to the late Victorian city. A sub theme of the latter is how those responses were used or not used by the advocates of modern town planning (all male) who were to become professionally concerned with the quality of the physical environment of cities. There was, of course, considerable overlap between concern for social welfare and concern for the quality of the physical environment in the late Victorian era. Often the same individuals, men and women, in towns and cities in all parts of Britain, were working to improve both. Yet while there is now a considerable historiography on the origins of the welfare state and the role of women in this, there is virtually nothing about their contribution to town planning and the quality of the urban environment. There are several reasons for this. Town planning was, after all, the 'cinderella' of social welfare policy. Tacked on to a housing act for the first time in the Housing and Town Planning Act of 1909, town planning was still only made permissive and there were serious doubts whether there was sufficient trained expertise in the country to carry out modern town planning schemes.[6]

This highlights another reason. Town planning at this time, as the

---

in *Twentieth Century Britain* (Harlow, 2001), pp. 262–77; C. Beaumont, 'Citizens not Feminists: The Boundary created Between Citizenship and Feminism by Mainstream Women's Organisations in England in the Interwar Period', *Women's History Review* 9(3) (2000), pp. 411–29.

[5] G. Bock and P. Thane, *Maternity and Gender Politics: Women and the Rise of the European Welfare States, 1880s–1950s* (London, 1994); Seth Koven and A. Chambers, 'Toward a Definition of Welfare History' *Journal of American History* 73 (September 1986); Seth Koven and Sonya Michel, 'Womanly Duties: Maternal Politics and the Origins of Welfare States in France, Germany, Great Britain, and the United States, 1880–1920', *American Historical Review* 95(4) (1990); Seth Koven and Sonya Michel (eds), *Mothers of a New World: Maternalist Politics and the Origins of Welfare States* (London, 1993).

[6] Helen Meller, *Towns, Plans and Society in Modern Britain* (Cambridge, (for the Economic History Society), 1997).

manipulation of the physical environment, was seen by city administrators as a matter of public health and by-law regulations. The 1909 Act was concerned with town extension schemes. Even the public-spirited women, hoping to demonstrate their qualities of citizenship, who got themselves elected onto town councils in increasing numbers by the end of the nineteenth century were very rarely appointed to sit on the public health committee.[7] Drains, water supply and environmental nuisances were not seen as the province of women. Yet the quality of an urban environment was not only a matter of by-laws for roads and housing and the provision of drains. The fact that the majority of the population now lived in cities, a sizeable proportion in large cities, made the late Victorians particularly sensitive to the idea that there was a social and cultural aspect to urbanization which had to be addressed. This is not an easy subject to explore. Factors influencing social adaptability to the changing circumstances of large cities in nineteenth and early twentieth-century Britain are myriad. But it has to be possible for historians to look at the means of creating and transmitting social knowledge, especially knowledge about how to live in a modern urban environment.

Defining the quality of life in cities, however, is not straightforward. It encompasses many basic questions such as how to find accommodation, how to bring up families, how to engage with the labour market, even how to cross the road! Less basic but no less essential are questions about the use of leisure, the availability of recreation and fun, all of which are constrained by place and space. Social adaptability to urban changes can take place at many different levels and did so. Yet what was considered acceptable and what was desirable were matters which raised questions about the expectations of what was possible in an urban environment. Answers to those questions were culturally determined. In an urban context where there was much poverty, concern over such matters depended on a non-materialistic, altruistic sense of caring and nurturing, the accepted gender characteristics of women. When, more than 30 years ago, I was exploring the efforts made by the Victorians to 'civilize' the city,[8] I was particularly conscious of two things. First, how little had been written about the 'civilizing' forces in the nineteenth-century city and, second, how what there was, was heavily 'gendered' in a way which largely excluded the humble, and often unpublicized, contributions made by women. From Matthew Arnold's polemic, *Culture and Anarchy* (1869), to Edward Edward's campaign for a penny rate for public libraries; from

---

[7] P. Hollis, *Ladies Elect: Women in English Local Government 1865–1914* (Oxford, 1987).

[8] H.E. Meller, *Leisure and the Changing City 1870–1914: A Study of Bristol* (London, 1976).

Canon Barnett's efforts to bring 'civilization' to the East End of London to the patrons, in cities up and down the land, who provided funds for civic art galleries and museums, the parameters of the subject, to use Catherine Hall's words, appear to be mostly 'white, male and middle class'.[9]

Yet research at a local level showed that women had had much to contribute in the task of 'civilizing' the city, especially helping to improve the quality of life of the poor. Nurturing and caring were both time-consuming and selfless, 'fitting' work for women. Seeking social roles before the acquisition of the vote, such work could be justified as displaying 'citizenship'. In nearly every city, public-minded women had been involved not just in the business of transmitting moral values, but in tackling the 'inhuman' elements of urban life, especially those related to families and children. They had been at the forefront of inventing ways of manipulating the physical environment of home and its surroundings (one of the primary concerns of the nascent town planning movement) to make a semblance of civilized life possible in inner city areas. Yet, subsequently, their activities were marginalized. Why were the achievements of women in improving urban life in the years up to the First World War sidelined in the inter-war period when town planning became a professional activity? How did the ideal of modern urban life get defined and by whom? Why did town planning develop more as a professional practice dependent on engineering and design? In the great expansion of new housing in the inter-war period and the renovation of old properties, women were conspicuous by their absence of influence in what was actually built, yet women residents and volunteers were often called upon to make new council estates 'work'.[10] Why were the social consequences of new developments not part of the brief of the architects and planners who created the new urban environments of the twentieth century? Why did they think they knew what everybody wanted?

Alison Ravetz has offered some answers in relation to public housing and its design. She suggests that tenants, both male and female, were not consulted by anyone because council housing was, on the one hand, a new activity of government and there were many local officials who

---

[9] C. Hall, *White Male and Middle Class: Explorations in Feminism and History* (Cambridge, 1992). There were honourable exceptions such as Enriqueta Augustina Rylands (1843–1908) who sustained the development of the John Rylands Library in Manchester: D.A. Farnie, 'Enriqueta Augustina Rylands (1843–1908), Founder of the John Rylands Library', *Bulletin of the John Rylands University Library of Manchester*, 71(2) (1989).

[10] J. Greatorex and S. Clarke, *Looking Back at Wythenshawe* (Timperley, 1984); A. Ravetz, *Council Housing and Culture: The History of a Social Experiment* (London, 2001), p. 101.

thought that their brief was to 'govern'. On the other hand, the architects and builders following local government by-laws were, nevertheless, influenced by ideas emanating from utopian sources – utopian socialism and communitarianism relating to the land question – which deeply influenced the nascent town planning movement.[11] With ideals to achieve (the difference between the inner city environment and the outer city council estate was suitably huge), what need was there for consultation? Such an explanation goes some way towards an answer to why women were not allowed much influence on what was built. But there is still the question of women and citizenship and why women volunteers still found they had a role to play in the new estates as they had done in the old inner city areas.[12] It has taken me a long time to get around to articulating these questions since my research interests have moved more firmly into the male-dominated domain of planning history. But as a young lecturer at the University of Nottingham, in the late 1960s and early 1970s, I was invited to contribute to the seminars run jointly by the Urban History Group led by Jim Dyos and the Victorian Studies Group led by Philip Collins at the University of Leicester. I was lucky. Here was a group of scholars who, while not particularly committed to women's history, were committed to an interdisciplinary approach and keeping an open mind on the study of cities. They listened patiently while I gave fairly incomprehensible papers on civilization and cities.[13]

This is where I first met David Reeder, who has remained ever since a much-valued friend and advisor. With his own studies of the education of city children,[14] he was working in a parallel (much better defined) theme and I was, and still am, always immensely grateful for his interest, considered comments and warm support. In the 1990s when the study of urban history regained its impetus, David was at the centre of the small group who reconvened the annual urban history conferences. These events provide a forum for the dissemination of new work and David's enthusiasm, coupled with his modesty, has made him both approachable and an inspiration for generations of young scholars. As probably one of the earliest in this category, I am delighted to offer this chapter to his Festschrift and hope he sees in it some continuity with those early days.

*

[11] Ravetz, *Council Housing and Culture*, p. 2; see also G.E. Cherry, *Pioneers in British Planning* (London, 1981).

[12] H.E. Meller, *European Cities 1890–1930s: History, Culture and the Built Environment* (Chichester, 2001), p. 241.

[13] An example was 'Cities, Salvation and the Middle Class Solution' a paper delivered in Leicester on 4th December 1969.

[14] See the list of David Reeder's publications in this volume, pp. 311–15.

Concern over the quality of the urban environment and the question of how the masses might adapt to modern life received a boost after 1859 and the publication of Darwin's *The Origin of Species*. The concept of evolution was based on the idea of an interaction of organism with environment as the determinant of the future. British social scientists, from Herbert Spencer to Francis Galton and Patrick Geddes, emphasized the importance of the biological sciences in providing the methodology for understanding change.[15] Both men and women were influenced by this and could see the possible connections between environment and behaviour. The Royal Commission on the Housing of the Working Classes of 1884 was commissioned as much because of concern over the question of incest in overcrowded living accommodation as it was because of the problem of working-class housing.[16] Did the pigs make the sty or the sty the pigs? What was the connection? Many middle-class women were to become involved in managing working-class housing in the hope that they could bring civilizing influences to bear on the barbaric poor. Such work though led to wider issues about poverty and the urban environment as a whole.[17] Women were just as interested in these issues but their role in exploring the quality of the physical environment was destined to be submerged for reasons which had much to do with gender and politics.

When the town planning movement gained momentum, it was male dominated. Thomas Coglan Horsfall, Ebenezer Howard, Raymond Unwin and Patrick Geddes were the leaders among the men who are credited with formulating a distinctly British component in the town planning movement,[18] a movement that was rapidly becoming international as the pace of urbanization increased in the industrializing world. Very few women trained as architects and none as planners before the First World War. Yet planners' perceptions of an ideal, or even a reasonably tolerable, urban environment were not neutral, professional matters. They were based on social and cultural value judgements, heavily influenced by gender. This was the formative period for modern town planning ideology, in which social and cultural values were strongly

---

[15] R.N. Soffer, *Ethics and Society in England: The Revolution in the Social Sciences 1870–1914* (Berkeley, 1978); Eileen Yeo, *The Contest for Social Science: Relations and Representations of Gender and Class*, (London, 1996).

[16] A. Wohl, *The Eternal Slum: Housing and Social Policy in Victorian London* (London, 1977).

[17] Evident in the *Report of the Interdepartmental Committee on the Physical Deterioration of the Working Classes 1904* (HMSO).

[18] A. Sutcliffe, *Towards the Planned City: Germany, Britain, the United States and France, 1780–1914* (Oxford, 1981).

articulated. There was much voluntary effort from men and women seeking to improve the social condition of cities. From Octavia Hill's experiments in working-class housing in Marylebone to the formation of pressure groups at the turn of the century such as the Garden City Association, which lobbied for state action on environmental planning, all had an underlying common objective which united them. Yet when the Town Planning Institute was formed in 1913, its founder members were drawn exclusively from architects, engineers and surveyors with the single exception of Patrick Geddes, who called himself a sociologist and town planner.

In Britain, the process of professionalization took place in a context that was distinctly different in comparison with these developments in other parts of Europe. In Germany, powerful mayors gathered experts from all walks of life to work on urban development. In France, networks of municipal officers and government officials developed to address urban questions.[19] Nowhere were women much involved in these activities. But the British version was particularly exclusive making interdisciplinary interaction far more difficult.[20] What was perhaps most astonishing was the inclusion of Patrick Geddes as a founder member of the Town Planning Institute, a man without training as an architect or an engineer. His influence rested on the fact that 'professional' town planners realized that their raw material involved people, society, the nature of cities, subjects which their earlier training had not encompassed. Raymond Unwin, arguably the most important figure in British town planning before the Second World War,[21] had brought Geddes to the First International Town Planning Conference in London in 1910 and given him the task of organizing the Town Planning Exhibition for this reason. Geddes's idiosyncratic museum in Edinburgh, the Outlook Tower, had been devoted to mapping the evolution of cities and society, and architects were responsive to his visual approach.[22] As Raymond Unwin moved to the Local Government Board to promote town planning and worked with

---

[19] B. Ladd, *Urban Planning and Civic Order in Germany 1860–1914* (Harvard and London, 1990), pp. 38–48; S. Magri and C. Topolov, 'L'habitat du salarié moderne en France, Grande-Bretagne, Italie et aux Etats-Unis 1910–1925', in Y. Cohen and R. Baudouï (eds), *Les Chantiers de la Paix Sociale (1900–1940)* (Fontenay/Saint Cloud, pp. 223–54.

[20] G. Cherry, *The Evolution of British Town Planning: A History of Town Planning in the UK during the Twentieth Century and the Royal Town Planning Institute 1914–74* (Leighton Buzzard, 1974).

[21] M. Miller, *Raymond Unwin, Garden Cities and Town Planning* (Leicester, 1992).

[22] H. E. Meller, *Patrick Geddes: Social Evolutionist and City Planner* (London, 1990), pp. 102–10.

his civil servant, George Pepler, Geddes seemed even more important in the struggle to justify their activities.

The same was true in the world of planning education. The only department of Civic Design in the country at the University of Liverpool, founded by William Lever in 1908, was facing the challenge of moving from garden city ideals to the whole question of urban and regional development. During the First World War, the incumbent of the Chair was Patrick Abercrombie, who had become increasingly receptive to Geddes's ideas. He had entered the competition set up by Geddes to produce the best plan for the regeneration of Dublin and had been awarded the prize.[23] After the war, Abercrombie joined forces with Pepler to promote the idea of regional development, as proposed by Geddes, and the role planners could play in future economic as well as social development. Geddes was thus a useful figure to many of the powerful players in the establishment of British planning practice. He had even given them the basic framework for training a professional planner. His mantra, 'Survey, Diagnosis, Plan', became the means for uniting the practical activity of planning with the context of the environment. Geddes, of course, offered his own definition of survey techniques that were not dependent on social and economic data.[24] He believed in a biological approach in which surveyors and surveyed would together achieve an understanding of evolutionary social development, enlightened by a kind of *élan vital*.[25] For his architect-planner followers, the haziness of his concepts could be accommodated. The important thing was to establish their profession. Town planning in Britain was thus an exclusive activity, dominated in its early days by architects (a resolutely male dominated profession) which drew disproportionately on the sociological ideas of Patrick Geddes and was largely indifferent to the experience of voluntary efforts to improve the social condition of cities over the last half century. Women's responses particularly were ignored.

---

[23] See M.J. Bannon, 'Dublin Town Planning Competition: Ashbee and Chettle's "New Dublin – A Study in Civics"', *Planning Perspectives*, 14(2) (1999), pp. 145–62.

[24] Patrick Geddes, 'Civics as Applied Sociology' (1905), reprinted in H.E. Meller (ed.), *The Ideal City* (Leicester, 1979), pp. 75–90.

[25] This concept was promoted by the 'vital' biologists led by Henri Bergson. For a sympathetic discussion of Bergson's ideas see H.J. Muller, *Science and Criticism: The Humanistic Tradition in Contemporary Thought* (New Haven: Yale University Press, 1964), pp. 246–50.

Before statutory planning

Before it is possible to assess women's responses to the late Victorian city, however, it is necessary to expunge from our consciousness any twentieth-century notions on town planning. It is important to remember that 'town planning' as a discrete activity was not given that term until 1908 when the lobby for greater control over the development of new urban areas made the term necessary. It was a demonstration of the fact that the British had not developed a system of the orderly extension of cities. The Germans, with better municipal administration, had already got many regulations in place governing the development of town extensions. In the late Victorian period, German towns were growing very fast and national competitions were held to produce the best plans for future development.[26] What to do about the physical environment of the city centre was another matter. National capital cities such as London, Vienna and Paris had already pioneered new ways of restructuring central areas.[27] What all these developments lacked, however, was any concern about the people who were displaced by such activities. There was a divorce between an appreciation of the quality of the physical environment and the social needs of the majority of people who lived in cities. In the gender divide which was inherent in all voluntary work, it was the latter concern which dominated women's contribution.

In provincial British cities, without the benefit of German municipal administration, the social problems of the inner city had to be addressed by voluntary efforts if they were to be addressed at all. Because such effort was voluntary, piecemeal and ill-funded, there was no question of wholesale redevelopment, except in those cities, such as Edinburgh and Birmingham, where public health conditions demanded greater effort from the local authorities. The Chambers Improvement Scheme for Edinburgh was given approval for action by Special Act of Parliament in 1867 and was to continue until 1883. It was to provide the context for Geddes to develop his special approach to the conservation and regeneration of the historic urban fabric of the Old City of Edinburgh. In Birmingham, Joseph Chamberlain instituted the famous slum clearance scheme in 1872 which was to create the major thoroughfare of Corporation Street right through the middle of some of the city's most delapidated areas of working-class housing. The 1875 Public Health Act made

---

[26] By the early twentieth century, these had become part of the normal planning process: Ladd, *Urban Planning*, 227–33.

[27] T. Hall, *Planning Europe's Capital Cities: Aspects of Nineteenth-century Urban Development* (London, 1997).

all local authorities responsible for the clearance of the worst public health hazards, including insanitary housing and all boroughs of more than 100 000 inhabitants were obliged to appoint a Medical Officer of Health. These developments, far from discouraging the activities of volunteers, in fact had the opposite effect. By making some parts of cities slightly healthier, it enabled volunteers, especially fairly robust women, to move around and to work in inner city areas with less danger to their own health.[28]

What occurred in Britain was a unique experiment in exploring ways of making the inner city less of a bleak, unhealthy and depraved environment for its inhabitants. The work was done either individually or through organizations (mostly socio-religious). Women volunteers put their minds on to the problems of adapting to living in a modern city, albeit in a manner that was sometimes sensitive but also sometimes arrogant, since this was a class-based activity with middle-class women working for the urban poor. The approach was the direct opposite of national and local improvement schemes which started out to demolish and reconstruct the physical environment. The volunteers began with the people and sought ways of making their lives better by minor improvements in the circumstances of their daily life. They were exploring the social consequences of urban change in the absence of any other means of finding out how people interact with their environment, given that the social sciences especially in Britain had not even begun to address the subject.[29] As Britain was the prototype of modern urban civilization, their efforts provided valuable insights.

Women, voluntary work and the modern city

To articulate an analysis of women's role in the city necessitates bringing together the historiography of urban history with women's history. In some respects, a gendered response to the social problems found in cities was less difficult in the late Victorian period than either before or since. By the third quarter of the century, the age of great cities was over and

---

[28] Edward Denison, pioneer voluntary charity worker in London's East End in 1867, supported the 'new' scientific principles which were to inform the work of the Charity Organisation Society set up in 1869. Denison himself, though, died of typhoid fever, caught while living in the East End.
[29] P. Abrams, *The Origins of British Sociology: 1834–1914* (Chicago, 1968).

suburbanization released the pressure of densities for some.³⁰ Better local administration had also made most cities physically safer in medical terms. By the Edwardian era, government investigations, such as the 1904 Interdepartmental Committee Report on the Physical Deterioration of the Working Classes and the great Royal Commission on the Poor Laws 1905–9, demonstrated the inadequacies of social work in the face of poverty and ill health. Such official interest helped to dry up the creativity of the volunteers in their search for new solutions to old problems.³¹ By the First World War, those at the forefront of defining ideas of public duty and citizenship for women who had, themselves, been nurtured in the philanthropic tradition, now sought public office and struggled to find a woman's role within the mainstream of male-dominated politics.³² Yet in the preceding quarter of a century, things had been different. There had been a hope that if enough women could be persuaded to undertake voluntary work, whole neighbourhoods of the inner city could be uplifted.³³

The social and cultural context within which the women volunteers worked was vital. Women, of course, did not work apart from men. Although they were to number a vast army, still most of the positions of influence in their organizations were taken by men. There was, however, the gradual development of gendered responses. Gerda Lerner wrote a couple of decades ago about how philanthropic work could affect the women who undertook it. She suggested that the experience could be a learning one and one in which a feminist consciousness is developed.³⁴ This does not mean that women philanthropists in cities were 'feminists'. Many most emphatically were not. Yet this kind of work, which was outside the norms of their own home lives, made them think all the harder about the special qualities women might bring to addressing particular problems. The work of women volunteers in the local context of their home cities very often moved, using Lerner's terminology, from being women-oriented to being women-defined. Josephine Butler

---

[30] C. Pooley, 'Patterns of the Ground: Urban Form, Residential Structure and the Social Construction of Space', in M. Daunton (ed.) *Cambridge Urban History of Britain*, vol. III: *1840–1950* (Cambridge, 2000), pp. 429–66.

[31] M. Simey (1951) *Charitable Effort in Liverpool in the Nineteenth Century* (Liverpool, 1951), pp. 143–6.

[32] Pugh, *Women and the Women's Movement*.

[33] The annual *Year-book of Social Progress 1913–14* (London, 1914), published for the first time in 1912–13, gave a confident review of the combined activities of the state and voluntary sector. There was no mention of any particular contribution made by women.

[34] G. Lerner, *The Majority Finds its Past: Placing Women in History* (Oxford, 1979), pp. 160–62.

had lamented in her preface to the volume on *Women's Work and Women's Culture* that she published in 1869, that middle-class women were experiencing a sense of loss in their perception of themselves within society. She wrote:

> The great tide of an imperfect and halting civilisation has rolled onward, and carried many triumphantly with it. But women have been left stranded, so to speak ... Their work is taken out of their hands: their place – they know not where it is. They stretch out their hands idly.[35]

But she herself, in her own work for higher education for women and in the leadership of the Ladies National Association for the repeal of the Contagious Diseases Acts, personified the first shift in consciousness. Also, by the time this work was published, the number of women who were beginning to work in the poorer areas of large cities was growing.

Over the past couple of decades, many scholars have contributed to our understanding of the significance of voluntary work of all kinds in defining gendered views on citizenship.[36] Such work forged a sense of personal and social identities, provided the context for friendships between women living in different places but promoting the same cause, or living in the same city and being involved in a range of activities. There is yet more work to be done, especially on women's networks and their exchanges of ideas and support, though June Hannam has begun to address this in her researches on the women of Bristol.[37] What is still needed, however, is more research not only into how women tested and extended the realms of a social existence determined by convention, but also how they played a part in exploring and shaping the urban environment. This has a contemporary resonance. Since the 1980s, women have been making a more concerted effort to break into the masculine worlds of architecture and town planning.[38] Yet those trying to fight their way

---

[35] J. Butler (ed.), *Women's Work and Women's Culture* (London, 1869).

[36] For example, J. Rendall (ed.) *Equal or Different: Women's Politics 1800–1914* (Oxford, 1987); M. Poovey, *Uneven Developments: The Ideological Work of Gender in Mid Victorian England* (London, 1989); J.R. Walkowitz, *City of Dreadful Delight: Narratives of Sexual Danger in late-Victorian London* (London, 1992); F. Prochaska, *Women and Philanthropy in Nineteenth Century England* (Oxford, 1980); M. Luddy, *Women in Ireland 1800–1918: A Documentary History* (Cork, 1995); P. Joyce, *Democratic Subjects: The Self and the Social in Nineteenth Century England* (Cambridge, 1994).

[37] J. Hannam, 'An Enlarged Sphere of Usefulness: The Bristol Women's Movement, c1860–1914', in M. Dresser and P. Ollerenshaw (eds), *The Making of Modern Bristol* (Tiverton, 1996).

[38] Clara Greed, *Women and Planning: Creating Gendered Realities* (London, 1994).

into the town planning profession and gain some say in the future manipulation of our physical environment find that while feminist theory is on their side, history is not.[39] There is as yet no clear historical framework for exploring women's responses to the city.

Women and the urban environment

One place to start is perhaps with the perception that women's work tended to be people centred and place specific. The women who worked in the religious missions to the poor of the 1860s and 1870s found themselves trying to make contact by offering 'womenly' support to the poor in terms of mothers' meetings, visiting homes and providing entertainments. What they discovered was that the condition of working-class housing precluded the possibility of decent living standards.[40] Housing became a central issue. The most famous example of women's response on this issue is the Hill sisters, Octavia and Miranda, who worked in London from the mid-1860s. Jane Lewis has provided us with a nuanced analysis of Octavia's work in the context of her character and beliefs and the tasks that she set herself.[41] She and her co-workers, who included members of the influential Charity Organisation Society of 1869 of which Hill was a founder member, wanted to help the poor by rehabilitating the individual. Far less attention has been paid to Miranda and the organization she founded, the Kyrle Society. This organization, named after John Kyrle, the Man of Ross who had been noted for his efforts to improve the amenities of his native town, was devoted to social and environmental improvements, the context for a better life. The Kyrle Society aimed to bring pleasure into dull lives by any means that was possible within the framework of urban conditions, limited funds and massive enthusiasm from volunteers.

The stated aims of the society, which was founded in 1876, were six. These were to decorate with mural and other paintings, carved brackets and so on, rooms used by the poor for social purposes, such as clubs, schoolrooms and mission rooms; to make gifts of pictures and flowers for the homes of the poor; to lay out gardens on any available strips of waste ground, and to encourage the cultivation of plants; to organize choirs of voluntary singers; to cooperate as far as possible with the Commons' Preservation Society in securing open spaces in poor neighbourhoods to

---

[39] Ibid., pp. 70–87.
[40] Meller, *Leisure and the Changing City*, pp. 122–205.
[41] Jane Lewis, *Women and Social Action in Victorian and Edwardian England*, (Aldershot, 1991).

be laid out as public gardens; to further any effort at abating the smoke nuisance in manufacturing districts. It was a manifesto dedicated to environmental improvement and a nurturing approach to place and people. The Kyrle Society and a sister organization, the Home Arts and Industries Association of 1884, were supported by female aristocratic philanthropists such as Lady Lovelace, who were drawn to the arts,[42] and male artists and architects interested in Arts and Crafts, including William Morris, C.R. Ashbee and Charles Voysey.[43] It was a winning combination of aristocratic social influence in conjunction with the artistic avante-garde that could be delivered by amateur female volunteers.

'Bringing gleams of sunshine into the lives of the toilers and workers' was, at one and the same time, an object of philanthropy and a critique of the ugliness of an exploited urban environment. Octavia strongly supported her sister and her own work was influenced by these ideas.[44] The houses she managed in Marylebone could be easily picked out by visitors as they were surrounded by greenery: creepers, bushes, window boxes with flowers. In environmental terms, they appeared as an astonishing sight in the midst of a sea of brick. What the Hill sisters achieved was an understanding that housing alone was not enough. The houses themselves needed to have an improved context. There was need for space: small open spaces near homes for children to play in, larger open spaces within reach of all inhabitants for recreational purposes. Octavia's contribution to the founding of the National Trust for the preservation of areas of Outstanding Beauty was itself an outstanding contribution to environmental planning. Miranda's Kyrle Society was also the epitome of women-oriented environmental activity. What is interesting is how these ideas came to be transmitted to other towns and cities in Britain.

There is only space for details from one example. In Nottingham, the Town and County Social Guild was founded in 1875 to coordinate charity work.[45] It was modelled on the Charity Organisation Society of

---

[42] Anne Anderson, 'Reconstructing Lives: A Case Study of Mary Stuart Wortley, Lady Lovelace (1848–1941)', unpublished paper. I am grateful to Anne for sharing her research findings on the Kyrle Society, which she is in the process of publishing.

[43] Morris's perception of the importance of the environment as a factor in social improvement was totally different from that of Patrick Geddes (Meller, 67–8) but he (and Ashbee) devoted considerable efforts to developing ideas of the importance of the environment to the social community. See D. Hardy, *Utopian England: Community Experiments 1900–1945* (London, 2000).

[44] Gillian Darley, *Octavia Hill* (London, 1990).

[45] Details of its aims and objectives are given in H. Meller (ed.), *Nottingham in the 1880s: A Study in Social Change* (Nottingham, 1971), pp. 22–8.

London but it divided its activities into two distinct organizations (though often the same people were engaged in both). One was the Nottingham Society for Organising Charity. The other was the Kyrle Society, designed to bring refining influences into the lives of the poor. In fact as time passed, it was the latter organization that appeared to make more impact. The depression of trade and industry in the town in the 1880s made the problems of poverty seem overwhelming. Yet the Kyrle Society's activities – competitions for flower growing, window boxes, a People's entertainment society for the encouragement of music, day trips to local beauty spots and a plethora of other activities – met with considerable success. The spin off from this was that local people became more familiar with their locality at a time when the city was growing fast. There were no statutory powers to preserve areas of outstanding natural beauty but custom acted as a strong counterweight. It was not until the 1960s that the destination of many of the Kyrle Society outings, Clifton Grove, was developed as a private housing estate.

How did all this feed into the town planning movement? The answer is muted. The four British pioneers of planning, Horsfall, Geddes, Howard and Unwin, took for granted the idea that women would support their schemes and breathe life into them.[46] Only Geddes actually articulated the importance of women's work for the environment. As a natural scientist whose first book, *The Evolution of Sex*, was to give scientific 'legitimacy' to gender differentiation, he was particularly aware of the balance of the sexes in nature. This he translated into human society in the following way. Through citizenship, women would take their place alongside men in achieving social development. Yet the sexually determined role of women was to support and complement men, offering the gift of their altruism and natural nurturing abilities.[47] In 1884, he went to London to look at the Hills' work at first hand. On his return to his own city of Edinburgh, he was a moving force behind the setting up of the Edinburgh Social Union in 1885. The model finally chosen for this was actually the Nottingham Town and County Social Guild. Geddes quickly lost interest in it when the Union became deeply concerned with the problem of housing. For him it was the total environment that mattered. In his work in Old Edinburgh, he recruited young male students to help him acquire properties and to repair and

---

[46] D. Hardy, 'Feeling a Way towards Women's Emancipation', *Town and Country Planning*, 56 (1987), pp. 153–4.

[47] J. Conway, 'Stereotypes of Femininity in a Theory of Sexual Evolution,' in M. Vicinus (ed.), *Suffer and be Still: Women in the Victorian Age* (London, 1972), pp. 140–54.

manage them. The women who came to his summer schools were given supporting roles, especially those relating to gardening. They cultivated small patches of waste ground in the Old Town, their efforts making a great visual difference to the city scene. Geddes's eldest daughter went on to become a professional landscape gardener.[48]

The pioneering work of Miranda Hill made Geddes's ideas on what ideals a woman could pursue in the city appear 'normal'. Geddes's activities in his Outlook Tower were highly idiosyncratic but the young men attracted to social work through him took his ideas elsewhere. They helped him set up his International Summer School in Paris at the World Fair of 1900. They took the material from the Outlook Tower to London for the First International Town Planning Conference exhibition in 1910. Some of them went on to more 'mainstream' philanthropic activities working in the Settlement movement in other cities. Margaret Simey in her recent autobiography writes of the large number of young men recruited to the new University College of Liverpool who came from Scotland and seemed to be inspired by Geddes' work in Edinburgh.[49] One, who had actually worked as the secretary of the Outlook Tower, T.R. Marr, went on to become the warden of the University Settlement in Ancoats, where he was responsible for a housing survey and work for environmental improvement in Manchester.[50] When Geddes went to America, he stayed at Hull House in Chicago and conversed with Jane Addams on cities, social welfare and environmental problems. Jane Addams was unusual in that she totally dominated the organization of her Settlement.[51] In Britain, women tended to keep the provincial university settlements going but usually under the direction of a male warden.

Cross-fertilization of ideas between individuals influenced by this environmental and social approach was common in different cities, given that the numbers involved in Kyrle Societies or philanthropic Settlements in each city were quite small. The key fact though, emanating from all these activities, was that the practical details of a nurturing concern for the environment still tended to fall into the female province. Such concern was not always connected to a primary interest in refining influences. There was within the Nottingham Town and County Social Guild a Ladies Sanitary Institution organizing lectures on public health and hygiene. This strand of female activity was again, in different places,

---

[48] Meller, *Patrick Geddes*, p. 14, n. 25.

[49] M. Simey, *The Disinherited Society: A Personal View of Social Responsibility in Liverpool in the Twentieth Century* (Liverpool, 1996).

[50] Biographical details of Marr in Meller, *Patrick Geddes*, p. 16, n. 31.

[51] A.F. Davis, *American Heroine: The Life and Legend of Jane Addams* (Chicago, 2000).

to lead to results concerned with the environment. In 1911, in the colonial context of Ireland, Lady Aberdeen, wife of the Viceroy and founder of the Women's National Health Association of Ireland, invited Geddes to Dublin to offer advice on social problems. The outcome was to set in motion the activities that were to lead to the articulation of modern town planning ideas, especially in the housing schemes for Dublin's poor.[52] It also led to the creation of a Housing and Town Planning Association for the whole of Ireland and a continental-style planning competition for the future development of Dublin, which provided very influential propaganda for the cause of town planning in Britain. But, of course, the competition was won by Patrick Abercrombie and his co-authors, S. Kelly and A. Kelly, and the judges were Geddes and Raymond Unwin.[53]

Town planning was effectively ruled out as a female occupation. Much of the blame for this has to rest, paradoxically, with Geddes who had been most sensitive to women's responses to the urban environment. His ideas on sex differences, promoted in his book, were enormously influential until well into the early twentieth century, when cell theory was replaced by modern embryology.[54] By the time his views on the biologically determined relationships between men and women were going out of fashion, the formative period of creativity in response to the urban environment was over. Voluntary work was giving way to state intervention and the development of the newly professional responses. Recognition of the scale of the problems of poverty and ill health and the rise of organized labour demanding a voice left women stranded once again, just as Josephine Butler had described 30 years before. The answer was to push for representation in mainstream politics. Then women-oriented activities became more focused on women and children, especially the welfare of infants and the health of wives and mothers. Before the First World War, it was the campaign to reduce infant mortality that dominated thinking about the quality of the environment,[55] after the war, it was the health of mothers in the light of high rates of maternal mortality and the exclusion of wives from medical care under the National Insurance scheme designed to help male workers.

But above all, the initiative for defining ways of improving the quality

---

[52] F.H.A. Aalen, 'The Working Class Housing Movement in Dublin, 1850–1920', in M.J. Bannon (ed.), *The Emergence of Irish Planning, 1880–1920* (Dublin, 1985), pp. 131–88.

[53] P. Abercrombie, S. and A. Kelly, *Dublin of the Future: The New Town Plan* (Liverpool and London, 1922).

[54] D. Rubinstein, *Before the Suffragettes: Women's Emancipation in the 1890s* (Brighton, 1986), Introduction.

[55] H. Jones, *Health and Society in Twentieth Century Britain* (London, 1994).

of the urban environment had moved away from piecemeal improvements of inner city areas to a vision of the modern cities of the future. Ebenezer Howard had published his monograph *Tomorrow: A Peaceful Path to Real Reform* in 1898. In 1899, the Garden City Association was formed which was to lobby for planning and garden cities up to the Second World War and beyond.[56] It was the ultimate articulation of the idea that a good environment would produce a good society. Howard had managed to combine an understanding of the fact that the further inevitable process of urbanization no longer needed to mean existing cities getting simply bigger and bigger. He developed a sound grasp of the financial implications of setting up new settlements and how these may be met. He had seen that modern technology, especially transport and communications, meant cities could be established where people wanted them. Through the ownership of the land, new cities could use increasing rateable value as the land was developed to finance the provision of civic services and amenities. The garden city was a model of the civilization of the future. The first attempt to put these ideas into practice came in 1903 with the foundation of the Letchworth Garden City Company.[57] Raymond Unwin and his partner, Barry Parker, were engaged as the architects for the project, bringing to the work their love of the British Arts and Crafts style and the idea that old settlements, such as the beautiful medieval towns of the Cotswolds, provided the best examples of socially cohesive urban design. Letchworth gave Unwin the platform on which to base his future career as Britain's leading architect-planner.[58]

The garden city idea became Britain's most influential contribution to the international town planning movement. The rejection of the sooty black industrial city of the nineteenth century and the reincarnation of a pre-industrial model, which had grown organically, in an age when the relationship between man and nature seemed more harmonious, were startling to contemporaries. It was also modern and hygienic. Unwin and Parker actually took their families and lived, for what was one of the happiest periods of their lives, next door to each other in Letchworth. Their wives and children lived in a suburban heaven, according to the social conventions of the day. Middle-class wives did not do paid work.

---

[56] D. Hardy, *From Garden Cities to New Towns: Campaigning for Town and Country Planning 1899–1946* (London, 1991).

[57] R. Beevers, *The Garden City Utopia: A Critical Biography of Ebenezer Howard* (London, 1988); M. Miller, *Letchworth: The First Garden City* (Chichester, 1989).

[58] F. Jackson, *Sir Raymond Unwin: Architect, Planner and Visionary* (London, 1985).

Children needed large gardens and a natural environment in which to play. Howard's garden city ideal was defined by class and gender though he wanted to bring his middle-class benefits to all. Howard also wanted the support of women. The Garden City Association made three attempts to recruit them by creating a Women's League.[59] The first was in 1903 but it soon failed. The second was in 1907. That also failed. The third was in 1920, when the second garden city at Welwyn had been started after the First World War. The last effort to relaunch the Women's League coincided with the 1920 Ideal Home Exhibition which had played host to a conference designed to highlight the importance of 'women's perspective in the great housing debate'.[60] This time the Women's Section of the Association concentrated especially on sanitary reform in rural areas and the work of women as property managers. However, by 1923 this focus had narrowed to labour-saving devices in the home and by 1924 the women's organization had collapsed again. Women had little room for initiative in a model that put women, children and the family first under a benign patriarchy.

Women, citizenship and planning after the First World War

The garden city experiment, however influential in terms of style and design, was very small. Just two garden cities were built, Letchworth and Welwyn Garden City (founded in 1919). The old established cities and their social problems were of far more significance. Margaret Simey, in her autobiography, wrote about a change she perceived in the quality of concern over the social condition of the poor in Liverpool in the early twentieth century. She writes, 'the turn of the century saw the unique coming together in Liverpool of the moral commitment of the merchant community, the idealism of the young University and the passion of women's demand for equal citizenship'.[61] This articulation of concern was not confined to Liverpool. It was to be found in many large cities and it fed into national politics. This was the transitional period when the balance between the state and the voluntary sector was changing in favour of the former. After the First World War, the transformation was complete. Jane Lewis quotes the words of Elizabeth Macadam, a volunteer who had begun her work in the settlement movement and become

---

[59] Meryl Aldridge, 'Garden Cities: The Disappearing "Woman Question"', in S. Zimmermann (ed.), *Urban Space and Indentity in the European City 1890–1930s* (Budapest, 1995), Working Paper Series 3, pp. 13–23.

[60] Hardy, *From Garden Cities to New Towns*, p. 163.

[61] Simey, *The Disinherited Society*, p. 23

involved during the war in a government initiative to investigate social work training. Macadam wrote of a 'new partnership' between the voluntary sector and the state, where voluntary work was seen as complementary and supplementary to that of the state.[62]

Lewis's argument is that with this change, the influence of women on the development of social work became marginalized. Before, with their commitment to citizenship, women could view their voluntary work as a mutually uplifting work for themselves and the recipients of their care. They were working for social change and improvement. State provision of social welfare, however, did not have these kinds of objectives. The professionalization of social work led to greater emphasis on case work and a perception that the role of the social worker was to provide expert aid to the maladjusted.[63] For women who had worked to improve the urban environment, however, this diminution in the scope of their work did not seem so obvious. This was partly because state policy on housing and slum clearance was never properly funded, and partly because their focus on the environment rather than the individual made their work of continuing importance. There was still room for voluntary effort despite the mounting volume of regulations controlling the quality of new buildings and the condition of the old. During the First World War, the Tudor Walters Report on the provision of housing for the working classes, commissioned by the Ministry of Reconstruction, had produced guidelines of a very high standard which remained intact, with minor modifications, up to the Second World War. These had been drawn up by Raymond Unwin, as town planning advisor on the Local Government Board, and were based on his belief in low-density cottage style development. They were accepted as ideal by all interested in housing reform.

When the London County Council began to build its first major estates of municipal housing in the early 1920s, these were located in the countryside, in such places as Becontree, Bellingham, Castelnau and Roehampton. People from the East End of London were decanted out to the new estates without any preparation for the changes they would find in everyday living.[64] It was just assumed that this was the best kind of environment for the future. As Birmingham, then Manchester and other large towns followed London's lead, women volunteers in the old

---

[62] Jane Lewis, *The Voluntary Sector, the State and Social Work in Britain: The Organisation Society/Family Welfare Association since 1869* (Aldershot,1995), p. 213.

[63] Ibid., quoting the words of R.M. MacIver, pp. 213–4.

[64] A. Rubinstein et al., (eds), *Just Like the Country: Memories of London Families who settled the New Cottage Estates 1919–39*, (London, 1991).

inner city settlements found a new role. They were asked to set up their activities on the new estates to offer help to those with the same kind of social problems they had formerly experienced in the inner city.[65] Poverty, unemployment and ill health did not miraculously disappear with the new environment and there were additional problems of loneliness and isolation, distance from amenities and coping with the hazards of living in what were often building sites. The volunteers found plenty of work to do.

Meanwhile, in all the major cities, there were still slums and overcrowding. Women as volunteers, supplemented by a very small sprinkling of newly professional women, could continue to think creatively about environmental improvements. In the inter-war period, the challenge now was not just to 'humanize' the urban environment but also to 'modernize' it. Local and central government were slow to come to grips with this issue. In London, where inner city problems could not be solved by town extension or even new 'cottage' estates, there was an enmeshing of the work of lady volunteers with the new professional women in productive partnerships. A key figure here is Elizabeth Denby and her work for housing improvements in London, culminating in the New Housing for Old campaign of the 1930s and her collaboration with modern architects such as Maxwell Fry to design new model housing incorporating modern best practice.[66] She was a professional, having gained her certificate in Social Science from the London School of Economics. Her first paid work, though, was as Secretary to the Kensington Council of Social Service, the umbrella organization responsible for voluntary work in the area, which she joined in 1923. Throughout London, there were a number of Housing Associations which were supported by volunteers but which also drew on the paid services of professional women. The St Pancras Housing Improvement Society, set up in Somers Town in 1924, was to hire two of the first women chartered surveyors, Irene Barclay and Eileen Perry.[67] Like the first female medical doctors, women in new professions did not always find it easy to get jobs.

The role of housing and town planning volunteer lobbyists remained

---

[65] Meller, *European Cities*, p. 241.

[66] E. Darling, '"Enriching and Enlarging the Whole Sphere of Human Activities": The Work of the Voluntary Sector in Housing Reform in Inter-war Britain', in C. Lawrence and A.-K. Mayer *Regenerating England: Science, Medicine and Culture in Inter-war Britain* (Amsterdam, 2000), pp. 149–178.

[67] C. Greed, *Surveying Sisters: Women in a Traditional Male Profession* (London, 1991), pp. 61–2. Irene Barclay (Kingsley Martin's sister) wrote an account of her work in I. Barclay, *People need Roots: The Story of the St Pancras Housing Association* (London, 1976).

strong throughout the inter-war period. The Garden Cities and Town Planning Association (GCTPA), under its vigorous secretary, F.J. Osborn, gained a new impetus.[68] In 1928, the GCTPA set up a meeting at the Magdalen College Mission in Somers Town to address the problem of slum housing. It was a coming together of old established volunteer organizations on an old issue, bad housing, which had been made worse by changing land use in inner city areas. As homes were destroyed to make way for shops, offices, new transport systems and so on, the problem of overcrowding of what housing remained became worse. This group of lobbyists helped to make the Minority Labour Government of 1929–31 pass the Greenwood Housing Act of 1930, encouraging local authorities to make greater efforts to build more public housing mostly on greenfield sites. Meanwhile Elizabeth Denby was focusing her considerable energies in another direction. She wanted to institute a new wave of regeneration of housing and building in the inner city itself. Between 1931 and 1938, five exhibitions devoted to New Homes for Old were organized, and had a wide impact on current opinion. The first of these was almost entirely Denby's work as she was chair of the exhibition committee.[69] It was a final flowering of a gendered response to housing in the urban environment which drew on women's work of the previous half century.

Elizabeth Darling has used her study of Denby[70] to highlight the ways in which this was the case. She outlines the four main sections of the first exhibition, all curated or designed by women. The first was devoted to giving a visual image of the slum. It was curated by Avice Trench, a member of Manchester and Salford Better Housing Council, and contained a 'Chamber of Horrors' contributed by the St Pancras Improvement Society. Graphs and charts demonstrated the connection between bad housing and ill health. The main section of the exhibition was the work of Denby herself. It focused on new building and the model flat. Denby's message was twofold. While the LCC 'cottage estates' were

---

[68] M. Hebbert, 'Frederic Osborn 1885–1978', in G. Cherry (ed.), *Pioneers in British Planning* (London,1981).

[69] Another interesting link in the volunteer housing and town planning world was provided by Lady Pentland who was a member of the committee. Her husband had been a resident of Toynbee Hall under Canon S. Barnett and was heavily involved in setting up the London Playing Fields Society. It was Lady Pentland's mother, Lady Aberdeen, who invited Patrick Geddes to Dublin in 1911 and Lady Pentland's husband, when Governor of the Madras States, who invited him to take the Cities and Town Planning Exhibition to India in 1914. Meller, *Patrick Geddes*, p. 199, n. 95, n. 96.

[70] Elizabeth Darling, 'The Life and Work of Elizabeth Denby', Ph.D. thesis.

healthy and beautiful, not all could live there, the problems of inner city living needed addressing. Second, there was no reason why local authorities should not give thought to the practicalities of social life in an inner city flat alongside the actual business of building model housing. There needed to be verandahs, playgrounds, gardens, community halls, nursery schools and so on to encourage a 'happy home life'. Drawing on examples from Germany, Austria and Sweden, Denby showed how, with forethought and planning, flat living could be made comfortable, convenient and low cost, with modern heating and cooking facilities and built-in furniture.

To reinforce this message another section of the exhibition displayed a model flat designed by two women architects, Jane Fletcher and Alison Shepherd. It was for a family of seven, had a modern kitchen and bathroom and built-in furniture. The question of where these flats should be located was not overlooked. The fourth section was devoted to town planning. This was the work of Jocelyn Abrams, the first woman member of the Town Planning Institute, who also had strong connections with Fulham Housing Association, and later the Housing Centre.[71] Her message, though, was the standard one of the town planning lobbyists: the preservation of the countryside and the improvement of the city environment must be accomplished alongside the development of new homes. The whole exhibition, and subsequent ones, which from 1932 were held within the national Building Trades Exhibition in Olympia, caused a considerable public stir and kept the slum issue politically alive. They also led to the setting up of the Housing Centre in 1934 as a coordinating propaganda and information centre and, in 1935, to the creation of the National Federation of Housing Societies to deal with the practical side of voluntary housing work. The issue of housing and the long history of charitable effort by women in this sector had given women a platform to air their views. But, as in the case of social work, women's influence on these matters was in inverse proportion to the activities of the state. Greater state effort marginalized their efforts after the Second World War.

In the case of the actual activity of town planning, women had barely had a chance to offer a gendered response. Jocelyn Abrams may have been able to gain membership of the Town Planning Institute, but the actual practice of town planning, where it was instituted, had, from the start, been in the hands of public sector local authorities who did not employ women for this work. In the voluntary sector, the Garden Cities and Town Planning Association had failed to attract women to support

---

[71] Darling, 'Enriching and Enlarging', p. 162.

its Women's League. Only in one area had the pioneer planners offered women an opportunity. This was in survey work, which was considered to be a basic plank in the planner's education and practice. In some ways, this was not a new idea. Women had played a useful role in the collection of data in Charles Booth's ground-breaking survey of the life and labour of the people of London, carried out in the 1880s and particularly concerned with levels of poverty.[72] Patrick Geddes's idea of the kind of survey appropriate for planning practice required even more dedication. He did not try to buttress his results with statistics. Geddes saw poverty in biological, not monetary terms. People without space, without gardens, without privacy, without civic institutions were, in his eyes, poor. So the purpose of Geddesian survey work was twofold. First, a geographical, economic and social survey was required to explore the use of space and local resources. Second, however, there were also issues of cultural evolution, the special nature of each locality and the need to build on the best of the past to achieve good results for the future and further social development.[73]

In practice, Geddes's survey techniques were thus vague and required a passionate commitment on the part of volunteers to undertake them. Women were ideally suited to this task. Le Play House, the sociological voluntary society set up to encourage survey work had as its secretary Margaret Tatton, who spent her time organizing 'survey' holiday tours for members each summer.[74] For women interested in their local region, and in the case of elementary school teachers now encouraged to teach the natural sciences, survey work provided a way into these subjects. The need for this work was obvious. There was little systematic charting of local history, economic activities and social change, and local flora and fauna. The Ordnance Survey maps so popular with inter-war hikers and ramblers provided a skeleton of information. Yet human and regional geography was still an infant science.[75] Geddes' use of survey for planning work, however, did attract two influential women who went on

---

[72] Beatrice Webb chose the profession of social investigator as one appropriate for a woman of her status and skills: B. Webb *My Apprenticeship* (Harmondsworth, 1938), p. 197.

[73] P. Geddes, 'Civics as Applied Sociology, Part I', *Sociological Papers 1904* (London, 1905); P. Geddes, 'Civics as Applied Sociology, Part II', *Sociological Papers 1905* (London, 1906).

[74] Meller, *Patrick Geddes*, pp. 307–8.

[75] Dr Marion Newbigin wrote a paper on regional surveys in 1913 in which she suggests that the idea of regional surveys based on the Ordnance Survey map was put forward by H.R. Hill in 1896, building on even earlier efforts of members of the Royal Geographical Society: M. Newbigin, 'Geography in Scotland since 1889', *Scottish Geographical Magazine*, XXIX (1913), pp. 477–8.

to become professionals. Jacqueline Tyrwhitt and Ruth Glass in very different ways were to make survey work the keystone of their response to the city. Jacqueline Tyrwhitt was interested in a holistic approach to planning, was a firm believer in the efficacy of Geddes' ideas and became, after the Second World War, an influential lecturer at the Architectural Association.[76] There she trained returning ex-servicemen in the skills of planning, creating the workforce to man the new national system of town and country planning being set up by Attlee's reforming Labour Government. She inspired the generation of post-war planners with the idea that the actions of a professional planner were survey, diagnosis and plan. It was just that in the post-war world, there was no time and money for the kind of 'blanket' survey activities demanded by Geddes.

Ruth Glass's approach to planning was that of the social scientist. She went, as a social science graduate and member of the Association for Planning and Regional Reconstruction, to work with Max Lock, the architect planner, on his commissioned project to produce a plan for Middlesbrough and its region. This was one of the most publicized instances of a local authority commissioning such work. Lock collected a team of experts (three out of the four town planners and architects he appointed were women) and Glass was given responsibility for exploring the sociological perspective. Jacqueline Tyrwhitt was appointed to carry out a comprehensive social survey and investigation. Glass's brief was to study local social structures, to ascertain the desires of residents and to consider the outcomes of possible planning decisions. Her work was given equal status to that of the planner architects. She carried it out in a thoroughly professional manner, analysing statistical data using methods developed by social scientists in the 1930s and conducting many in-depth interviews with citizens from every walk of life.[77] The Middlesbrough experiment was not copied elsewhere and later Glass angrily blamed this specifically on the damage done by Patrick Geddes with his woolly and amateurish ideas on survey techniques and, more generally, the British lack of interest in urban life and culture.[78] Neither Tyrwhitt nor Glass saw themselves as offering a 'gendered' response to cities. They worked with and alongside men but shared a passionate commitment to a 'people'-

---

[76] Much later she went on to become fascinated by the ideas of C. Doxiadis and edited a book of extracts on a holistic approach to planning: G. Bell and J. Tyrwhitt (eds), *Human Identity in the Urban Environment* (Harmondsworth, 1972).

[77] M. Lock, *The County Borough of Middlesbrough Survey and Plan* (Middlesbrough, 1946).

[78] Ruth Glass became an academic urban sociologist and strongly expressed her views on social surveys in R. Glass, 'Urban Sociology in Great Britain: A Trend Report', *Current Sociology*, IV (1955).

centred approach to planning. It was this approach, however, that fell victim to increasing state interference in planning activities. It was sustained by a group of volunteers who formed the Max Lock Centre for the encouragement of a people-centred planning practice.[79]

By the end of the Second World War, a gendered response to cities and the urban environment was impossible even to imagine. As professionals took over in housing and town planning, there was a tacit assumption that if women wanted to work in these fields, they had only to qualify. The fact that there were few women in senior or decision-making roles did not seem to matter. It was the end of an era when women had believed that they had a special perspective to offer on the challenge of improving the quality of the urban environment for all. It had been the voluntary sector that had largely sustained women's influence in activities in this area. Over the period 1870 to the Second World War, women volunteers had flourished because of the context in which they worked. The concept of citizenship had made the city where they lived a prime target for their attention. This had been strengthened by the British class structure which gave middle-class women the confidence to tackle the problems of urban life as a means of helping the poor. Educated women (almost totally from the ranks of the middle classes) similarly felt a need to ally their newly developed skills and knowledge to a gender specific response to the city.

This influenced especially the first generation of female professionals such as Elizabeth Denby and the causes for which they worked.[80] They had continued to flourish in the inter-war period as state action in the provision of housing and the development of town planning was always tardy. After the Second World War, there was a substantial change. State government began to work much more closely with local government in the provision of housing and town planning, and special concerns about specific localities and particular people were subsumed in broader issues of environmental policy and national targets.[81] Yet in the previous

---

[79] This is currently located at the University of Westminster.

[80] Denby worked alongside Maxwell Fry, architect and planner, to produce housing schemes such as Kensal House in 1937. The project was overseen by a committee of six. Denby was the only woman and non-architect. Her partnership with Fry was fruitful since she provided the ideas about community development and the requirements of an ideal housing project and Fry gave form to her ideas. Darling, 'Enriching and Enlarging', pp. 165–71.

[81] Feminist planners have called for a more inclusive approach to planning history: L. Sandercock (ed.), *Making the Invisible Visible: A Multicultural Planning History* (Berkeley and Los Angeles, 1998). This collection of essays has three major themes: all planning history of the past has focused on Great Men and the professionalization of planning; modernism is only suitable for the kind of power

half century many women in large cities all over Britain had had a chance to make a difference in some ways to the way people lived in cities and many of them had taken it. For a while, a gendered response to urban living, urban culture and the quality of civilization had been given a chance to exist.

---

structures espoused by nation states and rampant capitalism and should be rejected; and, finally, there is a need to champion the civil rights of citizens excluded from these power structures. This definitely includes women with an interest in the quality of the urban environment.

CHAPTER ELEVEN

Citizenship, civil society and quality of life: Sutton Model Dwellings Estates 1919–39

Patricia L. Garside

In his contribution to Jim Dyos' *Study of Urban History*, David Reeder emphasized the importance of comparative studies in understanding the 'theatre of suburbs' with their complex, varied social and physical development.[1] Mindful of these recommendations, this chapter will set out a broad basis for evaluating life on new working-class housing estates during the 1920s and 1930s. It avoids considering local authority estates in isolation and compares them with other model housing estates.[2] It views housing estates as one of the 'variety of social spaces' thrown up by urbanism and inviting the formation of associations and associational cultures.[3] Estates offered their inhabitants a physically and socially distinct locality, and a new domain in which to participate in local and public affairs. At the time, there was an expectation that the choice and self-direction available to residents would provide a clear basis for the development of new relations between individuals and society – a dwelling place 'free of the tyranny of both cousins and kings'.[4]

This chapter uses concepts of citizenship, civil society and quality of life to explore the links between individuals, their localities and society at large. These issues underpinned debates about the impact of urbanization and of democratization in nineteenth-century Britain. In the twentieth

---

[1] David Reeder, '"A Theatre of Suburbs": Some Patterns of Development in West London, 1801–1911', in H.J. Dyos (ed.), *The Study of Urban History* (London, 1968), pp. 253–79.

[2] In her latest book, *Council Housing and Culture* (London, 2001, p. 4), Alison Ravetz comments on the exaggerations and misinterpretations that have arisen because council housing is almost always looked at in isolation from other parts of the housing system and housing stock.

[3] R.J. Morris, 'Civil Society and the Nature of Urbanism: Britain 1750–1850', *Urban History*, 25 (1998), p. 292.

[4] Ernst Gellner cited in Morris, 'Civil Society', p. 290.

century, anxieties about consumerism and 'mass society' were expressed at the same time as political and social rights were being extended to the working class. From this perspective, it seemed that greater personal involvement in the market place, on the one hand, and the growth of state intervention, on the other, would erode associational life. Consequently, the non-market, non-state activities of civil society would be lost.

Olechnowicz has concluded that in the inter-war years, anxieties generated by the enfranchisement of the masses came to focus on the life of local authority housing estates. Studying initially the London County Council's estate at Becontree and subsequently Manchester City Council's Wythenshawe, Olechnowicz has argued that contemporaries came to judge these estates as civic failures.[5] Above all, this was because they did not meet the high aspirations set for them. They were deemed to be incapable of developing the necessary apparatus of 'citizenship' – a viable and responsible community life, with independent associations dedicated to public affairs and social improvement.

In this chapter, my aim is to explore and enrich arguments about citizenship, civil society and quality of life in the inter-war period by comparing the reputation of local authority estates with that of a different model – the housing schemes provided across England by the Sutton (Model) Dwellings Trust.[6] After 1919, the Sutton Trust became the largest but least known housing trust in England, building estates not only in London but also in virtually all the major cities.[7] By 1939, it had provided 7816 dwellings on estates from Newcastle upon Tyne in the north-east to Plymouth in the south-west. Social life on Sutton model estates contrasted very strongly with that on local authority estates. Most importantly, the vitality of their communal life was based on the trust's low key, non-political and non-sectarian principles.

How civil society flourished on Sutton estates and yet received little recognition are the main themes of this chapter. The explanation that will be offered is that it is possible to encourage social responsibility

---

[5] Andrezej Olechnowicz, *Working Class Housing in England between the Wars: The Becontree Estate* (Oxford, 1997) and Olechnowicz, 'Civic Leadership and Education for Democracy: The Simons and the Wythenshawe Estate', in Mark Clapson (ed.), 'Planning, Politics and Housing in Britain', *Contemporary British History* (Special Issue), 14 (2000), pp. 3–27.

[6] Between its foundation on the death of William Sutton in 1900 and 1927, the trust was known as the Sutton Model Dwellings Trust. The word 'model' was dropped in 1927 and it became the Sutton Dwellings Trust. This name was kept until 1973 when the name William Sutton Trust was adopted.

[7] See P.L. Garside, *The Conduct of Philanthropy: The William Sutton Trust 1900–2000* (London, 2000).

'from outside' provided that the organization concerned is experienced by those involved as efficient and trustworthy. Furthermore, in contrast to efforts on local authority estates, the success of the Sutton estates was built on modest goals in sympathy with tenants' actual experience and their own social and personal practices. Despite this, Sutton's achievements as a model for building associational life were not recognized and it can be argued that this had costly consequences for England's urban fabric. Their invisibility resulted from shifts in the balance of power between central government, local authorities and the voluntary sector during the inter-war period. Local authorities came to be presented as the sole agencies capable of improving worn out towns and cities. The primacy ascribed to local authorities undermined the valuation of Sutton's sociable and familial civil society. Subsequently, the physical damage caused to major towns during the Second World War strengthened the commitment to local authority planning and reconstruction, ensuring that the role of the Sutton Model Dwellings Estates remained unrecognized for most of the twentieth century.[8]

I shall begin by considering how concepts of citizenship and civil society were discussed and deployed in the inter-war period. Conclusions drawn at the time about the working class in general, and about estates like Becontree and Wythenshawe in particular, are compared with evidence from estates provided by the Sutton (Model) Dwellings Trust. In this discussion, I draw on recent social and political theory to illustrate the differences between the *statist* approach of large local authorities and the *associationalist* approach of the Sutton Dwellings Trust. Inter-war Britain, in common with modern developing and ex-communist countries, confronted the issue of whether democratic society can best be built by promoting, or by overriding, indigenous forces of social and political change.[9] It is clear that the relative value of formal and informal organizations in civil society continues to be a matter of wide international concern. Is the way forward to harness individuals to a grand democratic vision through active involvement in formal associations, or should the focus be on more modest goals that enable civil society to grow locally?[10] Finally, the longer term significance for Britain of pursuing a *statist* approach in the inter-war period and of ascribing dominance to local authorities in housing and urban renewal is analysed. The implications for the working class in the post-war welfare state are outlined.

---

[8] Ibid., ch. 7.
[9] J. Howell, 'Making Civil Society from the Outside – Challenges for Donors', *European Journal of Developmental Research*, 12 (2000), p. 20.
[10] Ibid., p. 14.

Determining the status and significance of life on working-class housing estates

The first half of the twentieth century has been described as a period when 'the ramshackle mass' of private institutions was supplanted by a wide-ranging state apparatus, not least at the local level. José Harris has documented this shift in the locus of public life and its profound effects on the mutual relations between society and the state.[11] For much of the nineteenth century, the state was held to be of secondary importance since the 'highest sphere' of life was expressed through voluntary associations and the local community. More extensive government was unnecessary, since a 'dense network' of agencies of civil society surrounded the citizen at every level – business, work, culture, family life, religion.[12]

The granting of universal suffrage in 1918 and 1929 revived anxieties about the need to ensure social stability in England's rapidly expanding and newly enfranchised towns. Concepts of citizenship were redefined and the response to local authority housing estates in particular was saturated with Greek classical ideals and above all by the model city-state of fifth century Athens.[13] In 1928, the National Council for Social Service (NCSS), created the New Estates Community Council (NECC) with a mission to provide community centres on every large council estate. The LCC estate at Becontree had 25 000 dwellings, Watling 4000 and Manchester's Wythenshawe had 6000 by 1939. The NECC's aim was to moralize and integrate what they saw as these 'semi-detached', marginal and potentially dangerous localities. Ernest Simon, founder of Manchester's Wythenshawe, feared that the estate's working-class tenants were not fit citizens. Left to themselves, he feared, they might present a political and social threat, whereas guided and educated in citizenship, they could be brought to 'believe in and love [their] city' as Athenian citizens had done.[14] He shared the NECC's view that a new civic spirit had to be created to overcome the discontent and instability of the 'undifferentiated mass' of tenants on new local authority estates.[15] The solution that the NECC vigorously pursued was to provide a network of community associations led and supervised by 'big men'

---

[11] José Harris, 'Society and the State in Twentieth-century Britain', in F.M.L. Thompson (ed.), *Cambridge Social History of Britain 1750–1950*, vol. 3: *Social Agencies and Institutions* (Cambridge, 1990).
[12] Ibid., pp. 67–9.
[13] Olechnowicz, *Working-class Housing*, p. 169.
[14] Olechnowicz, 'Civic Leadership', p. 13.
[15] The term 'undifferentiated mass' is from Mary Parker Follett, *The New State* (1918), quoted in Olechnowicz, *Working-class Housing*, p. 170.

'well-endowed with the qualities that make for leadership'. Believing that local resources were inadequate, it was felt that both the leaders and the buildings from which their programmes would be launched needed to be provided from outside.[16]

The NECC's vision for municipal housing estates was based on the operation of community centres. The centres would provide 'a new method of politics' through promoting community associations and a visible focus for the emerging community spirit. The objective was to link estate residents with local political structures and to modify electoral boundaries where necessary to give the new area a distinct administrative unity.[17] The focus of activities was to be 'education for citizenship', concern for general welfare and participation in local affairs.[18] Both the NCSS and the NECC emphasized the importance of community activity at local level for developing the kind of citizenship they sought to foster. It was through serious involvement in their own locality that new working-class citizens would grasp their 'paramount duty' – knowledge of how government worked.

The NECC shared the view that individual participation in the formalities of citizenship was the precondition for enhancing civil society and the quality of life.[19] Based on classical Greek ideals, it looked for uniformity, conformity and a single focus in its grand plan for citizen participation. In terms of boundaries and linkages, it placed the emphasis on individuals undertaking independent involvement in formal organizations and pursuing public issues of serious concern through the mechanism of local government institutions. Set alongside actual practice on estates like Dagenham, Wythenshawe and Watling, the NECC's aims were widely judged to be a lamentable failure. Individuals neither detached themselves from their families and homes nor adopted the independent civic involvement in the way that was required. Citizenship remained passive, civic society was confined to pubs, cinemas and football syndicates and in the eyes of the NECC the quality of life was culturally and politically impoverished. While it is easy to identify practical difficulties that prevented the achievement of the desired apparatus of citizenship, Olechnowicz concludes that failure was not so much

---

[16] The idea that working-class estates lacked people with 'the qualities which make for leadership' was widespread; see Olechnowicz, 'Civic Leadership', p. 18. By 1939, 70 estate associations were affiliated to the NECC and schemes for 200 community centres were in progress: Ravetz, *Council Housing*, p. 137.

[17] Olechnowicz, *Working-class Housing*, p. 117.

[18] In 1934, Ernest Simon of Wythenshawe founded the Association for Education in Citizenship which concerned itself particularly with problems on new estates: Olechnowicz, *Working-class Housing*, p. 166–8.

[19] See below, pp. 276–8.

an empirical reality as an ideological requirement. Working-class housing estates *had* to fail, he concludes, because social and political anxieties demanded that it should be so – the notion of their failure was necessary because it 'validated a form of state and society in which the working class, if at all possible, did not count'.[20]

Olechnowicz's contention is that on large London and provincial municipal housing estates it was not the newly enfranchised working-class citizens that failed but the unrealistic model against which they were being judged. By taking the different model of the Sutton Model Dwellings Trust, however, the verdict on working-class housing estates may be altered. Certainly, it seems that even on municipal housing estates, residents *did* participate in activities, but these focused primarily on home and family. Social links were established despite extended journeys to work, long working hours, lack of local facilities and the size and strangeness of the new areas. Indeed, many local authority practices actually undermined community identity – not only did they prefer to build vast estates but within these estates some authorities pursued a policy of breaking up groups of tenants with known previous links.[21] Given circumstances that often denied tenants street lighting, postal services, shops and schools for several years after houses were occupied, 'finding one's neighbourhood' was an immediate practical issue and not a philosophical question.[22] Despite these difficulties, civil society of a prosaic, mundane kind was established on inter-war municipal estates.

Evidence from Sutton estates will now be presented to show that tenants here encountered a much more manageable and supportive environment and enjoyed productive interaction with both their landlord and one another. Civil society, albeit of a distinctly different kind from that favoured by bodies such as the NECC, flourished, enhancing both quality of life and a sophisticated sense of citizenship. The two questions to be addressed are: how was active civil society generated on Sutton estates and what is the significance of the lack of recognition for their success?

Estates of Sutton Model Dwellings 1919–39

From both a legal and an operational point of view, 1927 was a critical year for the Sutton Trust. In that year, the trust was finally released from

---

[20] Olechnowicz, *Working-class Housing*, p. 192.

[21] For the mechanisms through which local councils achieved this dispersal, see Ravetz, *Council Housing*, pp. 133–4.

[22] Ernest Barker's question, set out in his *The Value of Life* (1939), summed up the 'great problem of the day' as understood by himself and the NECC.

the control of the Court of Chancery. For the first time since its founding in 1900, the trustees were able to make independent, though not unconstrained, decisions about their activities. With all its very considerable original assets realized, as well as access to public funding and more favourable building costs, the 1930s saw the trust engaged in a greatly increased scale of building.[23] Whereas only three estates were completed in the 1920s – London (Islington), Stoke–on-Trent (Trent Vale) and Manchester (Gorton) – there were 14 in the 1930s. Only one of the 1930s estates was in London (St Quintin Park), and the rest were overwhelmingly provincial, suburban, low-rise and low density. The trust's provincial schemes ranged between 200 and 500 dwellings in size and their layout, though spacious, tended to be conventional, unspectacular, even dull. Nevertheless, the estates conveyed a village-like appearance in keeping with contemporary preferences and whilst only one in eight William Sutton houses had a parlour at this time, there is no evidence that its residents were dissatisfied. The houses were well-equipped, with separate bathrooms, basic furnishings (window blinds, dressers, larders and hanging cupboards), outside storage, hot water and drying facilities. Increasingly, electricity was installed and, above all, there was privacy inside and outside the home. These amenities, Mass Observation noted, were what many a housewife of the day asked for but few possessed.[24] Indeed, one young Sutton resident who moved to the Bradford estate in 1934 remembered:

> It was very wide, very well laid out. Everybody had a garden and there was all this grass at the front. It was really spacious, wide roads with grass verges and trees.[25]

Compared with many local authority inter-war estates, Sutton's were plain rather than progressive. They compared well, however, with contemporary Peabody and Guinness schemes and also with private suburban building. One Sutton tenant reported:

> We were envied by other people because there was a list a mile long of people wanting to come on the Estate. We were getting all the same facilities that people that had more money and buying their own houses were getting, but as I say for 5/- [25p] a week (for a three bed-roomed house).[26]

---

[23] The assets bequeathed by William Sutton to establish his housing trust were valued at more than £2 million – four times those of the Peabody Trust and ten times those of Guinness (Garside, *Conduct of Philanthropy*, p. 1).

[24] Mass Observation, *Enquiry into People's Homes* (1943), pp. xii, xvii, 141–2.

[25] G. Bridgeland (ed.), *Laisterdyke Roundabout* (Bradford, 1992), p. 124.

[26] Ibid., p. 126.

Though sometimes criticized for their lack of aesthetic appeal and observance of town planning principles, Sutton estates of the time clearly met Seebohm Rowntree's essential standards for working-class accommodation: 'a properly constructed house, with three bedrooms, a fair-sized living room, a scullery-kitchen and a bathroom'. As one tenant who was 'thrilled to bits' to move onto the trust's Birmingham estate in 1939 put it,

> You didn't keep up with the Jones' because the Jones had got no more than we'd got.[27]

Residents on Sutton estates saw their situation as a desirable one. They suffered fewer restrictions than tenants of other philanthropic trusts because of their superior amenities and the privacy they enjoyed in their everyday lives. Their need for work in or close to home was acknowledged. 'Barrow sheds' were provided for a small rental on London estates, and workshops 'for men' were built in Hull.[28] Taking in and drying washing was allowed as long as it was discreet,[29] and gardens and allotments were encouraged. Though garden shows were organized on estates to improve appearances, the attitude towards gardens was largely utilitarian. One Birmingham tenant described her father keeping chickens, a billy goat and pigeons, even though every tenant also had an allotment.[30]

The policy of Sutton trustees was to 'temper the wind to the shorn lamb' rather than to mould its tenants according to some community ideal. This very striking objective reflects the aim of the founder, William Sutton, who insisted that his 'model' estates should be free from political and religious influence. From the beginning, social reformers were refused permission to set up moral or educational centres on Sutton estates. Even more important was William Sutton's determination to house the very poorest urban dwellers. Despite the modification of his aims through the interventions of central government and the Court of Chancery, it is clear that this objective was, nevertheless, successfully

---

[27] Tenant interview, Birmingham 6. On the Birmingham estate, planned prior to the First World War but not occupied by Sutton tenants until the early 1920s, only 30 out of 230 houses had a separate parlour.

[28] The Sutton Dwellings Trust, *Annual Report 1915*; London Metropolitan Archives, Acc 2983, The William Sutton Trustees' Minutes, 2 July 1930.

[29] By contrast, the Guinness rules of tenancy explicitly forbade the taking in of washing 'from persons who are not living in the buildings' (Rule Number 4, *General Rules of Tenancy*).

[30] Tenant interview, Birmingham 9.

pursued.³¹ Consequently, Sutton tenants were drawn from among those with extremely low incomes, people who would certainly not have been accommodated on estates provided by local authorities or by other trusts.³² Despite a trend to relatively higher incomes among new tenants in the low activity period of the 1920s, during the 1930s the degree of poverty amongst Sutton tenants was severe. By this time, most tenancies were being granted to families of unskilled manual workers with young children. Unemployment was the major cause of their poverty, especially in the provinces. The average income of the trust's incoming tenants at this time fell below subsistence levels calculated by Rowntree and by Bowley.³³ Paupers were not excluded from tenancies short of total inability to pay, but true to the instructions of the founder, some rent was always required. Rebates were granted, however, even up to the point where tenants entered the workhouse. Many tenancies were short-lived and 50 per cent of new tenants left within five years. Such a turnover figure, however, is comparable with that achieved on more prosperous local authority estates including Watling and Becontree.³⁴ In general, local authority tenants could be distinguished by their 'well-to-do' financial status and by their 'mental and moral capacities'.³⁵ Sutton tenants, by contrast, stand out because of their poverty and their previous association with the kind of slum housing that was often thought to be a sign of mental and moral *in*capacity.

There is little doubt that the acquisition of a Sutton tenancy in the inter-war period severed the link between extreme poverty and seriously inadequate housing. Though enjoyment of the benefits could be short-lived, it was often young children who gained the advantages at a crucial

---

³¹ Much of the material on the characteristics of Sutton tenants in the inter-war period is derived from Garside, *Conduct of Philanthropy*, ch. 6. The findings are based on surviving tenant registers for eight provincial estates and six London estates. They contain information for 6036 tenancies – split almost equally between London and the provinces.

³² Olechnowicz, for example, concludes that 'Overall, Becontree was not for "the poor"' *Working-class Housing*, p. 45.

³³ Garside, *Conduct of Philanthropy* and 'The Impact of Philanthropy: Housing Provision and the Sutton Dwellings Trust 1900–1939', *Economic History Review* xxx (2000), pp. 742–66.

³⁴ R. Durant, 'Community and Association in a London Housing Estate', in R.E. Pahl (ed.), *Urban Sociology* (Oxford, 1968), p. 183. In 1930s Watling, Durant says, 'Almost every second of the families stayed there less than five years.' Olechnowicz calculates that in the 1920s, about 10 per cent of tenants removed annually, though this rate seems to have diminished in the 1930s *Working-class Housing*, p. 47.

³⁵ Durant, 'Community and Association', p. 162; Olechnowicz, 'Civic Leadership', p. 12.

stage in their development. In this respect, living on a Sutton estate provided a 'big leg up' to families who had previously been denied the material means to participate in civil society.[36]

Cultural provision on Sutton estates also had its own particular character. It differed not only from that of local authority estates but also from that of other housing trusts, such as Peabody and Guinness. By 1927, the Sutton trustees had been dissuaded from pursuing William Sutton's original plans for providing a wide range of cultural and welfare facilities on their estates. Previously, during the charity's sojourn in Chancery, the trustees had drawn up a number of schemes for its management. They all would have allowed for the 'fitting up' of libraries, schoolrooms, infant nurseries, laundries, baths and wash-houses, reading rooms, gymnasiums, 'and any other (necessary) ... to promote the health and moral welfare (of tenants)'. After repeated objections from the Local Government Board that local authorities were already supplying many of these facilities, the trustees agreed not to pursue their own provision.[37] In this regard, it is important to bear in mind that compared with local authority estates, amenities provided by the Sutton Trust were limited. Their residents did not rely on separately provided educational and welfare facilities. They were not isolated from existing schools, for example, and did not suffer from their absence as local authority tenants did – in some cases for several years.[38] The Sutton trustees turned their attention to other facilities '(including if thought fit) any shops or other profit earning buildings'.[39] After 1927, the trust's interest in estate facilities was marked by a robust, financially prudent and practical attitude. A good example is the decision to consider the need for shops.

Tenant access to shops for everyday needs was a primary concern of the trustees. They refused to consider sites for housing that were 'too far out for our class of tenants' especially where 'there is no good shopping centre near'.[40] The trustees would not have countenanced the situation at Watling, for instance, where shopping was 'half an hour away'.[41] Whilst the major concern was convenience for tenants, local shops also promoted sociability, neighbourliness and mutual recognition. New, purpose

---

[36] Tenant interviews, Birmingham 4 and Newcastle, Barrack Road 6. The phrase 'big leg up' belongs to the Newcastle tenant.

[37] London Metropolitan Archives, Acc 2983, 010/1–8, 26 March 1906; 27 August 1906.

[38] Durant notes, for example, that in Watling, some early inhabitants 'missed schooling for two years' ('Community and Association', p. 159).

[39] Scheme of Management 1927, Sutton Dwellings Trust, Clause 2.

[40] London Metropolitan Archives, Acc 2983, 011/1–27 Trustees' Claim for Year, 8 March 1924.

[41] Durant, 'Community and Association' p. 160.

built shops were included in four of Sutton's inter-war schemes 'for the benefit of tenants'.[42] Furthermore, the trustees restricted their shops to those providing basic services and especially food. The five shops on the St Quintin Park estate in North Kensington, for example, had to be. 'grocer, baker, confectioner, greengrocer and chemist, subject to offers received'.[43] There had to be a small return from shop rents, and this provided an additional resource for tenants as a whole. As well as these practical benefits, tenants gained from the possibility of building up credit with local shopkeepers, based on mutual confidence. Where modern, useful shops were provided on the estates themselves, tenants enjoyed the enhanced status that such novel facilities brought along neighbouring streets. Directly and indirectly, the Sutton Trust's policy on shopping built confidence – between tenants, between tenants and traders, between tenants and their neighbours beyond the estate boundaries, and between tenants and their landlord. Sutton tenants were less likely to suffer the strangeness, alienation and loneliness that afflicted tenants of large council estates while the trustees avoided being perceived as an inadequate, hostile and remote landlord.

The Sutton Trust reinforced its reputation as a sympathetic landlord through the manner in which it provided communal facilities. Later, tenants would claim that in the 1930s they 'got used to the good life' on their estates.[44] The estates were said to provide 'everything we wanted', and tenants claimed that life 'was self-contained. We didn't need to go off the estate.'[45] It is certainly true that their social opportunities were expanded by estate facilities that typically included social halls, sports pavilions, tennis courts and bowling greens. What is more important, however, is the manner in which such amenities were planned. They were not supplied as a matter of routine, nor did they reflect a philosophy on the part of the trustees about what was necessary 'for our class of tenants'. Unlike local authority community centres, they were not implanted from outside, but were self-generated by people living on the estate. Combining self-help with collective associations and sharing networks, the creation of these facilities was part of a process of adaptation to a new location. The trust itself was not acting 'philanthropically' or idealistically. The trustees offered support but not subsidy. They set clear financial limits and unlike local authorities and the NECC, they relied on local leadership and involvement. Responsibility for

---

[42] London Metropolitan Archives, Acc 2983 The William Sutton Trustees' Minutes, 6 May 1931.

[43] Ibid., 1 January 1930.

[44] 'The Golden Oldies are Content', *Yorkshire Observer*, 17 August 1969.

[45] Bridgeland, *Laisterdyke Roundabout*, p. 130.

communal activity clearly 'depended on the residents themselves being involved'.[46] Cultural 'means to be civil' were fostered by the trust but built by tenants, supported by the trust's local representative – the estate superintendent. If tenants failed to respond, this was regarded as a temporary misfortune. It was not taken to signify the ideological and moral incapacity of the working class as was the case with local authority estates.

In providing recreational and social facilities more often associated with private suburbs, the Sutton Trust's major concern was essentially financial. Though the trust frequently bore initial costs of provision, facilities were then leased to tenants. They subsequently had to pay an annual rent with agreed repayments of the principal 'until the debt was cleared'.[47] On the Leeds (Killingbeck) estate, a piece of land for a bowling green was identified but tenant members of the committee did 'all (the) work necessary'.[48] At Bradford, the trust agreed to build an institute, but only when they were convinced that 'we were making the job financially a success after 12 to 18 months'.[49] In Sheffield, the trustees agreed to provide a meeting hall, 'subject to agreement with a representative committee of tenants, superintendent and deputy superintendent to be members of the committee. Tenants to pay £15 per annum, and to be responsible for maintenance, cleaning, heating, lighting and rates.'[50] Clearly, the emphasis was consistently on financial rectitude rather than civic ideology. Nevertheless, it can be argued that the manner in which Sutton estate facilities were provided positively encouraged associational life by meshing existing informal links with new, more formal ones.

The need to generate a reliable source of income for the amenities, for example, led on a number of estates to the formation of groups of tenants who acted as 'roundsmen'. They collected individual subscriptions of a penny to support estate activities from a 'round' comprising a street or part of a street. In Bradford, one 'roundsman' remembered:

> I used personally to do mine on Sunday mornings, and it wasn't a case of just knocking on the door and taking the penny and marking a card – we used to go in, and I got used to spend probably half an hour with them and get really interested with the people. I remember

---

[46] Tenant interview, Birmingham 4.
[47] London Metropolitan Archives, The William Sutton Trustees' Minutes, 6 July 1929.
[48] Ibid., 6 July 1932.
[49] Bridgeland, *Laisterdyke Roundabout*, p. 127.
[50] London Metropolitan Archives, Acc 2983, The William Sutton Trustees' Minutes, 4 March 1931.

one old dear who'd been laid in her bed for years and years, and she used to be looking forward to when we went.[51]

The *Yorkshire Observer* called the Bradford estate tenants' association 'the most enthusiastic and progressive body of similar organisations in the city'. As well as special celebrations like the coronation of 1937 when 'over 500 children on the estate enjoyed a party in the open air' there were regular activities.

> A tennis court and a bowling green are provided; there is a swimming club and a harmonica band; an interest is taken in the welfare of all – if people are sick hospital gifts are sent along, if sickness occurs at home appliances for the sick room may be loaned to families – each year the association gives Christmas treats, and each year the children are taken to the seaside,[52]

Not all tenants' associations could claim such successes. In Leeds, the tenants' committee was said to be 'apparently composed of the worst elements of the estate' and was disbanded. It was later restored, but only after tenants' efforts in creating a bowling green showed that it was again operating 'on a proper footing'.[53] The Benwell association in Newcastle was also a disappointment to the trustees because although financially sound, members showed 'little interest apart from paying their penny a week contribution'.[54] Here, access to counter attractions in surrounding areas clearly played a part and the trustees felt that estate activities would only revive in periods of unemployment.

These examples show that the trustees' aims were not solely financial. They were looking for activities that brought tangible benefits to tenants and that linked them to one another and to the trust's representatives on the ground – the superintendents who lived on the estate with their families. Promotion of communal activity was undoubtedly seen as part of the estate superintendent's job while their families were expected to provide a model for tenants. When things were working well, besides access to facilities and activities, associations offered advice from 'the super' on dealing with everyday hazards like burst pipes, woodworm infestation, gardening problems, pensions and benefits. They arranged for cheap deliveries of beers and mineral waters, lime, manure, 'all your

---

[51] Bridgeland, *Laisterdyke Roundabout*, pp. 127–8.

[52] Ibid., pp. 128–9.

[53] The William Sutton Trust, Records of the Leeds York Road Tenants Association, File KB 82.

[54] The William Sutton Trust, Benwell Tenants' Association, Superintendent to Secretary, 23 January 1947.

gardening goods' and coal. Pianos, invalid chairs, tennis rackets and balls were made available on hire or credit terms.[55]

How far these 'trivial' (that is, personal, mundane and non-political) activities are relevant for the creation of civil society is an issue to be discussed further in the final section of this chapter. I would suggest here that the evidence of the Sutton estates shows a progressive culture developing among tenants who had previously been severely disadvantaged. Some tenants could demonstrate high levels of organizational and interpersonal skill and handle abstract, public issues with an impressive degree of sophistication. Organizers of events and competitions gained experience of handling large sums of money (the Stoke Trent Vale Association had assets of over £800 by 1946). Annual seaside visits involving hundreds of children required considerable and sustained effort over many months. When conflict arose over these kinds of social events, it was the tenants' organizing committee that had to negotiate and implement a strategy to resolve the difficulty. The Stoke (Trent Vale) Committee tackled one such problem by requiring a notice 'to be placed in the Institute notifying dance patrons that permission must be had from the M.C. to sing at the microphone on dance nights'.[56] Though the regulation of inappropriate singing at a local dance might border on the trivial, it formed part of a larger issue of the boundaries of considerate public behaviour and respect for one's fellows. It also has to be seen in its wider context. The appeal of the facilities and activities extended beyond the estate itself, and where it was considered advantageous and financially prudent, people from neighbouring areas were welcome to join in – provided they behaved appropriately. Sutton estates, therefore, unlike local authority estates, were seen as a local resource – outside organizations rented estate facilities 'at normal retail price'; people from neighbouring areas came for entertainment and sport; children 'played on the Sutton's'.[57] The Sutton Trust strategy of encouraging community responsibility had the effect of integrating their estates with their surroundings rather than setting them apart.

Through their own experiences, tenants assessed the significance of the social and public links that resulted. Some showed a shrewd sense of the boundaries of this 'civil society'. In Stoke, the tenants' association committee from the Trent Vale estate considered their role following the

---

[55] The William Sutton Trust, Records of the Leeds York Road Tenants' Association, File KB 82.

[56] London Metropolitan Archives, Acc 2983/226 Stoke on Trent (Trent Vale) Tenants Association Minutes, 27 August 1939.

[57] The William Sutton Trust Archive, File 82, Leeds York Road Tenants Association. Tenant interviews, Newcastle Barrack Road 11; Birmingham 11.

declaration of war in 1939. They recognized both their own position in local society and the boundary between their responsibilities and those of the state. They expressed the view that

> The people on the estate and the district looked upon the Sutton Committee as the leaders of social welfare ... to safeguard the people in the vicinity.[58]

Nevertheless, they concluded that in this case they should not act independently. They reasoned not from practical or financial considerations, but from constitutional principle. Civil defence, they reasoned, was properly 'a local government or national responsibility'. They therefore agreed to approach the local council and the St John's Ambulance and to seek their collaboration in setting up an Air Raid Protection Post and a first aid station on the estate. Sutton tenants as well as trustees, it seems, adhered to principles of communal and financial rectitude, and held back from grand ideals of social welfare and civic duty.

The Sutton Dwellings Trust was apparently very successful in developing formal and informal links on its estates and beyond. It did not seek to foster 'worthy' as opposed to popular communal activities, nor did it seek to exert control over tenants' activities to the extent that local authorities did.[59] Its communal activities meshed with and reinforced tenants' pre-existing social links not only on the estate but also in the surrounding neighbourhood. In both these aspects of the Sutton strategy, resident superintendents and their families played a key part. Through their very visible day-to-day presence, they acted both as role model and catalyst. It was the superintendent who regulated standards of public and private behaviour among tenants, and who in part ensured social cohesion, especially through the selection process. Though decisions on applications for tenancies were made centrally in London, the superintendent was a very important local link. They advised, visited, assessed and recommended potential tenants. One tenant whose father had been a superintendent on the trust's Bradford estate in the 1930s described her father's technique as 'cherry picking', not least in favouring tenants with the potential for promoting the

---

[58] London Metropolitan Archives, Acc 2983/226 Stoke on Trent (Trent Vale) Tenants' Association Minutes, 31 October 1939.

[59] The extent of local authority intervention is described in Ravetz, *Council Housing*, pp. 139–42. Not all went so far as Sheffield where the warden of the Manor estate's community centre 'removed the billiards and card tables and turned the recreation room into a reading and debating room, to provide "the foundations of an intellectual and self-contained community"' (p. 142).

associational life of the estate.⁶⁰ Sutton superintendents had to balance the interests of the tenants and the trust. Through their involvement in communal activities, they aimed to 'know what was happening and . . . look after the interests of the Trust'.⁶¹ By shaping tenants' status and significance in the functioning of the estate, superintendents and their families reinforced people's sense of belonging. They assisted in the development of a new social order that was based on tenants' own notions of what was enjoyable and desirable.

Compared with local authority estates of the time, Sutton's clearly possessed what many council estates appeared to lack. The principles and strategies employed by the trust avoided many of the problems that apparently beset local authority estate associations. Its tenants enjoyed high status locally, good relations with their landlord, social homogeneity, participation in estate-based organizations and confidence that 'the ordinary, routine services' necessary in their new location would be established and maintained. A building to accommodate their activities might follow, provided that it was self-financed, tenant-led and based on well-supported leisure and social interests. Local authority tenants, by contrast, experienced local hostility,⁶² an antagonistic landlord, alienation both on and off the estate, 'many failures of the powers that be',⁶³ absence of community buildings and a 'disjointed tangle' of competing societies.⁶⁴ Most important was the question of image and mutual respect. The Sutton Trust saw its tenants as brought low by circumstance ('shorn lambs'), but it worked on the assumption that they had the capability to be 'civil', albeit under the guidance of the estate superintendent. Local authority tenants, on the other hand, were expected to satisfy levels of political and ideological commitment that were 'in the last resort unrealisable'.⁶⁵ Mutual expectations between council tenants and landlords were very high but confidence in one another's capabilities was low. Though 'home-grown' leisure activities did appear on local authority estates, Olechnowicz argues that they were undermined and undervalued by the rhetoric of citizenship promoted by the NECC. Consequently, the LCC concluded that in practice building model com-

---

⁶⁰ Tenant Interviews Newcastle, Barrack Road 7 and 9, Birmingham 3, 9 and 14, Chelsea 11; Bridgeland, *Laisterdyke Roundabout*, p. 127.

⁶¹ Letter, W.L. Mills (Superintendent, Sutton Estate, Hillsborough, Sheffield to Secretary, Sutton Dwellings Trust), April 1948.

⁶² The residents' association at Watling was set up in response to an offensive letter about the estate in the local press: Durant, 'Community and Association', p. 167.

⁶³ Ibid., p. 179.

⁶⁴ Ibid., p. 177.

⁶⁵ Ravetz, *Council Housing*, p. 4.

munities was more trouble than it was worth.[66] While local authority tenants refused to shoulder the 'unrealistic and damaging' version of citizenship expected of them,[67] the Sutton 'cherries' were encouraged to find familiar and congenial ways of enhancing their individual and collective lives.

Building civil society

Between the wars, local authority and Sutton estates provided contrasting examples of building communal life among the poor. The two models were based on fundamentally different assumptions about what was needed and what estate dwellers themselves could provide. The final section of this chapter explores these assumptions further by focusing on current debates about the process by which 'civil society' can be built. Drawing on the evidence of English inter-war estates, it examines the arguments of political and social scientists, anthropologists and historians.

As we have seen, determining empirically whether civil society exists in a particular locality depends on the definitions that are used. Civil society remains an elusive concept, often defined by what it is not rather than by what it is. Civil society has been said to occupy a 'gap' or a 'space' though its boundaries are often indistinct. Kumar reports that civil society has been found

> in the economy and in the polity; in the area between the family and the state, or the individual and the state; in non-state institutions which organise and educate citizens for political participation; even as an expression of the whole civilising mission of modern society.[68]

Accounts of inter-war housing estates have shown that the primary concern of local authorities at the time was with educating individuals for political citizenship. Commentators emphasized the need to separate the family from civil society while at the same time drawing a firm line between civil society and government. Individual citizenship was seen as the goal and to achieve this family ties had to be subordinated to abstract, formal civic duties while the state occupied another, separate sphere. The prevailing view of civil society was of a distinct, narrowly defined entity, whose limits were fixed by ideological boundaries and

---

[66] Olechnowicz, *Working-class Housing*, p. 199.

[67] Olechnowicz, 'Civic Leadership', p. 5.

[68] K. Kumar cited in G. Morton, 'Civil Society, Municipal Government and the State: Enshrinement, Empowerment and Legitimacy. Scotland, 1800–1929', *Urban History*, 25 (1998), p. 348.

determined by the 'proper', that is, separate and independent, relationship between individuals, families, associations and the state. These values and relationships were to prevail, above all, on local authority housing estates.

The normative picture, however, was at odds not only with how people behaved in the early twentieth century but also with how the boundaries of civil society were in practice determined.[69] For working-class members in particular, family, household, kin and neighbourhood were closely linked through myriad social and economic ties. To recognize only 'individual' acts as participation in civil society *by definition* effectively ruled out a major part of working-class group activity.[70] Furthermore, to separate the state from civil society ignores the part that the state repeatedly played in structuring, protecting and delimiting the realm of civil society.[71] Such a narrow formulation of civil society certainly obscures the state's role in regulating the voluntary sector in England between 1900 and 1939 and one effect of this is to mask the achievements of bodies like the Sutton Dwellings Trust.[72]

The operation of civil society

Historians have recently begun to assess the character of civil society in Britain. Its mechanisms have been studied by historians of eighteenth century Edinburgh, nineteenth century Bristol and twentieth century Glasgow.[73] In these three different locales, Morris, Gorsky and Morton have analysed how civil society functioned. Morris stresses the importance of civil society as an arena for the individual citizen to exercise choice and self-direction in the interest of the public good. From this flowed personal development, class solidarity and civic order to the benefit of Edinburgh as a whole. Gorsky, on the other hand, tested claims that in the nineteenth century civil society operated so as to generate 'social capital' – self-help, trust and social cohesion. He cites

---

[69] Morris, 'Civil Society', pp. 289–90.
[70] Richard Hoggart in his classic account of working-class life, *Uses of Literacy* (London, 1957), noted that 'Most react instinctively against consciously planned group activities; they are used to a group life, but one which has started from the home and worked outwards in response to the common needs and amusements of a densely packed neighbourhood'; quoted in Ravetz, *Council Housing*, p. 166.
[71] Morton, 'Civil Society', pp. 350–51.
[72] Garside, *Conduct of Philanthropy*, ch. 4.
[73] R.J. Morris, M. Gorsky and Graeme Morton, 'Civil Society in Britain', *Urban History* (Special Issue) 25 (1998).

Green who has argued that friendly societies functioned in this way in relation to welfare by encouraging solidarity between members, promoting civic engagement and acting as nurseries of democracy while cultivating independence and self-help. Gorsky is more equivocal. He emphasizes the special characteristics of friendly societies – their origins in mutual welfare and in conviviality, where democracy was tempered with respect for status and hierarchy. Bristol friendly societies had a broad social base and though some members used them as a training ground for activism, Gorsky finds there is little evidence that they were 'nurseries of democracy'. Nor does it seem they invariably operated to reinforce or create mutual trust – conflict over benefits was marked. Furthermore, members were tactical in their reliance on friendly societies. Societies were the first resort for unemployment risk but the Poor Law remained the ultimate safety net, particularly in old age. Indeed, Morton stresses the permeability of the boundaries to civil society that some theorists have held to be inviolate, not least in the period between the wars.

These historical accounts highlight fundamental issues about the structure of the urban world and its governance that are important for evaluating the evidence from local authority and Sutton estates in the inter-war period. They suggest that urban associations in Edinburgh, Bristol and Glasgow produced an array of conflicting, sometimes incompatible, outcomes – these include personal enrichment, class solidarity, civic integration, social capital, political engagement and enhanced public decision-making. Similarly, social scientists studying contemporary phenomena in developing countries and in Eastern Europe's post-communist states have variously described civil society as hierarchical (evangelism/educational) but also as horizontal (self-help/sociability); open and transparent as well as closed and secret; divisive as well as socially cohesive; permeable as well as separate; a bulwark against state expansion as well as a creature of the state and its manoeuvrings in the urban setting.[74] In these settings, as in the new housing estates of inter-war Britain, the emphasis is often on 'making civil society' in untried ground.[75] The problems are indeed similar – how are new social and political organizations to be formed to promote the cohesion of these

---

[74] There is an extensive literature on the development of ideas around civil society. For a general account, see Chris Hann, 'Introduction', in C.M. Hann and E. Dunn, *Civil Society Challenging Western Models* (London, 1996) and also John Hall, 'In Search of Civil Society', in J. Hall (ed.), *Civil Society: Theory History Comparison* (Cambridge, 1995), pp. 1–32.

[75] See, for example, Howell, 'Making Civil Society from the Outside', pp. 3–22.

	Primary focus	→ **Intermediate stage**	→ **Final stage**
Model A	individual citizenship	→ civil society	→ quality of life
Model B	civil society	→ citizenship	→ quality of life
Model C	quality of life	→ civil society	→ citizenship

11.1 Models for building civil society

segregated groups?[76] The answer historians and social scientists give to this question depends fundamentally on the primacy given to one of three elements – individual citizen, civil society and quality of life. Depending on which of these is made the primary focus, very different conclusions may be drawn, as illustrated by Figure 11.1.

Many commentators today agree with the NECC and its prevailing inter-war view that individual participation in the formalities of citizenship provides the precondition for enhancing civil society and the quality of life. Individual citizenship has to be the primary focus (Model A). This view, however, is opposed by others who consider that such a focus on citizenship will erode, rather than build, civil society. The anthropologist Adam Seligman, for example, has argued that such a concept of citizenship 'undermines that concrete mutuality and shared components of the moral community upon which trust is based'.[77] For him, civil society is the component on which all else depends and has to come first (Model B). Furthermore, on the basis of empirical data from Britain in the twentieth century, Peter Hall has challenged the view that social trust and civic engagement depends on the level of individual involvement in formal associations. Causal links between patterns of political engagement and social networks of trust, Hall argues, are less clear than an emphasis on individual 'citizenship' has suggested. Indeed, others have argued that civil society is *not* dependent on the public and political sphere, but can 'start anywhere' – wherever people come together in social encounters or in modest pursuit of their own or more general interests.[78] Such encounters develop loyalties and personal capabilities that can be deployed in the political realm, building active citizenship and improving the quality of life. Sutton estates appear to exemplify the value of modest encounters as building blocks for active community life.

Some commentators, however, have sought to locate civil society at

---

[76] See David Eversley's concluding remarks following discussion of David Reeder's contribution in H.J. Dyos (ed.), *Study of Urban History*, pp. 278–9.

[77] Seligman cited in Hann, 'Introduction', p. 4.

[78] V. Perez-Diaz, 'The Possibility of Civil Society', in Hall, *Civil Society*, pp. 106–7.

an even more basic level. They emphasize the primacy of quality of life, arguing that it is this that determines involvement in both civil society and political life[79] (Model C). Chris Bryant has concluded that in some cases, 'an underclass is denied the very material and cultural means to be civil'.[80] From this perspective, making civil society has to begin by ensuring a sufficiency of basic resources for individual members and validating everyday participation in a wide range of social activities. It is grounded in

> precarious groups of people who spend a few decades of their lives doing what they consider to be decent and sensible things often enough to produce a modicum of social trust in their social encounters ... they develop loyalties to each other and to the people who come before and after them and in so doing they cling to several traditions ... that support them in their own identities.[81]

It could be argued that it was the material contribution made by the Sutton Dwellings Trust in housing thousands of the very poorest urban dwellers that constituted its major contribution to building civil society.

Imagining civil society

Recent historical and sociological studies prompt the conclusion that identifying and constructing civil society is undoubtedly an ideological matter. It follows that determining the presence or absence of civil society, true citizenship or improved quality of life is also a matter of perception as well as of evidence and experience. Particularly relevant to assessments of the inter-war period is the distinction that has been drawn between a 'Greek' and a 'Roman' interpretation of citizenship and civil society.[82] The Greek model is typified as one that seeks uniformity, conformity, a single focus and a grand plan for citizen participation. The Roman model, by contrast, looks for diversity, experimentation, diffusion and local initiative in public life. The Greek notion suggests that there is one ideal form of civil society for the whole community while the

---

[79] Hall cites R.D. Laing who in 1965 commented that a working-class youth in Britain was more likely to spend time in a mental institution than to attend university: Peter A. Hall, 'Social Capital in Britain', *British Journal of Politics*, 29 (1999), pp. 417–61; Peter Loizos, 'How Ernest Gellner got mugged on the Streets of London or: Civil Society, the Media and the Quality of Life', in Hann and Dunn, *Civil Society* pp. 50–63.

[80] C.A.G. Bryant, 'Civil Nation, Civil Society, Civil Religion', in Hall, *Civil Society*, p. 153.

[81] Perez-Diaz, 'The Possibility of Civil Society', p. 107.

[82] P.B. Clarke, *Citizenship* (London, 1994), pp. 4–9.

Roman favours a more contingent, instrumental approach resulting in a multiplicity of forms reflecting local circumstances. While the Greek civic ideal underpinned the philosophy applied to local authority estates, it is tempting to place Sutton estates in the alternative Roman camp.

The 'Greek' formulation of 'proper' linkages between formal 'significant' organizations and active public life has been challenged, not only by historians like Ravetz and Olechnowicz but also by commentators concerned with the structure of modern societies. Without belittling the task of 'becoming civil', Chris Bryant has celebrated the value of tokens of interpersonal respect and consideration and has endorsed what others have preferred to call 'trivial', 'secondary values' such as pragmatism, cooperation, fair play, compromise and tolerance.[83] Bryant rejects the pursuit of primary, universal values as the path to the realization of civil society. Anthropologists studying societies in Africa, Turkey and China have also criticized this view of civil society on the grounds that it emphasizes formal structures and neglects beliefs, values and everyday practices. They argue that such a view privileges male, middle-class groups and masks the informal coping strategies of other (often female) groups based on kin, friendship and reciprocal assistance.[84] Clearly, the alternative approaches demonstrated by local authorities and the Sutton Dwellings Trust in the inter-war period resonate today in the experience of old and new democracies alike.

Structuring the role of local authorities and the voluntary sector

I would argue that in the 1920s and 1930s, widely shared ideologies about the nature of citizenship made it impossible for Sutton estates to be recognized as a 'success'. Not only did the 'Greek' ideals of the NCSS and the NECC enjoy support among conservatives, but in their emphasis on the importance of individual engagement by citizens with the political process, they also found common ground with some on the left. Herbert Morrison, for example, advocated active membership of political organizations and an informed interest in voting as marks of true citizenship. G.D.H. Cole, however, criticized the atomistic basis of Morrison's notion of 'proper' participation. In terms that reflected much more closely the kind of society encouraged on Sutton estates, Cole argued that

---

[83] Loizos, 'How Ernest Gellner got mugged', p. 50; K. Tester, *Civil Society* (London, 1992), pp. 146–7.

[84] Jenny B. White, 'Civic Culture and Islam in Urban Turkey', in Hann and Dunn, *Civil Society* pp. 14–16: Howell, 'Making Civil Society from the Outside', p. 15.

local government must rest upon small and manageable cells of real neighbourhood organisation ... with a constant and real contact between members of the neighbourhood group and those that represent it upon the larger civil authority.[85]

Daunton has argued that in twentieth-century Britain, the choice between these alternatives was determined by the view that it was local authorities rather than central government or semi-autonomous bodies that 'would be the most "trustworthy" and amenable to influence'.[86]

The Sutton Dwellings Trust's experience between the wars shows three important elements in the resolution of this question of power.[87] First, the immense wealth and unrestricted remit of the trust to house 'the poor' was not welcomed by existing charities, landowners or central government. Its very capability for breaking the existing mould of housing provision and for providing an independent alternative agency provoked not confidence but hostility. For central government, the greatest problem appeared to be its lack of control, especially over the trust's relations with local authorities. Well before 1919, the Local Government Board was intervening to prevent local authorities from negotiating directly with the Sutton Trust, hinting that powers and financial help would follow, provided they withdrew. Second, parameters for voluntary sector housing in the 1930s were set by the close alliance between central and local government and by the 'taming' of the Sutton Trust, formalized in its 1927 scheme of management. Despite periodic efforts to revive and extend it, the role of the voluntary sector remained subservient to that of local authorities and the private sector.[88] Some housing trusts, and especially the Sutton Trust, chose to operate *as if they were a local authority*, obeying much the same rules and taking advantage of government grants and subsidies. Others acted as 'gatekeepers' for local authority housing, pre-selecting and training prospective tenants. Though Daunton sees this as 'collusion' by voluntary bodies, the Sutton experience shows that there was active influence by government to subvert any independent role on their part. Finally, by 1939 emerging democratic ideals reinforced the importance of individual citizenship and the political organization of local authorities. Above all, it was the physical emblems of civic improvement, especially slum clearance

---

[85] Cited in M. Daunton, 'Payment and Participation: Welfare and State Formation in Britain 1900–1951', *Past and Present*, 150 (1996), pp. 204–5.

[86] Ibid., p. 214.

[87] P.L. Garside, 'Reassessing Voluntary Action in English Housing Provision Post-1900', *Journal of Social Policy*, 30 (2001), pp. 613–36.

[88] P.L. Garside, 'Central Government, Local Authorities and the Voluntary Housing Movement 1919–1939', in A. O'Day, *Government and Institutions in the post-1832 United Kingdom* (Lewiston/Queenston, 1995).

and planned redevelopment of civic centres that came to represent the new order of citizenship.

The structure of power brokered in urban areas, therefore, meant that the Sutton Dwellings Trust had been rendered a 'non-starter' – a 'non-entity'. It had been schooled to act as a 'virtual' local authority, enjoying no independent profile and ignored not only by central government but also by the rest of the voluntary sector. Its status was ambiguous. Standing between the voluntary and the state sectors, the trust had emerged finally from Chancery in 1927 as a supposedly 'independent' body. Its trustees, however, were predominantly drawn from the Ministry of Health and from councillors of large English cities. Furthermore, it agreed to drop the word 'model' from its title on the grounds that this emblem of the voluntary sector had come to have 'unpleasant connotations'.[89] Nevertheless, enough of William Sutton's view of what was required to house the poor remained to make living in one of his 'model dwellings' a successful step in realizing a better quality of life. Sutton estates offered people the chance to cooperate in providing common facilities and activities, based on the routines of daily life, local centres and regular association. Their achievements, so desired by the NECC on council estates, nevertheless gained no recognition. This was an inevitable outcome since the manoeuvrings of the central state and its willing allies in local government had relegated the 'princely trust' of William Sutton to a minor and insignificant role in urban affairs. The 'top-down' Greek model of civil society prevailed because it meshed with the central role being accorded to municipal authorities through the inter-war period. Creating modern cities, their citizens and their model dwellings were all tasks reserved for local authorities. The theoretically respectable and well-supported alternative version exemplified by the Sutton estates was therefore set aside. The low-key, sociable, home grown process of community participation to be found there was held to be of no account in the realization of citizenship and civil society among the poorest sections of the working-class.

The statist British structure remained in place until the 1980s. Defensiveness and passivity marked life on post-war housing estates, no matter whether they belonged to local authorities or to those voluntary 'housing associations' that continued with an active building programme, including the Sutton Dwellings Trust. Post-war affluence, however, reduced anxieties about the changes in working-class life that moves from slum to housing estate required. Local authorities and their planners pursued the creation of communities through physical means. 'Community building'

---

[89] Garside, *Conduct of Philanthropy*, ch. 4, p. 42.

through social means became a marginal concern, surviving among small groups committed to self-help and cooperatives. The 1990s, however, saw a resurgence of interest in conditions on local authority housing estates. Social exclusion, poverty and deprivation brought calls for a renewal of 'active citizenship' and for more tenant participation in the management of estates, now increasingly freed from local authority control. Today, once again, the proper relationship between citizenship, local loyalty and consumerism is being keenly debated as local authorities retreat from direct housing provision. While it would be inappropriate to draw direct lessons from Sutton Dwelling Trust estates in the inter-war period, it is worth highlighting the positive contribution they made to communal life through organizational trust, pragmatism and modest and sympathetic goals. In addition, however, the fate of the Sutton Dwellings Trust's model demonstrates the importance of ideology in furthering civil society, and particularly the values promoted by government at national and local level.

CHAPTER TWELVE

When we lived in communities: working-class culture and its critics

Robert Colls

> Contracts give rise to obligations which have not been contracted for.
>
> (Emile Durkheim, *The Division of Labour*)
>
> The great challenge to the urban historian ... is to assess the impact of the city as an independent variable.
>
> (David Reeder, *Exploring the Urban Past*)

'Community'

In the beginning, I didn't know I belonged to a 'culture', but at the moment when I realized I did, I felt estranged. This was a paradoxical condition, not willingly sought at the time and only half-grasped since. This chapter is an attempt to come to terms with it.

South Shields was the place and I think it was the early summer of 1965. I was 16 years old. Imagine a street of Tyneside flats, two sides facing each other, one street in a grid of hundreds like it, all banking steeply down to the river. From an upstairs bedroom window on the higher side, imagine looking down across 20 yards of cambered road to kerb and pavement, then a yellow doorstep and set of front doors up to an upstairs bedroom window the same as mine only slightly lower and facing me. My bed was wedged sideways against the window. I lay on it looking down. It was Saturday, late afternoon, around five o'clock. Over the way, some of the older residents were sitting on their doorsteps calling out to neighbours on my side doing the same. One man was reading the *Shields Gazette*. I recall he had a cup and saucer by his slippered feet. Up the road, the milkman's horse was pulling the cart and clopping and stopping, as she was trained to do, while Tommy got his money. I could hear some kids playing. Later, in the early evening, there would be quite a bit of coming and going from the front doors, the girls high-heeled and glamorous, with bouffant hair, the lads red-scrubbed and Brylcreemed. Because there were so few cars, you could hear the clack of heels and the rattle of talk. We all talked the same in Laygate Lane. Only teachers and BBC announcers talked differently. To the right, about a hundred yards up and on the other side of the road, a knot of older women stood at the corner shop, talking calmly, all arms-folded except for one who, arm out straight, gently rocked a pram. Mothers like these held the streets from first morning message to last evening call.

What I saw that afternoon was a normal scene in a very small world. I knew it in every line and movement. I knew the cracks in the warm summer pavements, as I knew the stepped slate roofs with blue shipyard cranes beyond and the familiar river noises off – welding, blasting, drilling, with screeching seagulls wheeling in. It seems now that through it all a reddish sun was low and slanting.

I am trying to get this right, but I can feel my mind moving into a different register. There's a mood coming on. Do I remember what I actually saw? Can I know what I actually felt? Do I begin to feel like this because of how others have written about working-class communities, or because of regret at what was to happen later to my own? Above all, *is it true?* Certainly. (Though in more ways than one can tell.)

Then something happened. It took long enough just to think it. I saw that what I was looking at from the window was indeed a 'community'. More, I saw that that community was, or had, or lived, or somehow encompassed, a culture. This flash of realization had everything to do with the book in front of me and nothing at all to do with what was happening down in the street – a street, I may say, that I had never thought about even though I had stepped into it a million times. The book was *The Uses of Literacy* by Richard Hoggart – a book with whole chapters devoted to people whom I took to be like those down there, saying that the lives they lived were cultured, and worthy of attention. Reading this book was like seeing, or I should say hearing, Geordies on the television: a rare enough event in those days and one guaranteed to bring the family herding into the room. Only it was better than that because Hoggart's astonishingly astute acts of recognition were embedded in an argument about the English working class as a whole, how their urban world was under pressure, and cracking, and how that was going to mean a terrible loss of some sort. I didn't see the loss part of his argument because I didn't know its place in a tradition of writing about England, but I *did* recognize immediately the life Hoggart so brilliantly illuminated. For the first time in my life I felt I was learning about what I already knew:

> Home may be private, but the front door opens out of the living-room on to the street, and when you go down the one step or use it

12.1 Laygate Lane, South Shields 1930

as a seat on a warm evening you become part of the life of the neighbourhood.

To a visitor they are understandably depressing, these massed proletarian areas; street after regular street of shoddily uniform houses . . . But to the insider, these are small worlds, each as homogeneous and well defined as a village. Down below, on the main road running straight into town, the bosses cars whirr away at five o'clock to converted farm-houses ten miles out in the hills; the men stream up into their district. They know it, as do all its inhabitants, in intimate detail – automatically slipping up a snicket here or a shared lavatory block there; they know it as a group of tribal areas.

This is an extremely local life, in which everything is remarkably near. The houses . . . open on to the street, the street itself, compared with those of suburbia or the new housing estates, is narrow; the houses opposite are only just over the cobbles and the shops not much farther.

There are varieties of light he will know: the sun forcing its way down as far as the ground-floor windows on a very sunny afternoon, the foggy dew of November over the slates and chimneys, the misty evenings of March when the gangs congregate in the watery yellow light of the kicked and scratched gas lamp. Or the smells: the beer and Woodbine smell of the men on Saturday nights, the cheap powder and cream smell of . . . grown-up sisters, fish and chips.[1]

No celebration. Not a flicker. Not a word. I didn't tell anyone for there was no one to tell. Yet it was fairly big news for a grammar school boy who, at the time, was being trained to purge himself of who he was and where he came from. From that moment on I started looking differently at these people in the street, seeing their life as somehow external from mine, though not apart from it, and valuable, though not necessarily by them. What for me had been loose and ill-considered, now became screwed tight with meaning. 'Structure' in the sense of 'social structure' had entered my feelings. Indeed, it belonged there. Hoggart had made me literate. All was new.

I do not want to give the impression now, for I certainly did not have the impression then, that this community was all cosy and decent or, as the saying goes, 'traditional and homogeneous'. There were neighbours who didn't speak, doors that were firmly shut, men and women who wouldn't work (or want), and hard lads who were not averse to spreading a bit of misery. There were layers of ignorance difficult for outsiders to penetrate and, what is more, this was a working class that wasn't all white, though those Yemenis who had married and settled were most certainly Geordie. These were seamen, mostly, and their lodging houses dotted the neighbourhood. The rest were shipyard workers – tank cleaners in our street's case – and they lived, as well they might, at the bottom end. Not everyone was friends with them, but there again, not everyone was friends with everybody else. Our back lane was understood to be *ours*, ('wors' in the dialect) in the way that siblings were – *wor* Carole, *wor* Billy, *wor* street and so on. Not theirs. All this was territorial; nothing to do with persons. Same with boys and girls: they played their games and we played ours, you in your small corner and me in mine. Occasionally, everybody would play together, but only if you 'knew how to play', and you weren't too young. A back lane game of cricket would end the moment someone wouldn't let you get your ball from their backyard ('six and out'). A back lane game of football ('doors') would end when residents got tired of some pretty poor defending and the umpteenth violent thump of the ball against their backdoor. A back lane line of washing could be carried off by a filthy coal wagon which couldn't be bothered to wait. Sometimes, mainly on Friday and Saturday nights, quarrels spilled out into the street. There

---

[1] Richard Hoggart, *The Uses of Literacy: Aspects of Working-class Life with Special Reference to Publications and Entertainments* (Harmondsworth, 1958), pp. 41–3, 47. Hoggart was writing about Hunslet 30 years before.

12.2 Back lane girls, Lyton Street, South Shields 1938

12.3 Back field boys, Eglesfield Road, South Shields 1957

was a working men's club just over our 'back field' (a ripped up coal track and embankment between two back lanes). After closing time, my brother and I would lie and listen to the antics in the street below. Sometimes punches were thrown, but usually it was just the beer talking. I can't remember any violence being done to women, but then I was not in a position to know. I suppose there was: men were expected to hit men, so it was to be expected that they would hit women too. But I saw no sign of it and if there was nastiness and quarrelling, there was also a lot of self-knowledge and stoicism as well. We lived in same streets. We went to same schools, at least up to 11. Most of the fathers of the boys I knew worked in the same two or three occupations, the same half dozen trades, as did the women who, however, were more expected to be mothers than workers, as were the girls, most of whom were social mothers long before they were biological mothers.

I am talking, then, of a community put together by where people lived. I am not talking, at least not yet, of associations, or friendship groups, or voluntary clubs, or virtual communities or even imagined ones – important as they may be. I am talking about street life as a local resource that was open to all provided they accepted its laws, the laws Hoggart uncovered. In fact, community in this sense was very close to those 'laws which affect only the inhabitants of particular districts' as outlined by Sir William Blackstone in his *Commentaries on the Laws and Constitution of England* (1765–9). Blackstone described ways that were peculiar, continous, compulsory, civil and reasonable to themselves.[2] As Richard Hoggart recognzed for his own district, the boundaries were well marked and people knew where to draw the line. We knew each other only too well. I never thought of 'community', indeed the word had not entered my vocabulary, but there again I knew who I was.

Or at least, I thought I did. The trouble is, once you start looking *at*, rather than *with*, everything changes and the moment of realization is also the moment of estrangement. Hoggart preferred to talk of 'life' but, as I was to learn later, in modern times when we were supposed to have lived in such things, I had lived in a 'traditional working-class community'.

Revisionists

In 1994 the Birkbeck historian Joanna Bourke declared her intention to investigate working-class community from a new angle:

---

[2] *Blackstone's Commentaries on the Laws and Constitution of England: Abridged for the use of Students, and Adapted to Modern Statute and Decisions*, ed. John Gifford Esq. (1765–9; London, 1820), pp. 8–11.

> The intellectual fascination of British social history is found in elegant tomes elucidating the development of working-class consciousness as experienced in the waxing and waning fortunes of trade unions, workingmen's clubs, community pressure groups, and political parties. This book approaches the social history of the working class from a different angle: what does 'working class' mean when our vision focuses on the individual stripped of these institutional affiliations?[3]

According to Bourke, the idea of the traditional working-class community was a 'retrospective construction', made up in the 1950s by socialist intellectuals who, in their writings, wished it on the historical experience of people who had never actually lived it. 'Community' in this sense flourished, Bourke says, mainly as 'a rhetorical device'. It could not explain outsiders, it was bad at explaining insiders who opted out and, given its heavy (male) institutional overlay, it was never meant to include either.[4] Against 'community', she drew attention to what was 'private . . . feminine and . . . discordant'.[5]

Bourke was right to see community as too vague a concept, especially when in the hands of politicians and policy-makers who used it to suit themselves.[6] And she was right to detect lazy thinking in too many socialistic histories of the working class. By concentrating instead on individual choices and personal strategies, Bourke got to places many historians never reached. On the other hand, there is a difficulty with her reasoning, and addressing it will take us further.

She criticizes the concept of the working-class community for the way it implied that people were generally similar in the way they lived.[7] Practical, everyday lives were complex and diverse, she tells us, and 'the concept of "community"' 'cannot help us understand these diverse responses'.[8] For there were multiple and enduring differences between

---

[3] Joanna Bourke, *Working-class Cultures in Britain 1890–1960: Gender, Ethnicity and Class* (London, 1994), p. 1.

[4] Ibid., pp. 138, 151.

[5] Ibid., p. 4.

[6] Too vague? George A. Hillery, Jr came up with 94 definitions in 1955 – 'all the definitions deal with people. Beyond this common basis, there is no agreement': Colin Bell and Howard Newby, *Community Studies* (London, 1971), p. 27. In the hands of policy-makers? Peter Golding and Andrew Sills, 'Community Against Itself', *Community Work and Communication*, 20 (1983), p. 187. Generally the word has been used in a desirable sense, but German Jews in the 1930s had reason to hate it, and Orwell drew attention to Ingsoc's loathsome 'community centres': Victor Klemperer, *I Shall Bear Witness: The Diaries of Victor Klemperer 1933–1941* (London, 1999), p. 281, George Orwell, *Nineteen Eighty Four* (1949; Harmondsworth, 1973), p. 21.

[7] Bourke, *Working-class Cultures*, pp. 138–9.

[8] Ibid., p. 151.

the people – differences at many levels, including their ability to communicate, to agree and disagree, to get on together, to intermarry, to live comfortably, to be religious, to like or dislike the neighbourhood and so on. Because of these essential differences, she argues that the working-class neighbourhood was essentially a *contracting society*, bidding for scarce commodities and resources. Bourke's critique of community, then, starts not with what was lived in common but rather with what was held apart and brokered by a series of 'individual transactions', 'reciprocal rights' and 'power relations':

> It is not enough to specify the interaction of two individuals as being between two members of a particular class who belong to the same 'community': rather we must look at how these two individuals define their relationship (as an acquaintance, a neighbour, a friend, or a member of a family) and how the exchange is conducted (through latent exchanges of rights and obligations, gifts or the cash nexus).
>
> Living in a particular neighbourhood does not simply entitle an individual to access to specific spatially restricted resources . . . rather it enables individuals to bid for these resources by increasing information and raising the costs of searching for resources elsewhere. By examining networks between individuals, we can expose a complex of power relations instead of merely describing a broad stratum of alleged consensus . . .[9]

Bourke's book was important in the turn against writing social history of the class and community type. In 1994 Mike Savage and Andrew Miles explained how the turn happened.[10] It began in the 1980s, they say, and behind it was the decline of manual labour coincident with the weakening of the trade unions, the fall of Communism, the rise in 'identity histories' and the emergence of the notion that the key to understanding the past lay not so much in a narrative of real events and experiences, but in the analysis of the languages, texts and discourses – the so-called 'linguistic turn'. As Patrick Joyce put it in 1991, the idea that 'the category of "experience" . . . is in fact not prior to and constitutive of language but is actively constituted by language, has increasingly been recognized as having far-reaching implications'.[11] Moreover if by the 1990s people had stopped using the language of class and community (and perhaps they

---

[9] Ibid., pp. 149–52.

[10] Mike Savage and Andrew Miles, *The Remaking of the British Working Class 1840–1940* (London, 1994), pp. 3–19. E.P. Thompson, *The Making of the English Working Class* (London, 1963) was the key text in post-war class and community history.

[11] Patrick Joyce, *Visions of the People: Industrial England and the Question of Class 1848–1914* (Cambridge, 1991), p. 9.

never had) what was the point of continuing with it? Why persevere with the residual thought processes of a fading socialist era? The revisionist implications of this 'seemingly simple recognition' were startling. As Savage and Miles put it: 'It has become increasingly unclear what the point of working-class history is, if class seems to mean so little to people, whether in the past or the present.'[12] Since 1994, the revisionist case has grown. In their 1999 study of working-class London and on the basis of research into 28 100 households in 38 boroughs carried out in the late 1920s, Baines and Johnson concluded:

> The new data provide little evidence of occupational continuity or low levels of social mobility, as might be expected of a 'traditional' working-class community in the 1930s, and as was assumed to have existed in the community-based studies of the immediate post-war period. This raises two possibilities and an agenda for future research. Either working-class society in London had, by the 1930s, already changed from a stable homogeneous community towards the more individualized and dynamic society observed in the post-war period, or homogeneous working-class communities had never been the norm in Britain.[13]

Of course, a lot depends on what Baines and Johnson mean by 'homogeneous', but if referred to that Laygate Saturday back in 1965, the revisionist response would surely invite me to think again about what I thought I saw while reading Hoggart's neo-socialist 'retrospective construction' of working-class culture. Residents were not so much enjoying the common life of the neighbourhood in the late afternoon sunshine, but were partaking in the altogether more wintry business of reciprocal dealing.

True, these things are not mutually exclusive. Nor can it be denied that contract offers one way of looking at social relationships. Nor can it be denied that Bourke provides examples, though as in all scholarship much depends on her methods of argument and categories of classification.[14] But I want to ask not whether Joanna Bourke is right or wrong in

---

[12] Savage and Miles, *The Remaking of the British Working Class*, p. ix.

[13] Dudley Baines and Paul Johnson, 'In Search of the 'Traditional' Working Class: Social Mobility and Occupational Continuity in Interwar London', *Economic History Review*, lii (4) (1999), p. 712.

[14] First, her 'not necessarily' line of argument where she is not necessarily saying that there was community, and she is not necessarily saying that there wasn't. Second, her 'change of meaning' line of argument where she takes out historical meaning and inserts her own – as, for instance, the claim that children went to Sunday school for 'leisure' rather than for community or religious purposes. Third, 'the slip', as on page 148 when skilled manual workers suddenly slip out of the working-class category. Fourth, 'selectaquote', which all historians indulge in, but the same page gives a roaring example. Fifth, the 'set up' where

her emphasis on contract but, whether, after all those contracts have been accounted for, there is anything more to say.

Is there anything more to say? Tönnies and Durkheim

In 1887 Ferdinand Tönnies published *Gemeinschaft und Gesellschaft* and helped set the agenda for the coming academic discipline of Sociology. For him, family, language, the contiguity of households and the shared knowledge of occupation and neighbourhood all constituted the 'mutuality' (*verstandnis*) and the 'unity' (*eintracht*) of 'community' (*gemeinschaft*). Alongside *gemeinschaft*, Tönnies offered *gesellschaft*, or 'society' – a more calculating, individualistic kind of life based on contract and exchange. Tönnies's description of this life is close to the version offered by Joanna Bourke:

> to be understood as a multitude of natural and artificial individuals, the wills and spheres of whom are in many relations with and to one another, and remain nevertheless independent of one another . . . This gives us the general description of 'bourgeois society' or 'exchange Gesellschaft' . . . a condition in which, according to the expression of Adam Smith, 'Every man . . . becomes in some measure a merchant . . .'.[15]

Gemeinschaft and *gesellschaft* have tended to be cast as opposites: if contract and exchange is true, community must be false and vice versa. But for Tönnies, the two forms were not opposites but obverses intended not so much to represent the real world as to provide models prior to its representation. For him, they indicated existing mental constructs, twin poles of thinking, about how to live in a society in the throes of modernization (*burgerliche gesellschaft*). Tönnies offered his forms as tendencies, projections, remote goals – 'in the process of becoming', 'like an emanation'.[16]

For Emile Durkheim, writing around the same time, modern society

---

Bourke enjoys target practice at some particularly weak conceptualization (set up by her).

[15] Ferdinand Tonnies, *Community and Association* (London, 1955), trans. Charles P. Loomis, pp. 48–54, 87–8, 37. 'Association' here seems an odd translation for *gesellschaft*, if for no other reason than *both* conditions are seen by Tonnies as associational forms: *gemeinschaft* – 'real and organic', *gesellschaft* – 'imaginary and mechanical'.

[16] On ideal types 'intended to aid empirical analysis' by placing structures rather than facts, see Martin Bulmer, 'Sociological Models of the Mining Community', *Sociological Review*, 23 (1975), pp. xix, 88 and Raphael Samuel, *Theatres of Memory* (London, 1994), vol. I, p. 431.

was based on 'powerful machines . . . great concentrations of forces and capital . . . extreme division of labour'. With all the differentiation and competition such a dynamic society must produce, Durkheim believed that contracts served as a truce between competing parties. As social 'similitudes loosen', and individual contracts took their place, he wanted to know by what means the mass of individual contracts could hold if in modern society there was no deeper, greater, social contract to underpin them:

> the conception of a social contract is today difficult to defend, for it has no relation to the facts. The observer does not meet it along his road, so to speak. Not only is [sic] there no societies which have such an origin, but there is none whose structure presents the least trace.[17]

'Contracts give rise to obligations which have not been contracted for', said Durkheim. In a society dependent on individual contract but with no apparent or tangible social contract to underwrite the extra-contractual obligations, Durkheim found that contract *in society itself*. In other words, beneath the myriad of momentary private wills where 'interest relates men . . . never for more than some few moments', and, indeed, outside the individual consciousness of those wills, Durkheim thought that in regular practices and experiences, in moral traditions, in known histories and in the representation of these things, lay the subliminal sustaining aggregate of society itself – the 'social contract'.[18] Edmund Burke called it, or something very like it, 'an entailed inheritance', 'wisdom without reflection'.[19] Raymond Williams and Terry Eagleton would come to call it 'culture' by reference to a certain social wholeness, or completeness, in what it was and what it stood for.[20] But Durkheim saw it as the minute regulation of the contracting parts by the contracted whole: 'In sum, a contract is not sufficient unto itself, but is possible only thanks to a regulation of the contract which is originally social.'[21]

This was Durkheim's major contribution to Sociology as a discipline concerned not only with experiences and actions which could be observed, as it were, on the surface, but also, and most especially, with what they added up to as a whole, as an independent variable. In this sense, working-class culture cannot be denied by reference to diverse and

---

[17] Emile Durkheim, *The Division of Labour in Society* (1893; New York, 1964) pp. 39, 202.

[18] Ibid., pp. 212, 215.

[19] Edmund Burke, *Reflections on the Revolution in France* (1790; Harmondsworth, 1978), pp. 119, 171.

[20] Raymond Williams, *Culture and Society 1780–1950* (1958; Harmondsworth, 1978), p. 16; Terry Eagleton, *The Idea of Culture* (Oxford, 2000), p. 13.

[21] Durkheim, *Division of Labour*, p. 215.

discordant acts because it is not the acts which constitute the culture as the culture which constitutes the acts.[22] For instance, at the bookie's there is nothing more private and contractual than a bet, but *betting* is the cultural, communal and whole form, the social contract which allows the bet to happen. For some men, indeed, betting was 'a studied art'.[23] In this way, operating beneath the frenetic surface of men laying bets, betting is best seen, according to Durkheim, as concerned 'not with simple incidents in personal life but with regular and constant practices, residues of collective experiences, fashioned by an entire train of generations'.[24] And what is true for the humble bet is true for great national institutions as well. Banking and taxation, for example, or the operation of the British constitution, also depended on regular and constant practices and residues of collective experiences fashioned by an entire train of generations – basic assumptions about how to do things that Walter Bagehot called the 'common sense of the nation'.[25]

Durkheim did not intend culture to preclude difference, but he did intend it to preclude non-recognition of what is commonly understood to be particular about living in one place as opposed to living in another place. It is hard to believe that in Bourke's working-class London, or in her industrial cities, relationships were so ad hoc, or so fleeting, or so anonymous, that they were unable to produce cultures common enough 'as to constitute a shared identity'.[26]

Three disciplines

In 1857, John Stuart Mill reckoned that most Englishmen had nothing in their lives but work, and it is from around this time that historians date the making of a working-class community in north-east England.[27] They identify it in the concentration of marine engineering, shipping and shipbuilding, coalmining, and chemicals, banking and finance in inte-

---

[22] I am following here Durkheim on moral codes as in Lewis A. Coser and Bernard Rosenberg's *Sociological Theory* (New York, 1976), pp. 88–93.

[23] Ross McKibbin, 'Working Class Gambling in Britain 1880–1939', *Past and Present*, 82 (February 1979), p. 171.

[24] Quoted in E.A. Tiryakian, 'Emile Durkheim', in Tom Bottomore and Robert Nisbet (eds), *A History of Sociological Analysis* (London, 1978), p. 202.

[25] On banking and taxation: Donald Winch, 'Introduction', *The Political Economy of British Historical Experience 1688–1914* (Oxford, 2002), pp. 21–4; on the constitution: Conor Gearty, 'How We Declare War', *London Review of Books*, 3 October 2002.

[26] Bourke, *Working-class Cultures*, p. 169.

[27] J.S. Mill, *Principles of Political Economy* (1857; London, 1921), p. 105.

grated business sectors, and in the dense urban settlements that spread down the banks of Tyne, Wear and Tees and out into the coalfield itself. The rate of inward migration into Northumberland and Durham was at its most intense in the 1860s and 1870s. Industrial investment was at its most intense after that, up to 1914.[28] From the census enumerator's returns, sometime between 1869 and 1879 George and Susannah Colls moved with their two young children from Potter Heigham, in Norfolk, to Tyne Dock, in South Shields.[29] Whatever life this little family left behind it in agricultural Norfolk was clearly a life that did not match the rough and ready opportunities of the place they headed for. After the 1890s, the rate of north-east inward migration and investment calmed down and what had initially been thrown together as industrial districts began to congeal into what came to be called an urban conurbation. My grandfather, George Colls, grandson of Norfolk George, was born in 1900. In 1921, after military service, he followed his father and uncles into the shipyards. In 1923 my father was born, and in 1939 he followed his father into the yards. In one generation, therefore, the Colls family had moved from the worst paid labour in England to the best. In two generations, they had made it a family tradition.

For most of the nineteenth century, English working people were considered incapable of forming their own institutions. Investigators and missionaries said things about Jamaican plantation workers that they also said about Durham miners: they were excitable, ignorant, outspoken, childish and in need of great reform or, at least, in need of a schooling that would instil great reform.[30] In particular, their 'psychology' was cast as unstable and lacking discipline. In the event, first discipline turned out to be a greatly expanded labour market, which wanted its labour cheap, flexible and free from custom,[31] and the second discipline turned out to

---

[28] J.W. House, *North Eastern England: Population Movements and the Landscape since the Early 19th Century* (1954; King's College, University of Durham, 1960), pp. 3, 14, 50–53.

[29] High wages in coalmining and shipbuilding pulled the people in. Between 1851 and 1911 Northumberland and Durham, along with South Wales, were the fastest growing regions: E.H. Hunt, *Regional Wage Variations in Britain 1850–1914* (Oxford, 1973), tables 1–7, 4–10, 7–1, fig. 6–1. For the north-east of England, see essays by Ellis, Lendrum, Vall and Barke in Robert Colls and Bill Lancaster (eds), *Newcastle upon Tyne: A Modern History* (Chichester, 2001).

[30] Robert Colls, '"Oh Happy English Children!" Coal, Class and Education in the North East', *Past & Present*, 73 (November 1976), pp. 86–96; Catherine Hall, *Civilizing Subjects: Metropole and Colony in the English Imagination 1830–67* (Cambridge, 2002), ch. 5.

[31] And in the north-east the battle over labour began early: David Levine and Keith Wrightson, *The Making of an Industrial Society: Whickham 1560–1765* (Oxford, 1991).

be self-reliance, which was partly what individuals did for themselves (in the manner of Samuel Smiles and Joanna Bourke) but which was also achieved by an expansion of what workers did for each other, in organized ways. This was not 'collectivism', or 'class consciousness', or 'community' in the reified way such terms have been used by academics, but practical steps by those who could not gain their protection in any other way.[32] What eventually came to be called 'Victorian Values' was in fact largely the attempt of one class to discipline another, but by the 1880s, when it was becoming clear that the class to be disciplined was disciplining itself in the self-insuring, friendly and trade societies, there was a distinct shift in attitude. Gradually, Tyneside came to be represented more positively, as a region defined by its labour power and represented in the associational life of certain key trades who controlled the pace, the quality and, to a degree, the volume of industrial production.[33]

In shipbuilding, the primary lines of modern trade solidarity were introduced from the 1850s when the construction of ships by iron, and then mild steel, rendered the wood-based crafts untenable.[34] *John Bowes*, the iron screw collier launched at Jarrow in 1852, was the first successful modern cargo ship.[35] By 1914, there were over 90 new and adapted trades in the shipyards – 'ironmen' in the lead. Ironmen included platers, angle-iron smiths, rivetters, drillers, caulkers and fitters: all of them time-served and apprenticed.[36]

In coal, the main division was between hewers and the rest, a division essentially between men and boys.[37] It was well observed that the coalfield

---

[32] In extreme need people relied upon each other far more than on the poor law. On the failure of the Poor Law Unions to recruit paupers; see K. Gregson, 'The Operation of the Poor Laws in the Hartlepool Poor Law Union 1859–1930' (M. Litt., University of Newcastle, 1976 p. 76; R.G. Barker, 'Houghton le Spring Poor Law Union 1837–1930' (M. Litt., University of Newcastle, 1974), p. 47.

[33] The rise of mass trade unionism in Britain was more occupationally and geographically concentrated in the north-east than in any other region, where its craft principles dominated the movement: D.H. Aldcroft and M.J. Oliver, *Trade Unions and the Economy 1870–2000* (Aldershot, 2000), ch. 1.

[34] 'During the five years which have elapsed since publicatioin of the first edition of this work, steel has almost entirely replaced iron in ship construction': Samuel J.P. Thearle, *The Modern Practice of Shipbuilding* (Glasgow, 1891), preface.

[35] Norman McCord, *North East England* (London, 1979), p. 113.

[36] Paul L. Robertson, 'Demarcation Disputes in British Shipbuilding before 1914', *International Review of Social History*, xx (1975), p. 222, 226–8. For craft ethos, see Ian Macdonald and Len Tabner, *Smith's Docks: Shipbuilders 1908–1987* (Cleveland, 1989).

[37] 'The hewers are like the cabinet council of the county, governing and directing': William Whellan, *History, Topography and Directory of Northumberland* (London, 1855), p. 129.

was an itinerant community. Housing usually accompanied the job, intermarriage was frequent, collieries came and went, as did migration chains. There had always been high rates of migration, and therefore common knowledge, all across the coalfield. Inside the villages, no one doubted the status of the hewers and, best of all, the 'pitmen' – a historic term denoting technical skill and instinct. Knowledge such as this was power, and was not always to the owners' liking, but it existed in all occupations with strong craft and locational ties.[38] Indeed, for 400 years it is possible to discern in the coalfield Durkheim's same regular and constant practices: large-scale capital operations; ruthless commodity markets; widespread environmental damage; water and ventilation dangers; poor industrial relations; dramatic wage variations; finely graded divisions of labour, including sexual divisions of labour; and dense cultural networks, not only in the villages but across the coalfield as a whole.[39]

Alongside the disciplines of the labour market and the trades was a third discipline, that of gender. Work and wages were the elemental tests of manhood. Organized into squadrons of the skilled and unskilled based on a revitalized system of industrial apprenticeship, a new masculinity emerged.[40] One only had to be a man, or a boy, to share its connotations.[41]

Women's labour had a greater claim to be elemental. When industrial production moved away from households, if family finances allowed, most working-class mothers opted to stay at home. This was a pattern that prevailed from at least the 1840s to the 1940s, and in the north-east it probably started sooner, and lasted longer, than in any other region.[42]

---

[38] See, for instance, John Daglish to Lord Vane (n.d. 1864?), Durham County Record Office, D/Lo/C217. On recruitment and migration; see Michael Sill, 'Hetton le Hole: The Genesis of a Coalmining Landscape, 1770–1860', MA, University of Durham, 1974; G. Patterson (ed.), *Monkwearmouth Colliery in 1851: An Analysis of the Census Returns* (Durham, 1977); Roy Church, *History of the British Coal Industry 1830–1913* (Oxford, 1986), vol. 3, pp. 229–32, 614–17.

[39] Levine and Wrightson, *Whickham 1560–1765*, and Robert Colls, *The Pitmen of the Northern Coalfield: Work, Culture, Protest 1790–1850* (Manchester, 1987).

[40] 'and the boys, by their hard labour having a right to indulgence soon become the masters': G.A. Cooke, *Topographical and Statistical Description of the County of Durham* (London, 1824), p. 54. Major Durham occupations were men only, with 417 320 women rendered 'unspecified': *Census 1911*, x, pt 1, pp. 168–72, 238–42. Between 1911 and 1951, there was very little relative change in men's employment: see *Census 1951*, occupational tables, pp. 152–5, 620.

[41] George Parkinson, *True Stories of Durham Pit-Life* (London, 1912), pp. 16–17; Jack Lawson, *A Man's Life* (London, 1946), p. 46.

[42] Up to the 1930s most working-class women 'saw their emancipation as being a move away from paid work outside the home towards staying there'; in 1911 only about 13.7 per cent of married females were in full-time work in

Mother was 'the centre of the household, the mainspring on which all depend', and daughters were apprenticed to her from as soon as they could help.[43] Even if women's formal capacity to collectively organize their labour was weak, there can be little doubt that by making the household operational, their labour enabled the male associations to function. In this regard, for Middlesbrough in 1907 it was calculated that about half of mothers succeeded.[44]

Women were streetwise. They kept clear the channels of communication. They knew who was who and where they lived, and they drew on all this as common knowledge. Right down to the 1930s it was still a walking society and the streets remained safe. Children virtually lived there, especially in the summer, and sustained a powerful culture of play right into the 1950s.[45] To the men, women's street talk was just gossip. But to those who needed information about a job, a useful contact, or local resource, or a house swap ('key money'), women's gossip was a standing committee on public safety. David Reeder and Richard Rodger once famously referred to cities as the 'information superhighways' of their age. At street level, where the flow of information was heaviest, no one knew this better than the mothers.[46] What came to be called community was simply another way of referring to their world.[47]

England and Wales, and far fewer in County Durham: Elizabeth Roberts, *Women's Work 1840–1940* (London, 1988), p. 16, tables 1.2, 3.1. See also George Joseph, *Women at Work: The British Experience* (Deddington, 1983), fig. 3.5.

[43] Margaret I. Balfour and Joan C. Drury, *Motherhood in the Special Areas of Durham and Tyneside* (London, 1935) p. 10. For a Bedlington household apprenticeship in the 1920s, see Mary Wade, *To The Miner Born* (Stocksfield, 1984). Between 1911 and 1951 the region's major occupational groups had the highest fertility levels in England and Wales: M.R. Haines, 'Fertility, Nuptuality and Occupation', *Journal of Interdisciplinary History*, viii (1977–8), pp. 256–7; Simon Szreter, *Fertility, class and gender in Britain 1860–1940* (Cambridge 2000) ch. 7, fig 7.1. Szreter identifies strong community patterns behind similar fertility levels – or what he calls 'distinctive form[s] of generic community from a socio-economic and demographic point of view'. (p. 322).

[44] Lady Bell, *At the Works* (London, 1907), p. 171.

[45] Madge and Robert King, *Street Games of North Shields Children* (Tynemouth, 1930); Iona and Peter Opie, *The Lore and Language of Schoolchildren* (Oxford, 1959).

[46] David Reeder and Richard Rodger, 'Industrialization and the City Economy', in M. J. Daunton (ed.), *Cambridge Urban History of Britain*, vol. III: *1840–1950* (Cambridge, 2000), p. 554. Colin Smith represents markets as dealing as much in urban information as the price of things: 'The wholesale and retail markets of London, 1660–1840', *Economic History Review*, lv (February 2002).

[47] For a comparable community, see Trevor Lummis, *Occupation and Society: The East Anglian Fishermen 1880–1914* (Cambridge, 1985), p. 76.

Women's communication networks did not lie over the neighbourhood like a grid. Rather, they were embedded, with all connections open.[48] Outdoor parties, bus trips, chapel teas, child care, park outings, the daily borrowing and sharing according to a strict housework rota (the female division of labour), as well as the street minding that went on all day, every day, just seemed to happen, as if out of nothing. In fact it came out of deep female networks. My grandfather got his gold medal, award of The Amalgamated Society of Boilermakers, Shipwrights and Blacksmiths, presented 'by the executive Council for long and faithful service to the Society, 19 August 1971'. Grandmother was never so honoured. There was no Amalgamated Society of Female Menders and Moulders to call her Sister Doris, or to acknowledge the part she played in the social contract, but mending and moulding is what she did. There is no street-corner, blue-plate memory of these women.[49]

New Civil Society

By the end of the nineteenth century it was clear to all, particularly to a government which had just completed a Royal Commission on the subject, that 'Labour' was in the process of building an entirely new civil society based on free association. In 1889 the Austrian deputy J.M. Baernreither described this as 'a gigantic development of associated life':

> England is at present the theatre of a gigantic development of associated life, which gives to her labour, her education, her social intercourse, nay, to the entire development of her culture, a pronounced direction, a decisive step. The tendency towards the union of forces and the working of this union are nowadays more powerful in England than ever, and more powerful than anywhere else. The free union of individuals for the attainment of a common object is the great psychological fact in the life of the people, its great characteristic feature . . . freed now from all [legal] fetters, and yet at the same time under discipline, it has become a mighty moving wheel

---

[48] 'society . . . may fairly be said to exist in transmission, in communication'; oral communication provided 'the lines of primary solidarity': John Dewey, *Democracy and Education: An Introduction to the Philosophy of Education* (New York, 1948), p. 5; Talcott Parsons, *Structure and Process in Modern Societies* (Glencoe, Ill., 1960), p. 269. On Tyneside, first mark of the communicant was in the dialect.

[49] Pamela Sharpe comments on how women are difficult to 'catch' in the sources of history: 'Continuity and Change: Women's History and Economic History in Britain', *Economic History Review*, xlviii (2) (1995), p. 354.

of social development in general, and especially in the elevation of the working classes.⁵⁰

Dr Brentano had studied the trade unions, Dr Rabbeno had studied the cooperatives and wholesale societies, and Drs Hasbach and Baernreither had made their observations with the friendly societies in mind (ten types). In France, the professor of Political Economy at Paris University concluded that they could not 'expect to teach many new ideas to our English cooperative comrades because it is from them that we have received almost everything'.⁵¹ A circle of historians known as the *Anglicistes* gathered, and Boutmy, Halevy, Mantoux and others found plenty to praise in English associations for their shaping of popular political *mentalites* – as would New Liberals at home like Hobhouse and the Hammonds, or New Socialists like Tawney, a key figure in the workers' education movement.⁵² At Walbottle Colliery, the migrant German coalminer Ernst Duckershoff observed that if two Englishmen wished to fight, they could hardly do so without squaring up in a proper ring with proper rules and due procedure. It was their 'capacity to organize themselves collectively and decently' which so impressed him.⁵³

It also impressed members of the Royal Commission. They saw miners' associations as direct applications of those everyday practices and principles learnt face to face on the ground (and under it). Northumberland and Durham miners' sliding scale arrangements were intended to maintain fairness in wages against prices. Their system of county averages maintained parity of wages between pits (the only coalfield ever to achieve it).⁵⁴ Their 'cavilling' agreements maintained parity of risk between teams by the quarterly balloting of work places, 'thus effectually preventing any exercise of partiality on the part of colliery officials'.⁵⁵ Their checkweighmen ensured fair weighing and payment, guaranteed from 1860 by acts of parliament.⁵⁶ Their Permanent Relief Fund looked

---

⁵⁰ J.M. Baernreither, *English Associations of Working Men* (London, 1889), p. 11.

⁵¹ Charles Gide, *Consumers' Cooperative Societies* (London, 1921), p. ix.

⁵² L. Goldman, *Dons and Workers: Oxford and Adult Education since 1850* (Oxford, 1995), ch. 4. Peter Clarke explains how New Liberalism was both collectivist and anti-statist, and Gurney explains its relationship with Cooperation: *Hope and Glory: Britain 1900–90* (London, 1997); *Cooperative Culture and the Politics of Consumption in England 1870–1930* (Manchester, 1996) pp. 123–4.

⁵³ Duckershoff, E., *How the English Workman Lives* (London, 1899), p. 67.

⁵⁴ W.R. Garside, *The Durham Miners 1919–1960* (London, 1971), p. 22.

⁵⁵ R.L. Galloway, *Annals of Coal Mining and the Coal Trade*, 2nd series (1904; Newton Abbot, 1971), vol. II, p. 358; Colls, *Pitmen*, p. 48.

⁵⁶ John Wilson, *A History of the Durham Miners Association 1870–1904* (Durham, 1907), p. 339.

after the old, the disabled, widows and children. In their county associations, Northumberland and Durham miners adhered to a density of membership and discipline unsurpassed by any trade union in the world.[57] In 1891, their Permanent Relief Fund had an income of over £1 million – £953 141 from them, £81 096 from owners – a revenue base guaranteed by total assocational membership. Since 1863 the fund had cared for 1823 widows, 3845 children of 3200 members killed, and a similar number permanently disabled. Long before the state got round to it, this institution was paying modest amounts to 5737 pensioners.[58] Evidence to the Commission suggested around 90 per cent coalfield membership of the Cooperative Wholesale Society. Like the *Anglicistes*, John Mitchell, the CWS chairman, understood how this the most powerful English working-class association provided a template for a new civil society. While giving evidence to the Royal Commission on behalf of the Society in 1892, he was heckled by some of its more sceptical members:

> He surprised some of the gentlemen by the enthusiastic descriptions he gave of the power of cooperation. He gambolled with millions of money in share and loan capital. He jauntily talked of fleets of cooperative steamers. He wrote down buildings and machinery by thousands of pounds annually, till some of his healers called for proofs of his statements. Balance sheets were handed round immediately.[59]

Seen in this light, the emergence of a Labour party and a parliamentary road to socialism looks less like the culmination of an existing working-class politics and more like the beginning of a new, and rival, form.[60] Nevertheless, the Labour party was nothing without the associations. In 1919 it captured County Durham through the miners' union. This was the first time the party had won a county council. And though they lost it in 1922 they recaptured it again in 1925 (and have not relinquished it

---

[57] The Durham Miners' Association insisted on total membership and compliance with the rules; so did the coalowners: evidence of Mr Lindsay Wood, President, Durham Coal Owners' Association, in *Royal Commission on Labour*, First Report, Digest of evidence taken before Group A, Parliamentary Papers 1892, vol. xxxiv, pp. 216–35. In the region as a whole, the Webbs calculated that 11 per cent of the eligible population were members of trade unions – the highest proportion in the UK (average 3.98 per cent): Sidney and Beatrice Webb, *The History of Trade Unionism 1666–1920* (London, 1919), p. 742.

[58] *Royal Commission on Labour*, summary of evidence received by Group A, Part 1, Mines and Quarries, Parliamentary Papers 1894, vol. xxxv, pp. 301, 307, 321–3, 310.

[59] William Maxwell, memoir of Mitchell, quoted in Stephen Yeo, *Who Was J.T.W. Mitchell?* (Manchester, 1995), p. 32

[60] Early Labour party leaders damned the cooperative movement with faint praise: Gurney, *Cooperative Culture*, pp. 182–4.

since). In the 1945 general election, every strand and faction came together for Labour to orchestrate its victory at all levels.[61]

Alongside Labour, there was a constellation of other institutions – primarily the nonconformist and Methodist chapels and Sunday Schools, the Cooperative Wholesale Society and Cooperative Union, and the national friendly societies, and after them, the allotment societies, the brass bands, voluntary bodies, sporting clubs, youth organizations and the like – which drew their members from the streets but which also projected their activities out on to a wider, civic world. Every working-class neighbourhood was thick with these institutions. Brian Simon's chapter in this volume on the locally elected school boards adds schools and teacher centres as new, though short-lived, fields of projection. Most of the voluntary institutions carried in their rules the concept of 'association', 'union', 'federation', 'guild', 'league', and 'connexion'. What Richard Holt says about the pleasures of belonging to sporting clubs can be said about clubs of every kind – particularly the part of those 'cheerful fanatics' who did the paperwork and kept things going.[62] In Throckley village the Cycle Club and the Mothers' Union might have differed in their pleasures as in their personnel, but they stood for the village as a whole.[63] Ever eager for recruits, these were the people who liked to show their colours. They were the ragged-trousers public moralists.[64]

After municipal reform in 1835, middle-class associational life was increasingly committed to taking responsibility for town government as a whole. At the municipal level it was a life that brought people together in commonly recognized procedures. Gatherings were taught how to agree, and how to agree to differ – all vital lessons in civic governance.[65] Although artisanal mutual aid societies were the largest associational

---

[61] This is the main theme in Kenneth Morgan's *Labour in Power 1945–51* (Oxford, 1951), p. 45, 500–503. See also Huw Beynon and Terry Austrin, *Masters and Servants: The Durham Miners and the English Political Tradition* (London, 1994), pp. 250–63.

[62] Richard Holt, *Sport and the British: A Modern History* (Oxford, 1989), p. 155.

[63] Bill Williamson, *Class, Culture and Community: A Biographical Study of Social Change in Mining* (London, 1982), pp. 230–31.

[64] 'part of a vocabulary of political analysis ... which insisted on the inadequacy of merely legal or consitutitional changes when unaccompanied by the necessary qualities and habits in the people': Stefan Collini, *Public Moralists: Political Thought and Intellectual Life in Britain 1850–1930* (Oxford, 1991), p. 107.

[65] R.J. Morris, 'Civil Society and the Nature of Urbanism', *Urban History*, 25 (3) (December 1998) pp. 289–301; Simon Gunn, *The Public Culture of the Victorian Middle Class* (Manchester, 2000).

group before, and after, 1800, the middling classes had been building their associations for just as long.[66] We might call their associations 'civic bourgeois' but it would be wrong to underestimate their capacity to represent beyond their memberships.[67] Consider the 'Lit and Phils', or, as in Williamson's chapter in this volume, the university extra-mural departments. They may have been small in size and few in number but they were highly influential in lending historical identity to the regions. The late Victorian political class were very keen on this, and, as Richard Rodger's chapter shows, they took every opportunity to promote it. Local governments ran programmes which working-class associations came to depend on. There could be no football without playing fields, no pigeons without crees, no gardening without allotments. The Women's Co-operative Guild asked for clinics, and everybody needed, even if everybody did not receive, affordable housing, decent health facilities and cheap public transport.[68]

Commerce is not always linked to associational life, but on Tyneside, the names of the great men and the companies they founded came as second nature. Up and down the river, everyone had stories to tell about working at Armstrong's, or Leslie's, Palmer's, Smith's, Swan's, Market Dock, Reyrolle's and a hundred others. While it is true to say that radical liberals and socialists tended to see commercial activity as a threat to democratic associational life (and so it has proved to be), at the time, the form of capitalism most typically represented by the business elite was not entirely different from other forms of middle-class voluntary association. Up to a point, limited companies were subscriber democracies proportionally represented in shareholders'meetings. Up to a point, they were locally based, locally capitalized, locally staffed and locally known, and therefore locally accountable – or at any rate more accountable than forms of capitalist commercial enterprise before or since. Similarly, great men's philanthropic offerings – the libraries, parks, colleges, galleries, museums and sports and social clubs which bore their name – were poised somewhere between self-interest and the public good. Pubs, newspapers and professional football clubs were explicitly offered as modern forms of popular representation. No one can doubt the

---

[66] Peter Clark, *British Clubs and Societies 1580–1800: The Origins of an Associational World* (Oxford, 2000), pp. 470–71.

[67] The area had a smaller middle class than the country generally: General Registrar Office, *Census County Report. Durham. Northumberland* (London, 1954), pp. xlvi, xliii.

[68] David M. Goodfellow, *Tyneside: The Social Facts* (Newcastle, 1942), pp. 15, 34–5.

multifaceted popularity of the public house; for nearly a hundred years Newcastle United and Sunderland FC have been sites of a remarkable (if rather one-eyed) regional identity;[69] newspapers were very important indeed because not only did they represent themselves, they represented everybody else as well.

We are describing, then, a new civil society in the making.[70] It wasn't free market capitalist, or central statist, or democratic individualist, nor was it seen as the work of any single class or group. Rather, it was associationalist based on what had been achieved already – eclectically so – and projecting federally forward with the half glimpsed intention to constitute a greater and greater share of what Mill called 'the collective business of society', business that can be performed, 'by the people themselves, without any intervention of the executive government'.[71]

Stripping the culture

I left South Shields in 1967 and have been coming back ever since. Travelling up from King's Cross never ceased to mark the changes. But journeys are never just geographical. They traverse maps of meaning too, and when from the 1980s Shields began to rust on its rails, journeys home became anxious days. On Tyneside as across all the older industrial regions, there were mass closures in manufacturing and a restructuring of the labour market which involved the virtual disappearance of the youth labour market and the trend towards flexible, part-time, unskilled, cheap, branch plant and service labour. As the big industrial employers

---

[69] James Walvin, *The People's Game: A Social History of British Football* (London, 1975), pp. 50–68; Tony Mason, *Association Football and English Society* (Brighton, 1980), p. 234; Holt, *Sport and the British*, p. 168–72.

[70] Stephen Yeo is *the* key thinker in the history and strategics of this new society. See his 'State and Anti State', in P. Corrigan ed., *Capitalism, State Formation, and Marxist Theory* (London, 1980). Graeme Morton provides an interesting discussion of the link between voluntary associations and Scottish local government in articulating civil society as an independent urban variable: 'Civil Society, municipal government and the state', *Urban History*, 25, 3, 1998.

[71] Eugenio F. Biagini, *Citizenship and Community: Liberals, Radicals and Collective Identities in the British Isles 1865–1931* (Cambridge, 2002), p. 30. Gurney describes the cooperative movement as 'a transformative social and economic strategy based on the association of workers . . . deeply involved in the construction of a culture': *Cooperative Culture*, pp. 22–3. In the north, up to 1914, this burgeoning imagined political community found its strongest sense among advanced Liberals like G.J. Holyoake, Joseph Cowen, W.E. Adams, Robert Spence Watson and the first generation of miners' leaders, particularly John Wilson and Thomas Burt.

shut down and more women went out to work in a greater variety of locations, the female fund of common local knowledge began to dry up. Fundamental shifts in the pattern of work and residence, including the end of apprenticeship, the bureaucratization of the labour market, the mortgaging of housing and the steep fall in the number of married households all conspired against family and street as a source and a means of communication.[72] Mass demolition and building programmes broke up grid housing and the means of community self-surveillance it had encouraged. Increases in traffic and traffic pollution broke up the streets as places to dwell. Street crime and drugs, and fear of street crime and drugs, broke up the moral authority of ordinary people, especially older residents.[73] Women lost, or ceded, the streets.

The more political forms of working-class representation did not survive the 1980s. As their core industries were decimated and their legal immunities removed, the trade unions weakened. Coalmining and shipbuilding were more or less wiped out in about 10 years, the coalmining unions in about 10 months. Forms of cooperative, religious and civic representation, including the very idea of such forms of representation, went into what appears to be terminal decline. Philanthropy turned into 'sponsorship' – a much less committed concept. Government agencies talked a lot about 'community' and employed professionals to foster it, but only as a sign that it was slipping.

At the national level, the working class lost what authority it had managed to win in 1945–51. In its claim on 'The People' as a self-determining majority, there had always been a nationalist dimension to working-class representation. The move in emphasis away from majority to minority rights, in England at least, severely weakened this view of the people as having moral authority. In addition, so pulverized were northern industries during this period that some historians even began to doubt that the north had a place in English identity. Paul Johnson denied its true Englishness by depicting the Industrial Revolution as a bizarre episode never to be repeated. Professor Rubinstein declared that in all British history manufacturing had been not only an aberration, but a

---

[72] Supporting evidence can be found in various forms in *Ministry of Labour Gazette* (1950); *Labour Statistics* (2002); OECD *Historical Statistics 1970–2000* (2001); *Birth Statistics 1837–1983*; *Regional Trends* (2002); and *Office of National Statistics* (2002).

[73] The local newspaper gives editorial prominence to accounts of vandalism and terror. Murray Kelso, its crime reporter, is a key figure in reporting the town. While he reports a wave of arson attacks on schools, the town's MP, David Miliband, who is Minister for Schools, writes a column telling people they 'should not be living in fear of crime': *Shields Gazette*, 8 May 2003.

fetish.⁷⁴ At the same time, in the minds of metropolitan intellectuals at least, new ideas about ethnic and gender variability began to replace older ideas about solidarity and things that were supposed to be held in common. In a post-industrial, post-colonial, post-masculine, post-Christian world of fluid identities, ethnic diversities and global markets, the position of white working-class men who stayed attached to one place and a certain way of doing things (their own) looked distinctly uncomfortable.⁷⁵ In the study of social history, as we have seen, the revisionists began to appear, and in 1994 Joanna Bourke joined the spirit of the age and announced her intention to write about working-class culture 'stripped' of its 'institutional affiliations'.⁷⁶

Social contract made conscious

To try and understand a community stripped of its institutions might be a useful critical exercise, but it is an odd way of writing history. It resembles no society that has ever actually existed. There is no obvious cut off between the minds of individuals and the lives of institutions. Over the long run, British working-class institutions celebrated the ideal of the common life, taking ideas from within their own experience *and* from the world of ideas. Examples are legion, ranging from Methodism to Marxism, from Shakespeare to Shelley, but 'Socialism' might serve, very roughly, to describe the high cultural expression of that ideal.⁷⁷ In other words, Socialism was Durkheim's social contract made conscious and, once it was made so, ideas could be fed into it without compromising the authenticity of the community it stood for. The paradox I described at the beginning of this chapter was not a real paradox. Hoggart's book was part of the high culture of the community he described. Like any high culture, the book enriched and sharpened the world if addressed, and was part of. In the same vein, Joanna Bourke was wrong to see socialist 'community' writing in the 1950s as somehow

---

⁷⁴ Paul Johnson, *A History of the English People* (London, 1985), p. 430; W.D. Rubinstein, *Capitalism, Culture and Decline in Britain 1750–1990* (London, 1994), p. 35.

⁷⁵ For an attempt to explain the historical significance of these sweeping changes, see Robert Colls, *Identity of England* (Oxford, 2002), ch. 21 and *passim*.

⁷⁶ Bourke, *Working-class Cultures*, p. 1.

⁷⁷ See the discussion between Richard Hoggart and Raymond Williams in *New Left Review*, I (January–February 1960) pp. 26–30. For some Shakespearian examples, see Jonathan Rose, *The Intellectual Life of the British Working Classes* (New Haven, Conn., 2001), pp. 80–83.

inherently apart from working-class experience. The best of it understood that experience, and made it more cultured.

Nevertheless, cultures do not carry on regardless. In the 1990s, the pit villages of County Durham were offered as examples of moral and material disintegration.[78] Only 20 years earlier, they had been offered as examples of culture and community.[79] A whole civil society had been allowed to unravel. Except for some particularly feral estates and inner city areas, post-industrial Britain in 2004 is a long way off Durkheim's 'anomie',[80] but all government agencies are aware of the unravelling and not one of them has a clue what to do about it.[81] Now that Durkheim's 'regular and constant practices' and 'residues of collective experiences' have been broken, it is difficult to measure the rate of the unravelling because it is difficult to know what to measure it against. For a time, it seemed as though Etzioni's new communitarian politics would show how to restore civil society. Yet, although he uses history as a backdrop for what he sees as the disastrous decline of community since the 1950s, in truth Etzioni shows little interest in historical communities that had once lived.[82]

Anyway, these things can be argued about. What I do know is that these days, when I go back to Eglesfield Road where I was first shown community, there are no old folk on the front steps; there are no kids on the back field, rebuilt now to look like a prison exercise yard; no gangs of men striding home for twelve o'clock dinner; no lines of washing; no knots of women holding the street as if they owned it. Whatever exists there now, and whatever aspects of this old civilization continue to exist in other places, it is not the street I knew. The world Hoggart described not so very long ago is a way of life as dead as that of the North American Plains Indian or the Mississippi sharecropper.[83]

---

[78] For a powerful rendition, see Mark Hudson, *Coming Back to Brockens: A Year in a Mining Village* (London, 1994).

[79] One example from many: Martin Bulmer (ed.), *Mining and Social Change: Durham County in the Twentieth Century* (London, 1978), pp. 13–5.

[80] 'conflicting multiple normative paradigms': Tiryakiau, 'Emile Durkheim', p. 211.

[81] 'Village companies' as forms of social housing active in ex-mining towns have their supporters: 'Buying into Hope', *Guardian*, 20 March 2002. The Home Office's campaign against what it calls 'antisocial behaviour' can be seen as a struggle against some of the consequences of processes described in this chapter.

[82] Amitai Etzioni, *The New Golden Rule: Community and Morality in a Democratic Society* (London, 1997), pp. 141, xiv; *The Spirit of Community: Rights, Responsibilities and the Communitarian Agenda* (London, 1995), pp. 24, 118.

[83] Thanks to Richard Holt, Gavin Kitching, and Roey Sweet for their historical wisdom.

David Reeder: career and publications

Career synopsis

David Reeder's long association with the University of Leicester dates back to 1952 when he became a student in the School of Education. During the 1960s, whilst pursuing a career in teacher training, he undertook part-time higher degree studies in economic history at Leicester, supervised by the urban historian, H.J. Dyos, culminating in a one year full-time research fellowship in the Department of Economic and Social History. His wife, Barbara (nee Hunt) had also graduated from the University College, Leicester, with a BA degree in Mathematics in 1954 and both his son and daughter went on to study for first degrees at Leicester in Geology and History respectively. His wife and daughter were also students in the School of Education.

In 1973 David was appointed to a full-time post in the School of Education with responsibilities for Diploma and Higher Degree studies. In 1982 he was promoted to a joint appointment in urban studies in the Victorian Studies Centre in which respect he contributed to the MA course on Victorian Studies and gave several public lectures on behalf of the Centre. In 1983 he was made an academic officer of the University with responsibility for overseeing undergraduate courses in the associated colleges of the University. In this capacity be became the University representative on the Nene College Teacher Consultative Committee. He took early retirement from his joint post in 1988 in order to move to the newly founded Centre for Urban History in the Department of Economic and Social History to which he was appointed deputy director on a part-time basis. During this period he combined teaching duties in the Centre with duties as a tutor in the Department of Adult Education, giving classes at Vaughan College for the Certificates in Modern Social History and Social Science, and the BA in Humanities and World Humanities. He lectured regularly on the BA annual residential course at Ruskin College Oxford organized by Robert Colls. In the University, he contributed to three taught MA courses – in the Centre for Urban History, the Victorian Studies Centre and the Department of English Local History –

and acted as an external examiner to higher degree courses in several universities. He was also consultant to an ESRC project on wealth owning in the East Midlands, led by Professor John Scott of the Department of Sociology, and held a number of other research awards. In 1993 he relinquished some of these duties, but continued to provide advisory and consultancy services to the Centre for Urban History as a research associate. He also continued to operate as a tutor for the Department of Economic and Social History, and Adult Education.

David Reeder has combined duties in education with research and writing in urban and education history. Prior to his appointment at Leicester he had acquired experience of teaching and educational administration in the Royal Air Force, and as a school teacher and college lecturer in history, and as superintendent of an Evening Institute. From the mid-1960s he was involved in teacher training, initially for further and adult education. In the later 1960s and early 1970s he became head of education at Garnett College of Education and sustained a role in vocational education more generally. He contributed to courses at Madingley Hall Cambridge and an Anglo-American summer course at the London Institute, pioneered a new course in further education at the London Institute and the first CNAA degree for teachers in further education, edited a journal, and acted as advisor to the education boards of a number of vocational institutions, including the City and Guilds of London Institute and the Royal Society of Chiropidists, of which he was made a Fellow in 1982. On his move to the School of Education at Leicester he not only acquired new administrative responsibilities but specialized in the academic study of the history of education, acquiring a reputation for promoting studies in the history of urban education. From 1973 he was an active member of the History of Education Society and a member of the editorial board of *History of Education* until 1998. During the early 1980s he was also a member of an Anglo-German working group on the diffusion of knowledge, based at the University of Bochum. In the early 1990s he collaborated with Professor Fogelman of the School of Education in an Anglo-American research project on educational change, based at Leicester and funded by the Spencer Foundation.

As an urban historian, David Reeder has written on the history of urban development, particularly the suburbs, urban estate development, urban government and politics, urban surveys, the urban economy and urban education. Although urban history was an avocation more than a vocation in the 1960s and 1970s, nevertheless he was recruited by H. J. Dyos to be a founder member of the Urban History Group. He was also a member of the editorial board of the *Urban History Yearbook* and contributed papers to Urban History conferences and to the Dyos seminars in the Department of Economic and Social History at Leicester.

He also collaborated with H.J. Dyos in a joint essay for the symposium on *The Victorian City*, which was subsequently reprinted by the Economic History Society as a classic in the subject. After the death of Jim Dyos, David Reeder took over a number of his teaching and publishing activities. He was editor of the *Yearbook* for nine years, and until 2002 remained on the editorial board of *Urban History*, edited by Richard Rodger. He was conference organizer for the Urban History Group for five years and still continues as treasurer. As a London historian he acted as chairman of the conference of West London Local History Societies and was an active member of the London Topographical Society. In 1982 he was also involved in the Channel 4 TV series *The Making of Modern London*. In the early 1980s he assisted Peter Clark of the Leicester Centre for Urban History and Herman Diederiks of Leiden University to establish a joint Anglo-Dutch course in urbanization. In 1988–91 he was English representative on an Anglo-French working group based at the Maison des Sciences de l'Homme. One product of this group was the European colloquium on 'cities of finance' that he organized with the help of Herman Diederiks and the Royal Netherlands Academy in Amsterdam in May 1991. This was a forerunner for the formation of the European Association of Urban Historians the following year. Since then, European engagements have included attendance at the bi-annual conferences of the European Association in Strasbourg (1994), Budapest (1996) and Venice (1998); the keynote lecture at a workshop on 'Best Areas: elite residential districts' in Berlin, organized by Professor Heinz Reif of the Technische Universität (1997); and involvement in the research project entitled 'Les mots de la ville', based at the University of Aix in France (1999). On the domestic front, from 1988 he has worked with Professor Peter Clark on a number of research and publishing projects, including an ESRC project on health care in the twentieth century and the histories of Leicester and Maidstone. More recently, with the aid of a Nuffield Grant, he has collaborated with Richard Rodger, the present Director of the Centre for Urban History, in research on the British industrial city.

Curriculum vitae and list of publications

Education and qualifications

Nunthorpe Grammar School, York, 1942–9
Hatfield College, University of Durham, 1949–52; BA (Dunelm) 1952
School of Education, University of Leicester, 1952–3; PGCE (Leicester) 1953

Part-time study for an external degree in economic history; B.Sc. Econ (London) 1957
Part-time postgraduate study, University of Leicester, 1959–64; MA (Leicester) 1961; Ph.D. (Leicester) 1964

Theses

'The Use of Short-term Building and Repairing Leases in the Nineteenth Century', MA, Leicester, 1961
'Capital Investment in the Western Suburbs of Victorian London', Ph.D., Leicester, 1965

Posts

Education Officer, Royal Air Force, 1953–6
School Teacher and Superintendent of an Evening Institute, Leicester, 1956–9
Lecturer in History, Westminster College, London, 1959–62
Senior Lecturer then Principal Lecturer, Garnett College of Education, Roehampton, 1962–6
University Research Fellow in Economic History, University of Leicester, 1966–7
Head of the Faculty of Education, Garnett College of Education, Roehampton, 1967–73
Lecturer and Senior Lecturer in Education and Urban Studies in the School of Education, and the Victorian Studies Centre, 1973–88 (acting Director 1987–8) and Senior Tutor in the University of Leicester, 1983–8
Deputy Director (acting Director 1989–90), Centre for Urban History, and Adult Education Tutor, University of Leicester, 1988–93
Research Associate (acting Director autumn 1996), Centre for Urban History, University of Leicester, 1993–8 and Honorary Visiting Fellow 1998–

Books

The Age of the Chartists (Brodies Aids to History) (London: Brodies, 1960), 85 pp.
English Social Conditions in the Second Half of the 19th Century (Brodies Aids to History) (London: Brodies, 1960), 103 pp.
Urban Education in the Nineteenth Century (London: Taylor and Francis, 1977), 144 pp.
Suburbanity and the Victorian City: The H.J. Dyos Memorial Lecture

(Leicester: Victorian Studies Centre, University of Leicester, 1980), 22 pp.
Charles Booth's Descriptive Map of London Poverty 1887 (London: Topographical Society Publication No.130, 1984)
Archives and the Historian (Leicester: Centre for Urban History, 1989), 35 pp.
Landowners and Landholdings in Leicestershire and Rutland, 1873–1941 (Leicester: Centre for Urban History, 1994), 65 pp.
Going Comprehensive in England and Wales: A Study of Uneven Change (with A.C. Kerckhoff, K. Fogelman and D. Crook), (London: Woburn Press, 1996), 287 pp.

Edited books

Educating Our Masters (Leicester: Leicester University Press, 1980), 240 pp.
Exploring the Urban Past: Essays in Urban History by H.J. Dyos (Cambridge: Cambridge University Press, 1982), 258 pp. (with David Cannadine)
The Government of Victorian London (Cambridge, Mass. and London: Harvard University Press, 1982), 622 pp. (by David Owen, edited with Roy MacLeod, Donald Olsen and Francis Sheppard)
Rethinking Radical Education: Essays in Honour of Brian Simon (London: Lawrence and Wishart, 1992), 319 pp. (with Ali Rattansi)
Leicester in the Twentieth Century (Stroud: Alan Sutton, 1993), 240 pp. (with David Nash, Richard Rodger and Peter Jones)
Cities of Finance (Amsterdam: Royal Netherlands Academy, 1996), 320 pp. (with H.A. Diederiks)

General editor

Themes in International Urban History (Cambridge: Cambridge University Press, 1992–8), 5 vols (with Peter Clark)
Readers in Urban History (London: Longmans, 1990–93), 4 vols (with Peter Clark)

Edited journals

The Vocational Aspect of Education (Oxford: Pergammon) 3 times yearly, 1968–1979
Urban History Yearbook (Leicester: Leicester University Press, 1978–87), 9 vols

Published writings

'The politics of urban leaseholds in late-Victorian England', *International Review of Social History*, 6 (1961) pp. 1–18

'"A Theatre of Suburbs": patterns of development in west London', in H.J. Dyos (ed.) *The Study of Urban History* (London: Edward Arnold, 1968), pp. 253–79

'The making of a Garden Suburb', *Urban History Newsletter 1969* (Leicester, 1969), pp. 5–13

'The development of Fulham, 1880–1900' and 'Fulham in the twentieth century' in P. Whiting (ed.), *A History of Fulham* (London: The Fulham History Society, 1970), pp. 150–64; 275–90

'Slums and suburbs' (with H.J. Dyos), in H.J. Dyos and M. Wolff (eds), *The Victorian City: Images and Realities* (London: Routledge and Kegan Paul, 1973), vol. I, pp. 259–86. (reprinted for the Economic History Society in P. Thane and A. Sutcliffe (eds), *Essays in Economic and Social History* (Oxford: Blackwells, 1986), pp. 216–46

'The history of urban education' and 'Predicaments of city children: late Victorian and Edwardian perspectives on education and social policy' in D. Reeder (ed.), *Urban Education in the Nineteenth Century* (London: Taylor and Francis, 1977), pp. 1–10, 73–94

'Keeping up with London's past: local history in the Metropolis', *Urban History Yearbook 1977* (Leicester: Leicester University Press, 1977), pp. 48–55

'Education and industry: a recurring debate', in G. Bernbaum (ed.), *Schooling in Decline* (London: Macmillan, 1978), pp. 114–48 (reprinted in R. Dale et al. (eds), *Schooling and the National Interest* (Brighton: Falmer Press for the Open University, 1981), pp. 177–204

'H.J. Dyos: an appreciation' *Urban History Yearbook 1978* (Leicester: Leicester University Press, 1978), pp. 1–15.

'Liberal intellectuals, education and the franchise' in D.A. Reeder (ed.), *Educating Our Masters* (Leicester: Leicester University Press, 1980), pp. 177–204

'H.J. Dyos and the urban process', in D. Cannadine and D. Reeder (eds), *Exploring the Urban Past* (Cambridge: Cambridge University Press, 1982), pp. xi–xix

'Perspectives on metropolitan administrative history' and 'Bibliography of London's governmental history' in David Owen, *The Government of Victorian London 1855–1889*, ed. Roy Macleod et al (Cambridge, Mass. and London: Harvard University Press, 1982), pp. 347–69, 416–54

'Annals of metropolis: beyond the Edgeware Road. An essay review', *London Journal*, 9 (1983), pp. 71–4.

'The reconstruction of secondary education in England, 1869–1920', in D.K. Muller, F. Ringer and B. Simon (eds), *The Rise of the Modern Educational System, Structural Change and Social Reproduction, 1870–1920* (Cambridge: Cambridge University Press, 1987), pp. 135–50

'History, education and the city: a review of trends in Britain', in R.K. Goodenow and W.E. Marsden (eds), *The City and Education in Four Nations* (Cambridge: Cambridge University Press, 1992), pp. 13–43 (reprinted in Roy Lowe (ed.), *Themes in the History of Education* (London: Woburn Press, forthcoming)

'The radicalism of Brian Simon' in A. Rattansi and D. Reeder (eds), *Rethinking Radical Education: Essays in Honour of Brian Simon* (London: Lawrence and Wishart, 1992), pp. 15–24

'Schooling in the city: educational history and the urban variable', *Urban History*, 19 (1992), pp. 23–38

'The local economy' and 'Municipal provision: education, health and housing' in D. Nash and D. Reeder (eds), *Leicester in the Twentieth Century* (Stroud: Alan Sutton, 1993), pp. 49–89, 121–57

'Representations of metropolis: descriptions of the social environment in Charles Booth's *Life and Labour*', in D. Englander and R. O'Day (eds), *Retrieved Riches: Social Investigation in Britain 1840–1914* (Aldershot: Scolar, 1995), pp. 323–38

'The Victorian and Edwardian town: the rise of public services' and 'The First World War and after' (with L. Murfin) in P. Clark and L. Murfin (eds), *The History of Maidstone* (Stroud: Alan Sutton, 1995), pp. 148–76, 205–40

'The industrial city in Britain: urban biography in the modern style', *Urban History*, 25 (1998), pp. 368–78

'Industrialisation and the city economy' (with Richard Rodger) in M.J. Daunton (ed.), *The Cambridge Urban History of Britain*, vol.III: *1840–1950* (Cambridge: Cambridge University Press, 2000), pp. 553–92

'Obituary: Brian Simon: a tribute', *History of Education*, 31 (2002), pp. 307–10

'The Education Act of 1902 and local governance: some reflections on Brian Simon's critique', *History of Education Society Bulletin*, 70 (2002)

Unpublished writings

'Metropolitan Open Spaces: the battle for the Commons 1855–1900', unpublished paper for the project Space, Nature and Culture in the City: the making and contesting of open spaces, Helsinki, 2001–4.

Articles on 'metropolis', 'slum', 'suburb', 'house', 'flats', 'neighbourhood' contributed to *Un Trésor des mots de la ville (Dictionnaire historique plurilingue)*, co-ordinators Christian Topalov and Jean-Charles Depaule, UNESCO in conjunction with the Maison des science de l'homme, Paris, in preparation.

Index

accountability 22–38, 40–5, 47, 196
administration
   educational 178–206, 212–30, 308
   public 2, 6–7, 20–45, 46–66, 98, 104, 150, 154, 160, 172, 241, 262
adult and continuing education 13–14, 207–30, 303, 308–10
   see also Schools, Evening Continuation Schools
   Access courses 225
   award bearing, non award 211–12, 220, 224
   continuing professional development 221
   life-long learning 211, 215, 225, 229–30
   part-time degrees 212, 220, 225
   philosophy of 215, 223
   pre-retirement, return to study 220
   teaching methods, tutors 213, 215–16, 218, 222
   New Opportunities for Women (NOW) 220
   Recreative Evening Schools Association 197
agendas 1, 147, 160, 172–3, 211, 213–14, 221, 226, 292
Aire and Calder Navigation Co. 30
America 1, 14, 103, 151, 167, 206, 246
anglicans 131, 134, 138, 180, 188
anti-urbanism 52
architects, architecture 161, 174–5, 207, 234–5, 237–8, 242, 251, 253, 255
   Architectural Association 255
aristocracy 150–52
arts and crafts 244, 248
   Morris, W., Ashbee, C.R., Voysey, C. 244

Ashburton 70
associational culture, *see also* organizations, voluntary societies 9–10, 12, 15–20, 39, 121–43, 152, 163–7, 231–55, 258–81, 283–307

Bagehot, W. 150
Banbury 90
Barking, Essex 69, 87, 89, 91
Barnett, Canon 234, 252n
Barnsley 135
Birkenhead 191
Birmingham 27, 29, 50–51, 90, 134, 154, 184–5, 219, 239, 250, 265
Bishop's Stortford 91
Blackburn 50, 90
Blackstone, Sir William 288
Board
   of Education 191, 201, 205, 215, 217
   of Guardians 37n, 65, 276
   of Trade 43, 146, 195n
Bolton 35, 135, 190
Booth, Charles 254
boundaries 143, 162, 172, 221, 227, 262, 268, 271, 274–6
   see also jurisdictions
Bourke, J. 288–92
Bradford 17, 51, 58, 107, 111–12, 154, 184, 202–3, 264, 269–70, 272
Braudel, Fernand 1
Bristol 50–1, 134, 136, 184, 186, 191, 219, 242, 275–6
builders 235, 264, 305
buildings, *see also* public works
   courts 126–7, 142, 281
   cultural 142–3, 145, 153, 155–6, 164, 172–3

buildings *cont.*
  military 164, 166n
  public 139, 142, 144–5, 153–4, 161, 172, 174
  school 186, 190–91 (Cockerton judgement) 199
  social services 167–8
  town hall, guildhall 142, 144, 155, 172
Burnley 36
businesses 99, 146–7, 163, 212, 261, 295, 303
  Chambers of Commerce 39
  trade societies 117, 147, 296

Cambridge 91, 134
capitalism 1, 21–45, 60, 121, 134, 163, 201–6, 212, 256n, 293–7, 303–5
Cardiff 191, 219
Carlisle 74
catholics 135
centralization 8, 52, 54, 63, 65, 96, 104, 108–10, 112–14, 187, 189, 201–6, 300, 304n
central-local relations 7, 12, 56–62, 63, 96, 152, 156, 158–63, 177, 201–6, 276, 280–81, 304
ceremonies, *see* civic
Chadwick, Edwin 6, 8, 24, 54, 62–3, 68, 70, 74–5, 94
Chamberlain, Joseph 239
chapels 126–7, 135, 302, 306
Chaplin, S. 208–9, 214
charities, *see also* voluntary organizations 18, 47, 54, 139, 141, 148, 161, 167–9, 244, 253, 280
  Nottingham Society for Organising Charity 245
  Town and Country Social Guild 244
chartism 60, 96, 99n, 100, 104, 117, 119
Churchill, Winston 158
cinema 262
citizenship 14–17, 64, 112, 144–77, 214–15, 229, 231–56, 258–82
city, *see also* urban
  gendered 15, 29, 104, 174, 184, 192, 231–57, 279, 297, 299, 304, 306
  growth xiv

improvements, *see* improvement
inner 3, 235, 239–41, 251–3, 281
civic
  ceremonies 136, 140–49, 150–61, 169, 172, 207
  honours 150–52
    freedom of the city 11, 150–52, 169
  hospitality 144–61
  pageants 150–58
civil society 8, 11–17, 103, 123–43, 144–77, 211–30, 258–82
  definition 274
class, class relations
  artisan 114, 185, 218
  middle classes 3, 9–10, 15, 38–9, 61, 97, 102–4, 111, 117, 123–43, 158, 204, 219, 234, 240, 242, 248–9, 256, 279, 302–3
  working class 39, 52, 54, 56, 61, 97–9, 102–3, 117, 132–3, 152, 180, 185, 199, 205, 237, 239, 241, 258, 261–3, 265, 269–82, 283–307
clubs 9, 135, 142–3, 163–6, 173, 175, 177, 243, 286–9, 302–3
  soccer 167, 303–4
coffee houses 9, 142
Colls, R. 12, 18, 308
commercial buildings 124, 127, 133, 135, 147
Commissioners
  Land 88
  Police or Improvements 7, 8, 33, 35–6, 41, 115
  Poor Law 241
  Sewers 63, 73–4, 76, 94
  Streets 100
commissions
  educational 180, 182–5, 196, 198
  housing 236
common good 11, 18, 106, 275, 144–77
communities 4, 5, 12, 14, 17, 19, 36, 61, 105, 107, 126, 139, 205, 207, 217, 220–1, 224, 226, 235, 243, 259–63, 265, 268–82, 283–307
competitions 164, 239, 245, 271
concerts 124, 146, 156
conferences 1, 11, 146–9

INDEX

consumers 33, 41, 43, 53, 133, 143, 147, 259, 282
co-operative movement 122, 216, 282, 300–301, 305
   Co-operative Union 216
   Cooperative Wholesale Society 301–2
   Royal Arsenal Co-operative Society 216
corruption 34–5, 53, 56, 63, 66, 109
Cottrell, P.L 5, 6
courts, *see also* law 25–30, 33, 40, 45, 109, 111–12
   Court of Chancery 264–5, 267, 281
Coventry 191
credit 39, 139
criminal justice system 8, 96–120
crown control 47, 62, 108–10, 169–70
Croydon 74

Daunton, M. 3
De Toqueville, Alexis 8, 10, 11, 12, 17
death rates 38, 45, 48, 50–51, 58
debts 29, 34
deference 133, 135
delegations 144–9, 162
democracy 96, 107, 111, 113, 179–82, 191, 205, 208–9, 228–9, 258, 260, 276, 279, 303
   political representation 21–45, 46–7, 52, 54, 57, 59–61, 96–120, 228, 303, 305
   subscriber 121–43
demography, *see also* mortality, life expectancy 51–2, 58, 226
Denby, Elizabeth 251–2, 256
Deptford 71
Dickens, Charles 23
directories 124
disease 48, 54, 56, 68
   epidemic 5, 33, 48, 50–51, 54, 62, 68, 72, 103, 121
   epidemiology of 48, 51, 55, 63, 66
Disraeli, Benjamin 4
donations 161, 163–5, 169
Doncaster 30
Dublin 134, 163, 238, 247, 252n
Durham, Miners' Gala 207
   mining villages 210, 224, 295, 300–301

Old Elvet 209
Durkheim, Emile 283, 293–4
Dyos, H.J. xiii, xiv, 1, 235, 258, 308–10

East India Company 21, 40
Eccleshall 61
economy, local 31, 39, 99, 128, 131, 139, 166, 227, 238, 245, 254, 274, 309
Edinburgh 11, 70, 80, 134, 144–77, 237, 239, 246, 275–6
   districts 153–4, 169
   Leith 154–5, 164, 170
   Portobello 153, 167
education
   acts 14, 178, 180–82, 187–9, 192, 196, 197–8, 201, 204
   and taxation 191, 196, 201
   Department of Education 187, 189, 191–2, 195, 199
   Science and Art Department 183–4, 191, 195, 197–8, 202–3
   grants 191–2, 195–6
   higher 211–12, 215, 218, 226–7
   Robbins expansion 221
   history of 97, 178–206, 207–30
   inspectors (HMIs) 193, 205, 222
   liberal 207–30
   pedagogical 186, 188–9, 193–4, 222, 225
   policy 187, 189, 194–5, 211, 228
   see also education acts
   qualifications 186, 197
   technical 183, 196–7, 200, 202
   university education 207–30, 308–10
      curriculum 213, 221, 224
      expansion xiii
      extension lectures 196, 215, 218
      graduates 190, 193
      public relations 220
      veterinary 162–3, 172
   women's roles, *see also* schools
      Butler, Josephine 241, 247
elections 100–102, 105, 115, 117, 163, 181, 191, 205, 228, 243, 262, 302
elites 121, 124–5, 135, 160, 194, 204–5, 209, 212, 214, 221
empire 152, 154, 160, 167
employers 26, 99, 117

empowerment 13, 64, 164, 197, 230
environment, built, *see also* businesses, manufacturing, housing 231–57, 258–82, 305
environmental conditions 5, 11, 27–8, 40, 43, 46–66, 68–9, 98, 106, 114, 172, 177, 224, 232, 245
 pollution by
  air 6, 21, 23, 25–31, 243, 248, 297
  rivers 22–3, 28–30, 68, 72–3, 88, 139, 297
Exeter 50, 146
exhibitions 11, 146–7, 149, 156, 249, 252–3
 Ideal Home Exhibition 249
 International Exhibition of Electrical Engineering 149
 International Exhibition of Industry, Science and Art 147, 149
external economies 3, 21, 24, 39, 40, 122
extra-mural, *see* adult and continuing education

family and kinship 5, 15, 134, 166, 231, 234, 261–3, 267, 270, 274–5, 286, 292, 295, 305
Farr, William 40
Ferguson, Adam 8, 11, 103.
Fieldhouse, R. 223, 228
Fitch, Sir Joshua 180–81
franchise 9, 21–3, 32–42, 64, 100, 104–5, 180, 228, 231–56, 259, 263
free trade 6, 21–4, 32, 39–40, 45, 228
friendly societies 121, 124–6, 148, 275, 296, 300, 302

Galton, Francis 236
garden cities 238, 248–9
 Letchworth Garden City Company 248
 Welwyn Garden City 249
 Organizations
  Garden Cities and Town Planning Association 252–3
  Garden City Association 237, 248–9

gardens, gardening 148, 153, 164–5, 175, 243–5, 248, 253, 265, 270–1, 302–3
 market 70
Garside, P. 16
General Registry Office, Registrar General 7, 11, 46, 55, 61
Georgian towns 3
Gibbs, H. H. 81–4
Glasgow 32, 58, 134, 154, 158, 167, 275–6
Glass, Ruth 254
Gorst, Sir John 17–80, 201
governance, *see also* urban government 3, 22, 34–5, 96, 276, 302, 309
Green, T. H. 13

Halifax 142, 184
Hastings 93
Hennock, E.P. 7
Hill sisters, *see* housing, philanthropic, and Kyrle Society
Hoggart, Richard 221, 226, 275n, 283–5, 286n, 288, 291, 306–7
homes 208, 252–3, 262–3, 283–4, 297
hospitals 16n, 46, 54, 129–30, 154–5, 172
 voluntary 54
 Yorkshire County 130
household 103–4, 275, 292, 297–8
 economy 15, 39, 166, 297
housing 114, 146, 171–2, 208, 233–4, 237, 239, 243–5, 249–53, 256, 258–82, 283–4, 303–5
 acts 232, 236, 252, 256
 amenities 17, 263, 265–8, 270, 283–8
 associations 16n
  Fulham Housing Association 253
  Salford Better Housing Council 252
  St Pancras Improvement Society 252
  Sutton (Model) Dwellings Trust 16–17, 258–82
  Sutton Tenants' Association 272
 betterment 45
 conditions 49–51, 59, 233–4, 236, 240, 243, 251–2, 270

council estates 16, 18, 154, 234, 250, 258–82, 307
  LCC estates: Becontree 259–61, 266, Watling 261, 266–7
  flats, tenement 147, 253, 283
  garden cities, *see* garden
  landlords 38, 102, 263, 268, 273
  leasehold system 45
  lodging 286
  model dwellings 16, 251, 253, 258, 265, 273, 281
  New Housing for Old 251
  philanthropic
    Guinness and Peabody Trusts 264, 267
    Hill sisters 15, 237, 243–6, 258–82
    Miranda 15, 243, 245–6
    Octavia 237, 243–5
  slums 1–3, 10, 45, 171, 239, 250–52, 266, 280–81
  superintendent 270, 272–3
  taxes, *see* taxation, ratepayers
    betterment 45
  tenants 16, 102, 146, 169, 234, 260–61, 263, 265–70, 273–4, 280, 282
    associations of 270–72
Hull 50–1, 134
Hume, David 11

ideology 60–61, 66, 96, 100, 110, 112–14, 116, 119–20, 132–33, 140–3, 163, 176–7, 207, 223, 229, 236, 262–3, 269, 273–4, 278–9, 282, 306
Ilkeston 193
improvements 34, 39, 56, 60, 108, 126, 141, 143, 153, 155, 171–2, 174–5, 240, 243, 248–9, 252–3
Improvements Acts 29, 98, 113, 239
individualism, *see also* Tönnies, Ferdinand 103, 176–7, 228, 292–3, 296, 304
industrial relations, *see* labour
industries 27–8, 30–1, 38–40, 123, 128–32, 137, 284, 296, 304–5
infant mortality 49, 51, 68, 247
institutions 5, 18–19, 31, 38, 46–7, 100, 103, 112–13, 115, 129, 147–9, 163, 165–72, 213, 228–9, 274, 289, 294, 306
  financial 77–95, 133, 139, 147, 152, 154, 294–5
international bodies
  UNESCO, OECD, EU 229
internationalism 145, 151, 162, 166, 173, 229, 239, 246, 253, 260, 276, 279, 299
Ireland 111, 119, 167, 247, 295
Ironside, Isaac 100–6, 108, 113–14, 116–17, 119

Jephson, Henry 56, 65
joint stock companies 124, 133
jurisdictions, *see also* boundaries 2, 104, 113, 162

Kay-Shuttleworth, Sir Ughtred 57, 65
knowledge xiii, 7, 9–10, 54–5, 103, 147, 196, 208, 223, 227–8, 233, 262, 283–8, 292, 297–8
Kyrle Society 15, 243–6

labour 99, 121, 125, 158, 172, 207–8, 218, 232–3, 254–5, 261, 265, 293, 295–6, 299, 300–302, 304
  colleges
    Central Labour College 222
    International People's College 229
    National Council for Labour Colleges 222
    Ruskin College 222, 308
    Working Men's College 217
  manual 214, 218–19, 266, 290
  movement 181, 205–6, 207, 222, 247
    National Union of Mineworkers 208
    National Union of Teachers 184
  professional, *see* professions
  relations 101, 108, 110, 224, 289–90, 296–7
  solidarity 158, 207, 275–6, 296
land use 6, 45, 114, 119, 163, 235, 248
landowners 26, 45, 73, 118, 131, 169, 173, 280, 309
language 97, 112, 117, 119–20, 123, 126, 129, 132, 163, 211–12, 228, 290–92

language *cont.*
  and literature, English 208–10, 212, 217, 224, 233
law, lawyers, *see also* courts 25, 27–9, 109–10
  common 24–5, 31, 108, 110–11
  contract 40–43, 45
  criminal 97, 111
  statutes 29, 31, 36–8, 65, 98, 111, 113, 115, 160, 232, 236, 239, 252, 256, 242, 300
Lawrence, D.H. 193
Leamington 91, 93
Leeds 9, 17, 29, 58, 70, 121–43, 154, 182–4, 186, 190–91, 205, 219, 225, 269–70
  housing estates, Killingbeck 269
  Auxiliary Bible Society 128, 131
  Ladies Auxiliary Society 130
  Public Dispensary 129–30
  Local Education Authority 219
Leicester xiii–xv, 19, 51, 90, 182, 191, 219
  Centre for Urban History xiii, xv, 308–10
  Victorian Studies xiii, xv, 308
leisure 19n, 145, 163–9, 177, 233, 262, 273, 298–9, 303
Letchworth 248
Lever, William 238
liberty 6, 23, 30, 45, 96, 104, 112, 208
libraries 105, 135, 153, 172–3, 208–10, 233, 303
  university 208–12
life expectancy 5, 51, 59, 61
life long learning, *see* schools, evening continuation centres
Liverpool 50–51, 58, 61, 124, 134, 136, 154, 189–90, 249
  West Derby 62
local government 3, 6, 21–45, 46–56, 96, 100, 106, 114–15, 121, 127, 231, 251–2, 260, 265–80, 303, 304n, *see also* urban government
Local Government Board 31, 48, 50, 64, 95, 196, 238, 250, 267, 280
localism 96, 113, 117, 119, 160, 178, 184, 192, 196, 231, 258, 261, 282, 303
London xiv, 1, 2, 4, 5, 9, 26, 33, 42, 46–66, 103, 134, 142, 152, 157,

161–2, 180–81, 189–91, 196–9, 202, 237, 239, 243–6, 251, 254, 263, 265, 272, 291, 294, 304
  boroughs
    Battersea 190
    Bermondsey 26, 50
    Camberwell 49
    Clapham 49
    East End 50, 53, 234, 240n, 250
    Finsbury 190
    Fulham xiv, 49, 253
    Hackney 49, 55
    Hammersmith xiv, 59
    Holborn 50
    Islington 28n, 89, 191, 264
    Kensington 49, 55, 195n, 201, 251, 264, 268
    Lambeth 49, 59
    Lewisham 59
    Marylebone 237, 244
    Paddington xiv
    Rotherhithe 49
    Southwark 49, 63n, 190
    St Pancras 55, 251–2
    Stepney 50
    Sydenham 89
    Wandsworth 49, 59
    Woolwich 194
  embankment 32–3
  government
    City of London Corporation 74, 79
    London County Council 47–8, 50, 54, 64–6, 201, 216–7, 250, 252, 259, 273
    Metropolitan Board of Works, *see* London organizations
    Vestries, *see* urban government organizations
    Metropolitan Police 9, 109, 117
    Metropolitan Sewage and Essex Reclamation Company 67–95
    London School of Art 191
    Trades Council 197
    Metropolitan Water Board 54, 65–6
    Port of London Authority 46, 65–6
    Thames and Lea Conservancy Board 46, 65–6

London Stock Exchange 80–82
Metropolitan Board of Works 5,
  33, 42–3, 46, 47, 54, 56, 59, 63,
  66, 73–6, 78, 80, 89, 92–3
Metropolitan Asylums Board 5,
  46, 54, 65
suburbs 49, 59, 61
Luckin, B. 5, 6

magistrates 8, 106, 109–10, 112–13,
  115, 146, 155–6, 170
Manchester 36, 41, 51, 58, 61, 134–6,
  183–4, 193, 202–3, 205, 246, 250,
  252
  Chorlton-cum-Hardy 61
  Gorton 264
  Wythenshawe 259, 261
manufacturing 3, 58, 61, 123, 126,
  137–40, 147–8, 151–2, 185, 244,
  304–5
markets, market forces 2, 3, 6, 9, 29,
  39, 83–95, 119, 122, 127, 139, 153–4,
  156, 171, 173, 226, 258
Mass Observation 264
Masterman, C. F. G. 217
meetings
  annual general 9, 121, 128, 136
  public 8, 9, 105, 109, 121–43, 243,
    253, 269, 271, 302
Meller, H. 15, 16
mentalités 2, 66, 300
merchants 126
Merthyr Tydfil 50
methodism 127, 135, 302, 306
metropolitanism 58–62, 64–6, 305
Middlesbrough 255, 298
Midlands 179, 182
migration 2, 4, 48, 58, 128, 286, 295,
  305
military 138, 144–5, 150–1, 164–6,
  169, 174
Mill, J. S. 7, 22, 45, 65, 294, 304
Ministry
  Education 218, 222
  Foreign 146
  Health 65, 281
  Reconstruction 250
    Adult Education Committee 215
missionary and bible societies 124,
  167, 243

monopolies, public 6, 21–45
morality 107, 231, 234, 261, 265–6,
  269, 277, 293–4, 302, 305–6
Morant, R. L. 184, 192, 205–6
morbidity 54
Morris, R. J. 3, 9–10, 19
mortality 50–5, 59, 61, 68, 247
municipal 3, 6, 10, 21–2, 60–2, 64,
  100–12, 144–77, 248
  history 174–5
  see also urban, local government
museums and galleries 172–3, 234,
  303
music 126, 130, 143, 145–6, 148, 157,
  175, 245
mutuality 5, 107–8, 122, 149, 163–9,
  176, 228, 261, 267, 273, 276–7, 292,
  300n, 302

neighbourhood 1, 4, 104–5, 109, 141,
  231, 241, 243, 267, 271–2, 275, 285,
  290–91
neighbours 176, 283–6
networks, see also associational,
    professional
  credit 39
Newcastle 134, 154, 191, 219, 259,
  270
  Benwell estate 270
newspaper rooms 124
night school, see schools, evening
  continuation centres
non-conformists 134–5, 206
Norwich 51, 134, 146
Nottingham 134, 184, 190, 203, 224,
  244–5
nuisances 22–33, 106, 114, 233, 244

occupations, occupational structure
  166, 185–6, 200, 219–20, 231, 288,
  292, 297, 304
officials, see also education, health
  coroner 110–11, 113
  inspectors 47, 55, 112, 193
  local 7, 57, 66, 103, 107, 113–14,
    117, 131, 146, 153, 162–3, 234,
    237, 241
  medical officer of health 55, 64, 240
  sanitary 50, 66
  water analyst, engineer 46

324 INDEX

Oldham 36
organizations and voluntary societies 148, 165, 167–8
  see also education, health, housing and town planning, labour
  see under individual place names
  charitable and cultural
    Amateur Musical Society 126, 130
    Association for Improving the Condition of the Poor 169
    Benevolent or Stranger's Friendly Society 127–8
    Charity Organisation Society 168–9, 240n, 243–4
    Committee for Feeding and Clothing Destitute Schoolchildren 167
    Mechanics' Institutes 101n, 126–7, 133
    National Association for the Prevention of Cruelty to Children 167
    National Association for the Promotion of Social Science 146
    National Council for Social Service 16, 261–2, 279
    National Union of Societies for Equal Citizenship 231
    New Estates Community Council 16, 261–3, 268, 273, 277, 279, 281
    Philosophical and Literature Society 126–7, 140, 164
    Social and Sanitary Society 169
  educational and instructional 148
    Adult Education Committee (Board of Education) 217
    Literary Institutes 217, 221
    British Institute of Adult Education 218
    Central Joint Advisory Committee on Tutorial Classes 219
    Educational Settlements Association 216
    Home Arts and Industries Association 244
    National Adult School Union 216
    National Education Association 185–6
    Recreative Evening Schools Association 197
    Tutors' Association 218
    Universities Council for Adult and Continuing Education 211, 220, 226
    Workers' Educational Association (WEA) 214, 217–18, 222, 227–8
  environmental
    Commons Preservation Society 243
    National Trust 244
  religious
    Church Missionary Society 131, 133
    Promotion of Christianity amongst the Jews 130
    Tract Society 129
    Young Men's Christian Association 216
  science and medicine
    British Association for the Advancement of Science 91, 146, 149
    British Medical Association 148–9
    Chemical, Meteorological Society 55
    West Riding Medical Charitable Society 126
  women's societies 130, 231, 251–6, 303
    Ladies National Association 242
    Ladies Sanitary Institution 246
    National Health Association of Ireland 247
    National Union of Women's Suffrage Societies 231
    Women's Institute 216
    Women's League 249
Otley, Richard 114
Owenism 60, 100, 128
Oxford 134

parents 106–7, 180, 185, 227–8
parks, open spaces 47, 127–8, 142, 153–7, 166, 170, 175, 243–4, 303

parliament 12, 41, 56, 59, 79, 120, 124, 132, 137, 161–3, 169, 177, 198, 201, 300–301
  lobbying 152, 160, 162–3, 177
pensions 167
philanthropy 18, 231, 241, 244, 246, 264–8, 303, 305
phrenology 103
place promotion 144–77
Plymouth 259
police 8, 97–115, 154, 158
  Watch Committee 101, 108, 116
policy, public 21, 55, 104, 160, 162, 187, 189, 212–14, 220–22, 224–7, 232, 234, 249–52, 258, 289
political
  action, protest 96–7, 100–101, 104–5, 107, 119, 158, 164–5, 222, 261, 273–4, 276
    public order 98–9, 106–7, 117, 122, 135, 158, 305n
  order 97, 107, 155, 158, 201–6, 208, 213, 228–9, 276
  philosophy 23, 60, 96–120, 158, 211, 215, 258, 260, 262, 268, 278–9
poll books 124
poor, poverty 4, 21, 34–6, 48, 58, 111, 119, 128–9, 156, 158, 166–9, 175, 233, 236, 241, 243, 245, 247, 249, 251, 254, 265–6, 278, 280–82
Poor Law
  Boards of Guardians 37n, 65, 276
  hospitals 46, 54, 154
  workhouse 127
population 2, 5, 21, 58, 62, 99, 121, 123, 166, 233, 295
  density 49, 58
populism 107, 178
power, structure of 3, 7, 9, 22, 32, 97, 104–7, 112, 114–15, 120, 137–8, 149, 154, 163, 213, 227, 256n, 260, 281, 289–90
press 9, 102–4, 106–11, 113, 115, 121–5, 128–40, 142, 167, 201, 269, 283, 303–4, 305n
Privy Council 163, 195
procession 136, 143, 150–60, 175, 207–8
professionalization 55, 66, 96, 104, 124, 186, 192–3, 229, 236–7, 250

professions 54–5, 66, 147–8, 185, 188, 212, 224, 234, 242, 255–6
  engineers 147–8, 234, 237
  medical 15, 54, 231, 251
  women 251–5
progressives 64–5, 181, 194
property 9, 25, 26, 30, 33, 35–6, 121–22, 146, 154, 158, 161, 169–73, 175
  qualification 36, 100, 117, 181
  rights 27–8, 30, 45, 154, 172
public
  dinners 136–7, 140, 144–6, 156–8, 175
  entertainment 144–54, 156, 158, 245
  expenditure 52, 109, 144–77, 187, 226
  houses 124, 126, 262, 303
public health, see also health, sanitation, regulation 6, 37–8, 48, 67–8, 90, 114, 233, 239, 246, 252, 266, 303
  General Board of Health 63, 69, 70, 95
  politics of 46–66, 240, 251
  sanitation 10, 22–40, 55, 67–95, 240, 246
public sphere 12, 122, 124, 226
public utilities 3, 24–45, 53–4, 63, 142, 144–5, 153, 160, 163, 172, 264, 303
public works 55, 58, 60–61, 63, 79–80, 87, 171–2

quality of life 258–82, 285–6
quangos 18–19, 66

race meeting 126, 207
radicalism 60, 97, 100, 102–3, 110, 112–15, 117–19, 124–6, 128, 131–2, 182, 202, 222, 230
railways 30, 40, 69, 124, 146, 163
rates, ratepayers 6, 23, 26, 33–8, 61, 100, 105, 107–8, 116, 135, 158, 162, 173, 181, 187, 191, 198, 233, 248, 269
Raybould, S.G. 214, 223, 225
Raynor, Thomas 100–101, 108–9, 112–13
Reading 90

recreation 156, 163–5, 233, 244, 262, 271, 286, 294, 298–9, 303–4
Reeder, David xiii–xv, 1, 4, 13, 45, 46, 67, 96–7, 105, 175, 178–9, 182, 188, 190, 201, 212, 235, 258, 298, 308–15
'Slums and suburbs' 1, 2, 10, 309
reform
  educational 178–206
  municipal 6, 10, 21–2, 60–62, 64, 100–12, 121, 302
  sanitary 38, 55–7, 68, 196, 246, 249
regulation(s) 98, 107, 114–15, 121, 134, 142, 160, 183, 195, 204, 233, 235, 250, 271, 275
relief, disaster 145n, 166–7, 175–6
rent 266, 268
respectability 97, 99, 103, 126, 141
rituals 121, 131, 136, 141, 158, 163–67, 172, 202
Rodger, R. 11, 298, 303, 310
Romford 89
Rowntree, Seebohm 265, 267
Royal Society of Arts 55, 91, 200
royalty 147, 150–51, 155–9, 169
Rugby 74

Sabbatarianism 105, 112
Salford 252
sanitation 6, 29, 33, 55, 59, 68, 79–80, 87, 95, 105, 114, 240
  reformers 38, 55–7, 68, 196, 246, 249
school 25, 154, 288, 205
  attendance 183, 186, 198, 200
  Boards 13–15, 47, 178–206, 302
    elections 181, 191
  curriculum 13–14, 179, 183–6, 195, 197–201
  discipline 186
  equipment, textbooks 184, 186, 190
  examinations 184, 195, 198, 221
    City and Guilds 197
    Society of Arts 91, 200
  Code of Regulations 183, 195, 204
  fees 179, 184, 191, 197, 199–201, 204
  inspectors 180, 205
  leaving age 179, 180, 183
  log books 199
  pupils 180, 184, 187, 199

teachers 14–15, 148, 179–80, 183, 185–9, 192–3, 195, 197, 200, 203–4, 217, 254, 284
types of school
  infant 126–7, 179
  central schools 183–4, 186, 203
  comprehensive xiii, 184, 187, 226
  county secondary 205
  elementary 179, 182–4, 186–94, 197, 204, 254
  endowed grammar 179, 184, 186, 203–5, 286
  evening continuation centres (ECSs) 179–81, 189, 191–2, 194–201, 205
    numbers 198, 200
  higher grade (secondary) 13, 179, 182–7, 196, 201, 204–5
  industrial 167
  night schools, see evening continuation centres
  organised science schools 183
  public 205
  pupil-teacher centres (colleges) 179–81, 188–94, 204–5, 215, 218, 302
  schools of science 190–91, 198, 202
  schools, secondary 13
  technical (colleges) 190, 196, 203, 303
  voluntary (church) 180, 188, 202, 206
  women's roles 15
scientific community 52–4, 95
Scotland 14, 16n, 147–8, 154, 161, 163, 173n, 175, 206, 246, 254n, 304n
  enlightenment 176–7
seasonality 124–5, 152
sectarian 127–8, 135, 188, 202, 206, 259–60
secularization 14, 207
self-help 12, see also individuals
servants 135, 167
Settlement Movement 246, 249, 251
sewage and sewers 28–30, 32, 52–3, 59, 63, 67–95, 119, 233
  companies 68–90
    Liverpool Sewage Utilization Co 90

London Sewage Co 71
Metropolitan Sewage and Essex Reclamation Company 67–95
Sewage Utilization & Essex Reclamation Co. 76
South Essex Estuary & Reclamation Co 76
Towns Improvement Company 70
financial markets and sewage disposal 67–95
Royal Commission on 72
shareholders 24–43, 79–80, 86, 126, 133, 303
Sheffield 8, 9, 17, 50, 61, 69, 96–120, 134, 186, 190–91, 203, 269
Ecclesall 107, 109
Nether Hallam 105–6, 108, 114
Sheffield Democrats 8, 96–120
Central Democratic Association 114–16
shops, shopkeepers 36, 158, 217–18, 268
Simon, B. xiii, xiv, 13, 47, 302
slogans, protest 209
Smith, Adam 3, 4, 8n, 97, 177, 292
social
 capital 153–4, 163–9, 233, 250, 254, 259, 260–75, 284–6, 288–9, 299
 control 207, 280
 Darwinism 52, 236
 exclusion 4, 19, 49, 166–8, 186, 219, 221, 224, 227, 230, 282
 infrastructure 2–3, 5, 23, 32–9, 45, 55, 60, 143, 154, 163, 171–2, 175, 232–3
 segregation 3, 4, 51–2, 61, 111, 140, 194
 status 124, 126, 134–5, 139, 141, 185–6, 200, 219, 268, 273
 structure 35n, 140–41, 163–9, 180, 185, 190, 213, 217, 219, 248, 275–6, 286
 surveys 254–5, 265–6
 work 167–8, 173, 175, 177, 241, 243, 250
  city missions 167–8, 243, 252
  visiting 243
solidarity 156, 208, 305
South Shields 283, 295, 304

Southampton 219
sovereignty 7, 102, 119
Spencer, Herbert 40, 236
St. Helens 25, 27, 28, 30
state 212, *see also* centralization
statistics 7, 51, 54–5, 188, 198
steam engines 123
Stoke on Trent 264, 271
 Trent Vale estate 271–2
streets 15, 97, 114, 127–8, 139, 143, 158, 159, 175, 283–8, 298, 302, 305
students 208–19
 extra-mural 208–19
 mature 180, 199, 210
 undergraduates 215, 218, 220
 working class 210–11, 223
subscribers 121, 126, 129, 133–5, 141, 269
suburbs, suburbanization 1, 2, 5, 10, 53, 59, 61, 112, 163, 240, 248, 258, 264, 269, 285, 309
Sunday schools 302
Sutton, William 259n, 265, 281
Swansea 25, 30, 50

Tawney, R.H. 217, 300
taxation, local *see also* ratepayers 19, 21–45, 59–61, 104, 116, 135, 160, 162, 191, 198, 201, 206, 226, 233, 294
Taylor, A.J.P. 9
teacher training, *see* pupil teacher centres
tenants' associations 270–2
Thatcher revolution 226–7
Thompson, E. P. 223
Tönnies, Ferdinand 292, *see also* mutuality
Toulmin-Smith, J. 7, 96, 102–4, 107–8, 112–14, 117, 119–20
town planning 15, 150n, 187, 194, 226, 232–57, 265, 280
 organizations
  Town Planning Conference 237, 246
  Town Planning Institute 237, 253
 planners
  Abercombie, Patrick 238, 247
  Geddes, Patrick 15, 236–9, 245–7, 252n, 254–5
  Horsfall, T.C. 236, 245

328   INDEX

town planning *cont.*
   Howard, Ebenezer 236, 245, 248
   Parker, Barry 248
   Unwin, Raymond 236–7, 245, 247–8, 250
   report, Tudor Walters 250
   town extensions 233, 239, 251
trade unions 101, 108, 110, 147, 167, 224, 289–90, 296–7, 299–302, 305
   Amalgamated Society of Railway Servants 167
   National Union of Teachers 184, 205
Treasury 160, 192, 211
Trevelyan, G.M. 210
trusts, trustees 115, 121–22, 129, 133, 138, 142, 259, 264, 266, 269, 272–3, 275–7, 280, 282
   turnpike 7, 124
Tyrwhitt, Jacqueline 254–5

unemployment 121, 131, 135, 220, 251, 270, 276
unitarians 134
unity 136–7, 140
universities 179, 183, 190, 194, 196, 201, 207
   Cambridge 215
   Durham 207–12, 218
   Edinburgh 144, 172
   Leeds 214, 223–4
   Leicester xiii–xv, 212, 235, 308–10
   Liverpool 238, 246, 249
   London 178, 215
      London Institute of Education 178
      London School of Economics 251
   Nottingham 235
   Oxford 215, 222
urban 'variable' xiv, 1, 304n
urban
   economy 31, 39, 99, 128, 131, 139, 166, 227, 238, 245, 254, 274, 309
   government
      corporations 34–5, 42, 57, 74, 95, 100, 111, 115, 157, 163, 169–70, 172, 176
      town councils 7, 11, 25–6, 29–30, 59, 62–3, 101–4, 113, 144–77, 152, 239, 251, 302, 309

      committees 116–17, 152, 233
      councillors 60–61, 100, 109, 115–17, 144, 150, 153–5, 160, 169, 174, 281
      Lord Provost 144, 153
      vestries 35, 37, 47–50, 54, 56, 58n, 63–4, 66, 127
identity 1, 34, 124, 126–7, 133, 135–6, 140, 147–77, 164, 176, 228–9, 242, 263, 275, 283–307, 309
politics 22, 31–2, 46–66, 96–120, 123, 136, 176, 241, 247, 262, 265, 279, 289, 305, 307, 309
religion 127, 131, 134–6, 148, 180, 188, 206, 265, 302, 305–6
   Christian News Letter Group 178
renewal 153, 171, 174–5, 260, 281, 305
revenues, *see* local taxation, ratepayers
   'feu-duties' 170–71, 173
rhythms 2, 39, 156, 281, 285, 291, 307
Urban History Group xv, 235, 309
Urban History Yearbook xv, 309
urbanization 2, 6, 11, 23–4, 122, 171, 233, 236, 248, 258
utilitarian 128, 217
utopianism 52, 106, 235–6, 249

values 207, 213, 231–4, 236, 278–9, 296
visits, royal 152, 155–9
voluntary societies, organizations 121–43, 163–7, 175, 202, 217, 228, 250, 256, 260–61, 268, 275, 280–81, 303, 304n
   committees 121, 129, 134, 136, 140, 152, 205
   volunteers 167, 169, 234–5, 239, 243–4, 247, 251

War, First World 145, 209, 230, 234, 236, 250
ward-motes 8, 17, 103–6, 108–9, 111–12, 114–17
waste, *see* sewage
water

INDEX 329

companies, *see* public utilities
rights 28–9, 32, 106
supply 53, 75, 139, 233
    East London Company 53
Webb, S. and B. 6n, 16, 206, 301n
Weber, Max 122
welfare state 214, 232, 255
Welwyn 249
West Riding, Yorkshire 123, 126, 139
Wilkinson, Ellen 193
Williams, C. 7, 17
Williams, Raymond 221
Williamson, B. 13
Wirth, Louis 122
Wolverhampton 27, 58
women 107, 130, 135, 152, 167, 200, 218, 231–57, 284, 297–8, 304

debts 29
education of 15, 181, 215, 220, 231, 256
politics 104–5, 231
professional 251–6
rights 231
social knowledge 288, 290, 297–9, 304–5
societies 130, 216, 231, 242, 246–7, 249, 251–6, 303
volunteers 241, 244, 247
work 247
Worcester 190–91

York 134, 141
youths 104, 112, 148, 167, 180, 182, 278n, 285, 302, 304